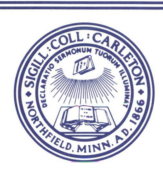

Sick Economies

Sick Economies

Drama, Mercantilism, and Disease in Shakespeare's England

Jonathan Gil Harris

PENN

University of Pennsylvania Press
Philadelphia

10 9 8 7 6 5 4 3 2 1

Published by
University of Pennsylvania Press
Philadelphia, Pennsylvania 19104-4011

Library of Congress Cataloging-in-Publication Data

Harris, Jonathan Gil.
   Sick economies : drama, mercantilism, and disease in Shakespeare's England / Jonathan Gil
Harris.
      p.   cm.
   Includes bibliographical references and index.
   ISBN 0-8122-3773-0 (acid-free paper)
   1. English drama—Early modern and Elizabethan, 1500–1700—History and criticism.
2. Economics in literature. 3. Mercantile system—Great Britain—History—16th century.
4. Mercantile system—Great Britain—History—17th century. 5. Shakespeare, William,
1564–1616—Knowledge—Economics. 6. Shakespeare, William, 1564–1616—Knowledge—Medicine.
7. English drama—17th century—History and criticism. 8. Great Britain—Economic conditions—
16th century. 9. England—Economic conditions—17th century. 10. Economics in literature.
11. Diseases in literature. I. Title.
PR658.E35H37 2004
822.3'3—dc22   2003055561

for my sister Naomi Harris Narev
(1968–2003)
—b'ahava raba

Contents

1   The Asian Flu; Or, The Pathological Drama of National
    Economy   1

2   Syphilis and Trade: Thomas Starkey, Thomas Smith, *The Comedy
    of Errors*   29

3   Taint and Usury: Gerard Malynes, The Dutch Church Libel,
    The Merchant of Venice   52

4   Canker/Serpego and Value: Gerard Malynes, *Troilus and
    Cressida*   83

5   Plague and Transmigration: Timothy Bright, Thomas Milles,
    Volpone   108

6   Hepatitis/Castration and Treasure: Edward Misselden, Gerard
    Malynes, *The Fair Maid of the West, The Renegado*   136

7   Consumption and Consumption: Thomas Mun, *The Roaring
    Girl*   163

8   Afterword: Anthrax, Cyberworms, and the New Ethereal
    Economy   186

Notes   191

Bibliography   235

Index   253

Acknowledgments   261

The Asian Flu; Or, The Pathological Drama of National Economy

At the end of 1997, newspaper readers around the world were treated to a striking journalistic diptych. Alongside reports of the outbreak of a new, possibly lethal strain of chicken influenza in Hong Kong, there appeared the first articles detailing the turmoil and collapse of East Asia's "tiger" economies. The juxtaposition proved quite suggestive. Although the new strain of influenza turned out to be relatively innocuous, the language it generated was altogether more contagious: in a matter of days after the Hong Kong outbreak, Anglophone reporters had dubbed the economic ills afflicting nations such as Indonesia, Thailand, and Korea the "Asian flu," or, with greater euphony, the "Asian contagion." The tigers were thus transmuted into morbid chickens, threatening to infect the economies of the West.

The "Asian flu" metaphor reveals a great deal. First, it bears witness to the constitutive role played by the body in shaping Western perceptions of the economic. One might think also of eighteenth-century French Physiocrat theories of the blood-like circulation of wealth; the word "inflation," which was originally a specialized medical term for "swelling"; the pathological connotations of "consumption"; Adam Smith's "invisible hand" of the market; or the organic etymology of "capital" itself.[1] Metaphors of infectious disease like the "Asian flu" similarly disclose the corporeal images that, even in an age where the archaic logic of resemblance between microcosm and macrocosm no longer holds sway, continue to organize popular understandings of the economic.

Just as strikingly, the metaphor lends expression to deep-seated fears about the vulnerability of national markets within larger, global networks of commerce. In these fears lurks an intriguing paradox. Fundamental to the notion of the nation's commercial health is an ambivalent conception of *transnationality* that works to naturalize the global even as it stigmatizes the foreign. The "Asian flu" metaphor embodies this ambivalence particularly clearly. By troping economic illness as a communicable condition that transmigrates across oceans, the metaphor attributes the cause of plunging stocks and evaporating capital around the world to specific foreign bodies rather than to global commerce itself, which is figured simply as the disease's indifferent medium. The trope of influenza thus works not just to *pathologize* the economic but also to *enable* it; contagious disease, in other words, provides the discursive ground for Anglophone understandings of national economy and transnational commerce. In the process, the tropological dimension of the "Asian flu" is accompanied by a narratological one. The "Asian flu" is not simply a metaphor; it is a character in a story, a story that, with its transoceanic setting and tale of hazards to be overcome, boasts the distinguishing generic features of dramatic romance.[2]

It is the early modern prehistory of this unlikely romance's most striking detail—the pathologization of foreign bodies as the enabling discursive condition for the globally connected nation-state—that I seek to clarify in *Sick Economies*. This has entailed my thinking about "the nation" in ways that are somewhat different from what is now customary in Renaissance studies. The growing body of scholarship on early modern discourses of nationhood has focused largely on political, legal, and linguistic fictions of England or Britain.[3] In doing so, however, it has almost entirely ignored an important genre of literature from the period: the so-called mercantilist writing of the early seventeenth century. In a series of treatises that endeavored to explain and manage the vicissitudes of international commerce, English mercantilists arguably offered the first systematic articulation of an object that now serves as one of the master tropes and characters of the drama of modern nationhood—the national economy.

Admittedly, the word "economy" did not acquire its modern, nation-specific sense of "*the* economy" until after World War II. In Tudor England, the term was used almost exclusively to refer to the maintenance of individual households and, by metaphorical extension, larger establishments and communities.[4] Nevertheless, the broad outlines of a discourse of English national economy are visible in the work of four early seventeenth-century writers, sometimes referred to as the "four Ms": Gerard Malynes, Thomas Milles, Edward Misselden, and Thomas Mun. Their treatises—now collectively regarded by economic historians as the canonical documents of early English mercantilism—mark the emergence of a recognizably modern, commercial conception of the nation. Significantly, the simultaneous naturalization of the global and pathologization of the foreign that is the hallmark of modern economic tropes like the "Asian flu" is anticipated by English mercantilist writing, in which metaphors of disease are likewise rhetorically central. Some of these diseases—canker, hepatitis—have subsequently lost their economic connotations. Others—most notably consumption—remain integral to the modern economic lexicon but have by and large shed their pathological senses. In early modern England, all these terms were key figures in a double helix of medical and mercantile signification. Pathology and economy, I shall argue, were interconstitutive domains of discourse. Each helped create the other's horizons of textual and conceptual possibility; changes in one helped produce changes in the other. By attending to the work of the mercantilist writers and their contemporaries, then, we can recover an important yet largely forgotten chapter in the shared prehistories of our modern notions of global commerce and disease.

The Discourses of Mercantilism

Mercantilism is, however, a highly problematic term. If "the early modern English economy" is an anachronistic or catachrestic signifier, calling into being a concept that had no precise label in the Renaissance, so equally is "mercantilism." Malynes, Milles, Misselden, and Mun did not regard themselves as "mercantilists," nor did their contemporaries view them as belonging to any coherent, let alone nameable, school of thought. On the contrary, the men regarded each other largely as ideological adversaries: much of what is now considered the mercantilist canon consists of Malynes's shouting matches with Misselden. Not surprisingly, then, many historians have questioned whether mercantilism ever really existed. "As a matter of fact," one scholar complains, "mercantilism was never an entity, never a system, never a coordinated or coherent body of policy or practice."[5]

This phantom "entity" or "system" was, in fact, born nearly two centuries after the fact. Mercantilism was for the most part the brainchild of Adam Smith, though he himself never used the term. The latter is a nineteenth-century neologism derived from the title of chapter 1 of book 4 of Smith's *Wealth of Nations* (1776), "The Principles of the Commercial or Mercantile System." In Smith's historical analysis, the mercantile system preceded the age of capitalism proper and was distinguished by the mistaken equation of wealth with money or bullion. For Smith, the system also entailed regulatory and monopolistic economic policies that he attributed to the "[self-] interested sophistry of merchants and manufacturers," straw men in opposition to whom he made his case for unimpeded free trade.[6] From the moment of its late eighteenth-century conception, therefore, "the mercantile system" was a loaded construct, serving a fundamentally rhetorical, not to mention political, purpose.

Such is the shadow cast by Smith in economic history, though, that a mercantilist epoch was for a long time an article of faith, and his assumptions concerning mercantilism went virtually uncontested. Smith's critical analysis of the mercantile system styled it as not simply a precursor of capitalism but also an exercise in statecraft. The system was more than a mode of commerce, therefore;

it was above all a mode of governmental *management* of commerce. This view was seconded even by Smith's fiercest detractors. Karl Marx regarded the mercantile system as a necessary, state-sponsored variant of the protocapitalist "Monetary System."[7] And Gustav von Schmoller, the nineteenth-century German *Kathedersozialisten,* characterized mercantilism "in its innermost kernel [as] nothing but state-making—not state-making in a narrow sense, but state-making and national-economy making at the same time."[8] In Smith's, Marx's, and von Schmoller's analyses, then, mercantilism was posited as a necessary, liminal stage in a teleological account of both economic and nationalist history—the system of governmental policies that provided the bridge from the petty bourgeois production of the urban city-state to the free market capitalism of the globally connected nation-state.

This view of mercantilism as a system of state policy persists in much scholarship on early modern culture. In her brilliant study of Francis Bacon's science and its relationship to economics, for example, Julie Robin Solomon characterizes mercantilism as "governmental strategies" that were designed to "control those facets of commercial culture not comprehended within older and more traditional or customary protocols."[9] But the Smithian perspective is not the only version of mercantilism that retains critical currency. A significantly different interpretation was advanced in the middle of the twentieth century by Eli Heckscher, the influential Swedish economic historian. Heckscher conceded that mercantilism was "a phase in the history of economic policy" and that "the state was both the subject and the object of mercantilist economic policy." But he deviated from both the mainstream Smithian position, that mercantilism was a system of state management of commerce, and the opposing extreme, that there was never any such thing. Instead, he argued that "mercantilism never existed in the sense that Colbert or Cromwell existed. It is only an instrumental concept which, if aptly chosen, should enable us to understand a particular historical period more clearly than we otherwise might."[10] In neo-Hegelian fashion, Heckscher proceeded to characterize mercantilism as less a material *structure* or *system* than a loose collection of seventeenth-century *ideas* about government intervention in foreign trade.

Heckscher may well have been right that the evidence discounts the historical existence of a mercantile system as such, at least in the sense of any coherent, coordinated set of commercial policies implemented by early modern European nation-states. But, as Heckscher himself acknowledged, that does not mean there were no significant trends during the period in state policy regarding the practice of international commerce. There had been trade networks across Europe for centuries, of course, networks in which the state was increasingly implicated. But until the middle of the sixteenth century, international commerce tended to be seen as the activity less of nation-states themselves than of people or trading associations identified with specific urban locations. Merchants from London potentially competed as much with traders from Bristol or Norwich as with their counterparts from Antwerp or Venice. Certain developments in English state policy, however, had spurred the cultural production of new, economically based conceptions of nationhood. As early as 1275, the English crown began to develop a national customs system—the first of its kind in Europe, where tariffs and tolls had traditionally been administered by cities, towns, or parishes.[11] The English monarch's coffers, topped off by duties and subsidies imposed on goods both entering and leaving the country, came increasingly to be identified in mainstream political writing with the wealth and weal of the nation.

This identification was given considerable impetus by the Reformation and the resulting centralization of England's political power in the king and the state. Following the dissolution of the monasteries, England witnessed a sustained standardization of economic policy and practice, motivated in large part by the objective of ensuring a ready supply of royal treasure in the event of war against hostile European Catholic powers. The emergent discourse of England's national wealth was also bolstered by the opening up of new sea trade routes to the Americas, Africa, and Asia, and the resulting pirate wars waged against Spain and the Ottomans by crown-sanctioned privateers and freebooters such as Sir Francis Drake. Even though the main beneficiaries of such activities were the queen and the privateers themselves, Drake and his ilk were lionized as national heroes who had "enriched [their] Countries store."[12] The rise of new associations of capital for foreign trade also helped fuel a sense of economic nationalism. Like Drake, these associations were lent legitimacy by the crown as representatives of the nation: whereas earlier merchant adventuring companies had been identified with cities, a charter in 1566 was awarded to the Merchant Adventurers of *England*. The brace of new early modern English regulated and joint-stock trading companies—including the Muscovy Company (chartered in 1555), the Levant Company (1581), the East India Company (1601), and the Virginia Company (1606)—likewise claimed to represent the interests of the nation, even as they lined the pockets of their principals and major shareholders.[13] It is no accident that two of the mercantilists, Misselden and Mun, were officeholders in English trading companies—Misselden with the Merchant Adventurers and Mun with the East India Company.

As Heckscher argued, the growing alignment of mercantile interests with those of the English crown and nation hardly constituted a mercantile *system*. Yet his Hegelian alternative to the Smithian state policy paradigm seems itself problematic. To view mercantilism as primarily a set of ideas about commerce is to run the risk of parenthesizing its material forms and effects, whether eco-nomic or cultural. To the extent that mercantilism existed at all, it may be more accurate to understand what von Schmoller termed its "nation-making" power at the level not of ideas or statecraft but of *discourse*. This new understanding would entail recasting mercantilism as something more than simply an ideology and less than a mode of state-controlled production, accumulation, distribu-tion, or exchange. Throughout this study, I propose to analyze mercantilism as primarily a discursive rather than an ideological or economic system. It may not be a particularly coherent discourse but, like any other, it is characterized by cer-tain strategies of signification, by means of which it produces both knowledge and power. Here I follow the lead of Mary Poovey, who in her remarkable study *A History of the Modern Fact* analyzes mercantilism as a discourse in which nu-merical representation first became the epistemological bedrock of truth. In this, she signals a large debt to Michel Foucault's interpretation of mercantilism in *The Order of Things* as constituting a new mode of representation founded on precise exchange.[14] My analysis differs from both Poovey's and Foucault's, how-ever, inasmuch as I am interested in mercantilism as a discourse less of "factual" or "precise" representation than of transnational typology. It is this typology that has bequeathed the framework within which the West continues to imag-ine both national and global economy.

Understanding mercantilism as a discourse, however, necessitates a pre-liminary sketch of its admittedly vague ideological premises. The disparate body of work produced by Malynes, Milles, Misselden, and Mun is rife with disagree-ment, much of it vehement, about how England's economy was organized, the nature of its dysfunctions, and what the sovereign needed to do (or not do) to manage England's trade with other nations.[15] But all four writers shared funda-mental assumptions. Each saw the wealth of the nation as the responsibility of the state, and the prince as the *fons et origo* of the nation's riches, even as he is aided and abetted by merchants. And each assumed that the goal of mercantile activity is to increase the nation's wealth, less in the form of productivity or cap-ital assets than of money—that is, gold and silver treasure acquired from abroad. The early "bullionist" mercantilists of the 1590s and 1600s, Malynes and Milles, believed that the nation's treasure should be hoarded at all costs, and any export of bullion out of England vigorously discouraged. The later "balance-of-trade" mercantilists of the 1620s, Misselden and Mun, tolerated the export of limited quantities of bullion, but only as capital guaranteed to bring back more gold and silver into the country's coffers.[16] Despite these differences, all four writers subscribed to a zero-sum conception of global wealth, according to which one nation's gain was almost invariably another's loss. Foreign countries, then, were rivals and even enemies. Because of the conviction that global commerce entailed England's competing with other nations for finite quantities of bullion, mercantilist discourse displays a marked xenophobic tendency: Spain, the Ottoman Empire, and occasionally the "Jewish nation" and the Low Countries are cast as the villains from whom English bullion must be protected or expropriated.

Despite this hostility, all four men argued that England's wealth could be augmented only if England *joined* with other nations in observing certain universal laws of commerce. In doing so, they followed the doctrine of cosmopolitan universal economy advanced by classical writers from Plato to Plutarch, according to which global commerce followed inevitably from the dispersal of necessary resources and commodities around the world. The difference was that the English mercantilists adapted this doctrine to explain trade between *nations*.[17] In *Free Trade, or The Meanes to Make Trade Florish*, for example, Edward Misselden makes the case that

to the end there should be a *Commerce* amongst men, it hath pleased *God* to inuite as it were, one Countrey to traffique with another, by the variety of things which the one hath, and the other hath not: that so that which is wanting to the *one,* might be supplied by the *other,* that all might have sufficient. . . . Which thing the very windes and seas proclaime, in giving passage to all nations: the windes blowing sometimes towards one Country, sometimes toward another; that so by this divine justice, every one might be supplyed in things necessary for life and maintenance.[18]

Likewise, in his voluminous treatise of 1622, the *Lex Mercatoria* (or the "Law-Merchant"), Gerard Malynes argues that despite the "great diuersitie amongst all Nations . . . in the course of trafficke and commerce," there is a "sympathy, concordance and agreement, which may bee said to bee of like condition to all people." These universal laws of global "trafficke and commerce" between "Nations," he insists, are "an inuention and gift of God."[19] Even as he attributes the doctrine of cosmopolitan economy to God, Malynes relies here—as he does throughout his treatise—on the Roman jurists' distinction between *ius,* or prince's law, and *lex,* or customary and natural law. His association of mercantile trade with the latter was part and parcel of the transformation of economics from a subset of ethics to an autonomous, protoscientific discipline. For the medieval scholastics, economics had tended to be a matter of individual morality; "good" practices of commerce avoided the sins of covetousness, miserliness, usury, and luxury. By contrast, the mercantilist appeal to the higher laws of "nature" helped ratify a new object of knowledge: an orderly, systematic sphere of transnational commerce whose workings could be ascertained through empirical observation.[20]

Perhaps the natural law that most distinguishes mercantilist conceptions of national wealth production is that of the balance of trade. Misselden articulates it as follows: "If the Natiue Commodities exported doe waigh downe and exceed in value the forraine Commodities imported; it is a rule that neuer faile's, that then the Kingdome growe's rich, and prosper's in estate and stocke: because the ouerplus must needs come in, in treasure."[21] Although this theory was explicitly outlined only in the work of the so-called balance-of-trade mercantilists, a version of it is also implicit in the work of the earlier bullionists. Malynes, Milles, Misselden, and Mun took it as a rule of thumb that selling native commodities to strangers brings treasure into the nation, while the import of foreign wares stands to lose it. To varying degrees, both the bullionists and the balance-of-traders tended to rail against the English consumption of "idle" foreign commodities and luxury goods. Increased national self-sufficiency was proposed as an ideal; Malynes, for example, advocated and even participated in mining ventures at home in the hopes of increasing the nation's reserves of bullion. Yet to accumulate wealth without foreign trade was seen as an impossibility. As Malynes argues in *The Maintenance of Free Trade* (1622), absolute self-sufficiency is the stuff of utopian imagination.[22] Hence the mercantilists understood the nation in terms of a potentially paradoxical pair of relations to the outside: England assumed its national identity in relation both to readily demonizable "forraine" bodies (other nations, their citizens, their goods), which potentially damaged its economic health, and to universal "rules" of transnational commerce, which sustained it.

This paradox was a crucial development in the emergent discourses of nationhood. Rather than a discrete geographical, linguistic, cultural, or legalistic entity defined sui generis, the English nation of mercantilist writing was now defined in terms of its wealth within a global framework. In this respect, the long-standing discourse of "commonwealth," which preceded the mercantilist discourse of the nation, influenced but also crucially differed from it. For political writers from John of Salisbury in the twelfth century to Thomas Starkey in the sixteenth, "commonwealth" was a term that tended to designate the nation's moral rather than economic condition. Thomas More lent "commonwealth" a literal financial sense in *Utopia,* but even for him the term retained a largely moral thrust: to hold wealth in common, Raphael Hythlodaeus argues, is the ethical basis of Utopian polity.[23] Here, as in nearly all its incarnations, the "commonwealth" is equated primarily with the internal, self-sufficient resources—ethical as well as financial—of the nation. By contrast, mercantilist formulations of the nation insist on how its wealth is necessarily the product of transactions across national borders. Although the mercantilists frequently referred to the English national economy as the "commonwealth," their chief investment was less in that term's "common" than in its "wealth," and specifically "wealth" as the outcome of international trade by private merchants. "What else makes a Common-wealth," asks Misselden in *The Circle of Commerce,* "but the private-wealth, if I may so say, of the members thereof in the Exercise of *Commerce* amongst themselues, and with forraine Nations?"[24] Even as it regards "forraine Nations" with suspicion, then, mercantilist writing repeatedly valorizes the global, although the forms of that economic cosmopolitanism are to be carefully monitored and controlled by the crown.

Early modern commerce's ambivalent relationship to the foreign, I shall argue, necessitated new narrative forms within economic writing. To modern eyes, one of the more striking aspects of early modern mercantilist discourse might be its theatrical register. Critiquing Malynes's allegations about the economic ills wrought by bankers and currency exchangers, Thomas Mun observes curtly: "I think verily that neither Doctor *Faustus* nor *Banks* his Horse could ever do such admirable Feats, although it is sure they had a Devil to help them; but wee Merchants deal not with such Spirits."[25] If Mun, like Marx, saw the history of political economy narrating itself in the registers of (Marlovian) tragedy and farce, other mercantilists tended to shape their analyses to the imperatives of another dramatic genre: romance. This is particularly so with Gerard Malynes, as is evidenced by the title of his first published pamphlet, *Saint George for England Allegorically Described* (1601). Unlike patriotic Tudor writers who glorified England's language, law, history, or geography, Malynes advanced an *economic* nationalism based primarily on praiseworthy practices of commerce. His unconventional brand of patriotism can be seen most clearly in *Saint George for England Allegorically Described,* in which he recasts the English patron saint as the champion of a damsel in distress, English Treasure, who is defined less by her location than by her vulnerability to the transnational dragon of usury.[26]

Other mercantilist writers may have avoided such overtly melodramatic fantasies of risk and rescue, but the language of romance is a recurrent feature of their writing nonetheless. In his treatise *The Custumers Alphabet and Primer* (1608), for example, Thomas Milles characterizes "Trafficke" (i.e., England's foreign trade) as "our swete . . . *Mistresse*" who, "distempered and distrest," is in urgent need of "remedy" from her male champions.[27] The connection between the languages of romance and commerce is equally evident in the mercantilists' use of the word "adventure." By the late sixteenth century, "adventure" had come to signify both romantic quest and commercial venture. The Merchant Adventurers of England arguably freighted the two meanings in their name; Thomas Mun wrote of the merchant's stirring "adventures from one Countrey to another," deliberately blurring the term's romantic and commercial senses.[28] A similar pair of connotations also attached to the word "hazard," which could refer not only to the risk taken by the romantic quester but also to a commercial venture and a popular gambling game.[29] The romantic conventions of perils overcome, (male) protection of distressed (female) parties, and treasure gained all lent a fairytale veneer to the mercenary ambitions of mercantilism. Just as importantly, the conventions of romance also allowed for the simultaneous demonization of foreigners and the validation of transnational laws of commerce.

The power of dramatic romance not just to accommodate but to articulate this mercantilist paradox is illustrated by the Belmont subplot of Shakespeare's *Merchant of Venice.* As many readers have noted, the entire play foregrounds the links between the "hazards" of merchant adventurism and of romance.[30] "In Belmont," says Bassanio, the man who must "hazard all he hath," "is a lady richly left" (1.1.160):

And many Jasons come in quest of her.
O my Antonio, had I but the means
To hold a rival place with one of them,
I have a mind presages me such thrift
That I should questionless be fortunate. (1.1.171–75)

Thus begins the play's insistent exposure of the commercial underpinnings of questing. As Bassanio suggests in this passage, a romantic venture needs venture capital. The fairytale-like subplot of the caskets is framed from the outset by its mercantile conditions of possibility: to enter the contest, this play's Prince Charming has had to obtain sponsorship from a sugar daddy. "We are the Jasons, we have won the fleece," brags Graziano in Belmont (3.2.240), but his turn as a romantic quester fails to conceal the commercial means—and ends—of that role. The Jasons' Argos, then, cannot help but blur into Antonio's argosies.

Like the mercantilists, the Venetian Jasons' quest has a nationalist as well as commercial dimension, not least because of the parade of suitors whom Portia inventories in the second scene of act 1. In what might seem like an unholy marriage of the Eurovision Song Contest and the Love Connection, Portia is both the M.C. and the prize in a game show that has previously attracted contestants from Naples, France, Germany, England, Scotland, and, if critics are right about the County Palatine's nationality, Poland. This contest is not in Shakespeare's nominal source, Giovanni Fiorentino's *Il Pecorone.* Nor are the two princes, Morocco and Aragon, over whom the Venetian Bassanio eventually triumphs. The latter pair are in some ways stock figures from romance—the swaggering Saracen who boasts of his violent exploits with his scimitar, the chivalrous Iberian aristocrat whom Cervantes was to pillory a decade later. But their inclusion also consolidates the play's transnational frame of reference, which corresponds to that of late sixteenth-century European commerce. In beating out Morocco and Aragon for Portia's hand, Bassanio is the winner in a contest against representatives of two of England's major trading adversaries, the Islamic North African states and Spain. Belmont thus attracts global adventurers who, for all their exoticism, are the specular images of Antonio and his more nakedly commercial ambitions, which dispatch argosies to Ottoman Tripolis and Spanish Mexico as well as to England and the East Indies.

Despite this national rivalry, Portia's suitors are bound by a universal law analogous to, yet different from, Malynes's *lex mercatoria*: the *ius patris* dictated by Portia's father, which governs the terms of the lottery. No matter how much Portia may revile her foreign suitors, she and they willingly accede to her father's law, which demands that they never marry if they choose the wrong casket: "To these injunctions every one doth swear / That comes to hazard" (2.9.16–17). Indeed, this uneasy but willing subjection to universally binding laws governing transnational "hazards" is one of the hallmarks of the play. It is evident also in Antonio's refusal to contest Shylock's suit on the grounds that "The Duke cannot deny the course of law," a law that recognizes how "the trade and profit of the city / Consisteth of all nations" (3.3.27, 31–32). This law may be imposed by the Venetian state and, to that extent, fall into the category of *ius*; but it is predicated on the natural *lex* of cosmopolitan universal economy. In the manner of mercantilist writing, then, the play imagines the pursuit of transnational "hazards" as proceeding only through the observation of global laws. Romance, moreover, provides the generic framework within which the foreign can be repelled and the global ratified. This pattern is evident in both subplot and main plot: just as Bassanio bests Morocco and Aragon while submitting to the *ius patris* dictated by Portia's father, so does Antonio triumph over Shylock while paying lip service to the *lex mercatoria* of global commerce.

If transnational economy in *The Merchant of Venice* has an explicitly romantic accent, it also has a more occulted pathological one. Old Gobbo misuses the term "infection" when he means affection (2.2.103), but his malapropism brings to visibility the pathological underbelly of desire, whether romantic or commercial, throughout the play. This underbelly surfaces most clearly in the courtroom scene. Bellario fails to appear in court because he is allegedly "very sick" (4.1.151); Shylock leaves the same courtroom complaining that he is "not well" (4.1.392); and Antonio calls himself a "tainted wether of the flock" (4.1.114), a diseased animal whose sorry condition, signposted in the play's very first line, foregrounds the dark side of a desire bifurcated between the imperatives of romance and trade. Theodore Leinwand has noted how Antonio's sadness exposes the affective component of commercial venturing.[31] But this component is also at root pathological, as is suggested by Graziano's advice to Antonio, couched in the language of humoralism: "fish not with this melancholy bait" (1.1.101). Indeed, *The Merchant of Venice*'s conjunction of pathology and commerce was made more explicit in a nineteenth-century American minstrel rewriting of the play; this updated version gave Antonio in the courtroom scene a case of "the mumps," for which he takes the splendidly efficacious "Mrs Winslowe's Soothing Syrup."[32]

The Merchant of Venice's mixing of the languages of trade and disease within the generic constraints of romance is especially significant. I would go so far as to suggest that this mixing is what distinguishes early modern English mercantilism as a discourse. In a manner strikingly reminscent of the "Asian flu" metaphor's freighting of the economic and the epidemic, the mercantilists' discourse of national economy was also a pathologically inflected one. All four writers repeatedly offered "remedies" for what they regarded as the nation's economic "sicknesses." Malynes titled one of his earliest works *The Canker of England's Commonwealth,* repeatedly compared the nation's economic ills to "gangrene" and "dropsy," and presented in his last treatise, *The Center of the Circle of Commerce* (1623), a sustained allegorical fable of the body politic's economic diseases.[33] Milles saw commercial trade as suffering from "dangerous fits of a hot burning Feauer" and a "Frensie," each of which he endeavored to cure with an "Apothecary Pill."[34] Misselden employed pathologies of the blood, and even coined the term "hepatitis" to figure obstacles to the circulation of wealth.[35] Mun styled idleness as a "general leprosie" that depletes the nation's treasure and developed the pathological metaphor of "consumption" in a way that heralded its modern, exclusively economic sense.[36] Most importantly, all four writers tended to imagine these sicknesses as the products less of internal economic problems than of exposure to foreign elements—whether people, goods, organizations, or practices—within the "natural" functionings of global commerce.

The mercantilists' obsessively pathological imagination may strike the modern reader as eccentric. But their conceptions of disease itself must seem far less so. We are habituated to political metaphors of invading cancers, plagues, or Asian flus. Susan Sontag and others have bridled at the xenophobic potential of such metaphors, but that is because these critics more or less take for granted that disease is usually transmitted by, and resides in, foreign bodies.[37] That the mercantilists repeatedly resorted to the language of pathological foreign bodies does not testify to disease's transhistorical figural power as an invasive entity. Rather, as I shall argue, mercantilist conceptions of economic pathology are possessed of a historical specificity born of changing material circumstances in the sixteenth and seventeenth centuries—in particular, the emergence of the nation-state and the growth of global trade. The mercantilists' language of economic pathology, moreover, provided one of the discursive fields within which disease could first be figured as a foreign body, "naturally" communicated from one organism to another.

Discourses of Pathology

So naturalized has the notion of disease as a foreign body become that it is easy to forget there once was a time when people's pathological fears were not figured in terms of viruses, bacteria, germs, or any other contagion. At the beginning of the sixteenth century, the dominant conceptions of health and disease in English culture looked decidedly different from our modern counterparts. Rather than an external, invasive entity, as it has overwhelmingly been conceived since Louis Pasteur formulated his theory of germs and Robert Koch discovered the bacillus that causes tuberculosis, disease was imagined as a state of internal imbalance, or *dyskrasia,* caused by humoral disarray or deficiency. An excess of melancholy, phlegm, or choler, or a deficiency of blood, was understood as both the immediate cause *and* the form of illness. The goal of the physician was not to prevent entry of any determinate, invasive disease, therefore, but to restore the body to a condition of humoral homeostasis, or balance. This model dates back to Hippocrates, although the notion of the humors was codified primarily in the writings of Galen. For nearly two millennia, humoral conceptions of disease held sway in Europe, northern Africa, and the Near East.[38]

The humoral model was occasionally challenged by other theories of pathogenesis, particularly during periods of epidemic illness. Because of its understanding of disease as an endogenous state, Galenic humoralism was never able to explain successfully the operations of contagion. To account for the transmission of plague and other epidemic diseases, medical writers frequently resorted to Hippocrates's miasmic theory of contagion or, more desperately, to arguments based on astrology or divine providence. Nonetheless, such deviations from the Galenic mainstream never seriously undermined the humoral model; indeed, they were usually accommodated within it. According to miasma theory, for example, polluted air or vapors were responsible for disrupting humoral balance. Disease might have external causes, therefore, but its form was understood to be endogenous, rooted in the complexion (or mix) of the body's internal substances.[39] Until and during the Tudor period, Galen retained a virtually uncontested monopoly in scholastic English understandings of disease and its transmission. Nearly all the academic and lay treatises on disease of the sixteenth century shoehorn illness into the glass slipper of humoralism. The Scottish physician Andrew Boorde's *Breuiary of Helthe* (c. 1540), for example, which was published in numerous editions in the sixteenth century, offers an exhaustive glossary of early modern illnesses, every one of which it endeavors to explain in terms of humoral composition and imbalance.[40]

The Galenic understanding of the physiology of the body, its humoral mix, and its appetitive functions provided a particularly rich metaphorical language for sixteenth-century writers. Economic writers were no exception: many articulated fledgling conceptions of national economy in the language of humoralism. In his *Dialogue Between Reginald Pole and Thomas Lupset* (c. 1535), for example, Thomas Starkey adduced eight primary illnesses of the body politic. The majority of these are economic ills that have a humoral tinge:

And like as the health of the body determeth [sic] no particular complexion, but in every one of the four by physicians determed, as in sanguine, melancholic, phlegmatic and choleric, may be found perfit, so this common weal determeth to it no particular state (which by politic men have been devised and reduced to four)—nother the rule of a prince, nother of a certain number of wise men, nother yet of the whole multitude and body of the people, but in every one of these it may be found to be perfit and stable. . . . For when all these parts thus coupled togidder exercise with diligence their office and duty, as, the ploughmen and labourers of the ground diligently till the same, for the getting of food and necessary sustenance to the rest of the body, and craftsmen work all things meet for maintenance of the same, yea, and they heads and rulers by just policy maintain the state stablished in the country, ever looking to the profit of they whole body, then that common weal must needs flourish; then that country must needs be in the most prosperous state.[41]

Here we can see the literal sense in which "common wealth" was often understood, as the wealth of the English nation. But this is not "wealth" as conceived by the mercantilists, derived from *foreign* trade. Starkey instead regards England's most "prosperous state" as a function of its *internal* economic operations—including labor, a category notably absent from mercantilist writing—for which the language of humoralism provides an appropriate vocabulary. Likewise, Galenic language suggested itself to the bullionists as a figurative resource for representing the *intrinsic* composition of the nation's alloy coins. Hence, Thomas Milles argues, "Money in a Kingdome, [is] the same that Blood is in the *Body*, and all Allayes but humors."[42]

The humoral model does not cut the body off from the world. If anything, it stresses the impossibility of separating the body from the external elements on which it depends—air, food, drink, even astrological influences. Crucial to its understanding of physiology are notions of input and output. As Thomas Laqueur has argued, "seminal emission, bleeding, purging, and sweating were all forms of evacuation that served to maintain the free-trade economy of fluids at a proper level."[43] For that reason, a humoral vocabulary is also evident in much early modern economic writing about the English body politic's commercial transactions with other nations. The all-important mercantilist notion of the balance of trade, even as it draws on the new model of Italian double-entry bookkeeping, resonates with humoralism's characteristic vocabulary of equipoise and homeostasis. So too does the recurrent mercantilist term "vent"; a synonym for the sale of domestic commodities abroad, it echoes the Galenic conviction that superfluous humors such as choler needed to be "vented" or expelled to restore complexional order within the body. As Margaret Healy has noted in her important study of Renaissance fictions of disease, mercantilists frequently employed a humoral conception of the "glutted, unvented" body politic; "wee must finde meanes by Trade," Mun observes, "to vent our superfluities."[44]

Nevertheless, to the extent that humoral pathology emphasized dysfunctions *within* the body's internal systems, its concepts and vocabularies were in many ways more useful for the residual discourse of "commonwealth"—that is, for the notion of the body politic as a primarily self-sufficient entity. It is perhaps telling that Gerard Malynes, nostalgically reflecting on the difference between the new, globally connected nation-state and the self-nourishing "commonwealth" of old, should resort to a metaphor from Galenic medicine to represent the political economy of the latter: "from the Prince as from a liuely fountain all vertues did descend into the bosome of that commonwealth, his worthy counsellors were with the magistrates as ornaments of the Law, and did ministrate (like Phisitions to the weale publicke) good potions for the ridding out of all distemperate humors."[45] Notably, this fantasy longs not for Laqueur's "free-trade economy" but for an isolationist program of ethical if not ethnic cleansing.

During the sixteenth and seventeenth centuries, the Galenic emphasis on the body's internal humoral balance was gradually if only very partially displaced by a new medical understanding of the body's vulnerability to invasion and infection by external foreign bodies. Regular outbreaks of epidemic illnesses such as plague, the sweating sickness, and, in particular, syphilis revealed the inadequacy of the conventional, Galenic understanding of disease as an endogenous state. Although providential and miasmic etiologies of epidemic disease retained popularity into the eighteenth century, physicians increasingly began to propose that illness was a determinate thing transmitted from body to body. This new exogenous model of disease, which I have examined elsewhere, was formally outlined in the first decades of the sixteenth century by the Veronese physician Girolamo Fracastoro and the iconoclastic Swiss physician Paracelsus.[46] Neither Fracastoro nor Paracelsus dispensed entirely with the theory of the humors; but in attempting to explain the transmission of epidemic illness, both radically reconfigured the very notion of disease itself. For Fracastoro and Paracelsus alike, disease was less an internal state of complexional imbalance than a determinate *semina* or seed, an external entity that invaded the body through its pores and orifices.

The idea was hardly an innovation of medical experts. Exogenous models of disease were part of folk medical lore, and religious rhetoric customarily embodied sin as a pathogenic *spiritus mali* that invaded the body through its sensory apertures.[47] But the notion of disease as an invasive entity was picked up with particular vigor in the century after Fracastoro and Paracelsus. Girolamo Cardano proposed in 1557 that the seeds of disease were infinitesimally small animals capable of reproduction.[48] With the growing Protestant reaction against classical Galenism and the championing of new "reformist" pharmacies, Paracelsus's model of pathenogenesis was refined and disseminated by many physicians, including the Belgian J. B. Van Helmont. This is not to say that there was any radical break with Galenism. Many writers, such as the English physician Robert Fludd, cheerfully accommodated the new Paracelsan model within the old humoral paradigm.[49] But other intellectual developments helped consolidate the new exogenous models of disease. The renewed seventeenth-century interest in the Roman Epicurean poet Lucretius and his doctrine of atomism helped writers like Lucy Hutchinson and Margaret Cavendish to reimagine disease as an irreducibly small, migratory entity.[50] And the invention of the microscope, which prompted Antony van Leeuwenhoek's discovery of minuscule parasites, potentially pushed reformist European medical science even farther in the direction of a pathological microbiologism. Even non-Protestants embraced the new models of disease: the Jesuit Athanasius Kirchner claimed to have observed a microscopically small organism that caused plague. The discovery of the bacillus that was the agent of bubonic plague, however, had to wait another two hundred years.[51]

To understand the emergence of these new exogenous etiologies simply in the idealist terms of philosophical and scientific discoveries, however, is to conceal much. In particular, it neglects the seemingly unrelated yet immensely formative political horizons within which the pathological objects of these new "discoveries" were first conceived. In the sixteenth century, the names of dangerous diseases increasingly become nationalized in order to denote their putative point of origin. Typhus fever, for example, was often called the *morbus Hungaricus,* and dysentery became known as the "Irish disease." England was not spared pathologization: the epidemic disease that attacked northern Europe in the 1520s was widely called the "English sweat," and rickets became known in the seventeenth century as the "English disease."[52] Such nationalized nomenclature was most evident, however, in the case of syphilis:

the Muscovites referred to it as the Polish sickness, the Poles as the German sickness, and the Germans as the French sickness—a term of which the English also approved (*French pox*) as did the Italians. . . . The Flemish and Dutch called it "the Spanish sickness," as did the inhabitants of North-West Africa. The Portuguese called it "the Castillian sickness," whilst the Japanese and the people of the East Indies came to call it "the Portuguese sickness."[53]

As this account hints, the global spread of syphilis prompted radically new etiologies of the disease. It had begun to be seen as not only a *state* of humoral disarray but also a *thing* that migrated across national borders. The above passage shows also how the perception of syphilis's migrations had an unmistakably economic tinge: the movement of the disease from Spain to Holland and North Africa, and from Portugal to the East Indies and Japan, delineated new, international trade routes. Communicable disease, in other words, was increasingly seen as an exotic if dangerous commodity, shipped into the nation by merchants, soldiers, and other alien migrants. Infection of the body politic by foreign bodies thus provided a template for infection of bodies natural.

The discourse of syphilis was not the only occasion for the pathologization of the foreign in late Tudor and early Stuart political writing. Moralist writers fired numerous jeremiads at exotic commodities, which they repeatedly lambasted as the agents of moral and economic illness alike.[54] With the help of some euphuistic alliteration, John Deacon wrote in 1616 of "our carelesse entercourse of trafficking with the contagious corruptions, and customes of forreine nations." In the process, he sketched an etiology of moral pathology that recalls the transnational nomenclatures and trajectories that distinguish early modern accounts of syphilis:

so many of our English-mens minds are thus terribly Turkished with Mahometan trumperies . . . thus spitefully Spanished with superfluous pride; thus fearfully Frenchized with filthy prostitutions; thus fantastically Flanderized with flaring networks to catch English fooles; thus hufflingly Hollandized with ruffian-like loome-workes, and other ladified fooleries; thus greedily Germanized with a most gluttonous manner of gormandizing; thus desperately Danished with a swine-swilling and quaffing; thus skulkingly Scotized with Machiavellian projects; thus inconstantly Englished with every new fantasticall foolerie.[55]

These diseases are not simply Turkish, Spanish, or French; by transforming European nationalities from nouns into transitive verbs, Deacon reimagines illness as exogenous conditions communicated across national borders. Such a conception of disease would have been arguably unthinkable outside the growing global networks of trade, migration, and information, which brought different cultures into potentially transformative contact. Even though his first examples are religious and moral, the underlying subtext of Deacon's catalogue of "contagious corruptions" is economic, referencing as it does the considerable influx into early modern England of foreign goods and migrants, such as Dutch cloth workers.

From a purely positivist standpoint, the mutually implicated histories of invasive disease and global commerce are apparent when one considers the twinned fortunes of trade and epidemics in antiquity and the Middle Ages. In a useful overview, Jean-Noël Biraben has identified six pathocenoses, or epochs of disease, in the history of the West since the classical age.[56] Nearly all of these are related to changing modes and infrastructures of commerce. Urbanization in antiquity led to epidemics; Roman roadbuilding to the Middle East brought smallpox and then leprosy to the center of the empire; and new trade routes to the Orient brought plague and other diseases to Europe in the thirteenth century. Jared Diamond has conversely shown how "germs," together with "guns and steel," were the West's primary weapons of economic as well as cultural conquest.[57] But such approaches, useful as they are, tell us little about why early modern English writers and not their classical or medieval predecessors were able to begin rethinking disease as a determinate thing in transnational motion.

Early modern England was not the first nation to experience epidemic disease or the dislocations of international commerce. But it did experience each as simultaneous novelties and crises that tested the limits of old vocabularies and demanded the production of new ones. The turbulent new modes of transnational commerce and the deadly epidemics of plague and syphilis each provided ready vocabularies for representing the forms and effects of the other. The relationship between discourses of disease and national economy, in other words, was not a simple, unidirectional one of cause and effect. Rather, numerous mutual influences obtained. Economic developments helped writers imagine disease as a foreign body (a theme that I will explore particularly with respect to Ben Jonson's fantasies of the plague); in turn, the new vocabularies of contagious or exogenous disease provided writers with the imaginative resources for an emergent discourse of national and global economy.

As Deacon's catalogue of "contagious corruptions" makes clear, new understandings of disease as residing in and transmitted by foreign bodies were insistently articulated in many nonmedical domains of early modern discourse. This is nowhere more evident than in the English mercantilist literature of the early seventeenth century. Inasmuch as this corpus of writing displays unprecedented attention to the vicissitudes of England's commerce with other nations—including the pathologies of trade imbalances, bullion flows, international currency exchange, centers of wealth production, and increased importation of exotic commodities—it displays a heightened interest in the foreign as the potential agent of both economic disease and health. Hence in the same passage where he laments the passing of an old discourse of "commonwealth" in which the prince would regulate the self-sufficient economy by the "ridding out of all distemperate humors," Gerard Malynes talks of a new world order in which foreign "contagion" has become the standard unit of both pathology and commerce.[58] Indeed, as I have noted, a significant number of the diseases that mercantilist discourse metaphorically invokes—including syphilis, taint, canker, plague, hepatitis, and consumption—are "contagious" ailments contracted from foreign bodies.

To this extent, mercantilist writers' fantasies of the body politic's diseases might seem to resonate with anthropologist Mary Douglas's highly influential characterization of the body as "a model which can stand for any bounded system."[59] The binary spatialities of "inside" and "outside," "self" and "foreign" that inform Douglas's analyses of bounded cultural systems have proved equally illuminating in anthropological studies of modern bacteriology and immunology. Emily Martin, for example, has written how "the notion that the immune system maintains a clear boundary between self and nonself is often accompanied by a conception of the nonself world as foreign and hostile."[60] As we will see, a similarly xenophobic opposition of self and foreign nonself suffuses mercantilist fantasies of economic pathology: Malynes identifies the commonwealth's "canker" with the predatory Continental "banker" who seeks to depreciate the value of English coin; Misselden attributes the nation's "hepatitis" in part to the "Turkish" pirate who plunders English bullion. Yet the binary structures that underwrite anthropological analyses of body metaphors present an insufficient picture of the complex typologies produced in mercantilist discourses of economic pathology. These discourses map not simply a binary opposition of "national" body and "foreign" diseases; as I shall show throughout this book, the latter pair of categories are crucially interarticulated with a third, the "global," which mercantilist discourse constitutes as the ecosystem within which the national and foreign must communicate (in both commercial and pathological senses). Diseases like Malynes's "canker" and Misselden's "hepatitis" may have fueled xenophobia, but they also helped legitimize visions of cosmopolitan economy; like the metaphor of the Asian flu, early modern mercantilist pathologies presumed "natural" patterns of migration across national borders that simultaneously stigmatized the foreign and naturalized the global.

My analysis of this tripartite mercantilist typology—the national, the foreign, and the global—also involves a rather different understanding of pathology from its previous theorizations in the influential work of Georges Canguilhem and René Girard. Both owe a significant if unspoken debt to Emile

Durkheim's *Rules of Sociological Method* and his protostructuralist analysis of social pathology.[61] In the work of all three theorists, disease tends to be hypostasized as a generic "disorder" that relationally ratifies "order," "normality," or "health." But as Michel Foucault writes in the preface to *The Order of Things*, "disease is at one and the same time disorder—the existence of a perilous otherness within the human body, at the very heart of life—and a natural phenomenon with its own constants, resemblances, and types."[62] The first part of Foucault's remark has become sacred writ in much writing about early modern representations of disease; but the second has been more or less completely ignored. Foucault's insistence that disease is also a "natural phenomenon with its own constants, resemblances, and types" remains a useful caveat not just to theorists of pathology but also to literary and cultural critics who have displayed a tendency to transform early modern diseases into Disease, and who overlook the "types" and distinctions that are the a priori ground of the very logic of "constants" and "resemblances." Those differences have often evaporated in accounts of the uniformity of disease in premodern discourses of pathology. One common view is that early moderns did not really differentiate between diseases: even a medical historian as scrupulous as Paul Slack argues that "there was little appreciation that individual diseases were separable entities before 1600."[63] It is hard to square this assessment, though, with the perspective of the early modern plague writer Thomas Dekker, who argued that "maladies of the Body, goe simply in their owne Habit, and liue wheresoeuer they are entertainde, vnder their proper and knowne Names; As the Goute passeth onely by the name of the Goute: So an Appoplex, an Ague, the Pox, Fistula, &c."[64] As we will see, many other early modern writers insisted on the multiple "types" of disease even as they adduced resemblances between them.

I wish, then, to offer a more historically and culturally nuanced understanding of early modern disease, one that attends to its status in the period as "a natural phenomenon with its own constants, resemblances, and types." I thus seek to illuminate not only diachronic transformations in conceptions of pathology but also the synchronic distinctions as well as resemblances between specific illnesses. Hence we will encounter here not Disease but a veritable gallery of early modern diseases—syphilis, taint, canker, serpego, plague, hepatitis, castration (widely considered a pathological affliction by early modern physicians), and consumption. In the process, I will attend to the enormous discursive productivity of these various ailments. Rather than simply ratifying the "normal" through a logic of binary opposition, these diseases could be productive in other, diverse ways. Syphilis, for example, offered writers various ways of imagining the appetite in the sphere of global commerce; taint provided a vocabulary for understanding the border confusions caused by the international flow of currency and people; canker and serpego metaphorically mediated the problem of the origin of money's value; plague helped figure the transnational migrations of commodities; hepatitis and castration raised questions about the centers of authority in the production and circulation of wealth; and consumption permitted a more comprehensive understanding of venture capital and import-oriented economics.

For all the differences between diseases that I am insisting on, there is still a unifying theme to my argument. By provisionally reimagining disease as a foreign body, people in the sixteenth and seventeenth centuries produced new epistemologies within which objects such as the national economy and the global laws of trade could be preliminarily conceived. Hence the early modern English "pathologization" of commerce for which I am arguing was by no means a straightforward *demonization*, as we might think it to be now. Although mercantilist writers frequently employed images of disease to stigmatize certain economic phenomena, these images equally served as the vectors for a more productive reimagining of international commerce and typologies of the national, the foreign, and the global. If he had been more attentive to the economic nuances of disease and the pathological accents of the economic in the seventeenth century, then, Foucault could have written a supplement to Marx's famous essay on money and *Timon of Athens* and called it "The Power of Disease in Bourgeois Society."

Dramas of National Economy and Disease

The growing seventeenth-century preoccupation with the foreign as a simultaneously pathological and economic phenomenon is evident not just in English mercantilist writing. As my discussion of *The Merchant of Venice* indicates, it is also prefigured in the drama of the sixteenth century, which repeatedly blurred the boundaries between what we now regard as the separate domains of the medical and the mercantile. This blurring can be seen as early as the Tudor interludes that preceded the drama of the professional London playhouses. In the early Elizabethan entertainment *An Interlude of Wealth and Health* (c. 1558), the mutual metaphorical implication of disease and economics is the play's governing conceit. The interlude for the most part imagines wealth and health in medieval fashion—as generic, allegorical concepts stripped of any historical or geographical specificity.[65] The character Health, for example, asserts that

>   Welth is good I cannot denay
> Yet prayse yourself so much ye may

For welth oftentimes doth decay
And welth is nothing sure. (28–31)

And Wealth likewise characterizes Health in generic terms: "I neuer marke this muche, nor understood / That Helth was such a treasure, and to man so good" (188–89). But lurking in the play is a counternarrative that looks forward to the mercantilist writing of the early seventeenth century. At times, Wealth and Health are presented as nationally specific, even nationalist, figures: "I am welth *of this realme*" (17, emphasis added); "I welth, am this realmes comfort, / And here I wyll indure" (157–58); "For here I [health] am well cherished" (163).

As soon as the two characters become nationally coded, moreover, they become close allies and even analogues of each other: "Welth for Lybertye doth loboure euer / And helth for Libertye is a great store" (270–71). The allegorical character Remedy observes,

welth, and helth, is your right names
The which England to forbere were very loth
For by welth and helth commeth great fames
Many other renlmes [*sic*] for our great welth shames
That they dare not presume, nor they dare not be bold
To striue againe England, or any right with holde. (544–49)

The logic of this passage is by no means mercantilist. Indeed, it arguably reproduces the premercantilist discourse of commonwealth, in which the health of the body politic is synonymous with its internally generated wealth. Economic as much as corporeal health is similarly understood here as an endogenous phenomenon, deriving from internal balance; hence even as "other renlmes" covet England's wealth and health, the latter seem initially to be assets generated entirely within the nation.

But the play also looks ahead to mercantilist understandings of economic health and pathology as corollaries of transnational commerce. The main threats to both Wealth and Health come from two allegorical characters, Illwill and Shrewdwit, who are coded as foreigners. Shrewdwit enters speaking French (350), Illwill speaks Spanish (845–46, 851–52), and both swear Catholic oaths. These two are not the only foreign bodies who threaten England's wealth and health. One of the interlude's characters, and indeed its only nonallegorical figure, is a Flemish immigrant named Hans. A mercenary looking for work in England, he is presented as a loutish drunk who speaks in a virtually incomprehensible stage-Dutch. Importantly, he is also linked to economic sabotage: he boasts that wealth no longer resides in England, for "welth best in ffaunders [Flanders], it my self brought him dore" (424). The discourse of the self-contained commonwealth is eclipsed here by that of mercantilist bullion-ism, according to which national wealth is synonymous with money and hence transferable across countries' borders. In order to restore health and wealth to a polity that is more nationally than universally coded, Remedy expels Hans from England, exclaiming, "There is to mainy allaunts [aliens] in this reale, but now I / good remedy haue so prouided that Englishmen shall / lyue the better dayly" (760–62). Thus is economic health reconfigured in nationalist terms as libera-tion from invasive foreign bodies. Yet such xenophobia anticipates the charac-teristic rhetorical gambit of mercantilist discourse: conflating the economic and the pathological, the play pointedly locates itself on the global stage, but within that stage, the "foreign" is deemed villainous.

In the wake of *An Interlude of Wealth and Health,* Shakespeare and his con-temporaries repeatedly plotted shifting links between the discourses of com-merce, disease, and national health. The foreign emerges in their plays as both a pathogenic and a commercial phenomenon, an invasive entity that threatens yet also is crucial to the health of bodies natural, politic, and economic alike. What Walter Cohen has termed the "drama of a nation" repeatedly lays bare the equa-tion of national wealth and health and subjects it to critical scrutiny.[66] If the "Asian flu" is not just a metaphor but also a character in a dramatic narrative, so too are the pathologized foreign bodies of the early modern stage. An analysis of how the plays of Shakespeare and his contemporaries resonate with mercan-tilist discourse can thus disclose the *dramatic* component of that discourse. To this end, *Sick Economies* considers the various, early permutations of the drama of national economy produced and refined in what I am calling the mercantilist drama of the late sixteenth and early seventeenth centuries.

This is not to say that such drama delineates an entity identical to what we would now regard as "the economy." Nor does it even represent the "English" national economy. Indeed, most of the mercantilist drama I will examine is lo-cated in Mediterranean city-states—Ephesus, Venice, Troy, Fez, Tunis—rather than in the English nation-state. Nevertheless, the mercantilist drama's preoc-cupations with commerce and disease entail the tripartite typology of the do-mestic, the foreign, and the global that distinguishes the economic writings of Malynes, Milles, Misselden, and Mun. By articulating this typology, the mer-cantilist drama of Shakespeare and his contemporaries also voices novel under-standings of desire, identity, citizenship, money, value, matter, motion, circulation, state authority, and capital, understandings that have provided the epistemological foundations for our modern, economic conceptions of the na-tion and nationalism.

Why was the theater the space for such dramas? One might cite historical, institutionally specific reasons for the irruption of economic and medical concerns into early modern English drama. As Jean-Christophe Agnew and Douglas Bruster have argued, the London playhouses were thoroughly implicated in the emergent forms of market capitalism, and these forms suffuse the plays that were staged in them.[67] Leeds Barroll has reminded us how the playhouses were equally the putative sites of disease, subject to repeated closures by the city authorities who feared that large audiences might be breeding grounds for plague.[68] It is tempting to speculate that an institution accused by its opponents of not only spreading but causing disease (the Puritan preacher Thomas White had claimed that "the cause of plagues is sinne . . . and the cause of sinne are playes: therefore the cause of plagues are playes") may also have had a special investment in debating the etiologies of illness.[69]

But to explain early modern drama's vocabularies of commerce and disease, we need to do more than just identify extradiscursive, historical "realities" that influenced Shakespeare and his contemporaries. No matter how much the nascent market economy and the plague may have touched the lives of early modern playwrights and their audiences, there is also something literally generic about the drama's obsession with mercantile and pathological foreign bodies. As I have shown in my earlier discussion of *The Merchant of Venice,* romance afforded Shakespeare and his contemporaries a medium in which to articulate new visions of global trade. Fredric Jameson has argued that romance from the twelfth century on entails the projection of an Other, a projection that ends when that Other reveals its "name."[70] As subsequent critics have noted, romance's projections and erasures of alterity provide the narrative template for many early modern English fantasies of empire and colonialism. Joan Pong Linton, for example, has demonstrated how romantic topoi mediate representations of Raleigh's exploits in Guiana and early English ventures in Virginia.[71] I wish to supplement Linton's analysis by showing how early modern romance's affiliations to dramas of nationhood are confined neither to the space of the American New World nor to the project of empire building. Romance's projections and erasures of alterity also offered mercantilist writers and early modern playwrights narrative strategies with which to imagine the commercial nation as well as its transactions with foreign bodies within an overarching global system.

Yet the plays I examine here are not romances in the conventional sense. Notably absent from this book are Shakespeare's late romances or the romances of Beaumont and Fletcher. The plays that have captured my attention are instead works in which romance is blended with other genres: the Plautine comedy, the Florentine novella, the nationalist epic, the Lucianic satire, the pirate adventure, the London city comedy. In all these generic hybrids, the transoceanic scope of romance serves to articulate and refract the play's commercial preoccupations. Such exercises in generic *contaminatio*—a term synonymous in the Renaissance with "infection"—also seem to come ready-fitted with a pathological vocabulary.[72] And this vocabulary is enlarged and refined by romance's characteristic "projections" of alterity.

Chapter 2, "Syphilis and Trade," attends to the mutual implication of early modern discourses of the pox and transnational commerce, with specific reference to *The Comedy of Errors.* In the process, I argue that the growth of global trade in the second half of the sixteenth century placed considerable pressure on conventional understandings of both pathology and economy. New understandings of syphilis as deriving from foreign nations came into conflict with residual conceptions of illness as an endogenous, appetitive, or humoral state; new understandings of the systemic operations of global commerce problematized the medieval conception of economy as a subset of morality. Shakespeare, I argue, reproduces these conflicts in his comedy. The language of syphilis provides him with a vocabulary that allows him to mediate, albeit problematically, conflicting understandings of trade. He does so, moreover, in a fashion parallel to the rhetorical gambits of protomercantilist economic writers of the sixteenth century such as Thomas Starkey and Thomas Smith.

Chapter 3, "Taint and Usury," considers how the economic pathology par excellence of medieval Christian ideology—usury—was reconfigured in three early modern texts: Gerard Malynes's *Saint George for England Allegorically Described,* the anonymous Dutch Church Libel of 1593, and Shakespeare's *The Merchant of Venice.* What is voiced in each text is less the conventional condemnation of usury as a form of unnatural breeding than a new, mercantilist problematic of transnational identity for which the "Jew" serves as the unstable signifier. Each text views the Jew as a palimpsest, in which discrete categories of national identity are fused and confused. The resulting transnational contaminations are registered pathologically, as "infections," "gangrene," and, most important, "taints." Yet in each case the hybridization of the Jew (as Turkish, Dutch, or Spanish) works to disavow the textual and historical hybridization of the "gentile" and/or English subject. Mercantilist discourse helps generate yet also subjects to immense pressure the myth of a discrete "national" subject in a time of unprecedented transnational fluidity.

Chapter 4, "Canker/Serpego and Value," examines the crisis of value prompted by what Malynes called "merchandizing exchange"—European bankers' playing of the foreign currency markets through the manipulation of rates of exchange. This raised the question: was the value of money intrinsic or extrinsic? Debates about the origins of disease provided writers a vocabulary with which to articulate the conflict over value's origins. Malynes refers to the problems of "merchandizing exchange" as a "canker," a disease that, like its close cousin "serpego," was understood to be both endogenous and invasive. Similarly, when Hector speaks in *Troilus and Cressida* of "infectious" valuation, he reproduces the disjunctions of the term in contemporary medical discourse, where it was used to designate both humoral disarray and contagion. Indeed, the play's extensive pathological and mercantile vocabularies repeatedly embody this uncertainty over whether the origins of disease and value are external or internal. Such an uncertainty, however, was one of the consequences of the growth of foreign trade and transnational practices of foreign currency exchange, and thus was symptomatic of the emergent drama of national economy.

These first chapters show how pathological language mediated mercantilist writers' and Shakespeare's understandings of the economic. In Chapter 5, "Plague and Transmigration," I argue that economic developments also affected dramatic understandings of the pathological. Ben Jonson found in the Pythagorean doctrine of metempsychosis, or transmigration of the soul, a richly suggestive figure for the dynamics of international trade. In *Volpone,* movement across the boundaries of national body politics, particularly via their ports, is both a constitutive principle and an occasion for considerable anxiety. A similar anxiety is expressed in medical tracts such as Timothy Bright's *Treatise: Wherein is Declared the Sufficiencie of English Medicines* and mercantilist treatises such as Thomas Milles's writings on national customs policies. Like Bright and Milles, Jonson lends expression to a fear of transmigratory foreign commodities contaminating the body politic through its ports. Jonson's heightened sensitivity to the transmigrations of things across national borders notably influences his vision of plague and, as a consequence, he brings to partial visibility the mercantile coordinates of what has been widely regarded as the most significant epistemic shift in seventeenth-century medical science: the eclipse of the old Galenic and Aristotelian cosmology of qualities, elements, and humors by the new mechanistic philosophy of quantifiable matter in motion.

Chapter 6, "Hepatitis/Castration and Treasure," examines how early modern physiologies of blood and semen underwrote economic models of the transnational circulation of bullion. In their extended pamphlet war of 1622–23 concerning the causes of the decay of English trade, Edward Misselden and Gerard Malynes both resorted to pathologies of the blood—most notably, hepatitis—to represent the pathologies of the national economy. Implicit in this exchange is a physiological understanding of the loss of treasure as analogous to castration by external forces, including (in Misselden's analysis) Turkish pirates in the Mediterranean. This understanding is made explicit in Thomas Heywood's *Fair Maid of the West* and Philip Massinger's *Renegado.* In both these plays' representations of Barbary piracy, the threat of Europeans' castration by Moors and Turks looms. Although the two plays' preoccupation with castration is usually read as expressions of an emergent Orientalist discourse of Islamic savagery, I locate it instead within a specifically mercantilist framework. In Misselden and Malynes's exchange, physiological analogies function ambivalently, vacillating between visions of the *corpus economicum* as a self-contained and self-sustaining physiological system with clear centers of wealth production and as a decentralized organism whose lifeblood (and semen) circulates in and out of it. Heywood's and Massinger's plays likewise corporeally figure bullion in ways that entail conflicting attitudes toward relations between the state and private venturers in the accumulation of national treasure.

Chapter 7, "Consumption and Consumption," examines the shifting valences in the early seventeenth century of a particularly important economic and pathological term. "Consumption" was employed in early modern economic discourse almost invariably as a negative pathological metaphor with which to heap opprobrium on commercial practices that depleted or "wasted" the nation's wealth. But it also brought to visibility emerging practices of *conspicuous* consumption, whereby exotic luxury commodities were purchased and flaunted by a new kind of subject, the cosmopolitan consumer. Although conventionally regarded as an endogenous, humoral affliction, consumption became increasingly freighted with the exotic in the early seventeenth-century imagination as a result of the growing trade in foreign luxuries. Such an association is visible in the influential economic treatises of the mercantilist writer Thomas Mun. Yet even as Mun vilified foreign luxury commodities, he also sought to reconfigure consumption as a necessary rather than pathological economic practice, and specifically as a mode of venture capital that benefited the English economy. Both these shifts are evident also in Middleton and Dekker's *Roaring Girl*, which pushed the meanings of consumption away from the purely domestic wasting of wealth toward the purchase and conspicuous display of foreign goods. Consumption is thus represented less as a wasteful, pathological phenomenon than as a medicinal process whereby a controlled encounter with foreignness safeguards the health of the body politic.

What I offer here, then, are several discursive etiologies of our modern notions of the national, the foreign, and the global. Indeed, the diverse meanings of the term "etiology" are of crucial importance to my argument. Throughout this book, I attempt to clarify the origins of the discourses of national and transnational economy. But inasmuch as etiology has more specifically become that branch of medical science concerned with the causation and origins of *disease,* I seek also to show how early modern debates about both the nature and the transmission of illness cannot be separated from the early modern emergence of economics as a discrete field of inquiry. In *Sick Economies,* I argue both that our modern notions of economy have a decidedly pathological provenance and that our modern notions of disease cannot be disentangled from the development of transnational capitalism. If the London commercial stage was the site of the "drama of a nation," therefore, its economic vocabularies betray traces of new, nationalistic etiologies of disease; equally, its pathological lexicons hint at multiple etiologies of the national economy. In these embryonic dramas, then, we might also see the egg from which the flu-bearing Asian chickens of modern commercial pathology have hatched.

Syphilis and Trade: Thomas Starkey, Thomas Smith, The Comedy of Errors

As critics have increasingly noted, images of syphilis cast a long shadow over Shakespeare's more mature drama, particularly the so-called problem plays of his dark middle period.[1] But what are we to make of the disease's presence in an early, ostensibly sunnier work like *The Comedy of Errors*? The play brims with references to the pox, to the point where it becomes a virtual leitmotif. The Syracusian Dromio and Antipholus joke about its effects, especially the loss of hair, at some length in 2.2.83–93; they banter about the same symptoms again at 3.2.123; and Dromio quibbles on the "burning" mode of its transmission at 4.3.53–55.[2] The disease also operates throughout the play at a darker, more metaphorical level. It haunts Adriana's extended lament about her own flesh being "strumpeted" by the "contagion" of her husband's seeming adultery (2.2.143); its hereditary nature lurks in Balthasar's assertion that slander can damage an "ungalled reputation" and "with foul intrusion enter in . . . For slander lives upon succession" (3.1.102–3, 105); and its effects can be recognized in Luciana's memorable question to her Syracusian brother-in-law: "Shall, Antipholus, / Even in the spring of love, thy love springs rot?" (3.2.2–3). Johannes Fabricius, the leading scholar of syphilis in Shakespeare's drama, has argued that the pervasive pathological imagery of the plays written in the period 1601–4—*Hamlet, Troilus and Cressida, Measure for Measure,* and *Othello*—points to Shakespeare's having contracted the pox at some time around the turn of the seventeenth century.[3] But any correlation one may attempt to draw between Shakespeare's syphilitic imagery and his personal health is quite confounded by *The Comedy of Errors,* written when the playwright was in his presumably healthy twenties.

In this chapter, I offer a different strategy for decoding the syphilitic references of *The Comedy of Errors*—one that divulges neither the biographical details of Shakespeare's life and pathologies, nor even the phenomenology of the syphilis epidemic in early modern England and Europe. I instead situate the play's treatment of the disease within a broader constellation of discourses and structures of feeling that accompanied the enormous growth of international commerce in the sixteenth century. When Adriana attributes her husband's seeming mental illness—one of the chief symptoms of syphilis—to "some love that drew him oft from home" (5.1.56), we can glimpse the playwright's calibration of the pathological and the economic. Throughout *The Comedy of Errors,* the appetite that lures one away from "home," whether domestic or national, is the necessary foundation of commerce: according to Luciana, men's "business still lies out o'door" (2.1.11). For Adriana, by contrast, such appetite is rather the source of disease, as is shown by her earlier complaint that her husband's pathological "ruffian lust" for women "out o'door" has left him (as well as her) syphilitically "possessed with an adulterate blot" (2.2.132, 139).

Adriana's remarks entail a potential semantic confusion, however, concerning what she perceives to be the cause of her husband's peregrinations and illnesses. Does the "love" that has led to his pathological alienation from "home" refer to his sexual and commercial appetite or to the *objects* of that appetite—the Courtesan and the exotic goods he covets? Does she believe his problem, in other words, to be internally generated or externally contracted? As I shall argue, this confusion resonates throughout *The Comedy of Errors,* and in a fashion that notably reproduces a disjunction endemic to premercantilist Tudor economic literature. In much the same manner as treatises like Thomas Starkey's *Dialogue Between Reginald Pole and Thomas Lupset* (c. 1535) and Thomas Smith's *Discourse of the Commonweal of This Realm of England* (1581), the play vacillates between a traditional view of commerce as a subset of ethics in which the appetitive subject assumes moral responsibility for his or her transactions and an emergent conception of commerce as an amoral, global system to whose demands the subject and the nation have no choice but to submit. As Adriana's ambivalent pathologization of her husband's extradomestic "love" suggests, moreover, this disjunction significantly mirrors—and is partly grounded in— late sixteenth-century medical discourse. Replicating the contemporary swirl of controversy concerning the etiologies of epidemic illness, the play flip-flops between representing disease as an interior state that the patient can avoid through self-regulation of appetite and as an implacable, invasive force that overwhelms its hapless victim. In both economic and pathological spheres, then, the play stages a contest between individual agency centered on internal appetite and ineluctable subjection to external control.

I shall argue that syphilis, a disease attributed by Shakespeare's contemporaries variously to appetitive immoderation and to contact with infectious foreign bodies, offered the playwright a ready-made vocabulary with which to mediate the disjunctions of a commerce that draws one "oft from home." The play's references to the disease serve to condense disparate anxieties about unchecked individual appetite and the potentially deleterious fiscal effects of trade with foreign nations—anxieties, in other words, about both moral and systemic economies. In the process, *The Comedy of Errors* offers an important glimpse of the extent to which the evolving premercantilist discourses of pathology and economy were entwined, and indeed helped transform each other's horizons of conceptual possibility.

Commerce of Errors

Modern criticism of *The Comedy of Errors* has repeatedly focused on Shakespeare's debts to classical Latin comedy source materials, specifically Plautus's *Menaechmi* and *Amphitruo,* with a resulting emphasis on details of dramatic and poetic form.[4] Though critics have noted the play's oblique topical allusions to the problem of French royal succession (3.2.123–24) and the Spanish Armada (3.2.135–36), they have done so primarily to date *The Comedy of Errors* early in Shakespeare's career, and hence to redouble attention to what evidence it may furnish about the young Shakespeare's classical reading. How the play might engage its contemporary political and economic contexts, though, has been largely ignored.[5]

The impulse to quarantine *The Comedy of Errors* from such contexts is, however, a comparatively recent phenomenon. Earlier readers of the play were highly attentive to its commercial dimensions, if only critically so. In the introduction to his 1723 edition of Shakespeare, for example, Alexander Pope lamented that the playwright's earliest works pandered to "*Tradesmen* and *Mechanicks,*" a tendency that he saw reflected in those plays' mercantile and artisanal characters.[6] Pope had in mind not just the principals of *The Merchant of Venice* or the "rude mechanicals" of *A Midsummer Night's Dream* but also the vast majority of characters in *The Comedy of Errors,* a play more rooted in the world of commerce than any other of Shakespeare's. The dramatis personae reveals a slew of "*Tradesmen* and *Mechanicks*": Egeon, a merchant of Syracuse; Balthasar, also a merchant; Angelo, a Goldsmith; First Merchant, friend to Antipholus of Syracuse; and Second Merchant, to whom Angelo is a debtor. Although they are not identified as merchants in the dramatis personae, the separated Antipholus twins are both engaged in commercial trade. If, moreover, one takes into consideration the sexual connotations of "trade"—which, I would argue, *The Comedy of Errors* actively encourages its readers and audiences to do—one might also add the Courtesan to the play's list of "*Tradesmen* and *Mechanicks.*"

Shakespeare places this collection of characters in a pointedly mercantile setting. If the Rialto and its commerce provides an appropriate backdrop for *The Merchant of Venice,* Ephesus's mart looms yet larger in *The Comedy of Errors.* Referred to no less than eleven times in the play, the Ephesian mart is not only the site of local commerce—the location, for example, of Antipholus of Ephesus's purchase of a chain for the Courtesan, crafted by Angelo the Goldsmith. It is also a window onto the globe, offering consumers a variety of exotic commodities after the manner of the Ephesian Antipholus's Turkish tapestry (4.1.104) or the Oriental "silks" that the tailor tries to sell to the bewildered Antipholus of Syracuse (4.3.8). The references to the mart, moreover, subtly align Ephesus with late sixteenth-century London and its own mercantile global connections: when Dromio of Ephesus summons his master "from the mart / Home to your house, the Phoenix" (1.2.74–75), the audience would have heard in "Phoenix" the name of a shop on London's Lombard Street, the banking district in which bills of foreign exchange were transacted.[7] Indeed, Ephesian commerce operates decisively in the register of the global. The merchant who has Angelo the Goldsmith arrested for defaulting on his debts, for example, does so because that merchant is "bound / To Persia, and want[s] guilders for [his] voyage" (4.1.3–4).

Most importantly, Shakespeare furnishes the play with an explicitly global mercantile framework unlike anything in his Plautine sources. Even as the story of Egeon contains coventional elements of romance—separation from and then reconciliation with his lost wife and children, in the manner of Pericles and Leontes—his is a tale that runs pointedly into the jagged rocks of international commerce.[8] Egeon is detained in Ephesus and threatened with capital punishment, because of a trade war between that city and Syracuse. The Ephesian Duke Solinus's opening speech to Egeon spells out the mercantile subtext of the play in no uncertain terms:

Merchant of Syracusa, plead no more.
I am not partial to infringe our laws.
The enmity and discord which of late
Sprung from the rancorous outrage of your duke
To merchants, our well-dealing countrymen,
Who, wanting guilders to redeem their lives,
Have sealed his rigorous statutes with their bloods,
Excludes all pity from our threatening looks.
For since the mortal and intestine jars
Twixt thy seditious countrymen and us
It hath in solemn synods been decreed,
Both by the Syracusians and ourselves,
To admit no traffic to our adverse towns.
Nay, more, if any born at Ephesus
Be seen at any Syracusian marts and fairs;
Again, if any Syracusian born
Come to the bay of Ephesus, he dies,
His goods confiscate to the Duke's dispose,

Unless a thousand marks be levied
To quit the penalty and to ransom him. (1.1.3–22)

International commerce thus frames the play. It is, moreover, international commerce of a recognizably late sixteenth-century complexion. As in England and on the Continent, foreign goods are retailed at specially demarcated "marts and fairs"; business is transacted across national boundaries, not by barter, but by means of a cash economy in which a Dutch coin, the guilder, has currency; and the terms of foreign exchange are organized around a standard denomination of weight in early modern western Europe, the mark.[9] Furthermore, foreign trade enters into the orbit of national sovereignty, as is witnessed by the warring dukes' attempts to control it through "statutes."

For all its *mercantile* subject matter, however, Duke Solinus's speech cannot be said to lend expression to a truly *mercantilist* conception of national economy—an ostensibly amoral (if self-interested) system of national wealth production that requires the intervention of the sovereign or the state to assure a healthy balance of foreign trade and maintenance of bullion reserves. Such a conception was to be fully articulated in England only in the economic treatises of the mercantilists in the early seventeenth century. Rather, the relationship between government and commerce is imagined by Solinus as being necessitated by transnational political "enmity and discord" rather than by any fiscal imperative to produce or maintain national wealth. Unless the Ephesian state's harsh edict against visitors from Syracuse—that any Syracusian discovered in Ephesus must pay a thousand marks upon pain of death—is implausibly interpreted as a canny tariff designed to boost the reserves of the state coffers, there is no discourse here of Ephesian national economy. Nevertheless, the conditions for such a discourse are discernible in Solinus's speech, although national economy emerges here more as a Syracusian than an Ephesian concern. Whereas the Ephesians have placed a ban on *all* Syracusians in retaliation for grievances against Solinus's "well-dealing countrymen," the Syracusian duke seems to have targeted his anger specifically at Ephesian *merchants*. Foreign trade with Ephesus, for reasons that are never disclosed, is regarded by Syracuse's sovereign as injurious to his nation's health.

The potential dangers of foreign trade are again invoked in Egeon's account of his estrangement from his wife. But here, the injury is registered at a personal rather than national level:

In Syracusa was I born, and wed
Unto a woman, happy but for me,
And by me, had not our hap been bad.
With her I lived in joy; our wealth increased

By prosperous voyages I often made
To Epidamium, till my factor's death
And the great care of goods at random left
Drew me from kind embracements of my spouse . . . (1.1.36–43)

Again, Egeon's transnational business is redolent of early modern commercial practice: as a foreign merchant, he relies on a local "factor," or agent, to broker his transactions in Epidamium.[10] But the critique of foreign trade that can be heard in this speech is not a fiscal one. Indeed, Egeon insists that "our wealth increased" as a result of his "prosperous voyages." Rather, he believes his international business to be at fault because of the damage it has done domestically, to his wife and to his marriage. Commerce in Egeon's life story thus entails what he considers to be a fatal error. The verb Shakespeare chooses here is revealing: Egeon's "great care of goods at random left"—that is, his mercantile appetite for neglected foreign goods—"*Drew* me from kind embracements of my spouse" (emphasis added). This is a term that Shakespeare often uses to suggest perversion of "kind," that is, natural, courses of action: it has a similar valence in Adriana's remark about "some love that *drew*" her husband from home.[11] Moral rather than fiscal economy is brought into play here, in other words; the agent of immorality is Egeon's appetite, which estranges him from his domestic as much as his national obligations.

In the Egeon story, then, Shakespeare articulates a highly ambivalent set of attitudes toward international commerce that serve to frame the details of the main plot. On the one hand, in the words of Solinus, commerce across national borders is a more or less innocent ensemble of "well-dealing" practices; on the other, it is viewed by the Duke of Syracuse as a potential threat to national health and by Egeon as a confirmed threat to domestic harmony. These negative assessments are informed by the ambivalences, in Adriana's words, of a "love that drew him oft from home." Is transnational commerce, as Egeon insists, a phenomenon born of the merchant's potentially excessive appetite, perilous only to himself and his family? Or is it, as the Duke of Syracuse hints, an external force that potentially damages the *nations* with which it comes into contact? In other words, is commerce simply a matter of individual or domestic moral health that necessitates prudence on the part of the merchant alone? Or does it have a potentially pathological impact on the fiscal well-being of nations, and thus require the judicious intervention of sovereigns? Significantly, such questions resonate with those posed in English economic writing of the sixteenth century. If the age of English mercantilism proper is dominated by the "Four Ms"—Malynes, Milles, Misselden and Mun—the century of premercantilist English thought is represented by the "two Ss"—Thomas Starkey and Thomas Smith.

Premercantilist Commercial Pathology: The "Two Ss"

It should be reiterated, of course, that the notion of "the" economy as a nationally bounded system engaged in transactions with global trading partners and adversaries is a twentieth-century, post-World War II innovation. What we might want to call economic writing prior to 1600 is rarely about the economy in the modern sense of the word: Tudor English writers, secular as much as ecclesiastical, tended to regard commercial activity as a subset of Christian ethics divorced from any national or global context, involving mostly individual transactions spiced with the sins of covetousness and usury.[12]

This focus on individual morality, however, was increasingly challenged in the sixteenth century by emerging practices of economic nationalism. Henry VII's victory in the War of the Roses resulted in the consolidation of central royal power at the expense of the feudal lords; the Protestant Reformation and the seizure of monastic properties by the crown further fueled a new ideology of the English nation-state in which not only religious and political but also economic power was centralized in the king.[13] This development was partly inspired by a financial crisis: throughout much of his reign, Henry VIII suffered from a drastic shortage of money. The necessity of full state coffers became even more pressing as England contemplated invasion by hostile Catholic powers. England's new religious nationalism, inspired by the break with Rome, was therefore accompanied by a worried economic nationalism, and writers supportive of the king looked for new ways to generate revenue and treasure.[14] This task was made all the more vexed by the economic crises created by rampant inflation in the 1540s and 1550s and devaluation of the nation's coin.[15]

Other factors contributed to the growing English awareness of and interest in national economy. Under the Tudors, English merchants and institutions wrested control of foreign trade from stranger merchants such as the Italian Lombards and the Hanseatic merchants of northern Germany; after the fall of Antwerp to Spain in 1576, new English joint-stock companies such as the Levant Company (chartered in 1581) and the East India Company (chartered in 1601) took control of the lucrative spice and silk trades, which had previously been dominated by the Portuguese.[16] English merchants' growing sense of themselves as players on the stage of global commerce also helped foster new perspectives among Tudor economic writers. In the decades following the London Merchant Adventurers Company's reincorporation in 1565 as the Merchant Adventurers of England, English economic writers—many of them merchants themselves[17]—likewise displayed a stronger sense of national as opposed to merely individual or familial wealth, together with an understanding of the systemic processes by which it might be accumulated or squandered.

Early Tudor protodiscourses of national economy are most legible, and were most sophisticatedly expounded, when they intersected with medicalized discourses of the body and disease. In the late 1530s, Henry VIII's political adviser Thomas Starkey penned a treatise titled *Dialogue Between Reginald Pole and Thomas Lupset*, in which he argued that the nation's wealth was diminished by metaphorical diseases such as "consumption," "palsy," and "frenzy."[18] But in resorting to such analogies, Starkey found it hard to identify with any coherence the causes of England's economic ills. On the one hand, the characters of his dialogue repeatedly excoriate the gluttonous appetites of English subjects in ways that reek more of the pulpit than of the mercantilist treatise. Pole, for example, attributes the nation's economic woes at one point to "excess in diet . . . For this may be a common proverb: 'Many idle gluttons make vittle dear' " (92). Similarly, he chalks up England's problems to the sins of "idleness and sloth" (93). On the other hand, however, Starkey sometimes offers analyses that anticipate a more modern conception of economic pathology—that is, he permits his two characters to regard England's ills as the product not of slipshod morality but of systemic problems that bedevil commerce with other nations.

The affliction of political "gout," for example, is caused by excessive foreign trade: "if we had fewer things brought in from other parts, and less carried out, we should have more commodity and very true pleasure, much more than we have now; this is certain and sure" (96). Starkey's suspicion of imports anticipates the mercantilist conviction that excessive consumption of foreign commodities depletes the nation's treasure. Also like the mercantilists, he complains about the export of English raw materials such as "lead and tin," which get converted into manufactures overseas, only to be retailed back to the English at higher prices (158). But Starkey does not share the mercantilists' valorization of exports as a means of acquiring bullion; instead, as the above examples make clear, his economic goal is the self-sufficient commonwealth. And this ideal often leads Starkey to collapse his more systemic analysis into moral outrage about the English appetite for all things foreign: Pole attributes what he calls the body politic's "palsy," for example, to "all such marchands which carry out things necessary to the use of our people, and bring in such vain trifles and conceits, only for the foolish pastime and pleasure of man" (82).

Starkey's conflicted paradigms of economic pathology delimit the conceptual horizons of subsequent sixteenth-century economic writing. On the one hand, his more medieval discourse of immoral appetite is replicated in the extensive body of Elizabethan literature bemoaning the unprecedented availability of sin-inducing foreign goods such as clothes, foodstuffs, spices, and drugs. In *The Anatomy of Abuses* (1583), for example, Philip Stubbes sought to locate the origins of economic pathology in the aberrant appetites of English subjects for such goods. Employing pointedly medical language, he offers a diagnosis of the body politic's ills that points the finger of blame specifically at "three cankers, which, in processe of time, will eat up the common welth, if speedy reformation be not had . . . daintie fare, gorgious buildings, and sumptuous apparel."[19] This diagnosis sets the tone for much of Stubbes's *Anatomy of Abuses,* in which individuals' venal appetites for exotic luxury goods are seen as the cause of economic as much as moral pathology. But even as he pathologizes the foreign, Stubbes firmly locates both the causes and the remedies for England's ills within England itself, or more specifically, within English people's *desires.* Thus is the moral discourse of commonwealth aligned with a humoral discourse of internal balance and self-restraint.

By contrast, Starkey's occasional attempts to understand national economic pathology as a systemic rather than moral problem are more fully realized in the important treatise *A Discourse of the Commonweal of This Realm of England* (1581), which Henry William Spiegel has characterized as proleptically "tinged by the preconceptions of the mercantilists." This treatise is of uncertain authorship; long attributed to the politican John Hales, the evidence would suggest instead the hand of Sir Thomas Smith.[20] A statesman and professor of law at Cambridge, Smith was also the author of a historical treatise on the value of Roman money, and many of the concerns in the latter work find fuller elaboration in the *Discourse.* Smith seeks to lend economic thought a prestige that it had not hitherto enjoyed, declaring it a branch of "Philosophy Moral."[21] At times, Smith's brand of moral philosophy can sound like Stubbes's. Warning against the appetitive sins of conspicuous consumption, he reminds his readers that "excesses [of clothing and food] were used in Rome a little before the decline of the Empire, so as wise men have thought it the occasion of the decay thereof. . . . I pray God this realm may beware by that example, especially London, the head of this empire" (82). Yet by theorizing the role of money in a nation's economic fortunes, Smith frequently suggests amoral explanations of the problems wrought by the growth of international commerce.

Written like Starkey's treatise in dialogue form, Smith's analysis pits a Doctor against a variety of characters, each of whom have somewhat different notions of the body politic's ills and their etiologies. The Knight, sympathetic to the Doctor, argues:

hereunto we have searched the very sores and griefs that every man feels, so to try out the causes of them; and the causes once known, the remedy of them might soon be apparent. . . . we have thus much proceeded as to the finding out of the griefs—which as far as I perceive stands in these points: viz., dearth of all things though there be scarcity of nothing, desolation of counties by enclosures, desolation of towns for lack of occupation and crafts. (32)

As this passage suggests, Smith is less inclined than either Stubbes or Starkey to locate the English economy's pathologies in moral or appetitive problems. It is instead systemic "sores and griefs" that occupy his attention. The most important of these, the Doctor goes on to argue, is the overvaluation of English currency, which has led to terrible inflation ("dearth," a term that in the above passage means dearness rather than scarcity). This diagnosis, however, involves a strange medley of moral blame and systemic analysis. When the Doctor attributes inflation to "the debasing or rather corrupting of our coin and treasure" (69), he sees this "sore" as partly the result of individual greed: money loses value because covetous people selfishly clip coins. On the other hand, Smith also presents the devaluation of English coin as the consequence of global commerce, including the flooding of European markets with American gold and silver (149). This more systemic brand of analysis is evident also in his claim that "we have devised a way for strangers not only to buy our gold and silver for brass and to exhaust this realm of treasure but also to buy our chief commodities in manner for naught" (69).

In the process, Smith comes very close to articulating the mercantilist theory of the balance of trade with other nations. Indeed, unlike Starkey, Smith rejects the notion of the self-sufficient nation: it was only "in such a country as Utopia" that one could "imagine" there to be "no traffic with any other outward country" (105). But for Smith as for Starkey, there remains confusion over the causes of economic pathology; it is sometimes the product of venal sin, sometimes the consequence of systemic economic problems. By calling for judicious fiscal "remedies" implemented and policed by the national sovereign (Starkey, 142; Smith, 95), however, both writers anticipate not only the mercantilist discourse of national English economy but also its distinctively pathological register.

Comedy of Eros

A mercantilist paradigm of national economy was not yet coherently available to Shakespeare in the early 1590s, of course. But he did have access to the two very different, medicalized notions of moral and systemic economic pathology that preceded it. The ambivalences that characterize Starkey's and Smith's conceptions of economic ills and their causes resonate with the questions raised by *The Comedy of Errors* concerning the nature and consequences of international trade. As we have seen, the framing story of Egeon entails conflicted conceptions of transnational commerce. Is it healthy or is it pathological? Does it fall into the orbit of individual and domestic moral economy, or is it the bedrock of amoral systemic economy? The play's main plot also poses such questions. Like the economic literature of the sixteenth century, it does so by means of a sustained embodiment and pathologization of notions of commerce. And like Starkey's treatise in particular, the main plot embodies commerce in two very different ways: it makes visible both the appetitive bodies of individual merchants or consumers and the global trading bodies constituted by nation-states. In the process, Shakespeare reproduces two radically different paradigms of pathology.

First, like Starkey, Shakespeare employs throughout *The Comedy of Errors* a broadly Galenic conception of physiology, according to which unchecked appetite leads to incontinence, humoral disarray, and sickness.[22] Dromio of Syracuse, for example, remarks that his master needs to avoid dry food to suppress his tendency to choler (2.2.61–62). With greater medical rigor, the Abbess attributes the Ephesian Antipholus's frenzy to "unquiet meals," which "make ill digestion; / Thereof the raging fire of fever bred, / And what's a fever but a fit of madness?" (5.1.74–76). Nell the kitchen-wench, that "mountain of mad flesh" (4.4.154), represents the play's most over-the-top incarnation of pathological appetite. Predating the copiously perspiring pig-wench Ursula of Jonson's *Bartholomew Fair* by some twenty years, her unrestrainedly sweaty desire for Dromio is characterized as a species of grotesque incontinence: "She sweats; a man may go over shoes in the grime for it" (3.2.103–4). Each of these remarks stigmatizes not appetite, however, but its excess. As Michael Schoenfeldt has reminded us in his invaluable study of early modern physiology, moderation rather than repudiation of appetite was the basis of Galenic moral economy.[23] If the discourse of appetite in *The Comedy of Errors* embodies any notion of economy, then, it would appear to be at the level of the individual, (im)moral subject rather than of the amoral nation.

Shakespeare nevertheless attends to the issue of the individual appetite in a fashion that serves to foreground the links between domestic pathology and national economy. Adriana's observation about the transgressive "love that drew" Antipholus "oft from home" invokes national as well as domestic "homes," inasmuch as the referent of her remark—unknown to her, of course— is just as much her seafaring Syracusian brother-in-law as her wayward Ephesian husband. In fact, "home" is a particularly charged and slippery word throughout the play. It acquires importance in the first act not just because of Egeon's own diagnosis of his turpitude in straying from his Syracusian "home" in pursuit of goods but also because of Solinus's question to him: "why thou departedest from thy native home?" (1.1.29). As we have seen, departure from domestic and "native" homes is for Egeon the basis of both successful commerce and familial grief. This tension recurs in Adriana and Luciana's first scene. While Luciana insists that men's "business still lies out o'door" (2.1.11), Adriana bewails her husband's absence from "home." His extradomestic "business" quickly begins to acquire associations of adulterous appetite: "unruly deer, he breaks the pale and feeds from home" (2.1.99–100). The alignment of commercial and sexual appetite is continued throughout the main plot. When Luciana says of Antipholus of Syracuse that he "swore . . . he was a stranger here," Adriana replies, thinking that her sister is speaking of her husband, "true he swore, though yet forsworn he were" (4.2.9–10). Adriana's quibble carries a lot of signifying weight: the "stranger" is simultaneously an adulterer and a merchant traveler, thereby aligning once again the domestic and the "native" home, as well as the appetitive subject's desires for extramarital relations and foreign goods. If the discourse of the appetite that "draws one oft from home" works to pathologize the individual's relation to his or her domestic space, therefore, it can nonetheless simultaneously disclose his or her potentially unhealthy international transactions.

However, *The Comedy of Errors* does not offer audiences solely the appetitive pathologies of Galenism. Elsewhere it provides glimpses of a quite different conception of disease: as an external, implacable force that invades its hapless victim. The latter is by no means coherently articulated in the play—and indeed, an exogenous conception of disease as an invading foreign body was far from systematically expounded at that time by physicians, let alone by Shakespeare himself. Rather, we find in *The Comedy of Errors* a patchwork ensemble of invasive pathologies figured in the language of possession or incursion. When Dr. Pinch attempts to exorcise Antipholus of Ephesus, for example, he regards his patient's condition as a pathological one, terming it "his frenzy" (4.4.81). Inasmuch as Dr. Pinch's proposed cure entails expelling the satanic foreign body "housed within this man" (4.4.54), he notably avoids conceiving of Antipholus's affliction as a product of endogenous appetite or humoral imbalance. In this, he is not alone among the play's characters: Balthasar likewise characterizes slander as an exogenous disease that will "with foul intrusion enter in" (3.1.103).

For all the vagueness with which it is articulated elsewhere in the play, however, the notion of disease as an intruding force appears with some clarity in the play's presentation of economic pathology. The extended set piece in which Dromio of Syracuse compares the body of sweaty Nell the kitchen-wench to the globe involves a conception of both corporeal and economic pathology that is recognizably closer to the modern paradigm of the invasive, communicable condition. Even as he pours scorn on what he regards as Nell's excessive appetite, Dromio imagines an embodied global system of circulation and exchange in which differentiated, sick national economies potentially infect each other. In the process, he develops the implications of Solinus's corporeal metaphor concerning "the mortal and intestine jars / Twixt thy seditious countrymen and us" (1.1.12–13). Like Solinus, Dromio distinguishes between nations while locating them in a unitary, if pathologized, global trading body. Although he begins his extended metaphor in a comic vein, identifying Ireland with the bogs of Nell's buttocks (3.2.117–18), his explanation of how various countries fit into her global *corpus economicum* becomes increasingly complicated. Take, for example, his ingenious anatomization of Spain and its relationship to the Americas:

S. ANTIPHOLUS
  Where Spain?
S. DROMIO
  Faith, I saw it not, but I felt it hot in her breath.
S. ANTIPHOLUS
  Where America, the Indies?
S. DROMIO
  O, sir, upon her nose, all o'er embellished with rubies, carbuncles, sapphires, declining
  their rich aspect to the hot breath of Spain, who sent whole armadoes of carracks to
  be ballast at her nose. (3.2.129–36)

Spain can thus be distinguished by the volume of precious materials it has acquired from the Americas. But Spain's "hot" blasts of breath, and the double meanings of "rubies" and "carbuncles" as inflammations and boils, work together to create an unmistakeably pathological frame of reference for Dromio's account of international trade. In the process, Shakespeare arguably acknowledges one of the greatest economic disasters of the late sixteenth century. Spain had considerably augmented its volume of specie thanks to its New World commercial activities, particularly its mining of silver and precious jewels; yet, as Thomas Smith had argued, the large influx of bullion into the state's coffers had paradoxically depreciated its actual wealth by prompting a spiraling crisis of inflation.[24] Dromio's remarks about Spain support such an explanation by styling its economic ills as a product not of individual pathological appetites but of contact with American goods that have infected and consumed it. Hence even as Dromio's extended analogy draws on a humoral understanding of disease as an endogenous state (the global trading body incarnated by the kitchen-wench is, like her, internally disordered), it nevertheless pivots on a vision of contagious transmission of ills across national borders.

    The two divergent notions of economic pathology visible in *The Comedy of Errors*—either a largely domestic condition stemming from an individual failure to regulate and moderate the internal appetite or a communicable disorder resulting from transactions between nations—are, I believe, integral to the play's presentation of syphilis. Shakespeare's treatment of the disease in this play is quite different from that of his later works; *The Comedy of Errors*'s often jocular references to the pox starkly contrast the much more bitter images of venereal disease one finds in *Troilus and Cressida, Hamlet,* or *Timon of Athens.* So why did Shakespeare keep invoking syphilis in this early comedy? It is, I shall argue, a disease that permitted him to mediate the striking conflict that we have witnessed, not only in English premercantilist economic writing, but also in Adriana's attribution of her husband's illness to "some love that drew him oft from home": namely, the competing convictions that ills proceed either from unfettered individual appetites or from systemic contamination by external forces. Which is correct? The late sixteenth-century discourses of syphilis offered Shakespeare a vocabulary that allowed him, if only provisionally, to answer: both.

Comedy of Hairs

To understand syphilis's meanings and—perhaps more importantly—its mediating power in *The Comedy of Errors* requires an understanding of the sixteenth-century discourses of the disease and, in particular, the debates, scholastic and popular, religious and lay, about its etiology. More than any other illness of the period, it prompted considerable uncertainty about the form and provenance of disease in general.

Syphilis was broadly considered to be a disease of the sinful or excessive appetite. This was certainly the religious explanation of the illness as early as its first epidemic outbreaks in the late fifteenth and early sixteenth centuries. In 1519, the London clerical reformer John Colet told the youth of his parish that "the abhominable great pockes" resulted from "the inordinate misuse of the fleshe."[25] The religious demonization of the syphilitic appetite often derived support from humoral theory: more than a century after Colet's sermon, John Abernathy remarked—in terms that freight the moral and the pathological— that "This burning lust spendeth the spirits and balsame of life, as the flame doth waste the candle: Whereupon followes corruption of humors, rotting of the marrow, and the joynts ake, the nerves are resolved, the head is pained, the gowt increaseth, & of times (as a most just punishment) there insueth that miserable scourge of harlots, The french Pockes."[26] With this assessment, Abernathy in large part echoes those Galenists of the sixteenth century who attributed syphilis to humoral disarray. The German physician Ulrich von Hutten, for example, was convinced that "this infirmite cometh of corrupt, burnt, & enfect blode."[27] The Scottish Galenist Andrew Boorde likewise attributed the disease to humoral overheating in prostitutes: "This impedyment dothe come whan a harlot . . . doth stand ouer a changyng dyshe of coles into the whiche she doth put brymstone and there she doth parfume her selfe."[28]

In a way that no previous disease had, however, syphilis tested the age-old assumption that illness was simply an internal, appetitive state. Although Galenic humoral theory acknowledged the existence of contagious diseases, it was often at a loss to account for their transmission, inasmuch as it regarded disease not as a determinate thing that invades the body but as a state of imbalance within it.[29] Yet syphilis's enormous contagiousness was what most compelled and horrified people: "The frenche pockes is a perilous and wonderfull sykenes," wrote William Horman in 1519, "for it infecteth only with touchynge."[30] As long as syphilis's contagiousness was believed to be confined to acts of sexual intercourse, the unbridled, intemperate appetite could remain the disease's putative origin. But many people feared that syphilis might be communicated by other, nonvenereal means to unsuspecting and even chaste victims, thereby raising the possibility that it was an invasive, amoral disease rather than a condition of the immoral appetite. Rumor had it, for instance, that Cardinal Wolsey had attempted to infect Henry VIII with syphilis by breathing on him; as the physician Peter Lowe wrote in 1596, the pox was believed to be contracted by "receiving the breath of such as are infected, and by sitting on the priuie after them, & sometimes by treading bare-footed on the spettle of those which haue been long corrupted."[31]

These accounts of the disease's contagiousness, which owe more to Hippocratic miasma theory than to humoral medicine, were accompanied by something of a crisis in the Galenic establishment. Even the usually indomitable Andrew Boorde was forced to conclude that his beloved Galenic authorities were incapable of shedding much light on syphilis: "The Grecians can nat tell what the sicknes doth meane wherfore they do set no name for this disease for it did come but lately into Spayne & Fraunce and so to vs."[32] Notably, Boorde's account of this new disease's transnational migrations resonates with the customary early modern names for syphilis. Sixteenth-century syphilographers were repeatedly fascinated by how the various national names for the disease chronicled its epidemic spread across national as well as corporeal borders. Ruy Díaz de Isla remarked in his *Tractado Contra El Mal Serpentino* (published in 1539):

The French called it the *Disease of Naples.* And the Italians and Neapolitans, as they had never been acquainted with such a disease, called it the *French Disease.* From that time on as it continued to spread, they gave it a name, each one according to his opinion as to how the disease had its origin. In Castilia they call it *Bubes,* and in Portugal the *Castilian Disease,* and in Portuguese India they call it the *Portuguese Disease.*[33]

In England, syphilis was dubbed the Spanish sickness, the French pox, or the Neapolitan disease; as on the Continent, therefore, the pox in all its nomenclatural guises was overwhelmingly understood to originate *elsewhere*, to reside in and be transmitted by foreign bodies that had infiltrated bodies politic and natural.

The perception of the foreign provenance of syphilis and of its transmission from nation to nation coincided with the emergence of radically new etiologies of disease in general. As I noted in Chapter 1, the Veronese physician Girolamo Fracastoro—who gave syphilis its name—proposed a new, ontological model of disease as a seed transmitted over a distance from body to body. Fracastoro developed this model to explain the plague, not the pox, for which he was inclined to regard astrological influences as primarily responsible.[34] Nevertheless, his understanding of disease as a determinate foreign particle rather than a state of imbalance found a number of significant counterparts in the corpus of sixteenth-century English literature on syphilis. Writing of the illness in 1596, for example, the surgeon William Clowes offers what looks uncannily like a microbiological account of infection: "the disease is taken by externall meanes . . . Any outward part being once infected, the disease immediately entreth into the blood, and so creepeth on like a canker from part to part." Still, even Clowes could fall back on a residual religious, appetitive description of the illness when he needed to; elsewhere in the same treatise, he writes, "I pray God quickly deliuer vs from it, and to remoue from vs that filthy sinne that breedeth it, that nurseth it, that disperseth it."[35]

As Clowes's vacillation makes clear, syphilis tended to be regarded as neither a univocally appetitive nor a univocally invasive disorder, but both simultaneously. Its bivalent etiology is evident in the *The Comedy of Errors*'s references to the pox, many of which conflate residual Galenic and emergent ontological understandings of the disease. Take, for example, Dromio's quibble about the syphilitic nature of prostitutes: "It is written, they appear to men like angels of light; light is an effect of fire, and fire will burn; ergo, light wenches will burn" (4.3.53–55). The colloquialism "burn," widespread in Elizabethan England, implies not only a humoral conception of syphilitic infection—recall von Hutten's remarks about "burnt blood"—but also an invasive one. This pathological bivalence is enabled by the grammatical confusion embedded in the verb, which can be read both intransitively (light wenches will burn in and of themselves) and transitively (light wenches will burn others).[36] The indeterminacy of "burn" finds a striking counterpart in Luciana's question to her brother-in-law: "Shall . . . / Even in the spring of love, thy love-springs rot?" (3.2.2–3). Again, if read intransitively, "rot" works to demonize the excessive appetite; if read transitively, it draws attention to the communicable nature of Antipholus's condition. In similar fashion, Adriana's remarks about her own afflictions suggest that she considers them to stem simultaneously from syphilitic appetite and external contagion:

I am possessed with an adulterate blot;
My blood is mingled with the crime of lust;
For if we two be one, and thou play false,
I do digest the poison of thy flesh,
Being strumpeted by thy contagion. (2.2.139–43)

The tension between appetitive "crime of lust" and communicable "contagion" is developed in her subsequent speech concerning the relationship between husband and wife. Here she enlarges on a standard metaphor in unexpected fashion:

Thou art an elm, my husband, I a vine,
Whose weakness, married to thy stronger state,
Makes me with thy strength to communicate.
If aught possess thee from me, it is dross,
Usurping ivy, brier, or idle moss,
Who, all for want of pruning, with intrusion
Infect thy sap and live on thy confusion. (2.2.173–79)

The gendered images of host and dependent work highly ambivalently here. The "stronger state" of the husband-elm makes the tree the source of the wife-vine's welfare; yet when the vine is "usurped" by other creepers, the elm is no longer the patriarchal origin of health but the vulnerable victim of contagious disease. Terms like "intrusion" and "infection" anticipate the discourse of contagious foreign bodies even as they work to pathologize the Ephesian Antipholus's appetitive "confusion."

In *The Comedy of Errors,* syphilitic pathology mediates the bivalent depredations of not just sexual activity, however, but commerce too. To understand how, one needs to consider the metaphorical uses to which syphilis was put in early modern nonmedical literature. Given its ready associations with prostitution, which was repeatedly lambasted for depleting men's pockets as well as health, the disease's commercial connotations were unavoidable. Hence in *Measure for Measure,* Lucio's quibbles about prostitution insistently link sexual and commercial trade:

LUCIO
  Behold, behold, where Madam Mitigation comes! I have purchased as many diseases
  under her roof as come to—

2ND GENTLEMAN
  To what, I pray?
LUCIO
  Judge.
2ND GENTLEMAN
  To three thousand dolours a year.
1ST GENTLEMAN
  Ay, and more.
LUCIO
  A French crown more. (1.2.41–47)

Lucio's monetary puns on the symptoms of and names for syphilis ("dolours/dollars," "French crown") figure the disease as a form of wealth that paradoxically entails a simultaneous depreciation of bodily and financial resources. This recalls Dromio of Syracuse's pathological vision of Spain acquiring American "rubies" and "carbuncles," which deplete rather than augment its treasure. Lucio's association of venereal and financial illness is also a feature of the cony-catching literature of the 1590s which, as Martine Van Elk has suggested, provides an important set of co-texts for *The Comedy of Errors*.[37] In *A Disputation Between a Hee and a Shee Conny Catcher* (1592), Robert Greene links the effects of visiting prostitutes not just to the pox's wasting of the body but also to the loss of wealth. The harlot's customers, he argues, "fish for diseases, sicknesse, sores incurable, vlcers bursting out of their ioyntes, and slat rhumes, which by the humor of that villainie, lept from *Naples* into *Fraunce* and from *Fraunce* into *England*." Just as importantly, her customers also "aime . . . at the losse of goods, and blemish of their good names."[38] Greene's account of the effects of syphilis is in certain respects commensurate with humoral and moral pathology: he fingers the unchecked carnal appetites of the harlot's customers as the source of their sundry ills, whether corporeal or financial. But his observation about the international trajectory of the disease, redolent of Ruy Díaz de Isla's account of the global etiologies of syphilis, invokes a broader canvas for his depiction of commercial pathology. The foreign origins of the pox, evident also in Lucio's remark about "a French crown more," facilitate the metaphorical conversion of its pathological effects into commercial afflictions of the body politic acquired from not just diseased appetites but also contacts with other nations.

One of syphilis's more visible secondary symptoms undergoes such conversion in *The Comedy of Errors*. Alopecia—the loss of hair, eyebrows, eyelashes, and beards—was among the most commonly joked about side-effects of the disease, and in a fashion that usually drew attention to its foreign provenance: "the French Razor shaues off the haire of many of thy *Suburbians*," Westminster tells London in Thomas Dekker's *Dead Tearme*;[39] "Some of your French crowns have no hair at all," remarks Bottom in *A Midsummer Night's Dream* (1.2.100). The symptoms of alopecia are twice referred to in *The Comedy of Errors*. In act 2, scene 2, the Syracusian Dromio and Antipholus joke at length about the loss of hair:

S. DROMIO
There's no time for a man to recover his hair that grows bald by nature.
S. ANTIPHOLUS
May he not do it by fine and recovery?
S. DROMIO
Yes, to pay a fine for a periwig and recover the lost hair of another man.
S. ANTIPHOLUS
Why is Time such a niggard of hair, being, as it is, so plentiful an excrement?
S. DROMIO
Because it is a blessing that he bestows on beasts, and what he hath scanted men in hair he hath given them in wit.
S. ANTIPHOLUS
Why, but there's many a man hath more hair than wit.
S. DROMIO
Not a man of those but he hath the wit to lose his hair.
S. ANTIPHOLUS
Why, thou didst conclude hairy men plain dealers without wit.
S. DROMIO
The plainer dealer, the sooner lost. Yet he loseth it in a kind of jollity. (2.2.71–88)

In pathologizing sexual and commercial "dealings" for the reckless sake of "jollity," Dromio—like Greene—invokes syphilis to represent the loss of financial as much as corporeal health, each of which is interchangeably figured as hair throughout this exchange. Alopecia has no international freight here. But Dromio develops the international, and specifically French, metaphorical possibilities of alopecia later in the play. While his extended conceit of the kitchen-wench as a globe conjures up a somewhat generic pathological vision of the depletion of national wealth, the economic sicknesses he imagines acquire at one point a specifically syphilitic dimension. In response to Antipholus of Syracuse's question about the location of France, Dromio replies that it is "In her forehead, armed and reverted, making war against her heir" (3.2.123–24). Shakespeare, as numerous commentators have noted, refers in this quip to the Catholic League's opposition to Henri of Navarre, the temporarily Protestant "heir" apparent to the throne in the late 1580s and early 1590s. But for all its political topicality, the remark is notable just as much for how it meshes with Dromio's larger, global vision of commerce. Dromio's pun on French "heir"/"hair" invokes alopecia partly to stigmatize the kitchen-wench's lust for him as syphilitic (she is balding) but also to bemoan the potentially communicable pathologies of nations. Within Dromio's analogy, therefore, syphilis operates simultaneously as an individual appetitive disorder and a systemic, transnational illness.

Lurking in Dromio's jokes about alopecia is a complex network of associations that can be discerned in other plays written by Shakespeare in the 1590s. In *Titus Andronicus,* for example, the depreciation of national wealth is likewise linked to the loss of hair. Titus's daughter Lavinia is subtly positioned throughout the play as Roman money by means of an elaborate, sustained series of images and analogies. Initially cast as "Rome's rich ornament" (1.1.55), she is later characterized as a "changing piece" (1.1.314) whose face value depreciates when she refuses marriage to the Emperor Saturninus. Later, at Aaron the Moor's urging, she is raped and mutilated—or, in Aaron's words, "washed and cut and trimmed" (5.1.95). This remark entails an extraordinarily elaborate pun. Each of Aaron's verbs is a term from the discourse of barbers, which helps sets up the association between "barber" and "barbarian" that some of the play's critics have noted. But these verbs all have a second, economic meaning: to "wash" referred to the sweating of gold or silver coins with acid; "cut" and "trim" were slang for the illegal clipping of coins.[40] The metaphorical loss of hair in *Titus Andronicus* is thus implicitly associated with the depreciation of coins' value and the depletion of national wealth. The discursive overlap of barbering, devalued national currency, and syphilis is made explicit by Harry in *Henry V:* "it is no English treason to cut French crowns, and tomorrow the King himself will be a clipper" (4.1.227–29). Once again, the customary associations of alopecia with the French permits Shakespeare to employ the symptoms of syphilis as figures for the vicissitudes of international transactions—although in this case, of course, Harry's aggressive "clippings" of "French crowns" are designed to improve rather than damage the health of the English body politic.

Amid these hairy tangles of commerce and disease, it is worth keeping in mind the homophonic possibilities of the "Errors" in *The Comedy of Errors's* title, which exceed even those of the more frequently discussed "Nothing" in *Much Ado About Nothing.* "Errors" was pronounced by Elizabethan Londoners in much the same ways as "hours"; the pun is apposite because of Shakespeare's uncustomary observation in *The Comedy of Errors* of the dramatic unity of time, which renders the play literally a "comedy of hours." But "Errors" participates within an even more suggestive homophonic chain that points in the direction of syphilis. This is, after all, a comedy of *whores* (the Courtesan and those other "light wenches" who "burn"), a comedy of *heirs* (the two Antipholuses who, like their father Egeon, do business "out o'door"—as a result of which one of them runs the quasi-hereditary risk of himself contracting his father's seemingly fatal sentence), and a comedy of *hairs* (those natural corporeal and commercial resources that are potentially depleted by a love, in both senses of the term, that "draws one oft from home").[41] The syphilitic subtext implied by the homophonic possibilities of the play's title is not, however, simply comic. It also discloses powerful structures of feeling pervasive in late sixteenth-century England: Shakespeare's "comedy of hairs" lends partial expression to, even as it attempts to assuage, deep-seated contemporary anxieties about a world in which the foreign body has increasingly come to rival the appetite as the origin of corporeal and commercial pathology.

The Syphilitic Economy

The Comedy of Errors is not merely a fantasy of pathology. It depicts also the pathology of fantasy itself—whether Adriana's delusions when speaking about her husband's illnesses or Dromio's when speaking about the kitchen-wench's. Both delusions are, of course, fueled by fatal perceptual errors and confusions of identity. But, as I have suggested, these pathological fantasies nonetheless reveal a great deal about the structures of feeling that accompanied the exponential growth of foreign trade in the latter half of the sixteenth century and the concomitant pressure placed on notions of "home." Each delusion lends expression to the same virulent fear—that by going abroad, men will forever change the homes they have left, partly because of their diseased mercantile appetites, but also because of the dangerous foreign forces to which they might expose themselves and, by contagious transmission, their homes. What *The Comedy of Errors* offers, then, is a compromise formation, one that mediates between a residual moral discourse of appetitive economy and an emergent systemic discourse of global trade. This compromise might be termed a syphilitic economy. It entails a protodiscourse of national economy in which the body politic is imagined, like the natural body that appears in the writing of sixteenth-century syphilographers, to be doubly vulnerable to internal and external threats. The syphilitic economy therefore anticipates even as it falls short of the more sophisticated mercantilist paradigms of commerce and nation that were to emerge in the early seventeenth century.

In his later, bitter plays, Shakespeare was to return to syphilis as a metaphor with which to lament the reduction of all human activity to the carnal desires occasioned by global trade. *The Comedy of Errors* is not, however, the bleak play that *Troilus and Cressida* or *Timon of Athens* is. It seeks to effect a reconcilation between the two sets of twin brothers, and in the process to disabuse Adriana of her delusions about sick appetite and foreign contagion. In doing so, the play ends up vindicating the transnational quests of the characters: Egeon is spared death and reunited with his family, Antipholus of Syracuse is reconciled with his long-lost brother, and the two Dromios leave the stage arm in arm. By the conclusion of *The Comedy of Errors*, then, "business out o'door" is no longer a challenge to the domestic; rather, it is the *deus ex machina* that ensures its miraculous reintegration. If the globe is initially condensed by Dromio into the diseased body of the kitchen-wench, it is at play's end refashioned as one happy, healthy, transnational family. Importantly, this reconfigured globe also necessitates a subtly transformed pathology.

The Abbess is doubly instrumental in this transformation. First she identifies the origin of the Ephesian Antipholus's malaise; then, having suggested a cure for her son, she takes her place as mother and wife in Egeon's reconstituted family. The language of syphilis might seem to reverberate in her diagnosis and cure, inasmuch as her understanding of Antipholus's ills similarly mediates invasive and appetitive understandings of disease. On the one hand, she attributes Antipholus's frenzy to his being constantly scolded by his wife, comparing his affliction to an exogenous condition such as rabies: "The venom clamors of a jealous woman," she asserts, "Poisons more deadly than a mad dog's tooth" (5.1.69–70). Yet even as the Abbess reproaches Adriana for corrupting Antipholus with her "venom clamors," she also models her son's illness as a melancholic disorder residing in his diseased, humorally imbalanced appetite:

Thou sayst his meat was sauced with thy upbraidings.
Thereof the raging fire of fever bred,
And what's a fever but a fit of madness?
Thou sayst his sports were hindered by thy brawls.
Sweet recreation barred, what doth ensue
But moody and dull melancholy,
Kinsman to grim and comfortless despair,
And at her heels a huge infectious troop
Of pale distemperatures and foes to life?
In food, or sport, and life-preserving rest
To be disturbed would man or beast. (5.1.73–84)

As much as the Abbess may reproduce the mediated disjunctions of syphilitic economy visible elsewhere in the play, her diagnosis entails a subtle but significant adaptation of that economy. Antipholus's is an affliction acquired not from a desire for foreign luxury goods that draws one "oft from home" but from disharmony within it. It is not appetite per se that is at fault, therefore, nor its objects; rather, it is the excessive restraints imposed on Antipholus's appetite that have made him humorally and morally sick. In accordance with Galenic and Christian ideals of temperance, therefore, the Abbess's cure is designed to permit if not unimpeded appetite for the extradomestic, then at least its moderate exercise.

Because the Abbess's advice to Antipholus is expressed in what seems to be an entirely moral or medical register, it is easy to overlook how it also has significant economic implications. I have argued that the play repeatedly recasts the domestic/extradomestic opposition in commercial terms, thereby allowing Antipholus's "business out o'door" to function as a catchphrase for both adultery and foreign trade. The Abbess's medical advice—that Adriana minister to her husband's health by giving him liberty to indulge in extradomestic "recreation"—works to transform his bivalently sexual and commercial "business out o'door" from a pathogenic into a prophylactic measure. With this counsel, therefore, she provides a retroactive justification less for his sexual truancy than for his mercantile activity in the agora and, more specifically, in the sphere of transnational commerce. The latter can now become a safeguard of rather than a challenge to the health of individual, family, nation, and globe.

But a powerful residue of anxiety lingers in Adriana's fantasies of syphilitic infection as well as the Abbess's Galenic solution to them, a residue that was to acquire an even more pathological strength in Shakespeare's problem plays. In those works, syphilis is the inexorable reality of a world in which commercial appetite is rampant and health a cruel dream; the pox, in other words, has become the stuff of horror. In the earlier *Comedy of Errors,* syphilis remains a nightmare from which one can still wake up, health and humor—in both senses of the word—intact. What this play shares with Shakespeare's later work and the mercantilist writing of the early seventeenth century, however, is a profound investment in the language of disease as a means of figuring new economic objects. In the next chapter, I turn to Shakespeare's *The Merchant of Venice,* in order to show how its pathological imagery resonates with an early mercantilist lexicon of infection that helped figure a growing economic phenomenon: the alienability of money and identity across national borders.

Taint and Usury: Gerard Malynes, *The Dutch Church Libel,* The Merchant of Venice

In February 1996, the Supreme Court of Arkansas delivered an opinion on a suit brought against a property vendor by two buyers who, unable to meet the unusually high rate of interest set by the vendor, had defaulted on their payments. Weighing the matter, the Supreme Court observed: "This case presents questions about usury." As quaintly archaic as the court's "questions" may seem, they had a sound legal basis. Arkansas is the only state in the union to set usury limits: Amendment 60 to the Arkansas constitution asserts that the maximum rate of interest on any contract entered into shall not exceed 5 percent per annum above the Federal Reserve Discount Rate. Clarifying the state's law before delivering its opinion, the Supreme Court wrote that "the express intent of Amendment 60 was that the *taint of usury* voids the agreement only to the extent of unpaid interest."[1]

If the Arkansas constitutional safeguard against usury sounds old-fashioned, the language of the Supreme Court's opinion might seem even more so. The "taint of usury" is a formulation that has a decidedly Shakespearean ring: it resonates with *The Merchant of Venice,* in which the Jewish usurer Shylock brings his "plea so tainted and corrupt" against the Christian merchant Antonio (3.2.75). There is a difference, however, between the Arkansas of 1996 and the Venice of 1596. If a "taint" is now simply a moral blemish, the term possessed a much wider array of meanings for Shakespeare and his audiences. In courts of law, a "taint" was a conviction for felony; hence when Antonio pronounces himself a "tainted wether of the flock" (4.1.113), he arguably accepts what he presumes will be the Venetian court's ruling against him.[2] Yet as this example demonstrates, "taint" also possessed a pathological meaning. The term could refer to an illness of animals, especially of horses, and its meaning shaded into that of "infection," whose etymology is almost identical to one of the senses of "taint"—a staining or contamination.[3] In this chapter I examine how both terms are used in the emergent mercantilist discourses of late Elizabethan England to recode the old crime of usury as a new economic phenomenon synec-dochally associated with Jews: the alienability of money and identity across national borders.

I read *The Merchant of Venice* in relation to two other "usury" texts with which it is not normally associated: Gerard Malynes's *Saint George for England Allegorically Described* (1601) and the anonymous Dutch Church Libel of 1593. Each text seems to cast its gaze in a decidedly non-Jewish direction. Malynes's treatise criticizes, from a recognizably mercantilist perspective, the depletion of England's bullion reserves; the Dutch Church Libel condemns London's substantial community of migrants from the Netherlands for all manner of religious, political, and economic crimes. Yet the Jew is made to play a significant rhetorical role in each text's vision of usury. What is voiced in both Malynes's fable and the Dutch Church Libel is less the conventional Christian condemnation of usury as a Jewish practice of sinful commerce or unnatural breeding than a modern, mercantilist problematic of transnationality for which "the Jew" serves as a fixing yet highly unstable signifier. This might help explain why neither text is usually considered part of the canon of anti-usury literature, where the moral or scriptural interpretations of usury have tended to be privileged. As I shall show, the mercantilist problematic of usury is also central to Shakespeare's *Merchant of Venice*. Malynes, the anonymous author of the Dutch Church Libel, and Shakespeare all produce the usurer as a palimpsest, within which discrete categories of national and religious identity have been fused and confused.

Notably, the language of disease mediates all three texts' production of usury as a species of transnationality. Yet in each case the pathologies identified with usury invoke not specific foreign bodies, as was often the case with syphilis, but states of *contamination* ("colour," "gangrene," "infection," "taint"). Such pathologies work to fashion the foreign less as a determinate thing than as a corrupted site of "Judaized" hybridity or indeterminacy by means of which the nation's wealth is covertly expropriated. Importantly, these Jewish hybrids (whether Dutch or Iberian, Catholic or Turkish) work to displace the reader's attention from both the textual and the historical hybridization of the non-Jewish and/or English subject. In a time of unprecedented transnational fluidity of goods, coin, and people, however, early mercantilist discourse subjected to immense pressure even as it helped generate the myth of a pure national identity. Critical attention to the mercantilist recoding of usury permits a new reading of *The Merchant of Venice*—a reading in which neither "usury" nor the "Jew" seems quite as fixed or as transparent as earlier criticism of the play has often assumed both of them to be.

Color: *Saint George for England Allegorically Described*

The importance of usury in the mercantilist lexicon is, at first glance, somewhat surprising. One of the standard views of mercantilism is that it eclipsed medieval understandings of moral economy with far more amoral conceptions of commerce. As a consequence, this view maintains, the oldest economic sin became defensible; Thomas Wilson may have published his well-known critique of usury in 1572, but early modern English state policy and literature increasingly supported the charging of interest, even if rates of more than 10 percent were frowned upon.[4] In his essay "On Usurie," for example, Francis Bacon enumerates its "discommodities," but he counters these with its many advantages, recommending that interest rates be set at 5 percent. "Few have spoken of usury usefully," he asserts in a telling pun, for it is precisely usury's commercial usefulness that mitigates it: "there [should] bee left open a meanes to invite moneyed men to lend to merchants for the continuing and quickning of Trade."[5] Despite such *mercantile* recuperations of usury, however, the so-called mercantilist writers themselves—with the notable exception of Thomas Mun[6]—condemned the practice fiercely. And although the mercantilists' condemnations differed from those of medieval theologians, "the Jew" remained symbolically central to their imagining of usury as a crime.

As any student of *The Merchant of Venice* knows, the enduring association of Jews with usury stemmed from their temporary "welcome" into medieval European cities to practice a trade that Christians regarded as sinful. For Thomas Aquinas in the *Summa Theologica,* the biblical proscription against charging interest on loans to "brothers" (Deuteronomy 23: 20–21) meant that, thanks to the Christian ideal of universal brotherhood, no true believer could practice usury. But in the later Middle Ages, Europe's merchants increasingly needed ready sources of credit for capitalist ventures at home and abroad; to accommodate them, scholastics identified in the Deuteronomic proscription an ingenious, if xenophobic, loophole—*Christians* could not recoup interest on loans, but *Jews* could do so when lending to Christians, because Jews sinfully yet conveniently regarded gentiles as "others" rather than "brothers."[7] This loophole was put into practice in England for only a relatively short time. But for centuries after the expulsion of Jews in 1290, English writers continued to regard "usurer" as a synonym for "Jew." The association is especially noteworthy in early modern drama. In addition to Shylock, we find a Jewish usurer, Gerontus, in Robert Wilson's *Three Ladies of London* (c. 1584); Barabas admits to a past career in usury in Marlowe's *The Jew of Malta* (c. 1588); and the Jew Zariph lends to Sir Anthony Shirley in Wilkins, Rowley, and Day's *Travels of Three English Gentlemen* (c. 1608).[8]

Critical discussions of these plays and of *The Merchant of Venice* tend to reference the conventional moral arguments against usury. Hence analyses of Shylock's first scene frequently note the Deuteronomic proscriptions against charging interest on loans to "brothers." These references are sometimes accompanied by citation of Francis Bacon's essay on usury and, in particular, one of the several "discommodities" that Bacon identifies with the practice: "They say . . . that it is against nature for money to beget money; and the like" (133). Bacon glances here at another customary condemnation of usury. In his influential treatise "De Moneta," the fourteenth-century French theologian Nicholas Oresme had argued that "it is monstrous and unnatural that an unfruitful thing should bear, that a thing specifically sterile, such as money, should bear fruit and multiply of itself."[9] This argument about unnatural reproduction was arguably the dominant discourse about usury in the Reformation. Luther was particularly pithy on the matter: "Money is sterile."[10]

Yet as Marc Shell and other readers have noted, such theological arguments about money's sterility do not provide the only framework for understanding Jewish usury in *The Merchant of Venice*.[11] On the contrary, Shylock forcefully asserts his "thrifty" ability to make money breed as fast as did the biblical Jacob's "rams and ewes" (1.3.88). According to Shylock, Jacob's skillful manipulation of Laban's sheep and their "work of generation" was an exemplary act of usury, yielding him interest in the form of a flock of "parti-coloured" (spotted) lambs (1.3.74, 80). Antonio, however, focuses instead on the criminality of charging interest to friends:

If thou wilt lend this money, lend it not
As to thy friends, for when did friendship take
A breed for barren metal of his friend?
But lend it rather to thine enemy . . . (1.3.124–27)

Antonio here invokes both the familiar Lutheran image of money as a "barren metal" and the Deuteronomic opposition between lending to "friends" and lending to "enemies," each of which conforms more straightforwardly to the customary Christian discourses of usury than does Shylock's prolix parable about the breeding of "parti-coloured" eanlings. In attempting to make sense of *The Merchant of Venice*'s discourse of usury, readers have tended to focus their attention solely on Antonio's Christian-inflected denunciation of Shylock's moneylending practices. Hence in his influential study *The Idea of Usury*, for example, Benjamin Nelson interpreted the play's presentation of usury within an exclusively moral framework, as inimical to a fading Christian ideal of friendship.[12] By contrast, I will argue that when read together with Shylock's parable of Jacob and his "parti-coloured" lambs, Antonio's speech drives to the heart of an anxiety that loomed large not just in rearguard defenses of moral economy but also in the emergent mercantilist discourse of national wealth.

Of particular importance here is the "brothers and others" typology of Deuteronomy, though I shall argue that its relevance to mercantilist discourse has to do less with Christian than with economic nationalist ideals of brotherhood.[13] Inasmuch as the Deuteronomic proscriptions against usury prohibit the charging of interest to "brothers" from one's own tribe, the activity definitionally entails a contract across national boundaries, however these may be defined (religiously, politically, economically). The Anglican divine Henry Smith, in a sermon delivered in the late sixteenth century, argued: "of a stranger, saith God thou mayest take usury, but thou takest usury of thy brother; therefore this condemneth thee, BECAUSE THOU USETH THY BROTHER LIKE A STRANGER."[14] Smith believed usury to entail a confusion or contamination of discrete categories: all Christians are brothers, yet any act of usury by a Christian "useth" a "brother" as if he were a "stranger" (i.e., a foreigner). Religious thinkers like Smith expressed such contamination in the register of moral economy. But early modern mercantilists such as Gerard Malynes tended to refashion the brother/stranger confusion of usury in the terms of transnational economy. As we will see, the usurer of mercantilist literature is accused less of sinful behavior than of political and economic sabotage. Francis Bacon, for example, echoes two standard mercantilist arguments when he asserts that usury "bringeth the treasure of a Realme of State into a few hands" and causes "the decay of Customes of Kings or States" (134). According to Bacon, then, usury deprives the state of bullion, diverting it into private and foreign coffers. The nationalistic inflection of Bacon's argument is evident also in his recommendation that "these licensed lenders [should] be in number indefinite, but restrained to certaine principall cities and townes of merchandizing; for then they will be hardly able *to colour* other men's moneyes in the country" (136; emphasis added).

Bacon's choice of verb here is fascinating. "To colour" is synonymous in this context with "to dye" or "to stain" and hence, in a more metaphorically pathological sense, "to corrupt." The OED lists Bacon's use of "to colour" under the now obsolete sense of "to lend one's name to; represent or deal with as one's own." I would argue that this meaning of "colour" also sheds light on Shylock's otherwise enigmatic vision of usury. Although they are the offspring of Laban's sheep, the eanlings become Jacob's by virtue of his ability to (parti-) "colour" them, and hence "represent or deal with" them as his "own." Shylock instructively aligns Jacob's profit with the usurer's interest, therefore, by means of an image of staining; like Bacon's "coloured" money, the "parti-coloured" fleeces embody the lambs' categorical hybridity as goods that have become alienated from Laban to Jacob, or Israel, father of the Jewish nation. For Bacon and Shakespeare alike, then, "colour" is the mark of a national boundary transgression intrinsic to usury.

In the process, the "colouring" usurer generates a potential crisis of uncertain identity, goods, and coin. Paraphrasing Portia, one might ask: which is the merchant's, and which the lender's "moneys"? For the mercantilists, this question was of pressing importance when the lender was a stranger and English bullion stood to be alienated across national borders. Thomas Milles, for example, argues that "many merchants do collour the conueying of ready Money out of the Realme of England."[15] The transnational undecidability generated by the foreign usurer's "colouring" also informs the early modern phrase "to colour strangers' goods," which the OED glosses as "to enter a foreign merchant's goods at the custom-house under a freeman's name, for the purpose of evading additional duties" (*colour*, v., 4). Gerard Malynes uses this very phrase in his treatise *Lex Mercatoria* (1622): "a Factor or Merchant, doe colour the goods of Merchant Strangers in paying but English Customes."[16] For Malynes, such "colouring" is tantamount to usury, inasmuch as it involves a crafty profiting from transnational dealership less in goods than in money. In both Bacon's and Malynes's texts, then, the "colouring" effects of usury are made to figure a twofold indeterminacy that is the product of transnational commerce. First, the usurer "colours" goods and money in such fashion as to obscure knowledge of who owns them, and whether they are domestic or foreign (or both). Second, the usurer confuses national borders, both by merging with his host nation and by obtaining money from—or sending it to—uncertain destinations in which he has family, factors, or trading connections. The "colouring" usurer thus *both* embodies *and* transmits national indeterminacy.

The pathological dimensions of "colouring" and the nationally indeterminate usurer are particularly evident in Malynes's first published work, *Saint George for England Allegorically Described* (1601). Unlike his later treatises, the text takes the form of a brief allegorical fable about England's economic ills; to this extent, it may be seen as a boiled-down *Faerie Queen* set on London's Lombard Street. Malynes recounts a dream he has had, in which he visits a city ("Diospolus," or London) on a "most fruitfull Iland" ("Niobla," an anagram of Albion).[17] The country is suffering, however; a beautiful princess, whom Malynes equates with the nation's treasure, is tormented by a rampaging dragon, which he identifies with usury. Despite the fable's title, Saint George notably fails to make his promised appearance. England's patron saint is "allegorically described" by Malynes only in his opening dedication to Sir Thomas Egerton; here he asserts that Saint George is a type of both Christ and Queen Elizabeth, each of whom has been used by God "to performe the part of a valiant champion, delivering an infinite number of the diuels power" (sigs. A2v–A3). When Malynes turns to the narration of his fable, however, he devotes nearly all of it to an allegorical description not of Saint George but of *usury*. And just as Malynes invokes a Christian frame of reference in his dedication only to exclude the very type of Christ from his actual narrative, so does the traditionally theological explanation of usury figure in his fable as a striking absence, referred to but once in a parenthetical citation of passages from scripture (65). Malynes instead focuses the majority of his critique on usury's economic and political effects. The dragon is named "*Poenus politicum* [hardship of the polity]"; one of his wings is called "*Vsura palliata* [disguised usury]," the other "*Vsuria explicata* [explicit usury]"; the dragon's tail is called "inconstant *Cambium* [exchange rates]" (sig. A8). As this allegorical anatomy suggests, Malynes imagines usury quite differently from Aquinas and the medieval scholastics. He believes not only that usury takes multiple forms, overt and disguised; it is also—as his invocation of exchange rates suggests—intrinsic to the systematic practice of commerce across national borders.

Malynes does not entirely abandon the language of moral economy. At times, he blames the dragon for a brace of sins practiced by Niobla's inhabitants: usury has, for example, produced "a present greater abilitie . . . to liue licentiously, following whores, harlots, wine-tauernes, and many other vnlawfull games, to their vtter destruction" (21). But throughout the fable, the religious is overwhelmingly subsumed within the economic, and medieval sins are eclipsed by systemic modes of transnational commerce. Uppermost in Malynes's lengthy list of the dragon's crimes are dangerous practices of "merchandizing exchange" that have resulted in the flow of bullion out of the nation: "he maintaineth a league with forreine nations, and causeth them to serue his turne, by bringing in superfluous commodities at a deare rate, and they to feede vppon our natiue soile, to the commonwealths destruction. . . . He carieth out our treasure in bullion and money, empouerishing our commonweale." (42). Here Malynes emphatically refashions usury in accordance with the characteristic nationalist preoccupations of mercantilism.[18] As a consequence, "usury" begins to lose its traditional meaning. In the above passage and elsewhere in Malynes's fable, the term refers no longer simply to the charging of interest on loans but more generally to "money being made a merchandize" in the course of transnational trade (71)—in this case, merchant strangers' manipulation of rates of currency exchange in order to buy English commodities cheaply and to sell foreign commodities at exorbitant prices. What should be England's wealth, therefore, becomes "coloured" as foreign.

Throughout his allegory, Malynes employs a resolutely pathological vocab-

ulary to figure the usurious underbelly of transnational commerce. In his dedication, he compares statesmen to the "Phisitions of commonweales" whose job
is to heal "the biles botches, cankers and sores thereof"; chief among these is the
"venimous sore" of usury (sig. A7v). And in the fable proper, Malynes describes
the dragon of usury variously as a *"Gangrena"* (49) and "this contagion, wherewith we are infected" (13). Both of these latter pathological metaphors are, I
would argue, crucial to Malynes's vision of usury and the relationship between
the "domestic" and the "foreign." On the one hand, Malynes seems to figure the
dragon of usury as an invasive disease when he compares *"Gangrena"* to *"Syn-*
ons [the Trojan] horse" (49). To modern eyes, a presumption of invasive disease
may be yet more apparent in Malynes's use of terms like "contagion" and "infected." All these pathologies might suggest that he views usury as a practice specific to foreigners. But I would argue that each of Malynes's metaphorical
diseases implies less *foreign invasion* (though that is certainly one of their connotations) than a *corruption* or *mixing* of categories that is redolent of usury's
"colouring" indeterminacy.

Gangrene, which derives from the Latin "cancrena," was regarded as a per-
ilously advanced form of more mild skin ailments like serpego and canker (both
of which I examine in the next chapter). Renaissance physicians imagined gangrene as an invasive disease only to the extent that they recognized its ability to
spread rapidly through the body, "devouring" it bit by bit. They located its causes
not in foreign bodies, however, but in elemental factors such as extreme cold.
What most exercised physicians' imaginations was gangrene's blurring of a crucial medical distinction: they characterized it as a form of living death, a confusion of vitality and mortification. Bartholomew Traheron notes in his 1543
translation of Vignon's work on surgery, for example, that "Cancrena [gangrene]
is not taken for flesh deade altogether, but for that whych begynneth to putrefye
by lyttle and lyttle."[19] Gangrene muddles the boundary between what is proper
to the body and what is alien to it; thus seen, the affliction is both endogenous
and invasive. The confusion of categories that distinguishes early modern understandings of gangrene is even more notable in the sixteenth-century meanings of "infection." The term had not yet decisively acquired its modern sense,
that is, the communication of a determinate, exogenous illness. Although it was
increasingly associated with foreign bodies as a result of new explanations of epidemic diseases such as syphilis (as we saw in Chapter 2), the dominant meaning
of "infection" was contamination or pathological mixing. The term derives from
Latin "inficere," to stain or taint; for Galenic physicians, it came to mean corruption, including the miasmic putrefaction of water or of air, and hence the transmission of disease. But in the late sixteenth century, "infect" still retained vestiges
of its residual meaning, "to dye, tinge, colour, stain" (OED, *infect*, v., 1.a).

The gangrenous, infected dragon is thus "coloured" and "colouring," in both pathological and economic senses. As Malynes says, the dragon has a "compounded body" (56); he is "half a man & halfe a beast" (73). This pathological mixing figures the hybridity of the usurer's capital, which creates the illusion of an "imaginatiue wealth" even as it "hath transported our treasure into forraine parts" (71). The usurer thus "colours"—or alienates—the nation's bullion. As this might suggest, the dragon's infected state entails the fusion and confusion of discrete national identities. "His tridented toung," Malynes tells us, is "like vnto a Turkish dart"; but his body is "like an Elephant." Indeed, Malynes repeatedly associates the dragon with Islamic nations: the dragon's tail, he informs us, "is marked with the new Moon of the Turkes, like vnto the letter C" (57). Malynes is less invested in Islamicizing usury, however, than in simply exoticizing it. The crescent moon that he here retools as the badge of usury conveniently enables him to allegorize the dragon's tail as "the letter C," the initial of *Cambium* or foreign exchange rates, with which he allegorically identifies this part of the body: "with the operation of his taile," he complains, the dragon has "transported the moneys of our Iland, and within our land altered the nature and valuation of the money, making one hundred pounds, to be one hundred and ten pounds" (62).[20]

Yet even as Malynes exoticizes the dragon, he also brands it as a recognizably domestic villain. Its "compounded body" may have an Orientalized tail, but its head is marked with "an F, like a fellon" (57). Malynes's remark seems calculated to exploit "fellon"'s linked early modern legal and pathological associations. The term derives from the Latin *fel,* gall, and was used in early modern medical writing as a synonym for a carbuncle or boil. In law, however, a "felon" was originally anyone who breached the feudal bond of trust between man and lord; he or she was thus understood as a domestic disease, disrupting the internal balance of the body politic.[21] Interestingly, the OED tells us that a "taint" was a mark applied to anyone convicted of a felony. Hence Malynes's "fellon"-marked dragon is "tainted" in both pathological and legal senses. A conflation of exotic and domestic ills, the creature embodies Frances E. Dolan's model of the early modern "proximate other," a suppositious social threat that was perceived to be simultaneously foreign and domestic.[22]

In focusing explicit attention on the dragon's "compounded body," however, Malynes diverts attention from the extent to which the England of his fable is itself already hybrid. Niobla's beautiful princess is by no means nationally pure; rather, she sports a transnational, Oriental motley. She wears clothes that are "odiferous as the smell of Lebanon" (52); her cheeks are like "a bed of spices" (52); her "admirable body" is "covered with a garment of white silke Damaske" (53); and she is "this *Indian Phenix*" (55). Yet it is the dragon of usury that is made to bear the burden of transnational mixing and the "coloured" indeterminacy that underwrites it. In the most eerie passage of the fable, Malynes describes the literal impossibility of pinning down the dragon's precise location:

> albeit he seemeth with the *index* of the dyall not to moue, when he is continually moouing, and stirred in such sort, that when men begin to perceiue his motion, and pretend to runne from him: he doth so allure them, that the more they runne, the more he seemeth to follow them, as the moone doth to the little children, whereby his motion is the lesse regarded. (57–58)

The dragon is always in motion, but his most dangerous skill lies in his ability to create the illusion that he occupies a fixed location. This passage captures particularly well the distinctive qualities of the usurer as he is rhetorically produced in mercantilist discourse: for all his seeming fixity, he is a fluid shapeshifter, "continually moouing" across categorical and national boundaries.

In mercantilist writing about usury, the oscillation between fixity and fluidity is most at work in the seemingly firm attribution of usury to the figure of the Jew. Thomas Milles, for example, follows Malynes in imagining usury as a pratice of "merchandizing exchange" that alienates bullion across national borders; yet despite usury's global status, Milles insists that merchandizing exchange transforms "our Christian *Exchange* into Iewish *Vsury*."[23] The same strategy is evident at a crucial moment in Bacon's essay on usury. In his list of "witty invectives" against usury, he reports the view that "Usurers should have orange-tawney bonnets, because they doe judaize" (133). "Judaize" serves here as both a metaphor and an ostensible cure for usury's undecidability. On the one hand, the Jew was the master trope of national indeterminacy; as James Shapiro has argued, the waves of Jewish and Marrano migration from the Iberian Peninsula in the fifteenth and sixteenth centuries facilitated the birth of the legend of the Wandering Jew, a stateless, transnational vagabond.[24] But Bacon's use of the verb "Judaize" also lends a reassuring local name, if not habitation, to a practice that involves a transnational blurring of discrete categories: usurers should wear the orange hats mandated of Jews in the Papal States, not because they are Jewish, but because their practice "colours" them as Jews. "The Jew" thus both figures transnational fluidity and lends it a provisionally stable identity.

Something similar happens in *Saint George for England Allegorically Described*. Malynes makes reference to Jews only once; but this reference is rhetorically crucial to his demonization of the transnational Turkish/English dragon. Admonishing the supporters of usury, he asks: "Will not the daunger that the leaguors of this Dragon do runne into, give them warning, when as at one time fiue hundreth Iewes were transported with *Carons* boate the ferrie man of hell, which were slaine by the Cittizens of *Troynouant* for feeding him?" (65). It is difficult to know at which historical incident Malynes glances here, but it may well be the York Massacre of the twelfth century, when the citizens of that town conveniently dissolved their debts by murdering the Jewish population.[25] In any case, Malynes, like Milles and Bacon, makes "the Jew" the certain material in which to clothe usury's transnational uncertainty. Yet that very material, like Bacon's "orange-tawney" bonnet, exacerbates even as it attempts to stabilize the dragon's hybridity: "the Jew" becomes less a name for the palimpsested identities of transnational commerce than one of the layers in that palimpsest.

Malynes's chilling fantasy of retribution against Jews also recalls what was a much more recent phenomenon: the antiforeigner libels of the early 1590s. For many London citizens as for Malynes, Saint George needed to slay no dragon when an English mob could be relied upon to administer wild justice to strangers. One such libel of 1593 warns: "Be it known to all Flemings and Frenchmen, that it is best for them to depart out of the realm of England between this and the 9th of July next. If not, then to take that which follows: for there shall be many a sore stripe. Apprentices will rise to the number of 2336. And all the apprentices and journeymen will down with the Flemings and strangers."[26]

The antiforeigner libels of the 1590s are rhetorically close to Malynes's fantasy of punishment in another respect. Even as they ostensibly target "Flemings and strangers," the libels use "the Jew" as a figure with which to lend a name to the hybrid identities that were increasingly a feature of early modern Europe and its networks of transnational commerce. Understanding these libels, and the confluence of economic and pathological language that distinguishes them, is crucial to an understanding of the social and rhetorical horizons within which Shakespeare composed *The Merchant of Venice*.

Infection: The Dutch Church Libel

In May 1593, during a period of mounting hostility toward London's immigrant Dutch community, a libelous poem was affixed to the wall of one of the city's foreign Protestant churches. It directly addresses foreigners living in London:

Ye strangers yt doe inhabite in this lande
Note this same writing doe it vnderstand
Conceit it well for savegard of your lyves
Your goods, your children, & your dearest wives
Your Machiavellian Marchant spoyles the state,
Your vsery doth leave vs all for deade
Your Artifex, & craftesmen works our fate,

And like the Jewes, you eate us vp as bread
The Marchant doth ingross all kinde of wares
Forestall's the markets, whereso 'ere he goe's
Sends forth his wares, by Pedlers to the faires,
Retayl's at home, & with his horrible showes: Vndoeth thowsands
In Baskets your wares trott up & downe
Carried the streets by the country nation,
You are intelligencers to the state & crowne
And in your hartes doe wish an alteracion,
You transport goods, & bring vs gawds good store
Our Leade, our Vitaille, our Ordenance & what nott
That Egipts plagues, vext not the Egyptians more
Than you doe vs; then death shall be your lotte
Noe prize comes in but you make claime therto
And every merchant hath three trades at least
And Cutthroate like in selling you vndoe
vs all, & with our store continually you feast: We cannot suffer long.
Our pore artificers doe starve & dye
For yt they cannot now be sett on worke
And for your worke more curious to the ey[.]
In Chambers, twenty in one house will lurke,
Raysing of rents, was never knowne before
Living farre better than at native home
And our poore soules, are cleane thrust out of dore
And to the warres are sent abroad to rome,
To fight it out for Fraunce & Belgia,
And dy like dogges as sacrifice for you
Expect you therefore such a fatall day
Shortly on you, & yours for to ensewe: as never was seene.
Since words nor threats not any other thinge
canne make you to avoyd this certaine ill
Weele cut your throtes, in your temples praying
Not paris massacre so much blood did spill
As we will doe iust vengeance on you all
In counterfeiting religion for your flight
When 't'is well knowne, you are loth, for to be thrall
your coyne, & you as countryes cause to flight
With Spanish gold, you all are infected
And with yt gould our Nobles wink at feats
Nobles said I? nay men to be reiected,
Upstarts yt enjoy the noblest seates
That wound their Countries brest, for lucres sake
And wrong our gracious Queene & Subiects good
By letting strangers make our harts to ake
For which our swords are whet, to sheed their blood
And for a truth let it be vnderstood / Fly, Flye, & never returne.
per. Tamberlaine[27]

The libel has been usually read in either of two ways: as historical commentary on London artisans' xenophobic attitudes toward foreigners or as a titillating sequence of clues about the career and cultural influence of Christopher Marlowe, three of whose plays—*Tamburlaine, The Massacre at Paris,* and *The Jew of Malta*—the libel references.[28] I want to consider the libel from a rather different perspective: as a cultural production that partially reconfigures traditional economic crimes, particularly usury, in a new, mercantilist register of transnational identity and pathology. In this register, I will argue, the Jew again plays a crucial rhetorical role.

The libel is ostensibly an inflammatory response to London's Dutch immigrant community. This is most apparent in its polemic against the strangers' overcrowding of tenements ("In Chambers, twenty in one house will lurke"), which echoes a complaint repeatedly leveled against Dutch refugees in late sixteenth-century London.[29] But aside from this topical charge, the libel's xenophobia does not find expression in stereotypical anti-Dutch accusations, such as excessive drinking. Another libel of the same year, for example, stigmatizes the Dutch as "you, beastly brutes, the Belgians, or rather drunken drones, and faint-hearted Flemings."[30] Instead, the so-called Dutch Church Libel is notably obsessed with alleged economic crimes. Singled out for attention here are the strangers' practice of skills that usurp English labor; unregistered plying of multiple trades; bribery, rent-racking and profiteering; expropriation of English bullion; and, most starkly, usury. The libel thus fantasizes an English nation under siege by foreign artisans and merchants whose activities result in the decay of state and coin. In this respect, the libel anticipates Malynes's mercantilist model of nationhood, which attempts to explain England's economic weakness in terms of its loss of bullion.

The economic crimes enumerated in the libel would seem to constitute a polemic directed simply at the Dutch refugees, voicing common fears of the time about their negative impact on the body politic. Yet what is striking about the libel is how it hybridizes the strangers. They are compared to Jews, explicitly ("like the Jewes, you eate us vp as bread") and implicitly ("Weele cut your throtes, in your temples praying"; "Egipts plagues, vext not the Egyptians more / Than you doe vs"). James Shapiro has noted how the libel's overt references to *Tamburlaine* and *Massacre at Paris* can hardly disguise the more subtle yet pervasive influence of Marlowe's *Jew of Malta*: like Barabas, the strangers are accused of being "Machiavellian Marchants" who "counterfeit religion" and are "intelligencers to state and crown."[31] The libel's sustained debt to Marlowe suggests how the drama of the London commercial stage played a crucial role in the narration of nascent discourses of national economy. It also points to the occasional starring role of the Jew—as Machiavellian, as heretic, as spy, as usurer—in such dramas.

Even as they "Judaize," to use Bacon's term, the strangers are additionally accused of being "infected" with "Spanish gold." The Spanish slur may be surprising to modern readers, given that the members of London's Dutch community were nominal co-religionists of the Protestant English. But "Dutch" was by no means a straightforward synonym for Protestant. The term was a highly refractory one; it was used to designate people who lived in what is now Holland, Belgium, and even Germany. "Dutch" also possessed a Spanish connotation. Most of the Low Countries were under Spanish rule until the Protestant Revolt of 1572—Charles V had made Antwerp Spain's major trading entrepôt in the early sixteenth century—and by the time of the Dutch Church Libel, the southern Netherlands had fallen back into Spanish possession. These territories included both Flemish and French speakers; the French-speaking Walloons of what is now Belgium are variously described in early modern records as "French," "Dutch," and even "subjects of the King of Spain."[32] Hence it was comparatively easy for the author of the Dutch Church Libel to insinuate that although they may have fled under cover of religious persecution, the refugees from the Low Countries were in spiritual thrall to Spain.

The accusation of "infect[ion]" by "Spanish gold" is less religious, however, than political and economic. "Spanish gold" here is payola, which the libel casts as an invasive, harmful presence in the English body politic, funding "Upstarts" who "enjoy the noblest seates / That wound their Countries brest, for lucres sake." But the gold with which the strangers are "infected" is also intended to encourage the flow of bullion out of England: "Your Machiavellian Marchant spoyles the state, / Your vsery doth leave vs all for deade." The libel thus conflates the foreigners' mercantile activity with a usury that not only "spoyles the state" but also "Forestall's the markets." The allegedly deleterious effects of such practices are expressed in a string of gustatory images: "And like the Iewes, you eate us vp as bread"—an exhumation of the old anti-Semitic canards of ritual murder, cannibalism, and host desecration—"& with our store continually you feast." Criticism of the strangers' devouring of English "store" leads to another specifically economic accusation: "You transport goods, & bring vs gawds good store / Our Leade, our Vitaille, our Ordenance & what nott." The last complaint lends voice to one of the pet peeves of the mercantilists—that raw goods are shipped out of the country and get turned into manufactures overseas, which are then retailed back to England, resulting in massive loss of bullion. In a complaint that specifically fingered the Dutch for their finishing of English raw materials, for example, Thomas Milles asserted that "our *Woolls,* (some-times the wonder of the Worlde,) are now the *Trophees* of strange Lands, and signs of our shame, and turned into Cloth, our Cloth into nothing; at least nothing lesse then *Bullion*."[33]

The accusation that the strangers are "infected" with Spanish gold is most striking, though, for its pathological language. As in Malynes's *Saint George for England Allegorically Described,* the term "infected" arguably works to fashion the foreigner as less a determinate *agent* of disease than a transnational *site* of undecidable identity, a diseased hybrid of Dutch, Jew, and Spaniard. In this pathological hybridity, moreover, lurks once more the color-full stain of usury. Bacon and Malynes argued that the usurer's capital collapses even as it depends on boundaries between "brothers" and "others," and such a collapse is hinted at in the suggestive line, "Your Machiavellian Marchant spoyles the state." "Spoils" here possesses an economic sense: to the victor the spoils. But its dominant meaning is again pathological: the Machiavellian merchant infects the state by "colouring" or alienating its bullion.[34]

The pathological hybridizations performed by the Dutch Church Libel are significant in two ways. First, they point to a rhetorical crisis of identity for which "the Jew" was dubiously both the symptom and the remedy. As in Bacon's and Malynes's writings on usury, the Jew functions as a signifier that lends a name to the otherwise indeterminate identity of the transnational stranger. But I would contend that the Dutch Church Libel's "Judaized" hybrids are more than simply the rhetorical products of xenophobic and/or antisemitic discourse. They hint also at historical realities: specifically, the emergence throughout Europe during the sixteenth century of new, protean forms of identity and affiliation. These mutable forms were to a large extent the coerced consequence of religious and political developments, including the Spanish Inquisition, the Protestant Reformation, and the wars in the Low Countries. I shall argue that they were equally a response to the rapid growth during the sixteenth century of transnational trading networks between the Iberian Peninsula and northern Europe. By examining what the historical archive can tell us about London's seeming "Dutch," we can also learn something about the pathological hybridity or undecidability of merchant, usurer, and "Jew" in early modern English writing and society.

Although there had long been a Flemish presence in London—merchants from Flanders had a monopoly on several trades by the end of the fifteenth century—the Dutch began to settle in London in large numbers only during the second half of the sixteenth century.[35] Throughout the reign of Edward VI, England welcomed refugees from the Low Countries whom it believed to be fleeing religious persecution at the hands of the Spanish. A Dutch Reformed church was set up in London with the support of the crown in 1550, although the ascension to the English throne of the Catholic Mary resulted in the church's temporary closure and the return of large numbers of refugees to the Low Countries. Levels of immigration increased again with the death of Mary and the coronation of Elizabeth; the numbers dipped after the Protestant Revolt against Spanish rule in 1572, only to rise exponentially following the fall of Antwerp in 1585. After that year, according to the antiquarian John Southerden Burns, one-third of Antwerp's "merchants and the workmen who worked and dealt in silks, damasks, and taffeties, and in baizes, sayes, serges, stockings, &c., settled in England, because England was then ignorant of those manufactures."[36]

As Burns's observation makes quite clear, people from the Low Countries migrated to England for economic as much as for religious reasons. And England's political authorities welcomed them not just for their ostensible Protestant sympathies but also for their supposedly productive impact on business.[37] Yet they were also widely perceived to have a negative effect on the English economy. London's artisans repeatedly protested what they saw as the usurpation of their labor by skilled strangers; the artisans' protests found support from people in high places, including Sir Walter Raleigh and, later, Sir Thomas Mildmay, who presented a suit in 1594 to the queen's Privy Council demanding the regulation of strangers.[38] Interestingly, Mildmay's suit focused on economic crimes similar to those of the Dutch Church Libel, including usury: "There be many known rich men among them, and others very able, (though not so greatly noted,) which live obscurely only to benefit themselves by usury and exchange of money, without doing good to our commonwealth" (300). Mildmay's emphasis on the strangers' allegedly unscrupulous pursuit of their commercial interests led him to doubt, as did the author of the Dutch Church Libel, their religious credentials. To voice his suspicions, Mildmay resorted to the identical term that Bacon and Malynes employed to represent the transnational undecidability of usurer's capital: "Even as her majesty, by her gracious favour, doth protect such as repair hither sincerely for their conscience sake and for religion, so is there no reason; but such as make religion the *colour* of their coming, and are in truth irreligious, and frequent no church at all, such be known and discerned from the other, as by this means they may be" (299, emphasis added).

Sir Thomas Mildmay's accusations against the "coloured" Dutch may have been born of xenophobic hatred and fear. But on the matter of the immigrants' religious loyalties, the evidence bears him out, if only partially. The many censuses of strangers taken in the late sixteenth century reveal that significant numbers of the "Dutch" were not committedly Protestant refugees, and that many did not worship at the Dutch Reformed Church. A census performed in 1568 determined that "the whole number of strangers, as well as denisons as not denisons, dwelling and remaining within the exempt jurisdiction and liberties adjoining to the city, together with the city of Westminster," was 2,598. The vast majority of these were Dutch (1,937); most of the rest were "French" (presumably Walloons and Huguenots). Of these, 835 worshiped in the English church, and 510 in the Dutch church; 423 worshiped in no church at all.[39] The figures from London tell a similar story. The total number of strangers in the city and in its liberties was 6,704. Again, the Dutch were an overwhelming majority: they numbered 5,225, while there were 1,119 "French." Of the observant strangers, 1,815 worshiped at the English church; 1,910 at the Dutch church; and 1,810 at the French church. But a grand total of 1,008 professed to worship at no church.[40] The figures for 1593, the year of the Dutch Church Libel, are even more startling. A survey of the stranger population that year registered over 7,000 Dutch immigrants in the capital. Yet according to this census, there were only 1,376 worshipers at the Dutch Church and 1,344 at the French Church.[41] While a large percentage of the remainder may have opted to worship at the Church of England, that still leaves many of the Dutch immigrants' religious affiliations (or lack of them) unaccounted for.

Could there be other reasons for these surprising figures? Were some of the nominal "Dutch" refugees non-Protestant—that is, crypto-Catholics, or even crypto-Jews? The possibility that some of the Dutch denizens secretly professed Catholicism is certainly one of the insinuations of Mildmay's suit. It is glanced at also by the Dutch Church Libel, both in its charge of Spanish "infection" and in its use of a metaphor that freights economic and religious crime: "*counterfeiting* religion for your flight / When 't'is well knowne, you are loth." Catholic merchants from Flanders had set up shop in England long before the Protestant Reformation; some of these merchants openly resumed their Catholic worship during the reign of Mary, and it is quite feasible that of these, several continued to profess Catholicism covertly during Elizabeth's reign.[42]

It is far more difficult to ascertain the second possibility—that London's migrant "Dutch" community included Jews. The Low Countries were ruled by the Spanish for most of the sixteenth century; hence the 1492 edict of expulsion applied there and was reinforced by subsequent bans in 1532 and 1549. To all intents and purposes, the Netherlands had been completely purged of its Jewish population by midcentury. Yet, as Jonathan Israel has noted, the Protestant Revolt against Spanish rule in 1572 allowed for policies of readmission and reintegration.[43] In 1577, the rebel States General, through the Antwerp city council, opened negotiations with the leaders of Frankfurt Jewry, inviting them to establish a Jewish community in Antwerp in return for financial assistance against Spain. William of Orange had planned also to readmit Levantine Jews in the hope of strengthening trade relations with Spain's other archenemy, the Turkish sultan. Although these latter negotiations proved fruitless, German Jews from Friesland settled in the northeastern parts of the Netherlands, particularly Groningen, in the 1570s and 1580s.[44]

To find a "Jewish" element in London's "Dutch" community, however, we need to follow trails that lead not to the openly observant Jewish community of Groningen but to the Portuguese Marrano population of Antwerp. By the 1570s, this city had become home to the largest Marrano community in northern Europe. The Portuguese had established a trading colony there in 1499; after the enforced conversion of all Portuguese Jews in 1497, Antwerp proved an attractive destination for many of the so-called New Christians or conversos. The city served as Europe's main entrepôt for the boom trades in Oriental silk and spices, and it made rich men of many Marrano merchants. The most notable of these in the first half of the sixteenth century was Diego Mendes, who formed a partnership in 1525 with another Portuguese Marrano, Johan Karel de Affaitati. Together they acquired a monopoly on the wholesale and retail spice trade of Flanders and forced their customers in France, Germany, and England to transact their business exclusively with them.[45] Mendes's and de Affaitati's careers reveal two important aspects of Marrano culture in the Low Countries. First, even as Dutch-based Marranos were widely referred to as the "Portuguese Nation," they had trading contacts and factors in many other nations, including England.[46] Second, they readily adopted the names of their host nations, as the Dutch first names of Mendes's partner, Johan Karel de Affaitati, make clear.

Antwerp's recapture in 1585 by the Duke of Alva on behalf of Spain technically made the city an unsafe place for practicing Jews. Nevertheless, a significant number of Antwerp's Marranos chose to remain there. Did those who stayed continue to practice Judaism secretly—as scholars who use the term "Marrano" have habitually assumed? Or did some of the Marranos take their "New Christianity" seriously? If some did continue to practice Judaism secretly, did they hold out hope that the Spaniards' recapture of Antwerp was a temporary state of affairs, even after the Inquisition was instituted there? Or was their primary focus on their economic rather than their religious activities? It was only in 1595, after the Dutch blockade of Antwerp, that the Portuguese Marranos migrated from the city en masse, and this was largely because it had lost its economic viability as an entrepôt. The traditional view is that Antwerp's Marranos mostly relocated to Amsterdam in the United Provinces. Allowed by that city's *Regenten* to practice Judaism openly, they soon became the most economically and culturally prosperous Jewish community in northern Europe, later producing the philosopher Spinoza and the rabbi Israel ben Menasseh, who would successfully argue for the readmission of Jews to England under Cromwell.[47] But not all of Antwerp's Marranos necessarily relocated to Amsterdam. Might some of them have joined the "Dutch" exodus to England referred to by Burns, whether after the blockade of 1595 or even after Antwerp's reconquest by Spain in 1585? In that year, almost twenty thousand merchants left the city. Herbert Bloom argues that "it is reasonable to suppose that there were some Marranos in the group, although, under their Catholic cloak, they would not have been driven from Antwerp."[48] Might it also be reasonable to suppose that some of these Marrano merchants went not to Amsterdam but to England, where they were identified not as Jews but as "Portuguese" or even "Dutch"?

There are a handful of clues that suggest a Dutch Marrano connection in London. Albert Hyamson has claimed that Sarah Lopez, wife of the ill-starred Dr. Roderigo Lopez, was from Antwerp (though other scholars insist that as the daughter of the Marrano immigrant Dunstan Ames, or Añes, she was probably born in London).[49] Moreover, names common to Portuguese Marranos turn up in registers of London "Dutch." When the Queen levied money from strangers to finance the war effort against Spain, for example, a list of the subscribers was made. Among many traditionally Dutch names, one finds a Peter De Coster and a Balthazar Sanctes; "Da Costa" and "Sanchez" are names that appear frequently in the records of Continental Marrano communities.[50] However, it is very difficult to place much credence in the "evidence" provided by names. This is partly because, as the case of Johan Karel de Affaitati suggests, many Marranos changed their names or went by various aliases. One such multiply named person for whom a paper trail has survived, even though it dates from later in the seventeenth century, is Manuel Lopes Pereira, a merchant who came to London from the Netherlands in 1655. In Holland he went by the name of Jacques Vanderperre; in transactions with factors in Portugal and the East Indies he passed as Manuel Velasquez; in the Amsterdam synagogue, however, he was known as Isaac Raphael Haim Pereira.[51] This suggests that Marrano "identity" could consist of multiple identities, strategically deployed for a variety of reasons in different locations. And although there has been a tendency to regard "Jew" as the Marrano's true identity and "Christian" as the duplicitous mask, scholars like Miriam Bodian have rightly warned against uncritically assuming any such schema.[52]

Take, for example, the story of Maria Nuñes. A daughter of two Portuguese Marranos arrested during the Inquisition, she was herself apprehended by the English in 1598 en route to Holland. Dutch legend had it that while detained in London, she charmed the queen and was wooed by a duke. Like Shakespeare's Jessica, she was adept at sexual shapeshifting: when captured, she was dressed in male attire. Memorialized in the late seventeenth century by the Amsterdam poet Daniel Levi de Barrios as a Jewish heroine, her identities—religious, gendered, national—appear to have been far less stable than the hagiographic version of her would countenance. Although she married the scion of a Marrano family upon her arrival in Amsterdam, she did not stay long in the Low Countries. Together with her husband, she emigrated to Spain, where he acquired a position of some considerable rank in the Spanish court—not a place one would expect even a covert practitioner of Judaism to seek a career. Were Maria Nuñes and her husband "really" Jewish, "really" Catholic, both, neither?[53] Despite Levi de Barrios's attempts to make Maria Nuñes a poster child for Amsterdam Jewry, her story underscores how people for a variety of undecidable reasons—economic, political, religious—shuffled transnational locations, identities, and names.

It is difficult, if not impossible, to distill social history from the moonshine of xenophobic polemic. Nevertheless, the Dutch Church Libel's hybridization of Low Country immigrant, Jewish usurer, and Spanish saboteur might point to historical realities—specifically, the existence of trading networks between the Iberian Peninsula and northern Europe that relied on merchants, factors, and artisans of uncertain, malleable nationality.[54] As the parallel shapeshifting biographies of Maria Nuñes and Manuel Lopes Pereira/Jacques Vanderperre/Manuel Velasquez/Isaac Raphael Haim Pereira suggest, early modern Iberian and Low Country identities were far less decidable, or (in the terms of the Dutch Church Libel) far more "infected," than is suggested by the determinate names we are now accustomed to use—"Portuguese," "Spaniard," "Dutchman," "Jew," even "Marrano."

If the Dutch Church Libel shows how the "Dutch" could be metaphorically "infected" by the "Jew," Shakespeare's *Merchant of Venice* might equally show how the "Jew" is likewise a transnational palimpsest, one of whose layers is "Dutch." In the following section, I shall attempt to tease out the Dutch subtext of Shakespeare's play about Jews and Christians in Venice. My point is not to suggest that Shylock is "really" Dutch, or is even an allegorical representation of a Dutchman. Rather, I shall attempt to show how "the Jew" is a far less transparent category of identity in the play than its readers have usually recognized. In a fashion that recalls the rhetorical strategies of Bacon, Malynes, and Milles, however, the transnational hybridity of Shakespeare's Jew is nonetheless recuperated as the "parti-coloured" taint of Shylock's usury.

Taint: *The Merchant of Venice/The Merchant of Amsterdam*?

Surveying the differences between Jewish life in the antisemitic Venice of the sixteenth century and the comparatively philosemitic Amsterdam of the seventeenth century, Martin D. Yaffe asks, why did Shakespeare choose to write *The Merchant of Venice* rather than *The Merchant of Amsterdam*?[55] It is a trick question, of course, because an anachronistic one. Nonetheless, certain events in Holland during the decade after the first performances of *The Merchant of*

Venice in approximately 1596 seem to lend the play an unlikely proleptic, shaping power across the channel. We have already encountered the story of Maria Nuñes—the "Jewish"/"New Christian" daughter who, like Jessica, escaped from her home dressed as a boy in order to be married. And then there is also the uncanny name of one of the first wealthy Jews in Amsterdam: when created a baron, he took the name "Belmont."[56] But one does not need to turn to such stories to tease out the Dutch subtext in *The Merchant of Venice.*

Antonio's trade interests, and his argosies, lead ineluctably away from Venice: Shylock reports that he has ventures abroad in Tripolis, Mexico, the Indies, and England (1.3.15–17). As several readers of the play have noted, however, Antonio's trading destinations cannot be those of a sixteenth-century Venetian merchant. In the nineteenth century, Thomas Elze singled out Antonio's trading links with Mexico and England as one of the "three unrealistic aspects" of the play; John Gillies has more recently noted that the Venetians never participated in the new oceanic trades, which were dominated by the Iberians.[57] Theodore Leinwand, by contrast, remarks on the *English* involvement in these trades, and in effect proposes Antonio as the title character in a cryptoplay called "The Merchant of London": "it certainly would have been possible in the 1590s, in the heyday of trade combined with plunder, to entertain such 'Elizabethan ambitions for London' and its great privateering merchants."[58] I would argue that if Antonio's global trading connections lend him a secret identity as a merchant of London, they can equally fashion him as a cryptomerchant of Antwerp or Amsterdam (otherwise known as the "Venice of the North").[59]

The play's submerged Dutch trading nexus at one point surfaces literally. As Antonio's ill fortunes at sea begin to accumulate, Salarino reports that "Antonio hath a ship of rich lading wrecked on the Narrow Seas; the Goodwins I think they call the place—a very dangerous flat, and fatal, where the carcases of many a tall ship lie buried, as they say" (3.1.3–7). The "Narrow Seas" was a name for the waters of the English Channel, and "the Goodwins" shoals upon which merchant vessels often came to grief. Around the time of the Dutch Church Libel, and only three years before the *The Merchant of Venice*'s putative date of composition, the Goodwins were the location of a major shipping accident, one that led to a political standoff between England and merchants of the United Provinces. On August 8, 1593, the queen's Privy Council read a letter addressed to Lord Cobham from "divers merchaunt straingers of Holland and Zeland." The Council observed that

we are crediblie geven to understand that there was in November and December last three shipps cast awaie uppon the Goodwin, namelie the St. Peter of Amsterdam, the Red Lion of London and the Golden Lion of Midleborough, being laden with manie packes of wax, linnen cloath, saies, grogrames and divers other merchaundizes apperteyning to merchauntes of the said cuntries of Holland and Zeeland, and that the same merchaundizes floatinge on the sea and coming on land in divers places alongst the sea coast, from the Isle of Thannett in Kent to the town of Rie in Sussex, have bin taken up, spoiled, imbeaseled, concealed and caried awaie by the inhabitantes adjoyning to the said seacoast and of other places, unconscionablie throwing them selves into the spooile therof without the regard of the miserie and affliction of the poore mariners and owners of the said shipps and goodes, and that notwithstanding divers letters written and divers orders given for the restitucion therof, yet great quantities of the said goodes and merchaundizes ar stil concealed and witholden from their proprietaries and their factours, to their great los and hinderaunce.[60]

We will never know whether Shakespeare was familiar with the details of this incident, which involved the English "spoil[ing]" and "imbeasel[ing]"—or "colouring"—of Dutch goods. Yet the tale of the three Dutch shipwrecks in the English Channel resonates eerily with *The Merchant of Venice*, and not only with Antonio's loss of an argosy on the Goodwins, but also with Salarino's earlier fantasy of shipwreck in the play's first scene. Here Salarino attributes Antonio's melancholy to causes reminiscent of those that afflicted the "poore mariners and owners of . . . shipps and goods . . . cast awaie uppon the Goodwin." In his fantasy, Salarino replays not only the Dutch traders' misfortune of losing their ships but also their horrified experience of seeing their "merchaundizes floatinge on the sea":

Should I go to church
And see the holy edifice of stone
And not bethink me straight of dangerous rocks,
Which touching but my gentle vessel's side
Would scatter all her spices on the stream
Enrobe the roaring waters with my silks . . . ? (1.1.29–34)

Crucial to Salarino's fantasy of shipwreck are the two commodities that, as we have seen, were the stock in trade of Antwerp. As Edward Misselden says in *The Circle of Commerce*, "*Spices, Silkes* . . . are the principall Commodities of the *Low Countries.*"[61] However, Salarino names the wrecked ship "my wealthy Andrew" (1.1.27), which editors usually interpret as a reference to the San Andres, a valuable Spanish ship captured by the English in 1596. What Salarino's fantasy invokes, then, are the perils not of Mediterranean commerce but rather of the Iberian/Dutch trading routes that are shadowed in the hybrid identities of the Dutch Church Libel.

Yet it is less Antonio's capital ventures than Shylock's cultural and legal status that most intriguingly points away from Venice to northern Europe. As Antonio remarks upon his arrest, Shylock is guaranteed certain privileges as a stranger:

The Duke cannot deny the course of the law;
For the commodities that strangers have
With us in Venice, if it be denied,
Will much impeach the justice of the state,
Since that the trade and profit of the city
Consisteth of all nations. (3.3.26–31)

Antonio's speech might well offer an accurate representation of "the commodities that strangers" enjoyed in sixteenth-century Venice. In 1561, the English visitor William Thomas was much taken by "the libertee of straunger's in Venice," claiming that "al men, specially strangers, haue so much libertee there, that though they speake very ill by the Venetians, so they attempt nothing in effect against theyr astate . . . whych vndoubtedly is one principall cause, that draweth so many straungers thither."[62] Yet for *The Merchant of Venice*'s earliest audiences, Antonio's defense of "the commodities that strangers have" may well have brought to mind a recent political debate concerning London's Dutch community. A month before the composition of the Dutch Church Libel, a bill seeking to regulate and limit strangers' practice of crafts and trades had been submitted to the House of Commons. The bill was fiercely opposed by some—Sir John Woolley argued that London's economic prosperity was in large part due to the strangers' skills—but it eventually passed the Commons by the wide margin of 162–82. The anti-stranger bill was decisively rejected, however, in the House of Lords, where the Dutch had many champions, including William Cecil, the Lord High Treasurer Burghley. From very early in Elizabeth's reign, Cecil had recognized the contribution that skilled immigrant workers could make to the nation's economic health, both by reducing England's dependence on foreign manufacturers and by preserving stocks of bullion in the realm. Even though Antonio is Shylock's adversary, therefore, he nonetheless tows the official line of the English state vis-à-vis strangers.[63]

But the play also lends voice to less accommodating English attitudes toward the Dutch. As James Shapiro notes, Shylock's "I will buy with you, sell with you, talk with you, walk with you and so following: but I will not eat with you, drink with you, nor pray with you" (1.3.28–30) is redolent of the claim that the Dutch immigrants were "an inward-looking society of their own deliberately cutting themselves off from their hosts."[64] Shylock himself lends a derogatory Dutch inflection to the subject of his usurious business practices: when he assures Antonio that he will "take no doit / Of usance for my moneys" (1.3.134–35), he refers to a Dutch copper coin of exceedingly small value (about half of an English farthing). During the fifteenth and sixteenth centuries, the coin had acquired illegal currency in England, where it became a proverbial token of cheapness. Yet it remained firmly associated with the Low Countries: John Taylor the Water Poet, for example, demeans "the Dutchmen" and their "base doyts and Stiuers."[65] Shylock's reference to the "doit," therefore, once more conjures up the ghost of *The Merchant of Amsterdam*.

There is another curious Dutch presence in *The Merchant of Venice*: Rhenish wine, to which the play refers twice. Rhenish—white wine from the Rhine region—was readily associated with Germany, which is why Portia invokes it as the bait with which she might lure an undesirable suitor, the drunken German prince, from the correct casket (1.2.78–79). Yet Fynes Moryson in his 1617 *Itinerary* says that Germans only "rarely drinke Rhenish wine."[66] Instead, Rhenish was associated proverbially with London's Dutch immigrants. In his *Travels Through London* (1636), for example, John Taylor lists four public houses that sell Rhenish and are frequented exclusively by Dutchmen; John Stowe insinuates in his *Survay of London* that London's Dutch publicans sell only Rhenish.[67] Fascinatingly, Rhenish is crucial to the play's figuration of Jewish identity. Salarino invokes the wine as he attempts to draw an absolute corporeal distinction between Jessica and Shylock: "There is more difference between thy flesh and hers than between jet and ivory; more between your bloods than there is between red wine and Rhenish" (3.1.33). Salarino's is a comparison ostensibly intended to rank fair over dark, quality over dross, New Christian over Jew, brother (or sister) over other. Yet his seemingly clearcut differentiation between red and Rhenish wines does not come without its complications. The syntax of the distinction works to equate Shylock the Jew with "red wine," which as a generically Mediterranean commodity would be the tipple more appropriate to Venice; Jessica the Christian-to-be is equated with "Rhenish," the foreign wine. Accidentally or not, the two wines also potentially invoke the two nations involved in the Low Countries wars, Spain and the United Provinces, hinting at an opposition of Catholic and Protestant that would render the Dutchified Jessica "one of us" to the English audience, but "one of them" to the Venetian characters. Even as Salarino seeks to distinguish Jessica from her Jewish father, therefore, he constructs both in a fashion that once again recalls the rhetorical gambits of the Dutch Church Libel, casting each not as a determinate stranger but as a Low Country/Iberian/Jewish hybrid.[68]

Such hybridity might seem to problematize "the Jew," making his or her identity far more refractory and transnationally palimpsested than critical responses to *The Merchant of Venice* have usually supposed. Yet I would argue that the play partially recuperates such hybridity as the condition of the Jewish usurer, and in ways that resonate with the mercantilist rather than the traditional Christian discourse of usury. This is particularly the case with Shylock's parable about Laban and Jacob's sheep, at which I have already glanced briefly. Shylock presents the parable as a myth of the origins of Jewish "thrift," the first enterprising "deed" of a presumably Jewish "kind":

> Mark what Jacob did:
> When Laban and himself were compromised
> That all the eanlings which were streaked and pied
> Should all as Jacob's hire, the ewes being rank
> In end of autumn turned to the rams,
> And when the work of generation was
> Between these woolly breeders in the act,
> The skilfull shepherd pilled me certain wands,
> And in the doing of the deed of kind,
> He stuck them up before the fulsome ewes,
> Who then conceiving, did in eaning time
> Fall parti-coloured lambs, and those were Jacob's. (1.3.69–80)

Critics have had enormous difficulty with this speech, puzzling over its relevance to usury.[69] In an otherwise insightful essay, for example, Elizabeth Spiller argues that "Shylock's use of the Jacob and Laban story becomes important not so much as an argument about usury but as a narrative about imaginative miscegenation."[70] Rightly noting that early modern readers repeatedly used the Jacob and Laban story to interject their concerns about not usury but racial impurity and intermixture, Spiller nevertheless neglects the extent to which such concerns were themselves integral to the mercantilist problematic of usury. As we have seen with Malynes's "Judaized" Turkish/English dragon of usury and the Dutch Church Libel's fantasy of usurious strangers "infected with Spanish gold," usury was repeatedly regarded as a stained and staining practice whose very condition was national and monetary hybridity.

In Shylock's allegorical reading of the Jacob and Laban story, there are two crucial levels of hybridity. The first is evident in Shylock's figuration of Jewry. Marc Shell has noted Shylock's puns on "ewes," "use," and "Jews" (or, as the Folio spells it, "Iewes"), citing these as examples of Shylock's "verbal usury"—the generation of semantic interest through punning and riddling.[71] As a result of Shylock's verbal usury, the "pied and streaked" offspring of *ewes* become the allegorical incarnations of *Jews*, a flock whose hybridity stains it in opposition to Laban's supposedly pure one. The homophonic connections between Jews and Jacob's sheep are consolidated by a telling lexical indeterminacy in the text of the folio edition: according to Shylock, the "parti-coloured" eanlings "were *Iacobs*"—thereby confusing the genitive and the plural noun forms of "Jacob" (or "Israel"). And indeed, the very phrase "parti-coloured" may have conjured up for the play's original audiences an association with Jews. Although Shake-speare could have found the phrase in Bishop Miles Coverdale's 1535 translation of the Bible,[72] it was also used to refer to the colored clothes that Italian Jews were notoriously forced to wear. In Henry Glapthorne's play *The Hollander,* for example, the Dutch gull Sconce compares his fellow countrymen to "the Jewes at Rome," who "weare party coloured garments to be knowne from Chris-tians."[73]

There is a second level at which "parti-coloured" hybridity is crucial to Shylock's parable. If Shylock equates the spotty eanlings with Jacob and *Jews,* he identifies the animals equally with the usurer's *profit.* As I have already argued, the "parti-coloured" fleeces of the sheep entail a specifically mercantilist pun: Jacob has "coloured" the sheep both physically and legally, in the sense of alien-ating them from Laban. Once again we see how the Jewish usurer not only em-bodies hybridity; he also transmits it, "colouring" money or goods to generate profit—which, in Jacob's case, takes the form of hybrid fleeces that are no less valuable than the "golden fleece" with which the play's romantic venturers asso-ciate Portia, Nerissa, and the wealth of Belmont (1.1.169, 3.2.240).

The language of disease does not figure explicitly in Shylock's parable of usurious interest, even though—as we have seen—the mercantilist term "coloured" participates within a string of similar words with pathological asso-ciations. But a later scene casts a retrospective, pathological light on Shylock's interpretation of Jacob's "parti-coloured" sheep. When Antonio famously refers to himself as a "tainted wether of the flock" (4.1.114), the text does far more than style him as a Christlike martyr, the lamb of God. Just as importantly, I would argue, he has here become a type of Jacob's "pied and streaked" sheep. Crucial to Antonio's self-representation is a language of pathological contamination and coloring that is highly redolent of the mercantilist discourse of usury.

"Taint" was itself a hybrid term. The OED tells us that it derives from two words of distinct origin that "appear to have run together in the formation of later senses" (OED, *taint,* sb.). The first word was an aphetic form of "attaint"—the past participle of "attain"—in the sense of "reach," "touch," or "strike." This produced the various meanings of a "hit" in tilting, a criminal conviction, and, significantly, a disease in horses (a pathology whose etymology recalls that of plague, which derives from *plaga,* the Greek term for "strike"). The second form of "taint" was derived from the Latin *tinctus,* meaning "tint" or "color." The in-terplay between "taint" as blow or animal disease and "taint" as color produced a variety of hybrid senses in Shakespeare's England, all of them with pathologi-cal connotations of varying degrees. First, "taint" possessed the still familiar sense of a stain, blemish, or spot; this was used almost invariably in a metaphor-ical sense, as in Viola's remark that she hates "ingratitude more in a man /

Than . . . any taint of vice" (*Twelfth Night,* 3.4.390), or in Maecenas's eulogy for Antony: "his taints and honours / Waged equal with him" (*Anthony and Cleopatra,* 5.1.30). Second, "taint" assumed the pathological sense of contamination or infection, as in *Henry 8,* where Gardiner speaks of "a general taint of the state" (5.3.28). And finally, "taint" became a more specialized medical term referring to a trace of disease in a latent state. This last meaning seems implicit in Antonio's description of himself as "tainted." Indeed, the OED lists two pathological meanings for the adjective "tainted"—"contaminated, infected, or corrupted"; and "having a taint of disease; infected with latent disease," for which it offers Antonio's remark in *The Merchant of Venice* as the first recorded example.

Yet the OED decisively fixes the meaning of the line in a way that is at odds with the play's fascination with the indeterminacy of "coloured" identities. I would argue, by contrast, that the "tainted" Antonio is physically *stained* as much as he is pathologically *infected,* and in a way that harks back to Shylock's justification of usury. If the usurer's skill lies in the production and expropriation of hybrid goods, the "tainted wether" Antonio has here become Shylock's "parti-coloured" sheep. The implication of Antonio's pathological self-representation, then, is that his very flesh has become Shylock's usurious interest. This interpretation is at odds with readings of the play inflected by the traditional Christian interpretations of usury. W. H. Auden, for example, insisted that insofar as it does not involve the taking of monetary interest, Shylock's bond is more typical of Christian jurisprudence and nonusurious conventions of lending.[74] But my suggestion that Antonio is Shylock's "parti-coloured" sheep is highly compatible with the mercantilist discourse of usury that I have sketched throughout this chapter. Like Malynes's dragon of usury, Shylock is a "proximate other" who is indeterminately Venetian and Jew, citizen and alien, Mediterranean and Dutch; moreover, he not only embodies but also transmits his hybridity. The "tainted wether" Antonio has become property alienated to Shylock, legally comparable to the lambs that Jacob usuriously expropriated from Laban. Hence Antonio's body is "tainted" or "coloured" in both economic and pathological senses of the terms. Even though Auden called his collection of critical essays *The Dyer's Hand,* his analysis of *The Merchant of Venice* is oddly color-blind to the images of dyeing/coloring/staining/tainting that are integral to the play and its reproduction of the mercantilist discourse of transnational usury.

There is a further metaphorical dimension to Antonio's usurious tainting that recalls mercantilist discourse. Shylock's pursuit of his bond with Antonio, as is routinely noted, acquires cannibalistic overtones. Despite his earlier refusal to dine with gentiles, Shylock finally accepts Antonio's dinner-party invitation, exclaiming that "I'll go in hate, to feed upon / The prodigal Christian" (2.6.14–15). Such a remark cannot help but raise the specter of the Jewish man-eater.[75] But as the Dutch Church Libel shows, the alleged expropriation of English bullion by strangers was itself readily figured as a rapacious, "Judaized" devouring of human flesh: "like the Jewes, you eate us vp as bread." Shylock's desire for a pound of flesh from Antonio's body and, more specifically, his desire for Antonio's heart ("I will have the heart of him if he forfeit" [3.1.100–101]) points to the play's repeated confusion of "purse" and "person" (1.1.137). It also connects to a powerful, recurrent mercantilist metaphor—blood as money, which I explore in more detail in Chapters 6 and 7. Gail Kern Paster has rightly noted the slipperiness of blood as a trope throughout *The Merchant of Venice*.[76] But inasmuch as Antonio's blood threatens to be alienated to Shylock, the trope in this instance cannot help but resonate with the mercantilist condemnation of usury as a practice that covertly depletes the nation's lifeblood, or bullion. Hence Portia's willingness to award Shylock Antonio's flesh, but not a drop of his blood (4.1.320–22), arguably spells the cancellation of the Jew's usurious bond and the restoration of Venetian economic sovereignty. This mercantilist-inflected nationalism is made explicit by the obscure statute that Portia invokes not only to cancel the bond but also to punish Shylock:

It is enacted in the laws of Venice,
If it be proved against an alien
That by direct or indirect attempts
He seek the life of any citizen,
The party 'gainst the which he doth contrive
Shall seize one half his goods, the other half
Comes to the privy coffer of the state . . . (4.1.344–50)

In a crucial reversal, therefore, Shylock's quest for Antonio's blood becomes the pretext for the mercantilist expropriation of "alien" bullion by the Venetian state.

The play thus seems to suggest that the threat of transnational hybridity originates in and ends with the Jewish usurer. Just as the stranger Jacob stains Laban's seemingly pure property, so does Shylock the Jewish usurer hybridize the Christian Venetians to whom he lays claim, in the process pathologically tainting them. Hence Antonio just as much as Shylock becomes the "goodly apple rotten at the heart" (1.3.93), tainted or "coloured" for usurious Jewish profit. But this reading ignores another possibility raised by the play. When decoding the transnational hybridity of the Jewish usurer, one might recall the hybridity of postcolonial identity as theorized by Homi Bhabha: that is, an imitation that displaces the supposedly pure origin by mimicking its very impurity.[77] Shylock famously remarks to Salarino that "the villainy you teach me, I will execute, and it shall go hard but I will better the instruction" (3.1.56–57).

In other words, Shylock has learned his villainy from the Christians, so that his hard "Jewish heart" (4.1.80) is arguably "coloured" Christian nastiness. To this extent, his vengeful mimicry reveals the already prior tainting of the supposedly pure origin.[78] In the courtroom scene, for example, Shylock follows Venetian example in justifying his ownership of Antonio:

You have among you many a purchased slave,
Which, like your asses and your dogs and mules,
You use in abject and slavish parts
Because you bought them. (4.1.90–93)

But even as Shylock reflects the *moral* taints within Venetian culture, he also embodies the more systematic *transnational* taints that comprise Venetian "identity." Antonio remarks that "the trade and profit of the city / Consisteth of all nations" (3.3.30–31). Venice is hybrid, both physically and rhetorically; it cannot help but blur the boundaries between itself and "all nations." Hence Shylock's Dutch-Mediterranean hybridity is not a unique trait of the "Jew." It is, rather, as we have seen, a local component of a larger "Netherlandish" subtext that equally stains Antonio's global capital ventures.

This suggests how even as the "parti-coloured" hybridity of the Jew ostensibly functions as a foil to the economic and cultural purity of the gentile, it can equally work to disclose the latter's own originary hybridity. In the courtroom scene, Antonio (who has adopted Shylock's script of "patient" suffering [4.1.11–12]), Graziano (who thanks Shylock for teaching him the word "Daniel" [4.1.337]), and Portia (who uses Shylock's literal interpretation of "justice" against him [4.1.317–18]) all seem to have "coloured" or expropriated the language of the Jew. At the end of the play, in a Belmont supposedly purified of the taint of Shylock, the Christian Lorenzo similarly identifies with the starving Jews in the desert, feasting on "manna" (5.1.294–95). Old Gobbo tells Bassanio that the protean Launcelot—who during the play not only trades his Jewish master for a Christian, but shapeshifts from morality play Everyman to born-again Jacob to "Hagar's" Arab offspring (2.5.42)[79]—has "a great infection, sir, as one would say, to serve" (2.2.103). Thus does the old man's compulsive habit of malapropism comically degrade his son's "affection," or desire. It is a revealing slip nonetheless. Given the play's fascination with "tainting" and "colouring," "infect" here cannot help but assume its residual sense of "dye, tinge, colour, stain." Launcelot, like his fellow Venetians, is thus an infected hybrid, possessed of no determinate national identity.

It is not only the Venetians who have "a great infection" in this latter sense. Perhaps the most notable instance is that of the English would-be suitor, whom

Portia imperiously dismisses in act 1, scene 2, along with her German, Neapolitan, French, Scottish, and Polish gentleman callers. In a satirical tableau of national stereotypes, Shakespeare represents the Englishman as wearing garments that derive from everywhere but England: "How oddly he is suited! I think he bought his doublet in Italy, his round hose in France, his bonnet in Germany, and his behaviour everywhere" (1.2.60–62).[80] This transnational motley, so redolent of the globally diverse garb of "English" treasure in Malynes's *Saint George for England Allegorically Described,* offers a subtle reminder of what both *The Merchant of Venice* and mercantilist discourse try so hard to disavow: in the universe of global trade, *everyone* is tainted by the multiple traces of transnationality.

Which Is the Englishman Here, and Which the Dutch?

My reading of the *The Merchant of Venice* is designed to put pressure on how we understand the meaning of "the Jew" in the play. Customarily, Shylock, Jessica, and Tubal are historicized in relation either to "real" Jews in Venice or to "real" English Jews and crypto-Jews, particularly Dr. Roderigo Lopez. Such historicizations are meant to arrive at certainty. Yet I have argued here that we can achieve greater historical richness by recognizing the national undecidability of "the Jew," whether in *The Merchant of Venice* or in other texts like Malynes's *Saint George for England Allegorically Described* and the Dutch Church Libel. This undecidability is partly a textual effect connected to the pathologies of usury, understood as a transnational infection or tainting. But it also suggests a mode of protean identity that had become a lived reality for many people, including the so-called Marranos, who circulated between the Iberian Peninsula, the Low Countries, and England. For many early modern Europeans as for Shylock, identity was not determinately univocal but multinationally palimpsested.

One such palimpsested identity, interestingly enough, was that of Gerard Malynes himself. Unlike other patriotic Tudor writers who glorified England's language, law, or geography, Malynes repeatedly subscribed—as *Saint George for England Allegorically Described* suggests—to an economic nationalism based on allegiance not to place of birth but to distinctive practices of commerce. This recoded Englishness quite possibly betrays a more personal anxiety. Malynes took repeated pains to stress his patriotism, claiming in one document to be an obedient subject of King James and telling the readers of the *Lex Mercatoria* that he was descended from a Lancashire family. But as Raymond de Roover has shown, Malynes was born in Antwerp and emigrated to England for unspecified reasons. Misselden mercilessly pilloried Malynes for his "Dutch mother tongue";

and his name appears (as Garet de Malynes) on the list of strangers from whom the queen levied subscriptions in 1588 to help defray costs for the armada preparations. Was Malynes really English? Or was he Flemish, Portuguese, even Marrano?[81] Malynes's movement across national boundaries, and his uncertain identity, eerily mirror the transnational hybridity of the usurious dragon that he reviles in *Saint George for England Allegorically Described.*

The three texts I have examined here hint at how "taint" and its related pathologies—"colouring," "infecting"—were literally symptomatic of mercantilist discourse and its fascination with transnational migrations. In the process, these pathologies contributed to a significant reimagining of the very notion of disease. Like the recoded "usury" of mercantilist writing, "taint" invoked the terminology of an earlier episteme to lend voice to a recognizably early modern problematic. On the one hand, "taint" entails a pathological mixing that recalls the standard humoral logic of "complexion" (derived from the Latin term for "mix"). On the other hand, "taint" evokes a very different kind of mixing, one closer to—though also different from—the Hippocratic theory of miasma, or pollution. This other mode of mixing belongs very much to the historical moment of the late sixteenth century: in all three texts, "taint" and its related pathologies designate mixings of the familiar and the strange, of the domestic and the foreign, of brother and other—in other words, the customary mixings of a mercantile age in which border crossings of various kinds had increasingly become the norm, and the foreign had acquired a much more dangerous, pathological power. To this extent, the "taint" of *The Merchant of Venice* looks forward to the more decisive recodings of disease as foreign body that we will see in later chapters.

Shakespeare's and Malynes's association of usury with diseased transnational mixtures betrays an economic anxiety that was to find fuller expression in the subsequent work of both men—an anxiety about the impossibility of innate, immutable value. In the next chapter, I turn to another economic treatise by Malynes and a later play by Shakespeare, each of which is preoccupied with the problem of value in the course of foreign exchange. And in both cases, a notable pathological vocabulary—albeit one somewhat different from the typology of the "coloured" taint of usury—mediates the two writers' fantasies of mercantile value.

Canker/Serpego and Value: Gerard Malynes, Troilus and Cressida

The Evil is Usury, Neschek *the serpent. . . .*
The canker corrupting all things, Fafnir the worm,
Syphilis of the State, of all kingdoms,
Wart of the commonweal,
Wenn-maker, corrupter of all things.

—*Ezra Pound, Addendum to Canto 100*

In his *Cantos,* written during his extended exile in Fascist Italy, Ezra Pound invokes a slew of pathologies with which to figure what he had come to regard as not only the moral "corrupter of all things" but also the bane of national economies: "Jewish" usury.[1] Absent from his pathological catalog are "taint" and the related early modern sicknesses I examined in the last chapter. Instead, heading Pound's list is "canker," a personified disease-cum-worm that he associates with usury throughout the *Cantos.* Even as his diatribes bear the unmistakable stamp of Italian Fascist monetary theory, Pound fascinatingly exhumes one of the conventional tropes in early modern English moralists' denunciations of usurious moneylending. In Robert Wilson's morality play *The Three Ladies of London* (1584), Conscience receives "cankered coin" from Usury.[2] The satirist Nicholas Breton branded the usurer in 1616 as "a kind of canker that with the teeth of interest eats the hearts of the poor."[3] And in his 1634 treatise *The English Usurer, or Usury Condemned,* John Blaxton approvingly cites the sermon of Bishop Sands, who denounced usury as "this canker" that "hath corrupted all England."[4]

The association of usury with "canker" is so commonplace in early modern English writing that it can be found even in *defenses* of usury. Although he supports interest rates of 5 percent, for example, Francis Bacon styles usury as "the canker and ruin of many men's estates."[5] The disease is also a recurrent feature of mercantilist discourse, where it is employed in tandem with the more customary pathologizations of usury as a "taint," "infection," or "coloring." In *Saint George for England Allegorically Described,* Gerard Malynes praises Licurgus for banishing the "canker worm" of usury from Sparta.[6] In *Free Trade, or The Meanes to Make Trade Florish* (1622), Edward Misselden compares "the want of restraint of the *Excesse* of the *Kingdome,* in *Vsury*" not only to "a *Viper* in a *King-*

dome that gnaweth through the bowels thereof" but also to "a *Canker* that fret-
teth and wasteth the stocke."[7] And as late as 1752, in his Malynes-inspired *Lex
Mercatoria Rediviva,* Wyndham Beauwes writes that "an extravagant interest . . .
is a sure Canker" to people's fortunes.[8]

Why did canker recommend itself to early modern English writers as a
pathological metaphor for the charging of interest? Money itself was associated
with the disease, thanks to Saint James's complaint that, in the words of the
Geneva Bible, rich men's "gold and siluer is cankred" (James 5:3). But the illness
had acquired additional metaphorical freight that made it particularly suggestive of usury. Like the latter, the disease was associated with unnatural generation *ex nihilo,* as John Aubrey's quip about Thomas Harriot's death from a nasal
canker—"a *nihilum* killed him at last"—intimates.[9] No doubt the link between
canker and usury was also suggested by the longstanding convention of representing usury as a "biting" serpent, a custom deriving from the double meaning
of the Hebrew *neshech,* which, as Pound's addendum to Canto 100 assumes,
means both "usury" and "to bite."[10] Indeed, in all the early modern English associations of usury with canker that I have cited, the disease is notably one that
eats, whether the pockets of the indigent poor, the consciences of good Christians, or the nation's reserves of bullion. But we can see in mercantilist usages of
canker more than simply the biting usury of moralists like Nicholas Breton or,
for that matter, Ezra Pound. Canker, like taint, also offered mercantilists a means
of representing transnational economy and the alienation of bullion across national borders. Such a use of the metaphor is hinted at in the second part of
Henry 4, when Bolingbroke—repeatedly described as a "canker" by Hotspur and
his faction—berates himself for the "cankered heaps of strange-achieved gold"
(4.5.72) that he has accumulated.[11] Adopting the phrasing of Saint James, Bolingbroke notably places "canker" in metonymic relation not only to gold but
also to the "strange" lands from which it has been conveyed.

It is not only the simple movement of bullion across national borders that
is figured in mercantilists' usages of "canker." Another transnational problematic
arguably lurks in their visions of what Wilson and Shakespeare call "cankered"
money: the mutability of financial value in the course of foreign currency exchange. The age-old Aristotelian ideal that coin must possess an intrinsic, fixed
value was placed under considerable pressure by the rise of national economies
with fluctuating foreign currency exchange rates, a development upon which
Malynes spilled considerable ink bemoaning the seeming evaporation of any
"gold standard" of economic value.[12] With the resulting commoditization of
and trade in national currencies, early modern merchants increasingly came to
see money less as an absolute yardstick of value than as a potential means to
making more money—a practice that Malynes denounced as "merchandizing

exchange" and, more brusquely, as "disguised usury." It is no coincidence, then, that Malynes gave the 1601 treatise in which he first formulated his critique of "merchandizing exchange" a pathological title redolent of anti-usury rhetoric: *The Canker of England's Commonwealth.*

Building on the influential studies of economy and semiology by Jean-Joseph Goux and Marc Shell, David Hawkes has convincingly demonstrated that seventeenth-century theories of money and language witnessed homologous shifts. The value of coins and signs alike came to be grounded not in their instrinsic telos, Hawkes argues, but in their socially imposed nomos: "economic and linguistic theory . . . historically developed in lockstep, moving away from intrinsic and toward nominal modes of evaluation."[13] Linguistics, however, did not provide the only template for shifting economic theories of value. As I shall argue in this chapter, the discourses of pathology offered early seventeenth-century writers an equally powerful resource with which to imagine rival models of value as inherent or extrinsic. To this end, mercantilists and dramatists employed not only canker but also another "eating" skin disease: serpego.

The figurative power of both canker and serpego in early-seventeenth-century writing stems in large part from conflicting early modern English understandings of their etiologies. We have already seen in Chapter 2 how competing understandings of syphilis as endogenous and invasive helped mediate rival attitudes toward the domestic effects of foreign trade. But the disjunction between humoral and exogenous conceptions of disease also proved discursively productive with respect to the issue of value. In this chapter, I illustrate the mercantilist codings of canker and serpego in extended readings of Malynes's *Canker of England's Commonwealth* and Shakespeare's *Troilus and Cressida.* The two texts share more than just their probable year of composition; both display strikingly similar preoccupations with, and uncertainties about, the migrations of disease and value across national borders. What follows is an attempt to join the dots of pathology and economics both in and between the two texts.

The Problem of Shakespeare's Creeping Serpego

In contrast to his more light-hearted mercantile comedies of the 1590s, Shakespeare's so-called problem plays from the early years of the seventeenth century can seem morbidly sick.[14] As numerous critics have noted, syphilis, its symptoms, and its colloquial discourses seem to have thoroughly infected the plays' vocabularies, whether expressly (the "pocky corses" of *Hamlet*'s graveyard scene, Lucio's banter about "French crowns" in *Measure for Measure,* the "French crown" fit for a "taffety punk" referred to by the clown in *All's Well That Ends*

Well, Thersites' caustic remarks about "Neapolitan bone-ache" as well as Pandarus's disclosure of his ailments at the end of *Troilus and Cressida*)[15] or more obliquely (the "tetter" that coats the poisoned body of King Hamlet and that crops up again in Thersites' railings, the "sciatica" and "serpego" referred to in both *Measure for Measure* and *Troilus and Cressida*).[16] But a battalion of other diseases are name-checked in the plays. *All's Well That Ends Well's* entire plot turns on the king's affliction with "fistula" (1.1.34). *Measure for Measure* offers us "gout" and "rheum" (3.1.31), "palsied eld" (3.1.36), and a "strange fever" (5.1.152). In *Hamlet* we encounter "contagious blastments" (1.3.42), a "vicious mole of nature" (1.4.24), a "leprous distillment" (1.5.64), "pestilent . . . vapors" (2.2.322–23), a "sense . . . apoplexed" (3.4.72–73), "the ulcerous place" (3.4.147), "the hectic in my blood" (4.3.66), "th'imposthume of much wealth and peace" (4.4.27), "plague" (4.7.13), "the quick of th'ulcer" (4.7.123), and a "canker of our nature" (5.2.69). And *Troilus and Cressida,* the most disease-ridden of them all, bequeaths to its audiences and readers an exhaustive compendium of early modern ailments: "ulcer of my heart" (1.1.54), "plague" (1.1.94, 1.3.96, 3.3.264, etc.), "jaundies" (1.3.2), "biles" (2.1.2), "botchy core" (2.1.6), "red murrion" (2.1.19), "scab" (2.1.29), "colic" (4.5.9), "tisick" (5.3.101), and, in one nonpareil of Thersitean virulence alone, "rotten diseases of the south, the guts-griping, ruptures, catarrhs, loads a'gravel in the back, lethargies, cold palsies, raw eyes, dirt-rotten livers, whissing lungs, bladders full of imposthume, sciaticas, lime-kills i'th'-palm, incurable bone-ache, and the rivell'd fee-simple of the tetter" (5.1.18–23).

When confronted with the extensive pathological vocabularies of Shakespeare's problem plays, modern critics have tended to adopt either of two distinct approaches. The first has consisted of occasionally lurid speculation about the state of Shakespeare's mind and health in or around 1601. In her enduringly influential study, *Shakespeare's Imagery and What It Tells Us,* Caroline Spurgeon notes that Shakespeare's interest in plague and hidden diseases such as cancer "became stronger in middle age," reaching its height in *Hamlet* and *Troilus and Cressida.*[17] Developing the implications of Spurgeon's observations almost half a century later, Johannes Fabricius suggests that the pathological imagery of these plays might be "explained as a predictable reaction to the poet's midlife crisis" but adds that the plays' pervasive disgust at sex and atmosphere of "rottenness, disease, death and corruption" point strongly to Shakespeare's having contracted syphilis.[18] By contrast, a quite different tradition of criticism has tended to view the plays' images of disease as metaphors for social and symbolic breakdown, whether universally or in turn-of-the-century Tudor England. This approach's most influential avatar is René Girard, who in a series of essays on mimetic desire and *Troilus and Cressida* offers variations on his more general claim that throughout literature, "plague is universally presented as a process of undifferentiation, a destruction of specificities."[19] Girard's ideas have been developed and lent greater historical context by Eric S. Mallin, whose brilliant topical readings of *Troilus and Cressida*'s and *Hamlet*'s pathological imagery are grounded in a specifically sixteenth-century assumption that "disease offers a structural template that produces unstructuring."[20]

As illuminating as these two very divergent strains of interpretation might be, they nonetheless share a substantial limitation: each tends to condense the plays' many diseases into Disease, either by interpreting illness as a generic metaphor with one symbolic valence (be it autobiographical or sociopolitical) or by implicitly regarding one disease—usually syphilis or plague—as the model for all others. But as careful scrutiny of *Troilus and Cressida*'s pathological imagery in particular makes clear, the play contains a multiplicity not only of illnesses but also of implied forms and etiologies of disease in general. The differences between these pathological models, I shall argue, are highly significant, and can be grouped into two broad paradigmatic camps.

There are numerous references in *Troilus and Cressida* to illnesses that demonstrate Shakespeare's familiarity with humoral discourse.[21] The play's Greek characters repeatedly suffer from complexional dysfunctions, to the point where it can seem as if the play was at least initially conceived of as a comedy of humors. Alexander describes Ajax as "a man into whom nature hath so crowded humors . . . He is melancholy without cause, and merry against the hair" (1.2.21–22, 26–27), a diagnosis that Ajax himself applies to Achilles (2.3.87); when Agamemnon asks his men "What grief hath set these jaundies on your cheeks?" (1.3.2), he alludes to a humoral condition commonly believed to be caused by obstruction of the bile; and "biles" is itself referred to at 2.1.2.

While these afflictions are all construed as endogenous states arising from internal imbalance, *Troilus and Cressida* also refers to certain illnesses that seem to offer a more modern conception of disease as a determinate thing contracted from an external source. This is particularly the case with the play's multiple references to syphilis, which—as we have seen in earlier chapters—more than any other disease tested the humoral assumption that illness was an internally derived state. Although Shakespeare displays no explicit knowledge of Fracastoro's theories of disease and only a passing familiarity with those of Paracelsus,[22] the emergent perception of syphilis as a determinate foreign body is powerfully present in *Troilus and Cressida*: Thersites anachronistically refers to it as the Neapolitan bone-ache (2.3.18–19), and Pandarus's concluding reference to the Winchester goose (5.10.54), a colloquial name for the pustules of syphilitic infection, notably figures the disease not only as an organism but also as migratory—an illness one might "bequeath," to use his term (5.10.56).[23]

There are other diseases mentioned in *Troilus and Cressida*, however, whose etiology is less easy to pigeonhole. The affliction of serpego (also rendered by Shakespeare's editors as "serpigo," "sapego," and "suppeago"), a creeping skin condition referred to by Duke Vincentio in *Measure for Measure* as well as by Thersites in *Troilus and Cressida*, provides a notable case in point. The Scottish physician Andrew Boorde believed serpego to have a humoral origin, arguing that it stems from "hote and corrupt blode myxt with coler"; the French physican Jean de Vignon associated it with an excess of phlegm.[24] Like other cutaneous afflictions, however, the disease had come increasingly to be associated with syphilis. In his *Breuiary of Helthe,* Boorde explains that "serpego" is the Latin term for the English "tetter," another common term for the syphilitic pustule.[25] The disease's association with pox led to its also being linked with specific foreign bodies. In Thomas Heywood's *Royall King and Loyall Subject,* for example, a virtuous captain scolds a prostitute whose customers include men who have "the French Fly, with the *Sarpego* dry'd."[26] Indeed, serpego's etymology— like its modern counterpart, herpes, it derives from the Latin *serpere* and the Greek *herpein,* to creep—helped model the disease less as an endogenous state of imbalance than as an affliction that migrates, both *in* the body and *from* body to body. Perhaps Shakespeare unconsciously picks up on serpego's etymology when he has Hector speak about the contagious fever of emulousness that afflicts the Greek army: "Their great general slept, / Whilst emulation in the army *crept*" (2.2.212–13; emphasis added). Serpego thus models a confusion that is pervasive in *Troilus and Cressida*. Diseases and their causes are contradictorily (dare one say problematically?) figured in Shakespeare's problem play; its illnesses are indeterminately humoral and ontological, endogenous and invasive.

The significant if incomplete displacement of humoral pathology in the sixteenth and seventeenth centuries by models of disease entailing the agency of foreign bodies cannot be disentangled from larger social developments and reorganizations of knowledge.[27] In the case of *Troilus and Cressida*, its pathological imagery evinces an uncertainty specific to the mercantilist moment of early seventeenth-century England. The contest between residual humoral and emergent invasive models of illness visible in Shakespeare's serpego, I shall argue, bespeaks a larger tension between differing paradigms of not just disease but also value—a tension strained to the breaking point by the growth of global trade and foreign currency exchange. The questions with which both *Troilus and Cressida* and mercantilist writing grapple are these: are the origins of disease and value endogenous or are they external? And if "the enterprise is sick," to borrow Ulysses's suggestive coinage (1.3.103), what exactly is the nature of economic sickness, and where does it originate? These questions notably surface also in Malynes's *Canker of England's Commonwealth.*

The Problem of Malynes's Banker Canker

In 1600, Gerard Malynes was appointed to the royal commission for establishing the true par of exchange—a monetary policy informed by the Aristotelian conviction that money's value must be grounded solely in its internal substance, that is, gold and silver. The fixing of value was a cause that exercised Malynes's imagination for the majority of his careers as merchant, statesman, and writer. In the 1590s, when he was still a private and by most accounts unsuccessful venturer, he served as one of the commissioners of trade in the Low Countries "for settling the value of monies."[28] Malynes had more opportunity to pursue this agenda after 1609, when he rose to the office of Royal Master of the English Mint. All his subsequent writings tirelessly reiterate the need for "settling the value of monies" on an international basis. His fervent advocacy of the true par of exchange might reek of the crackpot's belief in the all-purpose panacea. Yet it was also a response to genuine dilemmas and problems posed by the development of transnational networks of finance—a development that had transformed the very notion of the market.

Joyce Oldham Appleby's formerly influential assessment of the early modern market as an impalpable, alienating entity has recently been called into question by some social historians.[29] Craig Muldrew has painted a very different picture of a world in which mercantile activity was based on face-to-face relations, and credit entailed less impersonal finance than "social communication and circulating judgment about the value of other members of communities."[30] Building on Muldrew's work, Ceri Sullivan has argued that early modern English merchants often saw the market as an occasion not for alienation but for opportunity and affirmation.[31] Inasmuch as Muldrew and Sullivan focus on face-to-face relations of credit, however, they cannot help but construe the market as a highly personal, if not personable, agora. By contrast, Malynes's quixotic campaigns in support of true par tell another story. Sidestepping relations of credit, Malynes instead paints a portrait of an altogether more impersonal market, one in which money has become a transnational commodity of variable value with indirect yet draconian consequences for English citizens. Here, perhaps, we can see a version of Appleby's alienating, impalpable market—a market that, for Malynes, was less a personal than a systemic, global phenomenon.

This more impersonal market became visible largely as a result of economic problems that afflicted English and Continental commerce during the sixteenth century. As we saw in Chapter 2, Thomas Smith's 1581 *Discourse* offered a critique of England's economic woes in the decades after the Reformation, when prices soared to unprecedented levels. In Smith's analysis, the influx of gold and silver from the American mines was responsible for the general epidemic of inflation throughout Europe. But the "first cause" of England's economic woes, he argued, were the many debasements and revaluations of its coinage. Smith blamed coin-clippers and counterfeiters for the sorry state of the nation's currency, but he also boldly fingered the revaluations of coin authorized by its princes. Between 1542 and 1551, Henry VIII had endeavored to increase his revenue by systematically debasing the minted coinage—that is, by reducing coins' specie content and/or giving them a higher nominal value.[32] For Smith, such revaluation not only failed to recognize the intrinsic value of money; it also ignored how the nominal values of debased English coin could not be respected by foreign merchants:

It is not in the power of the prince to make the ounce of silver worth twain, nor yet of gold, nor of other metal. And I had as lief have a halfpenny called a halfpenny as have a halfpenny that should be called a penny. Well a man may change the name of things, but the value he cannot in any wise to endure for any space, except we were in such a country as Utopia was imagined to be that had no traffic with any other outward country.[33]

In the years after Smith's analysis, however, other developments helped not only to render the value of coin more fugitive but also to locate its origins outside the sphere of sovereign power. Sir Thomas Gresham's building of the Royal Exchange in 1566 was a landmark development, signaling the growing authority—albeit with nominal royal patronage—of private citizens in the new transnational money markets.[34] Princes may still have been responsible for the minting of coins, but merchants and financiers were increasingly determining the values of nations' currencies in the course of foreign exchange. In the late sixteenth and early seventeenth centuries, the quantity and the influence of currency brokers expanded throughout Europe. Following the model of the Italian city-states, cities in the Low Countries and Germany developed public banking systems that, taking advantage of fluctuating exchange rates, transformed foreign currency dealership into a lucrative vocation.[35]

It was in the midst of these turbulent reconfigurations of Europe's cash economy and the commoditization of money that Malynes wrote his *Canker of England's Commonwealth*. The treatise was published in 1601, the same year as *Saint George for England Allegorically Described*; it touches on many of the same issues, but does so in a very different fashion. Earlier analyses of England's economic ills took recognizably literary forms—Starkey and Smith wrote their treatises as dramatic dialogues, and Malynes's own *Saint George for England* is an allegorical fable on the model of Spenser's. By contrast, *The Canker of England's Commonwealth* represents a new phenomenon: the specialist economic text, borrowing from innovative economic writers on the Continent like Jean Bodin to explain in more precise, mathematical detail the exigencies of money and valuation. *The Canker of England's Commonwealth* was also published in the same year that many believe Shakespeare to have begun writing *Troilus and Cressida*. Regardless of whether Shakespeare had read it, Malynes's treatise conjoins analysis of international finance with images of disease in ways that are highly pertinent to a reading of Shakespeare's play.

Malynes endeavors to explain the causes of England's depletion of wealth, which he attributes partly to the unchecked outflow of specie from the country. English merchants, he argues, prefer to ship coin to their overseas clients instead of purchasing bills of foreign exchange; they do so because English currency is chronically undervalued, which means the pound sterling's international exchange rates are far poorer than the value of its component metals. Because merchants save more by sending their money directly to overseas factors instead of buying foreign currency at present exchange rates, England's supply of treasure cannot help but hemorrhage—and this, he argues, is the "unknowne disease of the politicke body."[36] To represent this "unknown disease," Malynes employs an altogether more ambiguous pathological metaphor than those favored by earlier sixteenth-century economic writers. Whereas early Tudor writers articulated an unequivocally humoral understanding of illness, implying that economic ailments derive entirely from internal imbalances in the body politic such as unequal distribution of resources or insufficient levels of production, Malynes resorts to a disease whose form and etiology in much sixteenth-century writing entail both humoral disarray *and* the agency of pathogenic foreign bodies: "canker." To this extent, he compounds the pathological confusions of "gangrene" and "infection" in his previous pamphlet, *Saint George for England Allegorically Described.*

Such confusion is not immediately obvious from Malynes's choice of disease. Since antiquity, "canker" or cancer had been believed to have an exclusively humoral and hence internal origin: Hippocrates and Galen both attributed it to an excess of *atra bilis,* or melancholy, a diagnosis that survived well into the sixteenth century.[37] Nevertheless, certain subtle semantic shifts in the meanings of canker had helped lend it new metaphorical possibilities. Early modern medical authorities frequently reminded their readers that the term derived from the tumor's resemblance to a crab, both in its physical appearance and in its migratory and gustatory habits; one English physician remarked that "it is called Canker because it goeth forth like a Crab."[38] Such images of a creeping, devouring crustacean invader doubtless contributed to the emergence in the fifteenth century of the term "canker worm," or simply "canker," to designate a parasitic caterpillar that destroys plants by eating their buds and leaves. Through a process of reverse influence, canker the parasite arguably began to affect popular perceptions of canker the disease. Instead of designating an exclusively endogenous, humoral disorder, the now multivalent term more readily suggested a hostile, even foreign organism that invades and consumes the body. And indeed, Malynes uses "canker" in both pathological and animal senses in *Saint George for England Allegorically Described*. He bemoans the "biles, botches, cankers and sores" of the commonweal and, as I have already noted, he also praises Licurgus for banishing the "canker worm" of usury from Sparta.[39]

An equally if not more decisive factor in the transformation of the popular etiology of canker was its association during the sixteenth century with the symptoms of syphilis. The pustules of syphilitic infection were known by a variety of names, including "bosses," "tetters," and the "Winchester goose"; they were also commonly called "chancres," French for canker. The French and English terms were, in fact, readily interchangeable. In his *Dictionarie of the French and English Tongues* (1611), Randle Cotgrave defines the "Bosse chancreuse" as "*A cankered byle; pockie sore, Winchester goose*";[40] as early as 1543, Bartholomew Traheron listed "lothsome cankers" as one of the prime symptoms of "that moste fylthy, pestiferous, & abominable dysease the Frenche or spanyshe pockes";[41] and Robert Wilson recognizably conflates the two diseases in *The Three Lords and Three Ladies of London*, when Simplicity wishes that Pleasure be consumed by "the French canker."[42] If the names for syphilis helped challenge the assumptions of humoral pathology by explicitly locating its origins in foreign agents, canker also acquired something of the disease's exogenous associations. This perception was to gain medical legitimacy in the early seventeenth century, when the German pathologist Daniel Sennert theorized that cancer was a communicable condition, and the Flemish Paracelsan J. B. Van Helmont suggested that the disease derived from an "external contagion"—an attitude that was in no small way responsible for European hospitals refusing admission to cancer patients well into the nineteenth century.[43]

Like that other "eating" skin condition, serpego, canker thus possessed twin connotations of complexional imbalance and external invasion. I would argue that it was precisely this indeterminacy that attracted Malynes to the disease. In his treatise, the cause of the canker of England's commonwealth might seem at first glance compatible with humoral etiology. He insists that England's illness derives from unhealthy imbalances within the body politic's internal mix of elements: "The right course of exchange being abused . . . causeth an *ouerballancing* of forrain commodities with our home commodities" (sig. C1; emphasis added). But it soon becomes apparent that Malynes believes such imbalances to stem from the plottings of malevolent aliens, bankers in league with Dutch merchants whom he accuses of manipulating the rates of exchange to England's detriment: "these Bankers which commonly are in league with the financiers of the low countries . . . do vse, or rather abuse the exchange, & make of it a trade for monies" (sigs. D8v, E4). This attribution lends Malynes's treatise something of a tabloidesque, scaremongering tone. Everywhere on the Continent that he casts his worried gaze, he spies evil foreign bankers conniving to destroy England's economic health: "But when the exchaunge goeth high, our merchants are inclined to buy forraine commodities, or to barter their commodities for the same, which oportunities is not onely obserued by the Bankers, but also procured. To which end they follow by the meanes of their factors, our merchants at all places, euen as the Eagle followeth her pray" (sigs. D5v–D6). Malynes's conspiratorial narrative of rapacious Eagle bankers and their hapless English prey sheds further light on his choice of pathological terminology: canker's semantic freight, not to mention its suggestive but perhaps unintentional rhyme with "banker," facilitates Malynes's attribution of economic illness to predatory foreign bodies.[44]

Malynes's invectives against the foreign Banker Canker betray an anxiety prompted by a good deal more, however, than the alleged depletion of England's treasure. The sense of emergency that pervades *The Canker of England's Commonwealth* is demonstrably fueled less by the *physical* migrations of specie out of the nation than by the more ineffable migrations of money's *value*—a phenomenon endemic to the growing, turbulent cash economy of the sixteenth century, which had witnessed not only the debasement of England's currency but also unprecedented volatility in international exchange rates. As a prophylactic measure against such turbulence, Malynes reiterates Aristotle's conviction that money should be a *"Publica mensura"* (sig. B6), or common measure of value, and hence exempt from fluctuation:

money was deuised to bee coyned of the finest and purest mettals, to be the rule or square, whereby all other things should receiue estimation and price, and as a measure whereby the price of all things might be set. And to maintaine a certaine euenhood or equality in buying & selling, and the same to haue his standing valuation only by publicke authority: to the end that all things might equally passe by trade from one man to another. (sig. B4)

For Malynes, money's capacity to measure value derives from the supposedly fixed, intrinsic value of its component metals, a conviction that he expresses also in his later, more extensive theorization of mercantilist philosophy, the *Lex Mercatoria* (1622): "the last propertie of Money is, to haue an internall value in substance, whereupon the Exchanges of Money are grounded."[45]

As the above passage from *The Canker of England's Commonwealth* concedes, however, the putatively endogenous value of money needs to be fixed by a "publicke authority"—specifically, the prince—who therefore functions somewhat paradoxically as both the protector of money's "internall value of substance" and the external *fons et origo* of such value. With this schema, Malynes brokers a deft compromise between the residual medieval model of intrinsic value, whose most influential formulation can be traced back to Thomas Aquinas, and the powerfully emergent intuition of the arbitrary, nominative nature of value.[46] In a subtle yet significant deviation from the traditional medieval scholastic distinction between the preexisting *bonitas intrinseca,* or metallic value of the coin, and the *bonitas extrinseca,* or face value given it by the prince, Malynes models the will of the prince rather than money itself as the gold standard that stabilizes exchange: in effect, it is now the *bonitas extrinseca* imposed by the prince that produces and protects money's fixed intrinsic worth.[47] Malynes is thus able to acknowledge implicitly the inadequacy of endogenous value while repudiating the epistemological dislocations to which an unreservedly exogenous model of value might commit him.

But this compromise stumbles upon one major obstacle. As Malynes recognizes, money's value is anything but fixed, even with the allegedly stabilizing influence of the prince. He regards certain cases of money's revaluation as inevitable and even desirable: the practices of clipping coins or transforming their ratios of gold to silver necessitate adjustments of money's value that reflect its component metals' intrinsic values as determined by "publicke authority." Malynes reserves his outrage for another widespread practice of currency revaluation, one notably based not on changes in the physical constitution of coins but on what he calls "merchandizing exchange"—that is, the alteration, authorized by foreign bankers, of national currencies' exchange values. For Malynes, this practice not only represents an egregrious usurpation of royal prerogative ("the valuation or alteration of money, concerneth only the soueraignty and dignity of the Prince or gouernor of euery countrey, as a thing peculiar vnto them" [sig. B7v]); even more problematically, it transforms value into something *transparently* external and arbitrary bestowed by private foreign agents—a canker— rather than a *seemingly* essential or intrinsic quality legitimized by "publicke authority." The currency revaluations entailed by "merchandizing exchange," he maintains, can lead only to crises of multiple or indeterminate value:

the merchandizing exchange which thus ouer-ruleth the course of commodities & mony, is intollerable: for we shall find in effect, that one summe of mony, of one sort and kinde of coine, hath two prices, & two valuations, at one time, exchanged for one distance of time; differing only by the diuersities of place & countrie: whereby priuate men alter as it were the valuation of coines. (sig. E4v)

Failing to respect ideals of intrinsic value, the stabilizing authority of princes, or the sovereignty of nations, therefore, bankers in effect make laws out of their own arbitrary wills or appetites.[48] This derogatory yoking of commerce and un-bridled private will aligns Malynes's economic "canker" at least in part with syphilis; as we have seen in Chapter 2, the disease's association with prostitution entailed a similar freighting of appetite and trade.

In Malynes's explanations of the origin of money's value, we can glimpse the outlines of a telling pair of related confusions, both of which testify to the increasingly transnational nature of early modern trade and disease. Malynes insists on money's "internall value in substance," yet complains that he (or the sovereign) is helpless to stop its revaluation by foreign agents; similarly, his cam-paign to secure the health of England's economy by balancing the mix of do-mestic and imported commodities as well as regulating exchange rates, both of which have pronounced affinities with humoralism, is at odds with the invasive paradigm of infection implied by the Continental Banker Canker. A compara-ble pair of confusions, I shall argue, afflicts *Troilus and Cressida*.

The Problem of Value

When Viola gives Feste a coin in *Twelfth Night,* he begs another: "I would play Lord Pandarus of Phrygia, sir, to bring a Cressida to this Troilus" (3.1.51–52). The comparison of Cressida and Troilus to money provides a suggestive point of connection with which to begin unraveling the more substantive links between Malynes's and Shakespeare's texts. Feste's remark makes explicit what is in *Troilus and Cressida* a perhaps surprising subtext: Shakespeare's play about the long-gone Heroic Age is obsessed with decidedly contemporary, mercantile is-sues of currency, trade, and valuation.[49] More specifically, both its principal fe-male characters are coded as public yardsticks of value who, like Malynes's *publica mensura,* money, are nevertheless themselves subject to revaluation in the course of foreign exchange. The play's concern with value has attracted con-siderable attention from scholars, who have often viewed Shakespeare as offer-ing a proleptic Hobbesian vision of market economy.[50] *Troilus and Cressida*'s ruminations on value, however, couched in the contradictory terms of a patho-logical discourse torn between exogenous and endogenous etiologies of disease, resonate much more closely with the language, concerns, and confusions of Ma-lynes's *Canker of England's Commonwealth.*

Malynes's anxiety about the unregulated private origins of value is echoed throughout the play. This may be the war of Heroes—but too many Heroes means too many sources of value, as becomes apparent in the epidemic of emu-lousness that has "crept" like serpego through the warriors of the Greek camp. The unlicensed production of value is the subject of the Trojans' forensic debate concerning Helen's worth. To Troilus's question, "What's aught but as 'tis valued?" (2.2.52), Hector replies:

But value dwells not in particular will,
It holds his estimate and dignity
As well wherein 'tis precious of itself
As in the prizer. 'Tis mad idolatry
To make the service greater than the god,
And the will dotes that is attributive
To what infectiously itself affects,
Without some image of th'affected merit. (2.2.53–60)

In insisting that any object's value ought to be "precious of itself" rather than arbitrarily derived from "particular will," Hector echoes Malynes's complaint that the overvaluation of currencies in foreign exchange produces "but an imaginatiue wealth, consisting in the denomination and not in substance" (sig. F6v).

Hector's characterization of "attributive" value ("inclineable" in the Folio edition) notably resorts to a pathological vocabulary: the will's fanciful imposition of value upon an object, he insists, is performed "infectiously." Early modern English usages of the adverb and its cognates participated within a decidedly slippery array of meanings that bespeaks the broader cultural confusion about the nature and origins of disease. As I showed in the last chapter, "infect" had retained the connotations of its Latin etymological root, *inficere,* to dye, color, stain, or pollute; in Galenic discourse and Shakespeare's plays alike, the term is often used to refer to the pollution of the body by ill or superfluous humors. A complexional understanding of infection is apparent in *Timon of Athens,* for example, when Apemantus characterizes Timon as suffering from "a nature but infected; / A poor unmanly melancholy" (4.3.202–3). A related but slightly different sense of infection, which can be traced back to Hippocrates' miasmic theory of pathogenic pollution, crops up frequently in early modern English writing about the plague, a disease often believed to be contracted by inhaling foul vapors that disturb the body's humoral balance; Shakespeare uses "infection" in this miasmic sense when Leontes asks in *The Winter's Tale* that "The blessed gods / Purge all infection from our air" (5.1.168–69).[51] By virtue of its exogenous model of pathogenesis, miasmic theory was conceptually closer to the more recognizably modern sense of infection that gained currency within the discourses of syphilis during the sixteenth century. As I noted in Chapter 2, most physicians regarded syphilitic infection less as a humoral imbalance than as the infiltration of a determinate, invasive disease. We might recall, for example, the surgeon William Clowes's characterization of syphilitic infection, which figures the latter in terms of the migratory properties of canker: "the disease is taken by

externall meanes. . . . Any outward part being once infected, the disease immediately entreth into the blood, and so creepeth on like a canker from part to
part."[52]

Hence by 1601, "infectious" was by no means a clear or self-explanatory
term: it variously designated bodies that were humorally imbalanced, miasmically polluted, or invasively contaminated by determinate, pathogenic entities.
These multiple possibilities present the reader of *Troilus and Cressida* with an
intriguing problem, one that has been insufficiently addressed: how to decode
the "infectiousness" of valuation. Is the attributive will's infectiousness humoral
and endogenous—a spontaneous disease confined to the subject and caused,
like "jaundies," by *dyskrasia*? Or is it ontological and exogenous like the Winchester goose, transmitted over a distance from the will to its object? In this confused and confusing play, it is arguably both.

It is certainly difficult to resist an exclusively exopathic reading of Hector's
infectious valuation. Fierce though Hector's commitment to the ideal of endogenous value may be, *Troilus and Cressida* struggles to present that ideal as a
viable alternative to the rival, exogenous codes that he critiques. Just as Malynes
is powerless to protect the value of money from the foreign Banker Canker of
unregulated currency revaluation, so the supposedly intrinsic values of *Troilus
and Cressida*'s objects are similarly vulnerable to external recoding; as goods cir-
culate from owner to owner, they change, seemingly infected by the wills that
evaluate them. Take, for example, the sleeve Troilus gives Cressida as a love
token; in the space of less than a hundred lines it degenerates from a "pretty
pledge" (5.2.77) to a "greasy relic" (5.2.159), its value altered less by its passage
from Cressida to Diomedes than by the unstable nature of Troilus's intense investment in it, an investment that barely conceals a pathological capacity for
disgust.[53] Something similar seems to take place with Hector's valuation of the
armor of the Unknown Soldier: the sumptuous casement, which he claims to
prize (5.6.28), reveals a "putrefied core" (5.8.1)—as if Hector's will has itself infected the armor's previously battle-ready occupant. Appetite, then, seems to
have the power to debase its objects throughout *Troilus and Cressida*. In an
equation perhaps typical of an age for whom venereal disease had irrevocably
transformed attitudes toward desire and its physical consequences, to "affect" is
to "infect," as Hector's earlier remarks in the Trojan debate about Helen's worth
imply.

If the exopathic reading of Hector's "infectiously" derives considerable
support from contemporaneous developments in early modern epidemiology,
the radical transformations of pathology that characterize the period were arguably linked also to concurrent economic developments. As Malynes's *Canker
of England's Commonwealth* hints, the steadily growing inclination of lay people

during this time to view diseases as originating less in internal states of imbalance than in determinate foreign bodies was, if not directly caused, then certainly facilitated by the growth of a global mercantile economy in which commodities, currencies, and individuals alike had become unprecedentedly migratory, and the sources of their market value extrinsic. Syphilis's customary names, French disease, Neapolitan bone-ache, or Spanish pox, found counterparts in the names of the growing number of continental goods available to early modern English consumers—for example, "French cloth," "Italian books," "Spanish fruit"—that acquired a widespread pathological valence in political and didactic writing as the external causes of the body politic's economic and moral ills.[54] Moreover, the very practice of foreign exchange necessitated the external attribution of variable value to any commodity, including money itself, according to fluctuating demand or appetite. And such revaluation is precisely what befalls the play's two exchanged women, Helen (taken hostage by the Trojans as a countermeasure to the Greeks' kidnapping of Hesione) and Cressida (traded to the Greeks in exchange for Antenor), as they cross their national borders.

Helen is the male characters' yardstick of value, the *publica mensura* of their exploits in war and in love. Her value is nonetheless extrinsic: "Helen must needs be fair," complains Troilus, "When with your blood you daily paint her thus" (1.1.90–91). As Linda Charnes has noted, this remark foregrounds the play's retroactive remodeling of Helen's *bonitas extrinseca* as inherent worth.[55] Like the unstable value of English coin in foreign markets lamented by Malynes, moreover, Helen's "painted" value is shown to vary across the national borders over which she has been transported. She is the "theme of honor and renown" (2.2.199) to the Trojan men, while the Greek Diomedes damns "every scruple / Of her contaminated carrion weight" (4.1.71–72). The latter's extraordinarily suggestive phrase freights the economic and the pathological: weighing her by the "scruple," or one twenty-fourth of an ounce, one of the standard units of measurement for apothecaries and merchants, Diomedes proclaims her "contaminated," a synonym—particularly in the discourses of venereal disease—for infected.[56] In what is for Diomedes an intolerable and even syphilitic mingling of rival valuations, therefore, Helen is pathologically marked by two men, Menelaus and Paris, and by two nations.

Similarly, even as Diomedes insists that Cressida "to her own worth / . . . shall be priz'd" (4.4.133–34), her value emerges not from her "own" intrinsic qualities but from patriarchal markets of fluctuating value and demand, as she herself realizes: "Men prize the thing ungain'd more than it is" (1.2.289). Such "prizing" is neither singular nor stable, thanks to the rival foreign agents who determine her worth. By the fifth act, Cressida is simultaneously Troilus's Cressida and Diomedes's Cressida, possessed of two extrinsic values; hence the "bi-fold authority" at work in Troilus's famous "This is, and is not, Cressid" (5.2.144, 146), which provides a striking counterpart to Malynes's complaint that "one summe of mony, of one sort and kinde of coine, hath two prices, & two valuations, at one time, exchanged for one distance of time; differing only by the diuersities of place & countrie: whereby priuate men alter as it were the valuation of coines" (sig. E4v).[57] Hence also what has been for many readers Cressida's distressing lack of agency as her location, loyalty, and worth are altered by "priuate men." Although Douglas Bruster has argued that Cressida attempts to control her commodity function and maximize her value as she is trafficked from Troy to Greece, she still cannot avoid becoming whoever her male evaluators determine her to be.[58] Ulysses's disgusted assessment of her while she is circulated among the men of the Greek camp—"There's language in her eye, her cheek, her lip / Nay, her foot speaks; her wanton spirits look out / At every joint and motive of her body" (4.5.55–57)—henceforth fixes her literal face value as "sluttish" (4.5.62) in her own eyes ("O false wench!" [5.2.71]) as much as those of the play's male characters, despite the discrepancy between Ulysses' evaluation and the Cressida of earlier scenes. What Ulysses attributes to Cressida's intrinsic character, or at least to her body, can be read critically as an act of ventriloquism; the "language" that "her eye, her cheek, her lip . . . , her foot" allegedly speak is, after all, his own. But this ventriloquism is the prerogative, perhaps even the constitutive principle, of a patriarchal economy in which the supposed *bonitas intrinseca* of women is the product of their male evaluators' infectious wills.[59]

Thus far, *Troilus and Cressida* might appear to articulate an unreservedly modern conception of value as exogenous and mutable. Ulysses's extended speech to Achilles about Time (3.3.145–90), for example, is not just a meditation on mutability but a proto-Marxian reflection on the market fluctuations of honor and virtuous deeds;[60] Cressida's exchange for Antenor, or Helen's for Hesione, corroborates Georg Simmel's insistence that economic value is an extrinsic, variable, but definite sum that results from the commensuration of two intensities of demand.[61] Inasmuch as *Troilus and Cressida* offers such striking parallels to modern conceptions of market value, it would appear to support the prolepticism that has characterized analysis of the play's economic preoccupations. W. R. Elton and Gayle Greene, for example, both see Shakespeare's play as anticipating Hobbes's assertion that "*value* . . . is not absolute; but a thing dependent on the need and judgment of another."[62] Hugh Grady goes farther, finding in *Troilus and Cressida* not only a "masculine prefiguration of Hobbes's state of nature" but also "a prescient exposition of the corrosive powers of instrumental reason and the related autonomous logic of Foucauldian power."[63]

Yet even as the play disqualifies the possibility of fixed and intrinsic worth, it is important not to forget that it also literally pathologizes attributive value. And in this respect, *Troilus and Cressida* offers a much more complicated, less prescient vision of modernity and the market than critics have on occasion intimated. The play's pathologization of externally derived value, I have suggested, is confusing and contradictory, resisting singular interpretation. At the same time as Hector's "infectiously" invites an exopathic reading, its meanings can be seen to derive at least in part from the discursive field of humoral pathology. This much is made clear by one of *Troilus and Cressida*'s other references to infection. Speaking of the metaphorical illnesses that have afflicted the Greek camp and rendered them incapable of winning the war against Troy, Agamemnon observes that

> checks and disasters
> Grow in the veins of actions highest rear'd,
> As knots, by the conflux of meeting sap,
> Infects the sound pine and diverts his grain
> Tortive and errant from his course of growth. (1.3.5–9)

Here the infection to which Agamemnon alludes is manifestly derived from an internal disorder, a pathological "conflux" of elements located in the "veins."

The humoral counterdiscourse of infection glimpsed in Agamemnon's speech surfaces elsewhere in the play's treatment of valuation. Thersites's mocking assessments of his superiors, for example, are revealingly imaged in humoral as well as monetary terms: Nestor refers to him as a "slave whose gall coins slanders like a mint" (1.3.193). Such humoral coding of the "coining" of value might also help explain a significant departure Shakespeare makes from his sources. Despite the seeming communicability of the infectious will elsewhere in the play, and despite her precarious status as the object of rival male evaluations, Cressida does not contract any overt infection as does her leprous counterpart in Robert Henryson's *Testament of Cresseid*, with her "bylis black ouirspred in hir visage."[64] Instead, the play's burden of disease is shouldered by one of the men: Pandarus. From where, or whom, did he contract the aching bones and "whoreson tisick" (5.3.101) of which he complains at the play's end? According to Frank Kermode, from himself. Alone among critics in arguing that the play's pervasive pathological imagery is symptomatic of the attributive will, Kermode offers a decisive diagnosis of Pandarus's ailments: "the war is being fought for Opinion, the delusive power which makes Helen seem what she is not—a valuable person, worth many men's lives. This disastrous error is produced by the dominance of blood over reason, imaged again and again as a disease of which Pandarus, at the end of the play, is a walking emblem."[65] Kermode thus sees the twin problems of externally imposed value and Pandarus's syphilitic ills through what amounts to a humoral prism; anyone suffering from unbalanced blood is captive to the infectious delusions of their own will. In this respect, Kermode echoes those few obstinate Galenists of the sixteenth century who persisted in attributing syphilis to humoral infection rather than to external agents; the German physician Ulrich von Hutten, we recall, remained convinced that "this infirmite cometh of corrupt, burnt, & enfect blode."[66]

To illustrate his point, Kermode cites Ulysses's diagnosis of Achilles's self-destruction, which is surprisingly redolent of von Hutten's language:

> Imagin'd worth
> Holds in his blood such swoll'n and hot discourse
> That 'twixt his mental and his active parts
> Kingdom'd Achilles in commotion rages,
> And batters down himself. What should I say?
> He is so plaguy proud that the death tokens of it
> Cry "no recovery." (2.3.172–78)

Ulysses presents infectious valuation as a complexional disease of the blood, and hence more lethal to the evaluator than to the object of value (unless, as in this case, the evaluator and the object are one and the same). He thus concurs with Nestor's observation that those Greek princes who aspire to speak with an "imperial voice"—that is, not only inflate their own worth, but also set themselves up as authoritative evaluators—are "infect" (1.3.187). In this reading, to "affect" is less to infect than to *become* infected. If Pandarus is for Kermode "a walking emblem" of the play's pathologies, it is because his will has succumbed to the disease of both coining and inflating market value, an affliction on display in his flagrantly flawed assessment of the Trojan heroes' relative worths in act 1, scene 2. Thus, when Pandarus "mark[s] Troilus above the rest" (1.2.183–84), it is arguable that he also infectiously "marks" himself—another term that potentially conjoins the economic ("mark" as a unit of measurement or currency) and the pathological ("mark" as a scab or pustule).

As this interpretation of Pandarus implies, the humoral reading of infectious valuation seems to leave open the possibility that an object can possess a *bonitas intrinseca* misapprehended or disacknowledged by the sick evaluator. Ulysses's speech about Achilles would certainly seem to corroborate Kermode's conviction that the "plaguy" Myrmidon, his body in a state of humoral disarray analogous to the internecine strife of civil war, has a deluded sense of self-worth fatally at odds with his true intrinsic value. Yet this is to make the essentialist assumption that Achilles—or any other object of deluded desire—*has* an intrinsic value, a position that the play repeatedly problematizes, not least in Ulysses's own insistence to Achilles that no man can "make boast to have that which he hath, / Nor feels what he owes, but by reflection" (3.3.98–99).[67] Whatever "true" value Achilles fails correctly to intuit remains suspiciously extrinsic and mutable, therefore, determined by "reflection" in another. Inasmuch as the consequences of will or appetite are repeatedly shown to be pathologically destructive to the desiring subject, Kermode is right to detect a residue of humoral discourse in the play's presentation of valuation; but his singularly endogenous diagnosis as much as any singularly exogenous reading of the infectious will speaks to only one side of *Troilus and Cressida*'s pathological transactions of desire. The viability of *both* humoral *and* invasive readings of the play's infectious valuations makes clear how *Troilus and Cressida*'s cankered wills infect inwardly as much as outwardly.

The Problem of Sovereign Will

Anxiously stranded between the failure of endogenous value and the double-edged infectiousness of imposed or attributed value, between a defunct (if ever extant) feudal order in which all things have a fixed *bonitas intrinseca* and the inescapably protean world of market capitalism in which price is calibrated with fluctuations of appetite and the dynamics of "merchandizing exchange," *Troilus and Cressida* concocts a compromise comparable to Gerard Malynes's: a theory of value that integrates the two opposed paradigms within a third, by means of which feudal stability can seemingly be reconstituted within the constraints imposed by the new mercantilist dispensation. The play thus gestures toward an alternative model of value that is neither quite intrinsic to the object nor quite derived from the external imposition of the wills of multiple, potentially competing subjects. Instead, value is assessed and fixed by a single, sovereign will that can be equated with the "publicke authority" of the prince in Malynes's schema. As is the case with its double coding of "infectious" valuation, however, *Troilus and Cressida*'s presentation of the sovereign will is mediated by a conflicted pathological vocabulary.

    The notion of the sovereign will may be glimpsed in Ulysses' critique of Ajax's and Achilles' idolatrous investment in the *machina* above the *deus* of war. "The ram that batters down the wall," complains Ulysses, "For the great swinge and rudeness of his poise, / They place before his hand that made the engine" (1.3.206–8). To Ulysses, the ram has no value in and of itself; rather, it derives its worth contagiously—not from the infectious wills of its evaluators, however, but from the "hand" of its creator. To the extent that Ulysses identifies the source of an object's worth in an external agent who "made" it, he seems to anticipate

Locke's, Smith's, and Marx's labor theories of value. But his model is different in one crucial respect: value is for Ulysses, as for Malynes, a product not of physical laborers but of an ineffable, sovereign designer.[68] This alternative model is more fully elaborated within Ulysses's Tillyardian set piece about degree. The latter might seem to suggest that everything has a fixed, intrinsic value within a cosmic hierarchy. But upon closer inspection, Ulysses's cosmos displays a pathological (and recognizably humoral) predisposition to disorder, one that is corrected only by the intervention of the sun-king:

And therefore is the glorious planet Sol
In noble eminence enthron'd and spher'd
Amidst the other; whose med'cinable eye
Corrects the ill aspects of planets evil,
And posts like the commandment of a king,
Sans check, to good and bad. (1.3.89–94)

The sun-king plays a contradictory role within this world picture: correcting the "ill aspects"—or sick face values—of wandering planets, he is both the protector of intrinsic order and its external origin. Ulysses's choice of pathological language to describe the curative effect of sovereign power, "med'cinable," works to model the sun-king's will as the polar opposite of Hector's infectious will. But here we might also recall Paracelsus's conviction that "every poison is good for some use."[69] There is little in fact to separate the sun-king's "med'cinable" will from the private agent's infectious one, other than its being the sun-king's. Like the infectious will of the private evaluator, the sun-king's "med'cinable" power entails, contrary to Hector's or Aquinas's conceptions of the origins of *bonitas intrinseca,* a value that "dwells . . . in particular will." Rather than being the straightforward conservative articulation of the Elizabethan World Picture that most readers have believed it to be—no matter whether they regard Ulysses as hierarchal degree's passionate advocate or as its Machiavellian manipulator[70]—the Ithacan prince's view of the cosmos is in fact very close to the mercantilist compromise of Malynes's *Canker of England*'s *Commonwealth,* according to which the "publicke authority" of the sovereign is likewise the sole, not to mention paradoxical, external source of intrinsic value in a universe composed of migratory, mutable elements.[71] Like Malynes's compromise between exogenous and endogenous theories of value, moreover, Ulysses's conception of the sovereign will has an explicitly transnational mercantile agenda: without it, he insists, there would be no "peaceful commerce from dividable shores" (1.3.105).

Also like Malynes's compromise, however, Ulysses's vision of "med'cinable" valuation proves unrealizable. Nowhere in the play does any putative sovereign will succeed in either stabilizing the worth of the elements under its jurisdiction or warding off the outbreaks of unlicensed, infectious attribution that render value fugitive within and across its national boundaries. Neither of the two camps' nominal sun-kings, Agamemnon nor Priam, is capable of stamping even any temporary order on the "ill aspects" of his polity; each is largely displaced by rival "imperial voices"—Agamemnon by Ulysses and Achilles, Priam by Hector and Troilus. The two leaders' surrogates fare no better, Troilus in particular providing a case study of the failed would-be sovereign will. In a revealing speech, he resorts to a decidedly Malynesian image of imperial creation, the production of coin's face value, to characterize his truthfulness. "Whilst some with cunning gild their copper crowns," he somewhat boastfully tells Cressida, "With truth and plainness I do wear mine bare" (4.4.105–6). Troilus vouches here for the enduring value of his currency, which here—at least metaphorically—is, and is not, Cressida. Troilus's very language, however, betrays the delusion of his will. His unwavering "truth" ironically damages rather than stabilizes his coins: in wearing them "bare" (ungilded) he "wears" them bare (depreciates their value). Every bit as much as Achilles, then, Troilus's "imperial voice" is terminally "infect."

The depreciating effects of the would-be sovereign will are brought to light persistently in *Troilus and Cressida,* and in a fashion that ultimately implicates not only the play's "orgillous" princes (Pr. 2) but also poets and playwrights as aspiring creators of enduring national literary value. The Trojan story and its characters provided writers across Europe with the materials for very different myths of nation and empire. Vergil mythologized the Trojan Aeneas as the father of Roman imperialism; Geoffrey of Monmouth propagated the apocryphal legend of the Trojan Brutus as the founding British patriarch; similarly, writers from France, Denmark, Ireland, and Saxony all traced their nation's origins back to characters in the *Iliad.* In a particularly insightful study, Heather James has characterized the Trojan myth as the coin of national identity formation, subject to competing "stampings" as it circulated through the literary marketplaces of classical, medieval, and early modern Europe.[72] What distinguishes Shakespeare's treatment of the myth in *Troilus and Cressida,* James argues, is how it makes explicit this history of rival valuation. Rather than simply performing another singular, nationalist stamping of the Trojan coin, Shakespeare deliberately highlights the multiple and mutually contradictory currencies he encountered in his source materials: "the play zealously exploits its various textual and generic resources with the goal of self-deformation."[73] As a consequence, *Troilus and Cressida*'s genre and characters alike are garish alloys minted from a treasury of ill-matched metals—among them, Homer's epic saga; Ovid's satiric debunking; Chaucer's romantic comedy; and Henryson's moral redaction.

The characterological disruptions wrought by Shakespeare's multinational literary sources have a pathological dimension. Consider Alexander's striking description of Ajax:

They say he is a very man *per se* . . . This man, lady, hath robbed many beasts of their particular additions. He is as valiant as the lion, churlish as the bear, slow as the elephant: a man into whom nature hath so crowded humors that his valour is crushed into folly, his folly sauced with discretion. There is no man hath a virtue that he hath not a glimpse of, nor any man an attaint but he carries some stain of it. He is melancholy without cause and merry against the hair; he hath the joints of everything, but everything so out of joint that he is a gouty Briareus, many hands and no use, or purblind Argus, all eyes and no sight. (1.2.15, 19–30)

This description is and is not humorous, at least in the early modern sense of the term. Alexander appears to describe Ajax's internal mix of elements, those "crowded humors" within which are blended complexional opposites such as "melancholy" and "merry" sanguinity. But upon closer inspection, the illusion of humoral interiority reconfigures itself as a bricolage of mutually contradictory versions of Ajax derived from the pens of multiple authors: Alexander's Ajax is an amalgam of the "valiant" Telamonian Ajax of Homer, the "churlish" aggressor of Vergil, and the "slow" dunderhead of Ovid.[74] In a fashion that both parallels the undermining of the play's Trojan and Greek "imperial voices" and implicitly rereads European literary history from the perspective of his own mercantilist moment, therefore, Shakespeare transmutes the sovereign wills of his predecessors into rival, infectious sources of value. Any assumption that the play's women alone are the protean, recodable coin of the realm thus becomes highly questionable. If *Troilus and Cressida*'s female characters are multiply marked by their Trojan and Greek evaluators within the play, so are its male characters multiply valued by their transnational authors within the Iliadic literary tradition. Here we might recall that for Feste, Troilus as much as Cressida is coin.[75]

Hence just as there is no one stabilizing sovereign will among *Troilus and Cressida*'s characters, neither does the play uphold any single authority among the rival purveyors of the Trojan legend. Whatever originary, fixing power Homer might command elsewhere within the Troy canon is dissolved in *Troilus and Cressida* by the play's many explicit transnational markings and contaminations of the *Iliad*. In this respect, Shakespeare's treatment differs greatly from that of George Chapman, who, insisting on the primacy of a sovereign, unpolluted Homer, sternly warned the readers of his translation of the *Iliad* against infecting its eminent author "with foul hands" or "other poet's slights" (which prompted his memorable and perhaps unique command that all readers should

"Wash here" before reading).[76] By contrast, Shakespeare's Homeric coin is already irrevocably infected by later "foul hands" and "poet's slights," as the medieval provenance of the Troilus and Cressida story makes clear. The transnational contaminations of Homer are pungently highlighted by the play's anachronistic references to those diseases whose names, postdating the *Iliad,* trace the historical and geographical trajectory of the legend from Greece through the Italian peninsula and finally to England: Thersites's "diseases of the south" (5.1.18) and "Neapolitan bone-ache" (2.3.18–19) yield at play's end to Pandarus's "goose of Winchester" (5.10.54).

Troilus and Cressida is not the only play in which Shakespeare subjected classical Greek and contemporary English settings to deliberately anachronistic and anatopistic mingling. But the final scene's Londonizing of Pandarus and his diseases is of a very different order from the celebratory Anglo-Athenian gallimaufrey of A Midsummer Night's Dream. The latter's mythical Greek aristocrats and English "rude mechanicals" spring from the tidily hierarchized worlds of court masque and antimasque. By contrast, *Troilus and Cressida*'s transnational contaminations reproduce the altogether more unstable, centrifugal universe of Gerard Malynes's Banker Canker, in which no object nor *publica mensura* of value can be secured against infection by private foreign bodies. Tellingly, Shakespeare's Troy meets a different end from Homer's, and by means of a very different agent of invasion. In *Troilus and Cressida*'s global marketplace of "traders in the flesh" (5.10.45)—an epithet that can be applied just as much to Shakespeare and his rival Iliadic storytellers as to Pandarus and his ilk—the majestic Trojan Horse has been superseded by the hissing Winchester goose.[77] For Shakespeare, therefore, Troy is irremediably contaminated by England.

The Problem of Troy Measurement

Interestingly, Troy was by 1601 not only an infected *publica mensura* of national literary value; it had also become an equally problematic gold standard for the measurement of weight. In The Canker of England's Commonwealth, Malynes asserts that Scottish coin is "inferiour vnto ours, and likewise their weight lesser then ours by foure peny weight full vpon the pound troy" (sig. F7v). Here Malynes invokes the troy system of measuring weight and bullion as a kind of meta-*mensura*, a yardstick with which to measure money's ability to measure value. But he does so to register the financial and epistemological crises generated by the *lack* of any standardized system of measurement. Sixteenth-century English minters and merchants tended to vacillate between three systems: the official mint or tower system, whose pound was equal to 5,400 troy grains; the avoirdupois system of general traders, more widely used on the Continent, which divided pounds into sixteen ounces and was equal to 7,000 troy grains; and troy weight itself, which posited a pound divided into twelve ounces and equal to 5,760 troy grains. Complicating matters further, the Scottish ounce was one sixty-fourth less than the English troy ounce. With twenty pennyweights to the ounce and twelve ounces to the pound in both systems, the difference between the two national pounds amounted to four English pennyweights, as Malynes acknowledges.[78] Such discrepancies in measurement of the pound inevitably rendered any conviction of money's fixed, intrinsic value—already substantially undermined by the sixteenth century's repeated currency devaluations and fluctuations of foreign exchange rates—all the more elusive.

The troy system probably derived its name from the French town of Troyes, not the city of classical legend. But that didn't stop Malynes's and Shakespeare's contemporaries from thinking otherwise, particularly when they sought to make sense of the confusions engendered by rival, nationally coded systems of measurement. In Middleton and Rowley's play *The Old Law* (c. 1618), a character observes that "Cressid was Troy weight, and Nell was haberdepoise [avoirdupois], she held more by four ounces than Cressida."[79] Here may be heard an uncanny echo of Malynes's remark about the disparities between English and Scottish coin that, finding personification in Shakespeare's Trojan and Greek women, serendipitously aligns the shared concerns of the two writers. Confronted in 1601 with the mounting dislocations wrought by foreign exchange as well as variable mercantile and literary systems of valuation, both Malynes and Shakespeare invoked—and found wanting—a gold standard named "Troy." With its allegedly prophylactic power comprehensively called into question, even multiply pathologized, the two writers' enterprises could not help but be sick.

Plague and Transmigration: Timothy Bright, Thomas Milles, Volpone

In the previous chapters, I have examined how Shakespeare and Malynes adapted emergent vocabularies of disease to articulate recognizably modern economic objects and problematics: the systemic nature of transnational commerce, the flow of money and people across national borders, and the origins of value. In this chapter, I wish to think about the reverse process: that is, how the growth of a global economy offered one playwright new languages and concepts with which to imagine an ancient and much feared disease not as a state of humoral imbalance, a miasmic irruption, or an act of God but as a discrete entity that migrates across the borders of bodies natural and politic. That playwright is Ben Jonson, and the disease is plague.

In his comedy *Volpone, or the Fox* (1606), Jonson paints a satirical portrait of universal greed in the lurid colors of physical as well as moral pathology. The confidence trickster Volpone, seemingly infirm and bedridden, accepts an unending stream of gifts from a swarm of legacy hunters who, believing him to be on the brink of death, hope to be named his heir and to inherit his fortune. As he cheerfully profits from those who seek to profit from him, Volpone proves himself a master of feigned illness. Perhaps his finest piece of sick theater occurs when he performs the symptoms of his imminent death for his delighted dupe, Voltore. Lying in bed, he wails: "I am sailing to my port, uh! uh! uh! uh!"[1] This remark splices two of *Volpone*'s most important thematic strands. The play's fascination with disease and its symptoms finds expression in Volpone's histrionic "uhs!" But the image of the ship sailing to port also resonates powerfully with another, seemingly unrelated preoccupation, one that befits *Volpone*'s Venetian location and its conventional dramatic connotations of merchant argosies: the exigencies and perils of foreign trade.

In what follows, I seek to unravel these two strands and their interconnections in order to show how Jonson articulates, through a variety of economic lenses, versions of what medical historians now call an ontological conception of disease—that is, disease conceived as an entity that migrates from body to body, and from nation to nation. To this end, I will argue, Jonson also makes effective satirical use of the Pythagorean doctrine of metempsychosis, or transmigration of the soul. The doctrine provides him with a richly suggestive model for the migratory nature of individuals, commodities, and diseases in a mercantile universe where movement across the boundaries of national body politics, particularly via their ports, has become both a constitutive principle and an occasion for considerable anxiety.

As I will show, the Pythagorean-inflected mercantile body politic of the play entails two related pathological dimensions. The first of these pertains to the type of migratory foreign commodity upon which *Volpone* lavishes the most attention: fashionable drugs of dubious efficacy imported from the Orient and the Americas. Jonson's dramatic treatment of luxury foreign medicines, I shall argue, demands to be interpreted in the light of early modern English economic debates about international trade and domestic protectionism, within which the comparative merits of imported and native drugs played a crucial role. For certain of Jonson's contemporaries, luxury foreign drugs were less medicinal remedies than potentially lethal agents of commercial as much as corporeal contamination, capable of disturbing national financial health and individual humoral balance in equal measure. The Galenic physician Timothy Bright makes this very case against foreign drugs and, in so doing, anticipates the rhetorical strategies of early bullionist mercantilists such as Thomas Milles. In his defense of England's customs system, Milles singles out the importing of foreign drugs as toxic drains on the nation's financial resources, but also as potential sources of income for the king. Bright's and Milles's writings, with their visions of transmigratory foreign drugs, provide an important pair of co-texts for Jonson's play.

The contaminating properties of foreign drugs are linked to the second pathological dimension of Jonson's mercantile body politic. In *Volpone,* international transmigrations of goods and people provide a metaphorical template for the foreign provenance of diseases, particularly plague. This involves an implicit, if only partial, rethinking of the dominant Galenic paradigm of illness as *dyskrasia,* or humoral imbalance. Rather than an endogenous state, disease in *Volpone* is often analogous to a migratory foreign commodity: it is imagined, in other words, as a determinate *thing* that invades the body rather than as a *condition* inside it. In an important set-piece, plague is presented by the English tourist Sir Politic Would-Be as an alien entity that is literally shipped into Venice as if it were a foreign commodity. Sir Pol's vision of plague as a quantifiable, dangerous entity migrating into the body politic through its ports is but one symptom of his characteristic paranoia concerning the cargos of mercantile transmigration. Yet even as Jonson satirizes Sir Pol's paranoia, he arguably partakes of it himself: *Volpone* presents a universe in which foreign trade is an economic necessity that nonetheless exposes the members of the body politic to both moral and physiological contamination.

With his vision of dubious foreign drugs and plague sailing to port, Jonson offers a revealing glimpse of how the early seventeenth century's emergent economic and pathological discourses of dangerous foreign bodies were in large part mutually constitutive. In a world where commodities, individuals, and diseases alike were increasingly perceived as possessing invasive powers to transmigrate across national borders—a perception that lent fuel to compensatory fantasies of both mercantilist and medical protectionism—the border dividing economics and pathology could not help but be porous. In his *Philosophy of Money,* Georg Simmel asserts that "the money economy first brought into life the ideal of numerical calculability," and that "the quantitatively exact interpretation of nature is the theoretical counterpart of finance."[2] Simmel's canny remark is lent weight by Sir Pol's fantasy of plague as a transmigratory commodity, in which the disease has become a measurable entity, subject to national customs surveillance and control as if it were any other imported good. *Volpone* thus brings to partial visibility the mercantile coordinates of what has been widely regarded as the most significant epistemic shift in seventeenth-century medical science: the eclipse of the old cosmology of qualities, elements, and humors by the new mechanistic philosophy of quantifiable matter in motion.[3]

Plague and Things in Motion

The pith of this new philosophy is arguably made visible in Shakespeare's *Troilus and Cressida,* and in a fashion that illuminates that play's presentation of disease. As part of his strategy to stir the Greeks' best warrior into action, Ulysses tells Achilles that "things in motion sooner catch the eye / Than what stirs not" (3.3.183–84). Ulysses speaks here of subjects rather than objects—of Ajax and his (supposed) popularity as a result of his dynamic feats in battle, which contrast those of the motionless Achilles, sulking in his tent. Nonetheless, Ulysses's description of "things in motion" also underwrites the play's vision of pathology. As we saw in the last chapter, the emergent belief that disease is a migratory entity rather than an internal state—a belief that increasingly underwrote afflictions like "serpego," "canker," and the "Winchester goose"—is pervasive throughout *Troilus and Cressida.*

Curiously, however, plague is not one of the diseases that the play embodies as "things in motion." In his famous speech on degree, Ulysses situates plague within an altogether more conventional cosmology:

> when the planets
> In evil mixture to disorder wander,
> What plagues and what portents, what mutiny! (1.3.94–96)

Ulysses may see plague as the astrological effect of planets in motion, but he does not regard the disease itself as a migratory entity; it is for him less a pathological than a cosmic disruption, commensurate with mutiny and anarchy. Despite the innovativeness of the play's ontological conceptions of diseases such as syphilis and serpego, Ulysses's speech typifies the dominant Elizabethan and Stuart attitude toward the plague, which likewise saw the disease as a generic if extreme disorder, devoid of any material or national specificity. As Thomas Dekker argued in his plague pamphlet, *London Looke Backe* (1630), "It hath a Preheminence aboue all others: And none being able to match it, for Violence, Strength, Incertainty, Suttlety, Catching, Vniuersality, and Desolation, it is called *the Sicknesse*. As if it were the onely *Sicknesse*, or the *Sicknesse* of *Sicknesses*, as it is indeed."[4] Like Ulysses, then, Dekker and a large number of his fellow English failed to understand plague as a determinate, pathological "thing in motion."

At first glance, this failure may seem baffling. Girolamo Fracastoro elaborated his radical theory of the *semina* of disease, according to which the vectors of epidemic illness were tiny airborne particles, to explain the infectiousness of the plague. Yet although Fracastoro's theory seems to have had some impact on English literature about syphilis, his ideas rarely surfaced in English physicians' treatises on the pestilence.[5] The absence might seem all the more puzzling, given that the Latin etymological root of plague, *plaga* (strike or blow), lends itself to an exogenous understanding of the disease. Paradoxically, however, this root is in large measure responsible for the early modern English failure to conceive of plague as a "thing in motion." Conventional religious dogma taught that the disease was a punitive "strike" of divine provenance; hence the biblical characterization of plague as "the arrow of God" (*Psalms* 38:2). This characterization informs the customary set of religious metaphors for the disease, which was referred to variously as not only an arrow but also a cannon, a dart, or a bullet. Thomas Dekker resorts to such rhetoric in *London Looke Backe,* where he remarks that "the cannon of the Pestilence does not yet discharge, but the small shot playes night and day, vpon the suburbes: And hath sent seauen bullets singing into the *Citty.* The arrowes fly ouer our heades and hit some, though they as yet misse vs."[6] This observation counters Stephen Greenblatt's notorious claim that disease conceived as "invisible bullets" was beyond the ken of the early modern English imagination, as does Dekker's earlier description of plague victims with "Arme-pits digd with Blaines, and vlcerous Sores / Lurking like poysoned Bullets in their flesh."[7] Yet these very visible "bullets" presupposed not a microbiological but a providential conception of disease. They were not material "things in motion," in other words, but marks of God's will.

Precisely because it was widely regarded to be a divine punishment, many English people refused to believe that the plague was contagious. As Stephen Bradwell observed, "though it may thus by the Learned be acknowledged to be *Venemous*; yet it is by many of the *Ignorant* sort conceited not to be *Infectious*."[8] Such a "conceit" was shared by Dekker. In his pamphlet *News from Graves End*, published immediately after the horrific epidemic of 1603, which killed a sixth of London's population, Dekker stridently rejects all theories of infection: "Nor . . . Can we belieue that one mans breath / Infected, and being blowne from him, / His poyson should to others swim." Instead, he favors the traditional providential explanation:

For euery man within him feedes
A worme which this contagion breedes;
Our heauenly parts are plaguy sick,
And there such leaprous spots do stick;
That God in anger fills his hand
With Vengeance, throwing it on the land.[9]

Hence even as providentialism created the template for an exogenous rather than a humoral explanation of plague, it frequently served to forestall speculation about the disease's material form and causes.

Despite the widespread belief in the providential etiology of plague, many early modern English physicians attempted to account for its form and mode of transmission in more material fashion than did Dekker in his pamphlets. Nevertheless, the notion of plague as a determinate "thing in motion" mostly eluded them. Some physicians explained the disease in the conventional Galenic terms of humoral disarray. In his *Treatise of the Plague* (1603), for example, Thomas Lodge asserts that the pestilence is caused by a "great repletion, or a general deprauation of the humours"; in the same year, Thomas Thayre argued that plague afflicted "those bodies wherein there is *Cacochymia*, corrupt and superfluous humours abounding."[10] Other physicians refined humoral physiology to explain the plague as a product of innate susceptibility to the disease. Thomas Sydenham, for example, grouped plague with other "epidemic distempers" such as smallpox and dysentery, all of which he believed to be caused by the coupling of atmospheric change with an individual's "epidemic constitution."[11]

More than Galen's humoralism or Sydenham's epidemic constitution, however, miasma theory offered physicians the most persuasive materialist explanation of the disease. Hippocrates' insistence on the pathogenic effects of contaminated air feature in virtually every sixteenth-century account of the plague. The Scottish physician Gilbert Skayne, for example, observed that "Ane pest is the corruption or infectioun of ye Air, or ane venmous qualytie & maist hurtfull Wapor thairof."[12] Like the providential model, miasma theory shifted the cause of the disease to external factors—chiefly air contaminated by dead carcasses—but its literally ethereal view of contagion did not readily permit plague to be viewed as a "thing in motion." As one writer argued in the notorious plague year of 1603, the plague was engendered by "a rooten and corrupt ayre by a hidden and secret properties which it hath."[13] If anything, the "hidden and secret properties" of miasmic air were more comfortably interarticulated with the providential etiology of the plague. Hence Skayne could argue, "Certaine it is, the first and principal cause may be callit, and is ane scurge and punishment of the maist iust God . . . the Heauine quhilk is the admirable instrument of God blawis that contagioun vpone the face of the Earth."[14] Skayne's "medical" opinion differed little from that of his ecclesiastical counterparts. In a lecture at York in 1594, at the height of the plague epidemic of that year, the divine John King attributed the "infection of the plague" to the "air," which "needs must be corrupted"; yet the familiar metaphor he used to represent the epidemic's spread makes clear his providential conception of plague: "For the arrows of the woful pestilence have been cast abroad at large in all the quarters of our realm, even to the emptying and dispeopling of some parts thereof."[15]

Influenced by Fracastoro, a tiny handful of early seventeenth-century English physicians struggled toward a notion of plague as a determinate "thing in motion." The enduring strength of the residual Galenic and Hippocratic explanations of pestilence, however, made it difficult for these doctors to articulate the notion with much clarity. Even as Lodge asserted that the immediate cause and form of plague is humoral imbalance, he also argued that its origin is "the ayre which we sucke, which hath in it self a corrupt and venemous seede, which we draw with our in-breathing."[16] As Margaret Healy notes, Lodge's etiology of the plague is an "eclectic soup of competing and complementary narratives."[17] Lodge's pathological gumbo is rivaled by Stephen Bradwell's confused and confusing explanation of the plague from 1636: "the Plague infects by all these wayes, and such sicke bodies infect the outward Aire, and that Aire again infects other Bodies. For there is a *Seminarie Tincture* full of a *venemous quality,* that being very thing and *spirituous* mixeth it selfe with the *Humors* and *Spirits* of the same Body also."[18] Like Lodge's, Bradwell's etiology of the plague mixes Galenic humoralism, Hippocratic miasma theory, and Fracastoro's notion of the *semina* of infection. Yet Bradwell's elaboration of the latter is too vague to be in any way groundbreaking. Even as his suggestive phrase "Seminarie Tincture" nods to Fracastoro, it also reeks of the much more materially vague, miasmic "taint"—with which "tincture" was etymologically linked—which I examined in Chapter 3.

Nonetheless, Bradwell's miasmic explanation of the disease's spread does suggest an intuition of "things in motion." "The *windes*," he argues, "doe sometimes transferre the Contagion from one region to another, as *Hippocrates* affirmes the *Plague* to be brought over the Sea from *Aethiopia* into *Greece*, by the *South-wind*."[19] Bradwell may defer here to the classical authority of Hippocrates, but his account of the plague's movement across national borders—so redolent of sixteenth-century writers' narratives of syphilis's transnational trajectories—points to a widespread suspicion about the spread of epidemics in the age of global mercantile trade, a suspicion shared even by those who professed an exclusively moral or providential explanation of disease. When he isn't blaming plague victims themselves for their sickness, for example, Dekker's impulse is to place the moral burden for the disease on foreignness, if not foreigners. Speaking of the "City-sin" of London, he exclaims:

And that she may not want disease
She sailes for it beyond the Seas,
With *Antwerp* will she drinke vp *Rhene*:
With *Paris* act the bloodiest Scene:
Or in pyed fashions passe her folly,
Mocking at heauen yet looke most holy:
Of Vsury she'll rob the Iewes,
Of Luxury, *Venetian* Stewes,
With Spaniards, shee's an Indianist,
With barbarous Turks a Sodomist.[20]

Dekker echoes here the sentiments of countless English moralists and priests: even if the plague was divine punishment for generic sins, these sins could nonetheless be imagined as the special prerogative of foreign nations. Yet Dekker's vision of plague "sailing beyond the seas" also resonates with a growing suspicion about one way in which the disease could be transmitted.

Flying in the face of the prevailing medical and religious explanations of the plague, English citizens and state officials often recognized that the disease could be transported from nation to nation by merchant ships and their cargos. One writer attributed the epidemic of 1630 to a "pack of Carpets from *Turkey*," and that of 1636 to a stray dog that had been a stowaway on a ship from the Netherlands.[21] Actions by state officials lent support to these lay suspicions. As early as 1580, Portuguese galleons were apprehended in the Thames, and their merchandise aired, under suspicion of carrying the plague. In the summer of 1602, when plague broke out in Holland, Lord Cobham barred Amsterdam ships from entering London's port.[22] And in 1636, the Royal College of Physicians issued the following recommendation: "neither men nor goods may come from any suspected places beyond the seas, or in the land, without certificate of health, or else either to be seent suddenly away, or to be put in the Pesthouse or some such like place for fourty daies (according to the custome of *Italy*) till the certainty of their soundnesse may be discouered."[23] As these examples show, state policy recognized the communicability of the plague. The queen's Privy Council, even as it acknowledged "these plagues and sicknes to proceede from the handes of God as a due punyshment of our synnes," also referred to it as "this contagious disease" and insisted that "we oughte to use all possible meanes by all good waies to prevente the increase of the same." Hence the council moved quickly to contain the epidemic's spread, on the assumption that it "cannot but increase by the common assemblie of people."[24] This was increasingly done, as the above examples suggest, through policies designed to control the movements of ships.

In other words, practical experience more than received medical wisdom created the conditions for a new understanding of plague as a "thing in motion," residing in and transmitted by foreign bodies. In the mercantilist age, ships sailing into port, and the cargo they carried, became objects of heightened anxiety—a phenomenon that we will witness also in Jonson's *Volpone*. Yet even as merchant ships may have provided an important stimulus to practical understandings of plague's transnational communicability, those few writers who sought to imagine the disease as a migratory entity also resorted to other, premercantilist discourses of "things in motion." In the absence of any empirical knowledge of the movements of the rats and fleas that were the vectors of the plague, let alone of the bacillus that transmitted it, early modern English writers rehabilitated conceptions of motion from antiquity. They found one such conception in the work of the Roman Epicurean philosopher Lucretius, whose materialist vision of the universe as comprised of minuscule particles in perpetual motion experienced something of a renaissance in the seventeenth century. In her pseudoscientific tract *The Blazing World* (c. 1657), for example, Margaret Cavendish debates at some length whether plague is caused by the complexional "imitation" of other infected bodies or by the infiltration of a pathogenic "body of little flies like atoms."[25] In using the Lucretian term "atom," Cavendish adapts his vision of "things in motion" less to imagine the physics of the universe than to reimagine pathology. A similar strategy was also employed, some fifty years earlier, by Ben Jonson in *Volpone*. As I will suggest, Jonson's play understands both mercantile and pathological movement in terms of an equally archaic doctrine of "things in motion": Pythagoras's metempsychosis.

Metempsychotic Episodes

Near the beginning of the play, Volpone's household grotesques stage an entertainment penned by his parasite, Mosca. The performance commences with a speech by Nano the dwarf:

For know [*pointing to* ANDROGYNO], here is enclosed the Soul of Pythagoras,
That juggler divine, as hereafter shall follow;
Which soul, fast and loose, sir, came first from Apollo,
And was breathed into Aethilades, Mercurius his son,
Where it had the gift to remember all that ever was done.
From thence it fled forth, and made quick transmigration
To goldy-locked Euphorbus, who was killed, in good fashion,
At the siege of old Troy, by the cuckold of Sparta.
Hermotimus was next (I find it in my charta)
To whom it did pass, where no sooner it was missing,
But with one Pyrrhus, of Delos, it learned to go a fishing;
And thence did it enter the Sophist of Greece. (1.2.6–17)

Nano proceeds to trace the progression of Pythagoras's soul through bodies natural and politic: it has transmigrated through not only animal, courtesan, philosopher, monk, lawyer, and Puritan but also Greece, Troy, and southern Italy prior to taking up residence in the Venetian body of Androgyno, Volpone's hermaphroditic fool.

The grotesques' interlude has baffled critics. On the one hand, Jonson's indirect source for it—Lucian's satirical dialogue "The Dream, or the Cock," which he probably read in Erasmus's translation—rehearses many of *Volpone*'s distinctive themes and preoccupations. Like the play, Lucian's dialogue offers a stinging critique of boundless wealth and self-serving legacy hunters. And, like the play, it does so in a context of disease: two of the illnesses feigned by Volpone, consumption and gout, are identified by Lucian as the ailments of the rich.[26] Yet for some reason, the grotesques' interlude takes as its focus not Lucian's more obviously pertinent economic and pathological themes but his seemingly less relevant account of Pythagorean transmigration. Why?

Few critics would now endorse Maurice Castelain's view that in performance, the interlude should be omitted altogether.[27] Since J. D. Rea's edition of 1919, Nano's speech about Pythagoras's soul has tended to be regarded not as an excrescence but as the play's keynote.[28] There has been little consensus, however, about exactly what note it sounds. Speculation has been divided between those who consider the interlude to offer substantive moral commentary and those who view its significance in largely formal terms. Harry Levin represents a good example of the first tendency; he suggests that Nano provides an etiology of modern evils, culminating in Puritan hypocrisy, that recalls Donne's *Progress of the Soul*.[29] By contrast, Douglas Duncan sees the interlude as Jonson's way of signaling his allegiances to the satirical models of Lucian and Erasmus.[30] I would like to offer a different reading, but one that supplements rather than disqualifies Levin's and Duncan's moral and formalist interpretations. By taking into account the contemporary historical nuances of transmigration, I shall suggest that Lucian's narrative of metempsychosis provides Jonson with a satirical template for the representation of overlapping economic and pathological phenomena: that is, the movement of people, commodities, and diseases across the borders of national body politics.

The term "transmigration" has a complex history in the early modern period. Although it was employed in its strictly Pythagorean sense by Shakespeare as well as Jonson,[31] its arguably dominant application was not cosmological but geopolitical. "Transmigration" had been used by theological writers since the thirteenth century to designate the forced removal of the Jews into captivity at Babylon; as a consequence, it had also acquired the more general sense of passage or removal of people or things from one place to another, and particularly one nation to another. Thus the term was used, for example, to designate the grand tours of the Continent customarily undertaken by young English gentlemen: Thomas Westcote referred in 1630 to "Gentlemen's younger sons, who, by means of their travel and transmigration are very well qualified, apt, and fit to manage great and high offices in the republic."[32] The OED dates the first occurrences of the more familiar terms "immigration" and "emigration" to only 1623 and 1677, respectively; in the early years of the seventeenth century, "transmigration" assumed much of the semantic baggage that these later, more specialized terms would carry.

The geopolitical meanings of transmigration are arguably part of the term's invisible cargo in *Volpone*. When these extra meanings are taken into account, the most salient details of the grotesques' interlude become the border crossings it traces, together with the commercial language in which these crossings are couched. The bodies in which Pythagoras has been reincarnated are repeatedly identified with *nations*—and when not specific nation-states, then the "profane nation" of Puritans (1.2.47) and the more praiseworthy "nation" of fools (1.2.66). The transmigration of Pythagoras's soul is, in other words, presented as an ongoing exercise in multinational identity tourism. In the process, transmigration sheds its more strictly spiritual associations. The metaphor Jonson uses to describe the rapid peregrinations of Pythagoras's soul, "fast and loose," refers to an early modern cheating game, one that involved "jugglers" tricking gulls out of money by inviting them to stab a seemingly substantial belt that was literally impossible to pin down.[33] The "fast and loose" soul thus acquires in Nano's speech something of the roving, mercenary quality of not only several of *Volpone*'s most important characters—the English tourists Sir Politic Would-Be, Lady Politic Would-Be, and the aptly named Peregrine, who typifies Thomas Westcote's "younger son" experienced in "travel and transmigration"— but also the play's objects, many of which are high-priced commodities transplanted from their original, exotic locations. Indeed, peregrination across national borders for the sake of profit is arguably *Volpone*'s leitmotif.

The transnational reading of metempsychosis is supported by the play's other reference to the doctrine. As Volpone attempts to seduce Celia, the wife of Corvino the legacy hunter, he offers her dazzling visions of the entertainments that he plans for them. In "changed shapes," he says, Celia will play a variety of roles:

Attired like some sprightly dame of France,
Brave Tuscan lady, or proud Spanish beauty;
Sometimes, unto the Persian Sophy's wife;
Or the Grand Signor's mistress; and for change,
To one of our most artful courtesans,
Or some quick Negro, or cold Russian;
And I will meet thee, in as many shapes:
Where we may, so transfuse our wand'ring souls,
Out at our lips, and score up sums of pleasures. (3.4.219–35)

The implied reference to transmigration in the last lines evokes the world of theater and its actors' shapeshifting power. Yet the most notable feature of Volpone's fantasy of "wand'ring souls" is, once again, its transnational axis: presented by Jonson as a hedonistic masquerade that tumbles "fast and loose" from Tuscan lady to Persian Sophy's wife and from Negro to Russian, theatrical impersonation blurs here into transmigration in its geopolitical sense. The effects of these border crossings, moreover, are notably presented in acquisitive terms. According to Volpone, to wander theatrically from one national role to the next is to "score up sums of pleasure"; the phrase suggests an accounting of libidinal riches accumulated through endless movement across nations.

The transnational dimension of metempsychosis is not confined to the play's "wand'ring souls"; as I have suggested, it extends to its commodities too. This much is made clear by one of Volpone's most effective impersonations. In order to attract the attention of Celia, he masquerades as a renowned mountebank, Scoto of Mantua. Tracing the origin and trajectory of Scoto's magical medicinal oil, Volpone sketches a path of transmigration closely paralleling that of Pythagoras's soul, which likewise has an Apollonian point of origin:

it is the poulder that made Venus a goddess, given her by Apollo, that kept her perpetually young, cleared her wrinkles, firmed her gums, filled her skin, coloured her hair; from
her, derived to Helen, and at the sack of Troy, unfortunately, lost: till now, in this our age,
it was as happily recovered, by a studious antiquary, out of some ruins of Asia, who sent
a moiety of it, to the court of France (but much sophisticated), wherewith the ladies
there, now, colour their hair. The rest, at this present, remains with me, extracted to a
quintessence. (2.2.236–44)

Volpone offers here an account of commodities strikingly close to that of
social anthropologist Arjun Appadurai. What makes an object a commodity,
Appadurai has argued, is not any property intrinsic to it, nor a specific mode of
production (such as capitalism) in which it may have been manufactured. The
commodity is instead constituted within and by a diachronic trajectory of exchange, or what he calls its "career." For Appadurai, then, objects do not simply
acquire meaning or value by virtue of their present social contexts. Rather, they
impart significance to those contexts as a result of the paths they have traced
through time and space. Using a phrase that in this context cannot help but
pointedly resonate with Ulysses's remark in *Troilus and Cressida*, Appadurai argues that "things-in-motion" transform "their human and social context[s]."[34]
Jonson's presentations of metempsychosis throughout *Volpone*, I would suggest,
articulate versions of Appadurai's account of commodities as "things-in-
motion" that shape their contexts. This is particularly true of the transmigrations of the play's mountebank commodities. Whether it is Volpone's "blessed
unguento" (2.2.94), which has journeyed to Venice from Greece via Asia Minor
and France, or the "vile medicines" that are transported and retailed, according
to Peregrine, by alien "quacksalvers" (2.2.16, 5),[35] the play's mountebank remedies tend to be viewed through the prism of their movements across the borders
of national as well as natural bodies. Jonson also universalizes the transformative power of the transmigratory commodity. As "blessed" cure or as "vile" poison, the medicinal "thing in motion"—like the commodity in Appadurai's
account—determines its present "human and social contexts": it produces
"firmed . . . gums" (2.2.238) and corpses (2.2.61), youthful-looking courts
(2.2.243–44) and "shrivelled" workforces (2.2.65). In the process, Jonson intervenes obliquely in an ongoing English debate about foreign drugs as transformative "things in motion," and the potential benefits and dangers presented by
the latter to bodies natural and politic.

Foreign Drugs and Protectionism: Timothy Bright

Volpone is teeming with drugs. In addition to Scoto's exotic magical oil, the play contains the predictable assortment of references to potentially deadly medications that one finds in much Jacobean drama featuring evil Italian Machiavels skilled in the art of poisoning.[36] The decrepit legacy hunter Corbaccio, for example, conspires to administer an opiate to Volpone (1.4.12–13); Volpone as Scoto scotches rumors that he has poisoned people with his "commodities" (2.2.41); Mosca proposes to sell Corbaccio's flesh "for mummia, he's half dead already" (4.4.14). Contrary to what one might expect, however, the most references to drugs are made not by any scheming Italian but by the unrelenting English busybody, Lady Politic Would-Be. In act 3, she cheerfully prescribes Volpone a cornucopia of drugs for his seeming ills:

Seed-pearl were good now, boiled with syrup of apples,
Tincture of gold, and coral, citron-pills,
Your elecampane root, myrobalanes . . .
Burnt silk, and amber, you have muscadel
Good i' the house—
              . . . I doubt, we shall not get
Some English saffron—half a dram would serve—
Your sixteen cloves, a little musk, dried mints,
Bugloss, and barley-meal— (3.4.51–54, 56–57, 58–61)

This pharmaceutical cocktail offers "remedies" for a bewildering variety of early modern ailments. Seed-pearl was conventionally prescribed for heartburn, and mint for general infections of the heart; elecampane root and bugloss were recommended for weakness; myrobalanes for melancholy; burnt silk for smallpox; saffron for jaundice, as well as many other humoral complaints; and coral for demonic possession.[37]

Lady Politic Would-Be's assumption of the role of Volpone's healer, daftly managed though it may be, accords with the expectation that English wives should know something about medicine. Indeed, some of the drugs to which she refers can be found in early modern English health manuals and herbals targeted specifically at housewives. Her remedies differ subtly yet significantly, however, from the literally domestic quality of housewifely medical lore purveyed by Gervase Markham and others.[38] For arguably the most striking aspect of Lady Pol's prescription is the transnational provenance of its contents. While humble bugloss, barley, and saffron derived from Lady Pol's native England, the more expensive coral, citron-pills, and muscadel were commodities from the Mediterranean and the Canary Islands; seed-pearl, cloves, musk, and myrobalanes were luxury imports from the Orient. The whole ensemble serves as a satirical portrait of the international goods favored by a relatively new type of fashionable cosmopolitan consumer. Indeed, Lady Pol's enthusiastic endorsement of international drugs is of a piece with her unabashed, if feckless, consumption of Italian clothes, cosmetics, and books. Her husband refers to her cosmopolitan curiosity as

a peculiar humour of my wife's,
Laid for this height of Venice, to observe,
To quote, to learn the language, and so forth. (2.1.11–13)

But Lady Pol's fetishization of foreign drugs is no mere "peculiar humour" confined to her. Sir Pol and Celia are both taken in by Scoto's magical oil, while Nano refers more generally to the widespread popularity not only of any "Indian drug" but also of relatively new medicines imported from the Americas: "tobacco," "sassafras," and "guacum" (2.2.126–28).[39]

Exotic drugs had, in fact, become popular metonymies for the goods imported into England from the Orient and the new worlds. Sir Thomas Elyot refers in *The Castel of Helthe* (1539) to the new "traffyke of spyce and sondry drouges" from the East; in order to blast the growing English love of commodities from abroad, William Harrison in his *Description of England* (1587) fingers his countrymen's "continuall desire of strange [i.e. foreign] drugs.... Alas! what haue we to doo with such Arabian . . . stuffe as is dailie brought from those parties?"[40] The very name of the Spice Islands served to conflate the wealth of the Far East with pharmacy: in the diet-obsessed humoral scheme, the boundary dividing food and medicine was thoroughly blurred, and spices were widely regarded as a species of drug. The trades of grocer and apothecary in late medieval England had tended to be covered by the generic term "spicer," and the lists of drugs in early modern English rate books include items that we would now regard simply as condiments, such as cardamoms, cloves, ginger, and turmeric.[41] Hence in *Paradise Lost*, Milton could speak of "merchants' spicy drugs."[42] Christopher Marlowe's *Jew of Malta*, which arguably exerted a considerable influence on Jonson as he wrote the opening scenes of *Volpone*, likewise conflates exotic drugs and spices as synecdoches for the bounty of international trade: when Barabas inventories the goods brought to him by his argosies, he includes in his list "warehouses stuffed with spices and with drugs."[43] Barabas had many real-life counterparts in sixteenth-century England who invested extensively in exotic medicinal commodities. Official state documents recording imported goods testify to the substantial increase during the late sixteenth and early seventeenth centuries in English consumption of foreign drugs and spices, including a good many of the confections listed by Lady Pol. The rate book of 1587–88, for example, includes among its inventory of imported drugs nearly £13 worth of myrobalanes, a large sum for the time, and no less than £1,500 of coral (it was not a good year for demons, evidently). Neither commodity was listed in the previous rate book of 1567–68.[44]

Drugs, however, were by no means England's largest import. How, then, did they acquire a symbolic importance that far outstripped their net commercial value in relation to those of other coveted foreign goods such as silk and gold? The heightened attention to foreign drugs and their transmigrations across England's borders was, I would argue, both symptomatic of and instrumental in the fashioning of a discourse of national economy. As I have shown in earlier chapters, certain infrastructural preconditions for such a discourse had been in place for some time. The suggestive associations of foreign drugs with transmigration, ingestion, health, and illness, however, arguably helped the emergent national economy to be envisaged in distinctively corporeal and, more specifically, pathological terms.

The greatly increased volume of imported drugs in the latter half of the sixteenth century testifies to their growing popularity. But foreign drugs were also regarded with considerable ambivalence. The national provenance of medicines was of special concern to seventeenth-century English herbalists; in his *Pambotanologia* (1659), for example, Robert Lovell distinguishes foreign from domestic medicinal plants with ominous asterisks.[45] As early as the mid-fifteenth century, however, the anonymous writer of *The Libele of Englyshe Polycye* protested against the evils of newly fashionable "Italian" drugs such as scammony: "for infirmitees," he claims, "In our Englande are such comoditees / Wythouten helpe of any other londe."[46] By the sixteenth century, suspicion of the exotic powders and oils of apothecaries and mountebanks notably combined opposition to them not only on nationalistic but also on a variety of other grounds, spanning the religious, the medical, and, most importantly, the economic.

The sixteenth century's most comprehensive elaboration of the various arguments against foreign drugs was undertaken by the physician Timothy Bright. In the opening note to the readers of his *Treatise: Wherein is Declared the Sufficiencie of English Medicines, for Cure of All Diseases* (1580), Bright underscores the overlap between discourses of bodies natural and politic:

I hope this my enterprise shall be a meanes to prouoke others to deal with the same argument more plentifully, and kindle in vs a greater diligence to inquire after the medicines of our owne countrie yeelde, and more care to put them in practise. The case is neither mine nor thine onely, but the commonwealthes, the benefite wherof all are bound who are members thereof, according to their place and calling, most diligently to seeke.[47]

Bright's "enterpris[ing]" exploration of diverse ways to augment the "benefite" to the English commonwealth of its medical substances and practices leads him to espouse a nationalism seemingly fueled by little more than religious jingoism: "the most of our Apothecarie ware is brought from the most vile & barbarous nations of the world, and almost all from the professed enemies of the Sonne of GOD: shall we say the Lorde hath more care, or setteth more store by them then by his owne people?" (sig. C4v). Bright's question is rhetorical, of course, for he insists that God has furnished "his owne" English people with an abundant supply of effective native medicines. "What can be more pleasant vnto thee," he asks his readers, "than the inioying of medicines for cure of thine infirmities out of thy natiue soyle, and countrie, thy Fielde, thy Orchard, thy Garden?" (sig. A4).

Such seemingly knee-jerk xenophobia in fact masks a sophisticated use of humoral dietary theory to justify the prescription of domestic medicines. Bright's resulting position might be described as a medicalized protectionism. Bodies differ from nation to nation, he argues, because of the food their peoples eat, "whereby ariseth great varietie of humours, and excrements in our bodies from theirs"; hence "the causes of diseases rising vpon breach of diet, (the diet being of an other sort) must needes be vnlike" (sig. B4v). Thus Bright abandons—at least from a medical point of view—his hierarchy of Christian and barbarous nations. Instead, he argues that God has provided each nation with not only food but also medicines that will minister to the humoral peculiarities of its bodies: "For as euerie nation hath a peculiar condition of the same disease, so must the medicine also needs be of an other sort. . . . The medicine varieth in respect of the complexion of the patient being other in one country, then in an other. . . . If it agreeth with the complexion of a *Moore* and *Indian,* or *Spaniarde,* then must it needes disagre with ours" (sig. F4v). Bodies natural and politic are thus universally protected through the scrupulous avoidance of foreign foodstuffs and drugs.

Paradoxically, however, this position leads Bright to an inventive explanation of the efficacy of certain foreign drugs. Many new diseases such as syphilis, he argues, are not native to Europe but derive from the worlds opened up by exploration and economic trade: the so-called French pockes is, according to Bright, in fact an "Indian disease" brought to Europe by Christopher Columbus, "who first discovered the West Indies" and "hath since infected the whole world." Because it is not native to Europe, this foreign disease cannot be cured by traditional European means. It necessitates a foreign cure, derived from plants in its lands of origin: "this straunge and Indian disease hath nature prouided remedie against . . . out of India, as the *Guiacum,* and *Salsa parilla*" (sig. D4v)—popular Caribbean remedies for syphilis to which Volpone also alludes (2.2.127–28).

Despite Bright's express commitment to humoralism, therefore, new conceptions of pathology are freighted with, and place pressure on, his Galenic theories. The conventionally endogenous model of disease that he articulates is offset by a new awareness of disease as a "thing in motion" that transmigrates infectiously from body to body, and from nation to nation. This leads him to articulate a taxonomy of disease's origins that differs slightly from that of his Galenic predecessors.[48] Although he reiterates the conventional Galenic dictum that "diseases are either in the complexion, or frame of the body" and that complexional ailments are "ingendred in the body," he notes also the existence of diseases "outwardly procured" through "infection passing from one to an other, as the French pockes" (sig. E2v). Bright's passing reference to the "French pockes" hints at one of the most revolutionary consequences of that new disease for early modern medical thought. As we have seen in earlier chapters, syphilis more than any other illness had placed pressure on the conventional understanding of disease as a state of *dyskrasia*, or complexional imbalance.

Bright shows no awareness of Fracastoro's innovative ontological theory of disease. But we can see him struggling toward a version of such a theory, even if only unwittingly. In his account of the origins of disease, he notably cross-hatches his new paradigm of "infection passing from one to another" with the noxious effects of foreign drugs, identifying "poisons" as one of the chief causes of diseases that occur "by outward occasions." Speaking of opium, for example, Bright observes that "the difference of our bodyes from those of straunge nations be so great, that the thing which helpeth them, destroyeth vs" (sig. C1v). For all the humoralism of his *Treatise,* therefore, the pathological model to which Bright repeatedly circles back is both ontological and exogenous. Whether they take the form of exotic opiates or syphilitic goods from America, transmigratory foreign bodies—"things in motion"—are what destroy England's domestic bodies.

A striking, recurrent image in Bright's account of such foreign bodies is of the traveler-trader sailing with his pathological cargo into Europe: we see, for example, Columbus returning from the West Indies with the "pockes" or the merchant returning from the Orient with dubious drugs. These instances hint at the mercantile coordinates of Bright's half-articulated ontological vision of disease. Conversely, they hint also at the pathological coordinates of his half-articulated conception of national economy. Indeed, economic and pathological discourses overlap substantially in his presentation of external threats to bodies natural and politic. The danger posed by foreign drugs, Bright argues, is not just to humoral balance but also to financial propriety: "For what hope is there to be had of the prouision made by Merchants? who buy to sell onely, and thereof to reape gaine, and by reason they be vnlearned" (sig. B2v). The pathological effects of foreign drugs upon bodies natural are thus supplemented by the more subtle pathological effects they have on the commonwealth at large: "Hath God so dispensed his blessings, that a medicine to cure the iawndies, or the greene sicknes, or ye rheume, or such like, should cost more oftentimes then one quarter of the substance yt the patient is worth? . . . is Physicke only made for rich men?" (sig. C4).

That foreign drugs, regardless of their efficacy, are a privileged form of treatment reserved for the rich was a commonly articulated grievance in the sixteenth century. A satirical set-piece of the time depicts the rich city gentleman resorting to the apothecary for pointlessly outlandish and expensive confections. In *A Quip for an Vpstart Courtier,* for example, Robert Greene observes that the decent but poor "cloth breeches" employs only local "Kitchen-Physicke," but the rich "velvet breeches" must "have his oyle of *Tartar,* his *lac virginis* ["virgin's milk," a cosmetic], his Champhire [camphor] . . . *Eringion, Oleum Formicarum alatarum, & aqua mirabilis,* often pound a pint."[49] Greene's satire resonates with the related fiscal argument that England stood to lose its financial health as a result of excessive imports of expensive exotic trifles. We have seen in Chapter 2, for example, how Thomas Starkey attributed one of the chief "diseases" of the body politic to "all such marchands which carry out things necessary to the use of our people, and bring in such vain trifles."[50] Such suspicion of "vain trifles" from abroad was one of the reasons why luxury foreign drugs were subjected to often steep customs duties. Bright's call for medical protectionism, therefore, neatly dovetails with mercantilist conceptions of economic protectionism. Foreign drugs, moreover, provide the common ground upon which each form of protectionism converges.

The Customer's Duty: Thomas Milles and Traffic in Motion

The economic implications of Bright's medical protectionism become more clear when considered in relation to the so-called bullionist movement within mercantilism, and in particular the writings of Thomas Milles.[51] Appointed the customer of Sandwich in the 1590s, Milles was no mere provincial functionary collecting duties on imports and exports; his position also cast him as a supporting player in the glittering theater of Elizabethan intelligence and espionage. Milles had been employed by Walsingham as an agent between England and Scotland in 1585; upon assuming the post of customer, he was employed by the government in the interception of foreign spies and correspondence.[52] His service to the state in combating suppositious foreign threats is of a piece with the somewhat paranoid bent of his economic writing, which seeks to expose mercantile rather than political conspiracies against the nation. In four pamphlets—*The Custumers Apology* (1599), *The Customers Replie* (1604), *The Custumers Alphabet* (1608), and *The Misterie of Iniquitie* (1611)—Milles argues for the threats posed by various transnational trading entities, practices, and goods, and the crucial role played by the customs official in the maintenance of England's economic health.

The English customs system was the first, and most comprehensive, of its kind. As early as 1203, during the reign of King John, national duties on foreign trade were instituted in the Great Winchester Assize of Customs; from 1275 to 1350, the Crown developed the national customs system that, in its basic outlines, persisted into Milles's day.[53] The system relied on the institution of the staple towns, "outports" that retailed certain local commodities (including wool, wool-fells, tin, lead, and leather) to foreign merchants. These commodities yielded the state a double source of revenue: primarily bullion paid for the staple commodities, but also extra customs and subsidies that helped top off the king's coffers. According to Milles, however, the growing power of regulated trading companies—particularly the Merchant Adventurers Company—had dangerously undermined the staple system. The Merchant Adventurers had acquired monopolies in the transport and retail of certain English staple commodities, especially cloth. By selling these goods to foreigners in European market towns rather than English staple towns, Milles argued, the company had damaged the national economy in several ways: (1) English outports were deprived of trade, and hence suffered economically; (2) the state was deprived of valuable customs duties and subsidies owed to it; (3) in the manner of Gerard Malynes's evil foreign financiers, the Merchant Adventurers manipulated foreign exchange rates for their private gain and to the detriment of England's wealth, thereby engaging in "merchandizing exchange" rather than fair commodity exchange; and (4) rather than attracting bullion from abroad, English commodities—undervalued as a result of the Merchant Adventurers' practices of "merchandizing exchange"—were now exchanged overseas for disproportionately overvalued foreign trifles, including drugs and spices.

Milles's views were fiercely rebutted in 1601 by the secretary of the Merchant Adventurers' Company, John Wheeler.[54] I am interested less in the substance or validity of Milles's specific accusations against the company, however, than in the epistemological underpinnings of his discourse of international trade and customs. Milles's writing is highly repetitive, and in any work he reiterates not only favorite phrases but entire paragraphs from earlier publications. For that reason, the four pamphlets read more as an extended narrative than as discrete texts. This narrative, I suggest, works to articulate a pathological discourse of "things in motion," one that additionally presumes extensive surveil-

lance and measurement of entities as they move in and out of the English body
politic. In my reading, Milles the customs official emerges as the political counterpart of Timothy Bright the physician, policing the transnational migrations
of potentially toxic, potentially medicinal commodities as a patriotic act of service to both nation and state.

Milles's mercantilist creed is grounded in a term that, throughout his writing, he uses more or less as a synonym for "things in motion": traffic. "The End
of *Money*," he argues in *The Custumers Alphabet*, is

to make all things vendible, by equalities of worth, and value of it selfe, for the quicker
dispatch and aduancement of *Trafficke*: and the *Ends* of *Trafficke* the Soueraignes *honour*, the Kidgdomes [sic] *peace*, and the Subiects *wealth*. Thus mouing and disposing all
means Endeuors, by willing Courses, and perpetuall Motions, to serue and worke for
ONE.[55]

Milles's vision of "mouing" and "perpetuall Motions" implicates not only the
agents but also the goods of traffic. In *The Customers Apology*, he writes that
"CUSTUMES are the Princes publike *Duties*, growing by TRAFFICK, on
Marchandize outward and inward, payable according to the *Equitie* of positiue
Lawes and forraine *Contracts*, freely and onely giuen *For defence of the Realme
and safe passage at Seas*."[56] As this remark shows, Milles's conception of traffic
not only entails a mercantile universe populated by "things in motion"; it also
depends on institutions that monitor, regulate, and extract profit from the objects of traffic. If these objects escape the gaze of the customer, Milles implies,
economic anarchy ensues.

As with all mercantilist literature, pathological metaphors dominate
Milles's writing. In each of his pamphlets, Milles solemnly intones his personal
mantra: traffic is "that generall *Restoratiue*, which easing all griefe in *Sores*, sup-
pling all *Sores* in *Diseases*, and curing all *Diseases* in particular Members, holdes
the whole Body of the *Commonweale* in perfect health."[57] Conversely, the decay
of traffic is repeatedly figured as a disease. In *The Custumers Alphabet*, Milles
pronounces English traffic to be "distempered and distrest with dangerous fits
of a hot burning Feauer," which he diagnoses as a condition "Not farre from
Frensie."[58] The discourse of plague subtly obtrudes into his analysis of traffic's
decay in *The Customers Replie*. For Milles, the old outports are the sites of an
epidemic if metaphorical disease: referring to England's custom houses in terms
that pointedly recall the way people fled from the plague, he asserts that "her
HOUSES as places infected . . . are either abandoned, or by extremities made
subiect to shifts."[59] What is this plague that has harrowed the outports?

Milles provides a ready answer: England's economic plague has been
caused by the monopoly given to the Merchant Adventurers to transport staple

goods to European market towns, thereby diverting traffic from the outports. But I would argue that Milles also assumes another, more subtle etiology of the custom-house plague, one that lends the disease the force of an invading foreign body. Given the widespread intuition in early modern England that plague might be carried by merchant ships and their transnational cargo, it is perhaps ironic that what seems to cause Milles's custom-house plague is a *lack* of ships sailing to (out)ports. Yet it is precisely the ships of the Merchant Adventurers that are the causes, if not the vehicles, of Milles's plague. By selling English goods abroad for foreign coin, which they exchange for foreign trifles that they then ship back directly to London, the Merchant Adventurers and their fleet have exposed England to an armada of dangerous, exotic merchandise that not only depletes the nation of specie but also escapes detection by the outports' vigilant customers.

Indeed, for all his Malynesian fulminations against the evils of a "merchandizing exchange" in which money becomes the object of trade, Milles repeatedly associates England's economic ills with the uncontrolled infiltration of its markets by exotic luxury goods. He laments the passing of a time when "there were not . . . so many forraine wares brought in againe into the Realme, as be at this day";[60] and he blasts the effects of "Forraine idle Commodities, brought in and obtruded vpon vs by Strangers, to the hinderance of our Trafficke in Trades, & decay of our Ports in Mariners and Shipping, which the wisedome of our State must always maintaine."[61] His argument against these "idle" commodities is redolent of an earlier generation of moralist writers like Philip Stubbes, who questioned such objects' use value. Milles similarly complains that "our *Returnes* (for the most part) beeing but toys and *Tabacco,* Bells or Bables, of things *needlesse* or *bootlesse,* doe shew how Strangers for better wares, can fat vs vp with pryde, or fodder vs with folly."[62] The critique may be old, harking back to Starkey's suspicion of "vain trifles," yet the appearance of tobacco in this list highlights how the new drugs imported from the Americas and the Orient figured prominently in Milles's vision of the diseased English economy. This vision is more clearly outlined in his later pamphlet, *The Misterie of Iniquitie,* by which time the newly incorporated East India Company had supplanted the Merchant Adventurers as his favorite bogeyman: "The new EAST-INDIAN Company, who finding our TRAFFICK thus by others made spiritlesse, pulselesse, and almost out of blood like confident *Emperikes* (that seeke but priuate profit at one hand or other) obtrude themselues, and offer to pouder her with Pepper, or turne her into *Mummy.*"[63] In this deft critique, Milles conflates mountebank physicians with the East India Company, both of whom he imagines hawking the questionably healthful effects—whether corporeal or financial—of pepper and mummia, two of the best-known Oriental drugs and spices.

Like Bright, then, Milles is suspicious of foreign drugs. Yet also like Bright, he is not entirely averse to them: they are acceptable, and even economically advantageous, so long as they are shipped to the appropriate destinations—England's outports—where they can be inspected by customs officials and subjected to duties or taxes. Without such scrutiny, he suggests, these commodities will engender an economic plague.[64] I would argue that the qualified medical and economic pathologizations of foreign drugs that we see in texts like Bright's and Milles's, together with the English government's careful monitoring and measurement of their transmigrations into the body of the nation, had an important twofold effect. First, the ambivalent attitude toward non-English medicines helped articulate the boundaries of a national economy whose "health" was potentially compromised or enhanced by the incorporation of foreign commodities. Second, this attitude facilitated the increasing tendency to regard the pathological, whether economic or natural, as quantifiable matter in motion. *Volpone* demonstrates both of these developments. As we will see, the play displays a heightened attention to the boundaries of national body politics. One of the enabling conditions for the latter perception, moreover, is the play's repeated positing of disease as transmigratory matter comparable to a foreign drug or commodity, in need of surveillance as it crosses national borders.

Plague, Ports, and Paranoid Plots

It is perhaps no surprise that Jonson, whose dramatic résumé begins with the so-called comedy of humors, should tend to conceive of illness in his plays in complexional terms—that is, as a state of internal imbalance. *Volpone* is no exception. It is populated by conventional humoral ailments such as the "flux of laughter" that Mosca warns Volpone against (1.4.134), the *"melancholia hypochondriaca"* (2.2.108) for which Volpone claims Scoto's oil to be a remedy, or the cooled blood from which Volpone claims to suffer as a pretext for luring Celia into his bed (2.6.64). But at times, the play also offers glimpses of an ontological conception of disease as a determinate, migratory entity. Not only does Volpone refer to syphilis (2.2.203), which he also claims Scoto's magical oil can cure; even more revealingly, he says of the legacy hunters that he "will be a sharp disease unto 'em" (5.3.117).

Any intuition in *Volpone* that disease is exogenous matter rather than a complexional state is arguably entangled with the play's presentation of drugs and other imported commodities as dangerous pathogens. When Volpone attempts to seduce Celia, she responds with a revealing request:

> flay my face,
> Or poison it, with ointments, for seducing
> Your blood to this rebellion. Rub these hands,
> With what may cause an eating leprosy,
> E'en to my bones, and marrow . . . (3.7.252–56)

Celia's retort comes after Volpone has offered her a "rope of pearl," whose every bead is "more orient than that the brave Egyptian queen caroused" (3.7.191–92). Thus in a revealing trajectory of displacement, she substitutes his exotic commodity with first apothecary "ointments" and then a contagious disease ("an eating leprosy") whose symptoms are redolent of that famously migratory transnational ailment, syphilis.[65]

By far and away the most vivid conflation of disease and the goods of foreign trade is offered by Sir Politic Would-Be. The English knight-tourist is a font of get-rich-quick schemes, all of which entail profiting from the dynamics of foreign trade. One of his more far-fetched yet compelling schemes concerns the detection of plague:

> How t'enquire, and be resolved,
> By present demonstration, whether a ship,
> Newly arrived from Soria, or from
> Any suspected part of all the Levant,
> Be guilty of the plague. (4.2.100–104)

Importantly, Sir Pol imagines plague here as a commodity literally shipped in from the Orient. This mercantilized conception of the disease, redolent as it is of Bright's and Milles's images of pathological cargo from the Americas and the East Indies, is a far cry from the orthodox providential and miasmic explanations that I have examined earlier in this chapter. What is most striking about Sir Pol's image of the plague as a "thing in motion" is how it mobilizes the tropes and practices of mercantilist protection as a means of disease prevention. Regarding plague as transmigratory matter rather than as a state of complexional imbalance or as a miasmic distemper allows him to imagine physically containing it:

> First, I bring in your ship, 'twixt two brick walls;
> (But those the state shall venture) on the one
> I strain me a fair tarpaulin; and, in that,
> I stick my onions, cut in halves: the other
> Is full of loop-holes, out at which, I thrust
> The noses of my bellows; and, those bellows
> I keep, with water-works, in perpetual motion,
> (Which is the easiest matter of a hundred).

Now, sir, your onion, which doth naturally
Attract th'infection, and your bellows, blowing
The air upon him, will show (instantly)
By his changed colour, if there be contagion,
Or else, remain as fair, as at the first. (4.1.113–25)

Sir Pol's ingenious contagion detector draws on the conventional folk remedy of onions for plague.[66] But there is much more than simple convention at work here. As transmigratory foreign matter, disease is for Sir Pol subject to the equivalent of customs and passport control as it crosses national borders (" 'twixt two brick walls" that "the state shall venture"); it is, in other words, a *measurable quantity*. In this Milles-like fantasy of surveillance and containment at the body politic's "outport," then, pathology has become an explicitly political as well as a mercantile phenomenon.

The cultural meanings of the port are crucial to Sir Pol's mercantilized conception of plague. As Michel Foucault notes in *Discipline and Punish*, ports acquired a special status as sites of boundary confusion during the global mercantile expansion of the seventeenth and eighteenth centuries: "A port . . . is—with its circulation of goods, men signed up willingly or by force, sailors embarking and disembarking, diseases and epidemics—a place of desertion, smuggling, contagion: it is a crossroads for dangerous mixtures, a meeting-place for forbidden circulations."[67] This makes clear how the port was seen as the site for "dangerous mixtures" and "forbidden circulations" of not only goods and individuals but also diseases: the port, in other words, was where the economic and the pathological most clearly intermingled.[68] Indeed, at the time Jonson wrote *Volpone*, Venetian authorities were highly attuned to the possibility of such intermingling. The quarantine system had been developed in Venice during the fourteenth century specifically to deal with the threat of plague: the term derives from *quarentina*, or "forty"—the number of days that individuals arriving in Venice from plague-stricken areas would be isolated by the city authorities. Quarantine regulations were targeted at merchant travelers and ships suspected of carrying the disease; the pathological and the economic, in other words, were thoroughly freighted in the city's laws.[69]

For Sir Pol, though, it is not just the port of the Venetian body politic that is prone to pathologized incursion. He also imagines the port of London as the site of attempted economic subversion by the enemy Spaniards, whom he accuses of planting a whale in the Thames in order to sabotage the returning fleet of the English Merchant Adventurers (2.1.44–52). This underscores the ambiguity of the port in *Volpone*: it is the necessary outlet for any nation's foreign trade, but it is also what makes that nation most vulnerable to external threats. Jonson takes this fantasy to ridiculous extremes with Sir Pol's conviction that Stone, the well-known London fool, was a dangerous spy in cahoots with sinister Continental agents.[70] The subversions with which Stone is entangled are imaged by Sir Pol as the hidden contents of transmigratory cargo shipped into England from the Netherlands:

SIR POLITIC
   He has received weekly intelligence,
   Upon my knowledge, out of the Low Countries,
   For all parts of the world, in cabbages;
   And those dispensed, again, t'ambassadors,
   In oranges, musk-melons, apricots,
   Lemons, pome-citrons, and such-like: sometimes
   In Colchester oysters, and your Selsey cockles.
PEREGRINE
   You make me wonder!
SIR POLITIC
   Sir, upon my knowledge,
   Nay, I have observed him, at your public ordinary,
   Take his advertisement, from a traveller
   (A concealed statesman) in a trencher of meat;
   And, instantly, before the meal was done,
   Convey an answer in a toothpick.
PEREGRINE
   Strange!
   How could this be, sir?
SIR POLITIC
   Why, the meat was cut
   So like his character, and so laid, as he
   Must easily read the cipher.
PEREGRINE
   He could not read, sir.
SIR POLITIC
   So 'twas given out
   In polity, by those that did employ him . . . (2.1.68–85)

In this exchange as much as in his plan for "outport" plague detection, Sir Pol emerges as the satirical doppelgänger of Thomas Milles. Both moonlight in the intercepting of supposed intelligence; both represent economic and political sabotage in the language of dietary pharmacy and pathology; both finger the Merchant Adventurers as leading players in the drama of England's infiltration by toxic foreign bodies; and both entertain fantasies of increasing the nation's profit through customslike surveillance of "things in motion." As Milles's fantasy about England's abandoned custom houses and Sir Pol's fantasy about

Venetian harbor pestilence detectors make clear, moreover, both imagine the commercial as well as pathological threats posed to their ports of residence as plagues "sailing into port," whose transmigrations parallel the global movements of those exotic commodities—in particular, drugs and spices—to which their fellow countrymen and -women are so partial.[71]

Even as he satirizes Sir Pol's and, by extension, Thomas Milles's paranoid theories about plaguy incursion through the body politic's ports, Jonson lends fuel to them. For if *Volpone*'s most corrosive satire is of its English characters, it is because of the latter's contamination by foreign agents—whether manners, goods, or ideas. In an important speech, Lady Politic Would-Be lectures Volpone about the pathological consequences of "incorporating" foreign bodies:

in politic bodies,
There's nothing, more, doth overwhelm the judgment,
And clouds the understanding, than too much
Settling, and fixing, and (as't were) subsiding
Upon one object. For the incorporating
Of these same outward things, into that part,
Which we call mental, leaves some certain faeces
That stop the organs, and, as Plato says,
Assassinates our knowledge. (3.4.104–12)

Lady Politic Would-Be's is a "politic body" in point: Jonson evidently wants us to view her as suffering from "assassinate[d] knowledge" as a result of her fatuous obsession with, and consumption of, fashionable "outward things" from around the world. A pathological discourse subtly haunts Lady Pol's account of the noxious effects of "incorporating" such "things" into "politic bodies." The etiology of mental illness that Lady Pol sketches involves a muddled adaptation not only of Plato[72] but also of humoral theory; as Michael Schoenfeldt has noted, "faeces" was a common seventeenth-century synonym for phlegm. The term, however, is itself part of a lexicon of illness that entailed an altogether different, ontological understanding of disease. The example cited by Schoenfeldt of phlegmatic "faeces" is taken from the *Utrusque Cosmi* (1619) of the English Paracelsan Robert Fludd, who, like his mentor, understood disease to take the form of exogenous *spiritus mali*.[73] With his choice of terminology, then, Jonson arguably makes Lady Politic Would-Be stray yet farther from Galenic convention and, like her husband, pay powerful homage to the pathological properties of foreign "things in motion"—be they spices, drugs, or the plague.

Infected Cargo

Lady Pol's version of Plato typifies Jonson's satirical strategy throughout the play. The dollops of bowdlerized classical philosophy that his characters dish up—Nano's version of Pythagoras's doctrine of metempsychosis as much as Lady Pol's version of Plato's physiology—are occasions for comedy. Yet, upon closer inspection, each can be seen to possess a larger validity in *Volpone*'s play-world, where matter ceaselessly transmigrates, often with pathological effects. Indeed, both Nano's updated Pythagoras and Lady Pol's bogus Plato serve as templates for Sir Pol's ontological paradigm of plague as matter in motion, one that notably departs from the humoralism of Jonson's earlier plays.

What ultimately enables Jonson's articulation of this new paradigm, however, is neither his satirical reworking of classical philosophy nor any more "scientific" understanding of disease that he may have acquired in the decade after he wrote *Every Man in His Humor* (c. 1598). Rather, as I have shown through my readings of Timothy Bright's and Thomas Milles's protectionist narratives, *Volpone*'s universe of transmigratory pathological matter is of a piece with the dawning universe of global, transoceanic economy. "Sailing to port" in early modern mercantile Europe as much as in Jonson's Venice and London always potentially entailed an interleaving of the economic and the pathological. Such interleaving may be witnessed in one of the subsequent meanings of "infection": in seventeenth-century legal discourse, an "infected" ship was one carrying contraband cargo between nations.[74] The transmigratory goods and diseases that *Volpone* fantasizes, therefore, were mutually determining phenomena: each provided the other with one of its constitutive grounds of possibility.

In this chapter, I have considered the linked discourses of goods and plague sailing *into* the body politic. "Sailing to port" was the natural concern of the bullionist generation of mercantilists, Gerard Malynes and Thomas Milles, who were obsessed with the alleged threats presented to the nation by foreign agents such as Dutch financiers and the exotic goods brought back to England by the Merchant Adventurers. In both cases, the purported threats entailed a usurpation of national sovereignty with regard to the production and valuation of the nation's wealth. For Malynes, the legitimate source of money's value was the king, firmly situated at the center of the body politic; foreign bankers illegitimately depleted England's treasure by undervaluing its currency. Milles adapted and partially displaced Malynes's more absolutist position by arguing for the economic importance of the customs officer situated at the nation's margins; yet for Milles, the authority of the outport customer was undermined by the covert machinations of the regulated companies, who, by shipping foreign trifles directly to London, avoided paying customs duties and thereby deprived the state of revenue.

But what about those mercantilists affiliated with the regulated and joint-stock companies, who were concerned with merchants sailing *out* of rather than *into* port? For such writers, bullion was accumulated less through the institutions of the crown such as the mint, the royal exchange, or the custom houses than through the efforts of individual merchants and associations of capital. How did this decentralization of the origins of the body politic's "lifeblood"— a recurrent metaphor, as we will see—square with the more absolutist creed of the bullionists? How did it influence understandings of physiology and pathology? And how may the latter also have helped shape the former? To answer these questions, the next chapter examines an important exchange between Gerard Malynes and one of the so-called balance-of-trade mercantilists—the deputy governor of the Merchant Adventurers' Company at Delft, Edward Misselden.

Hepatitis/Castration and Treasure: Edward Misselden, Gerard Malynes, The Fair Maid of the West, The Renegado

"Treasure" is a key term in two seemingly distinct genres: novels about pirates, as suggested by the title of Robert Louis Stevenson's *Treasure Island;* and early modern mercantilist writing, exemplified by Thomas Mun's *Englands Treasure by Forraign Trade.* To the twenty-first-century reader, the two genres can seem worlds apart. The plunder of fantastical pirates—stowed in the holds of Spanish galleons or buried on the shores of faraway desert isles—is the stuff of romance, measured in glittering pieces of eight and precious stones. The treasure of the early modern nation-state, by contrast, might at first appear altogether less glamorous. As numerically recorded in customs books, assizes of the mint, and the royal treasury accounts, seventeenth-century English wealth would seem to possess the abstract banality of the modern GDP. Yet such a view projects onto early modern English treasure the more disembodied forms that wealth now takes in the age of finance capital. Before the invention of paper money and electronic credit, the English nation's treasure was embodied—and repeatedly imagined—in forms that are indistinguishable from those of its pirate literature cousin. In this chapter, I argue that the seventeenth-century genre of pirate drama is throughly inflected by mercantilist discourse, particularly the latter's corporeal vocabularies of treasure.

Two early modern English plays whose plots dramatize privateering and corsair plunder off the Barbary Coast—the first part of Thomas Heywood's *Fair Maid of the West* (c. 1600) and Philip Massinger's *Renegado* (1623)—make explicit the links between the treasure of pirate literature and that of mercantilism. These links are in some ways transparently obvious: in both genres, the capture and plunder of European merchant ships in North African waters is represented as criminally depriving Christian nations of bullion by diverting it into the private coffers of renegado corsairs or the public treasuries of Barbary potentates. Yet early modern English pirate drama's mercantilist co-texts can also help illuminate a seemingly unrelated, and puzzling, preoccupation shared by Heywood's and Massinger's plays: the castration of Christians in Barbary Coast states. This preoccupation has been read as a distinguishing feature of early modern English Orientalist discourse about Islam and forced apostasy. I wish to read it less for what it may reveal about English attitudes toward North African religion and identity, however, than for how it is symptomatic of mercantilism's embodied conceptions of treasure, bullion flow, and the state.

These conceptions are repeatedly articulated in both mercantilist writing and pirate drama by recourse to medical language. Castration is, of course, a task performed by surgeons and their razors; hence the plays brim with predictable jokes and puns about Barbary barbers. But the procedure also falls under the purview of Renaissance physiology and pathology, linked as it is to theories current in the early seventeenth century about the circulation of the blood, the sources of the body's vital spirits, and the diseases of both. This is a period of great interest to medical historians, largely because the longstanding contest between Galenists and Aristotelians over which organ is the source of the blood (Galen argued for the liver; Aristotle favored the heart) was settled in 1628 with the publication of William Harvey's *De Motu Cordis,* in which he first announced his discovery of the circulation of the blood. Notably, the physiology of blood is also at the heart (or liver) of one of the most important exchanges of early English mercantilism: the pamphlet war of 1622–23 between Edward Misselden and Gerard Malynes, in which the two writers violently clashed over the causes of the decay of England's treasure. Misselden initially diagnosed the crisis as a "hepatitis" draining the body politic of its "lifeblood," or treasure, a condition that he partly attributed to Barbary piracy; Malynes responded with a fierce defense of what he believed constituted the virile "center" of a corporeally conceived commerce.

When read alongside the pirate plays, early modern medical and mercantilist debates about the physiology of treasure show how premodern fantasies of hepatitis and castration are informed by a decidedly different array of assumptions from those that underwrite their modern counterparts. Nevertheless, these fantasies also point to recognizably modern habits of medical and economic thought: namely, the attribution of diseases to foreign bodies and the naturalization of the global as the neutral medium of transnational commerce. "Treasure" is the overdetermined term through which such new conceptions of the medical and the mercantile were voiced. In the process, early modern English writers recast the Mediterranean's bloody robber seamen, and their Barbary masters, as robbers of the nation's blood and semen.

Misselden Versus Malynes: The Physiology of Treasure

The motor of early modern English economic growth was its cloth trade. With the patents granted by Queen Elizabeth to the Merchant Adventurers Company to control the export of unfinished cloths, overseas sales soared in the late sixteenth and early seventeenth centuries, and domestic productivity increased exponentially to meet the demand. The trade enjoyed an *annus mirabilis* in 1614, when the volume of textile production and export reached an all-time high. Five years later, however, this golden age had turned to brass. Textile production and retailing suffered a dramatic slump; by the early 1620s, England was also faced with a profound bullion shortage that helped precipitate a more general business depression. Modern economic historians have adduced multiple reasons for the crisis, including severe currency debasements in two of England's principal clothing markets, Poland and Germany.[1] Early modern English writers themselves generated considerable heat speculating about the causes of the depression. Most contentious was the bruising print exchange between two of the more prominent mercantilist thinkers, Edward Misselden and Gerard Malynes.

The exchange was initiated by Misselden, the deputy governor of the Merchant Adventurers at Delft, with the publication of his treatise *Free Trade, Or the Meanes to Make Trade Florish* (1622). Not surprisingly, his primary mission seems to have been to exculpate the Merchant Adventurers of responsibility for the crisis. Misselden delivers a long justification of the company's commercial practices and defends them against the charges of monopoly that, as we saw in the previous chapter, Thomas Milles had leveled two decades previously. He instead attributes the shortage of English treasure—which he terms a "hepatitis"—to several causes.[2] Some of these recall Malynes's earlier analysis of value and coin in *The Canker of England's Commonwealth*. Like Malynes, Misselden agrees that English coin is undervalued, which inflates the prices of foreign goods and encourages the flow of bullion out of the country. Unlike Malynes, however, he does not regard this undervaluation as a plot by scheming foreign bankers. "For it is not the rate of Exchanges," Misselden argues, "but the value of monies, here lowe, elsewhere high, which cause their Exportation: nor doe the Exchanges, but the plenty or scarcity of monies cause their values" (sig. H5). For Misselden, then, the value of money is not intrinsically fixed, nor can it be stabilized by a central authority or sovereign will; rather, it is subject to the uncontrollable ebb and flow of transnational commerce.

Nevertheless, Misselden does see certain aspects of transnational commerce as needing intervention, and to this end he identifies two chief causes of the loss of treasure—one domestic, the other foreign. The domestic cause is the export of English bullion by the East India Company, which received a license to transport treasure for the purchase of much-coveted foreign wares, including many of the drugs and spices I examined in the last chapter. Compounding the problem was the company's ongoing battle with the Dutch in the East Indies; by 1622, the Dutch had detained the English stock in Amboyna.[3] According to Misselden, the resulting loss of treasure and revenue had caused "the *body* of this *Common-wealth* to be wounded sore, through the *sides* of many particular members thereof" (sig. B7)—a corporeal image that seems to invoke less the depredations of hepatitis than of mutilation or castration.

For Misselden, however, the East India Company's dealings are not the only drain on the reserves of national treasure. The immediate foreign cause of the crisis, he argues, is Mediterranean piracy:

I will instance the warres of the *Pirats* of *Argier* and *Tunis,* which hath robbed this Common-wealth of an infinite value: the *crueltie* whereof many feele with *griefe*, others heare with *pittie,* but the *grieuance* remaine's. Needs must *Christendome,* and in it *England,* feele the want of money, when either it is violently intercepted by *Turkish Pirats,* the Enimies of *God* and *man*; or the instruments surprised, as *men, ships,* and *merchandize,* which are the channels to convey it to us. (sig. C1v)

Misselden refers here to Barbary corsairs, pirates operating from North African ports. These "Enimies of *God* and *man*" would seem to pose a very different threat to the nation's treasure from that represented by the East India Company. Yet, in Misselden's analysis, the two threats are intimately linked. Both entail the flow of bullion, not just out of England, but also beyond the pale of Christian polity:

For although the trades within *Christendome* are driuen with ready monies, yet those monies are still *contained* and *continued* within the bounds of *Christendome.* There is indeede a *fluxus* and *refluxus,* a *flood* and *ebbe* of the monies of *Christendome* traded within it selfe: for sometimes there is more in one part of *Christendome,* sometimes there is lesse in another, as one countrey wanteth, and another aboundeth: It commeth and goeth, and whirleth about the *Circle* of *Christendome,* but is still contained with the compasse thereof. But the money that is traded out of *Christendome* into the parts aforesaid, is continually issued out and never returneth againe. (sigs. C2–C2v)

In what amounts to a proleptic (if explicitly religious) fantasy of the European Union, Misselden condones the flow of treasure out of England only so long as it goes to other Christian nations, from which it will inevitably return according to the laws of bullion's "*flood* and *ebbe.*" Implicit in this fantasy, of course, is yet another defense of the Merchant Adventurers' commercial practices. Because the company exports cloth to the Continent and spends money on wares retailed by European merchants, Misselden implies, the Merchant Adventurers ensure the movement of bullion through a closed circuit of Christian exchange.

For all that Misselden's view of money's value and motion diverged from Malynes's, he might have avoided the latter's ire had he not openly critiqued the by now two decades old *Canker of England's Commonwealth* in a throwaway remark at the end of the pamphlet.[4] Malynes, stung, replied a few months later with a pamphlet of his own called *The Maintenance of Free Trade.* In it, he presented a boiled-down version of his earlier arguments in *Canker* and *Lex Mercatoria,* including a spirited defense of his pet project: the "true par of exchange," that is, fixed exchange rates based on the instrinsic metal value of nations' currencies. According to Malynes, Misselden had entirely missed the point. Malynes does not discount Misselden's arguments about the impact on England's economic health of the East India Company's bullion exports or the Barbary corsairs' raids. But he insists that even if England were to regain the treasure it has lost to the orient and North Africa, its wealth would continue to decay: "if *Pirates* did not take some of our monyes, it followeth not, that the same should come vnto vs *in specie.*"[5] Why? Because what Malynes terms "the overbalancing" of value—his old canard that foreign bankers and merchants manipulate exchange rates to increase their own profits—ensures the loss of English treasure. The only infallible nostrum for this quandary, he argues, is the imposition of "true par."

The next salvo in the quarrel was fired by Misselden, who answered Malynes with a second and longer treatise, *The Circle of Commerce.* This work's title refers to a well-known story about the artist Giotto, who drew a perfect circle without the help of a compass. Misselden thus implies that a perfect theory of commerce does not need a center like Malynes's conception of "par," which he laughingly ridicules as a "quacksalvers' . . . *Panchreston,*" or cure-all. Instead, Misselden once again insists on the mutable value of all commodities, including money: "*The plentie or scarcitie of moneys . . .* perpetually doth cause the Exchanges to rise and fall: and . . . doth as certainely, in forraine parts where monies goe vncertaine, rule their *Values* or denomination, as the plenty or scarcity of Commodities doth their *Price.*"[6] In one crucial respect, however, Misselden's argument is different from that of his first treatise. Since the publication of *Free Trade,* Misselden had worked on behalf of the East India Company as a mediator in its standoff with the Dutch. He thus recants his earlier critique of the company and instead chalks up England's depression to a poor balance of trade—the first time, in fact, that the theory was explicitly articulated in an economic treatise.

Malynes's reply, *The Center of the Circle of Commerce,* stubbornly reiterates his commitment to the doctrine of par. Malynes complains that Misselden's theory of bullion flow, like Giotto's circle, lacks a governing center. In a sense he is right. Misselden radically decentralizes transnational commerce by suggesting that abundance and scarcity, not imperial fiat, determine the value of money. To Malynes, however, the absence of a determining sovereign will in economic matters—as we saw in Chapter 4—is scandalous. He discounts the obvious objection that the balance of trade is Misselden's de facto center of commerce: "I answer, this imaginary Ballance is without a Parallell, as his Circle is without a Center; and may rather be termed the periphery or circumference of his Circle."[7] According to Malynes, a good balance of trade cannot by itself stem the loss of treasure. Instead, he proposes that the true center of commerce is "gain" on the level playing field of "par."

Malynes finishes his pamphlet with a lengthy allegory of the diseased body politic, one that in its vision of the nation's sick *"Hepaties"* would seem to affirm Misselden's initial diagnosis of the body politic's hepatitis.[8] Yet, for most commentators, it is clear how much the two writers diverged, not only in what they said, but also in how they said it. Economic historians such as Joyce Oldham Appleby have emphasized how the more modern-minded Misselden replaced Malynes's medieval cosmology, organized in relation to fixed points of value, with a new universe of flux and uncertainty.[9] Other scholars, following Michel Foucault, have also pointed out a more profound epistemological break performed by Misselden's economic writing. Despite the striking pathological metaphor with which he begins *Free Trade,* Misselden increasingly disregards the old analogies of microcosm and macrocosm in favor of a new discourse. Speaking of the balance of trade, for example, he says that "wee see it to our griefe, that wee are fallen into a great *Vnder-ballance of Trade* with other Nations. Wee felt it before in sense; but now we know it by science."[10] As Mary Poovey has argued, Misselden's "science" presumes an alternative epistemology founded less in analogy than in numerical representation. In *The Circle of Commerce,* he adapts the merchant's practice of double-entry bookkeeping to represent the nation's income and expenses. As a result, Poovey argues, Misselden's economic science takes a decisive step towards becoming the disembodied discourse based on quantitative analysis that it is today.[11]

Nevertheless, this epistemic rupture is neither as dramatic nor as total as Poovey's brilliant argument makes it out to be. Misselden might illustrate his theory of the balance of trade by invoking the logic of the double-entry ledger, but his writing is suffused with traditional modes of knowledge production. More from rhetorical expedience than from epistemological dogmatism, Misselden resorts to whichever textual strategy of legitimation happens to fit his argument at any given moment. Hence he uses corporeal analogies when they suit him. Likewise, Malynes employs numerical modes of representation when they serve his ends. Far more important than the two writers' competing modes of knowledge production—whether analogical or "scientific"—is that for all their disagreements about the causes of the decay of England's treasure, Misselden still advocates a transnational typology that Malynes more or less shares: foreign bodies (Muslim pirates or Continental bankers) are dangerous; yet global trade remains commerce's natural medium. And for all that Misselden's double-entry tables help illustrate this typology, both writers' favored mode of rhetorical legitimation—as Andrea Finkelstein has rightly noted—is corporeal analogy.[12] To obtain a better sense of the different ways in which such analogies work in the two writers' texts, I will examine more closely the disease that Misselden first invokes to represent the decay of England's treasure and that Malynes loosely adapts for his allegory of the diseased body politic: hepatitis.

Hepatitis as we now know it—an inflammation of the liver usually caused by any of five viruses (A, B, C, D, or E) or by drug or alcohol abuse—was not part of the early modern English or European medical lexicon. According to the OED, the first instance of the term appears in the mid-eighteenth century, though it was then associated not with any specific infection or epidemic condition but with generic liver damage and pleurisy.[13] Ailments of the liver were recorded in early modern England, but these are usually of a very different order from what we now think of as hepatitis. Gervase Markham, for example, asserts that "diuers diseases are supposed to proceed from the Liuer," all of which he attributes to "the grossenes of humors."[14] Andrew Boorde likewise notes that the liver has "dyuers and many infirmyties"; principal among the latter is "heat," for which he prescribes liverwort and the bleeding of two or three ounces of blood from the hepatic vein in the arm.[15] Even the more "scientific" William Harvey echoes the Parisian anatomist Jean Riolan the Elder's assertion, that a "special society" exists between head and liver, and those with head wounds are likely to have abcesses in the liver. He also associates the organ with hiccups.[16] What we would now call hepatitis, distinguished by various symptoms such as yellowing eyes and skin, high fever, swollen abdomen, and wasting of the body, overlapped but did not quite coincide with a variety of early modern pathological conditions: jaundice, distemper, dropsy, and consumption. "Hepatitis," in other words, was the invention of a later generation of physicians.[17]

What, then, is the object that Misselden calls "hepatitis"? Analogically juxtaposing the decay of trade with a diseased body, he writes in *Free Trade* that "thus the *Hepatitis* of this *great Body* of ours being opened, & such profusions of the *life blood* let out; and the *liuer* or fountaine *obstructed*, and weakened, which should succour the same; needes must this *great Body languish*, and at length fall into a *Marasmum*" (sig. B5v). This passage provides an outstanding example of how early modern discourses of economic pathology provided one of the horizons within which the objects of later medical "discoveries" could first be constituted. As Misselden uses it in this passage, the term seems to be his coinage, derived from *hepar,* the Greek word for liver. Hence he conceives of hepatitis as a problem afflicting the body politic's metaphorical liver and entailing a "great *Marasmum*" (from the Greek *marasmos,* wasting away) of the nation's "*life blood,*" money. The disease is not caused, as modern hepatitis is, by an invading entity; instead, it stems from a depletion forced largely by foreign agents, including infidel pirates. And this depletion presumes a usurpation or displacement of the nominal center of national wealth production, represented in Misselden's analogy by the liver.

The notion that the liver is the chief organ controlling the production and flow of the blood might strike the modern reader as counterintuitive. But Misselden's discourse of economic pathology in this passage lends voice to the conventional Galenic physiology of his time. Writing in polemical opposition to Erasistratus, who, like his teacher Aristotle, had held that the heart is the sole origin of the blood, Galen taught that the latter is instead formed in the liver. After raw food is digested in the stomach, the refined portion, or chyle, is conveyed through the portal vein into the liver, where it undergoes a second concoction and, completely purified, becomes venous blood, or "natural spirit." From the liver, the venous blood is transported through the veins (Galen's specific term for blood vessels originating in the liver) to all the parts of the body. The heart, according to Galen, is the organ where venous blood is exposed to air from the lungs, which carries the basic principle of life, *pneuma*; as a consequence, the venous blood is further concocted into arterial blood, or "vital spirit," and distributed through the arteries (i.e., vessels originating in the heart). The heart may perform a more refining function in Galenic physiology, therefore, but it remains chronologically secondary to the liver.[18] Most early modern English physicians subscribed to this Galenic hierarchy of the organs. According to Andrew Boorde, "a veine is a cundite that doth conteine the principal bloud in man, takyng theyr original or begynnyng of the lyuer."[19] Helkiah Crooke went so far as to provide a spurious etymology for the liver to emphasize its primacy: "the Liuer is called in Greeke *hepar,* from a word that signifieth *Want,* because it supplyeth the want of al the parts."[20] For those who belong to an age inured to the circulation of blood, it is easy to overlook the extent to which, prior to the publication of William Harvey's *De Motu Cordis* in 1628, the cardiocentric Aristotelian physiology was largely overshadowed by its hepacentric Galenic rival.

Misselden was not the only economic writer who parroted conventional Galenic lore to explain the origins of the the body politic's lifeblood. Barnabe Barnes compares the liver to the High Treasurer;[21] Thomas Milles writes that "the Cittie of LONDON, as the Liuer on the body receiuing the *Chylus* from all parts of the Stomacke, by detaining the bloud from the rest of the veines, is both inflamed & distempered in it selfe, and iniurious withall to all her fellow Members."[22] The most extensive mercantilist adaptation of Galenic physiology to explain the physiology of treasure appears in Gerard Malynes's *Center of the Circle of Trade*. In an extended allegory, Malynes compares the state of English trade to a diseased body. A team of economic physicians forensically scrutinizes the patient:

Considering the internal parts, they found the liuer (*Money*) obstructed, and the condinct pipes of *Bullion* and *Moneys* for importation stopt, whereby the *Hepaties* could not minister good bloud, with spirits sufficient to comfort the heart of (*our natiue commodities*) by a naturalle heate: for the gaule of *Customes and impositions* is ouerflown also, depriuing the stomacke of his appetie [sic]: hence the braine (*Exchange,* wanting sleepe) is distempered, whereby the body is ouertaken with a *trepidation* or shaking, shewing the very *Symptomes* of death.[23]

This passage, and the three pages of allegory that follow it, foreground the mercantilist tendency to embody treasure analogically. The sick liver, or *"Hepaties,"* is as readily available a metaphor for Malynes as it is for Misselden. The difference is that Malynes develops the metaphor to locate a privileged place for the par of exchange within a centralized national economy: "the obstruction of the Liuer, (*Money,* and the conduict Pipes of Spanish Royalls and Germaine Dollers) must be opened by the meanes of the Braine, (*Exchange*) to minister good Bloud and Spirits to the Heart of our natiue *Commodities,* to make a liuely Trade."[24]

As this diagnosis may suggest, hepatitis serves Malynes and his vision of national economy better than it does Misselden. After all, hepatitis—at least when understood as the pathology of a Galenic physiology of the blood—presumes a bodily center and thus lends itself well to the vision of national economy articulated by Malynes, who seeks to locate the origins of England's lifeblood within central institutions: the mint and the royal treasury. Bullion may derive ultimately from outside the body—as do those imported "Spanish Royalls and Germaine Dollers"—but it needs to be minted (or, in Galenic terms, concocted) by the liver before it can become the nation's lifeblood. Misselden, by contrast, embraces a much more decentralized understanding of the national economy's lifeblood—and in this respect, it is significant that he never equates the liver with any specific institution in the body politic.

It is perhaps equally significant that in his later *Circle of Commerce*, where he elaborates in more detail his decentralized conception of bullion flow, Misselden makes no reference to hepatitis. But he does analogically resort to the physiology of blood, if only indirectly. Misselden's conception of the "circle of commerce," which has been characterized as the exemplum of a mathematical rather than an analogical epistemology, has an easily overlooked corporeal dimension. Prior to Harvey's discovery of circulation, the circle was a powerful and recurrent figure in Aristotelian cosmology—one of the reasons Harvey may have been predisposed to look for the circulation of the blood in the first place. Earlier physicians, influenced by Aristotle, had proposed a rudimentary theory of the circulation of the blood, which they saw as ebbing and flowing like the tides.[25] This very analogy appears in Misselden's account in *Free Trade* of the *"fluxus and refluxus"* or *"flood* and *ebbe* of the monies of *Christendome"* (sig. C2). Misselden's Aristotelian vocabulary of circles and flows, together with Malynes's stated objection to it ("I am not to follow your method of circulation"), implies a corporeally embodied conception of money and its movement.[26] Yet despite the cardiocentric baggage of this alternative physiology, the doctrine of "circulation" allows Misselden to reimagine national economy as no longer grounded in a central institution such as the royal treasury or the exchange. In his analysis, as we have seen, wealth circulates less within the body politic than in and out of the nation according to global laws of scarcity and abundance.

Such a view has potentially subversive political implications. Not only does it suggest that the national economy is subject to systemic forces beyond the control of princes; it also elevates the status of merchant venturers, who are largely responsible for the transnational flows of goods and bullion. Even as mercantilist discourse yoked the interests of merchants and the crown, the alliance was always potentially an uneasy one; and whereas bullionist state employees (Malynes, the master of the mint; Milles, the customer of Sandwich) sought to subordinate the accumulation, valuation, and circulation of treasure to the sovereign will of the prince, those mercantilist writers who served the regulated or joint-stock companies often lent more naked expression to the private interests of the merchant venturers.[27] Little wonder that the more staunchly bureaucratic Malynes pronounced Misselden's theory of circulation to have no center; little wonder too that he partially appropriated the latter's Galenic theory of hepatitis to illustrate his own centralized conception of the true par of exchange.

As my analysis of Misselden's and Malynes's physiologies of treasure has made clear, their divergent forms of "hepatitis" are not ours. Each is grounded in the Galenic notion that the liver is the central organ controlling the production and flow of the blood; each also implies the agency not of an invasive organism, as modern viral hepatitis does, but of foreign elements outside the body that leech it of its lifeblood. I would like to develop the implications of this physiological analysis to suggest that "hepatitis" in both Misselden's and Malynes's writing also hints at another corporeal analogy for the loss of national treasure to foreign agents: castration. And this second analogy, latent as it may be, fits both writers' visions of national economy—Malynes's centralized one, inasmuch as it allows him to represent the loss of treasure as proceeding from the failure or absence of central monetary organs; but equally Misselden's decentralized one, because it permits him to represent the loss of treasure as an act of piratical violence against English merchants abroad, independent of royal authority and its economic institutions.

Castration: The Physiology of Purse Cutting

In our post-Freudian age, we tend overwhelmingly to imagine castration under the sign of the penis. But as Gary Taylor reminds us in his important study, *Castration: An Abbreviated History of Manhood,* Freud's account of castration is literally an urban legend.[28] Freud was writing as one of the first generation of European city dwellers who outnumbered their country cousins. Anyone born and raised in the largely agricultural economy of early modern England knew, however, that animal castration involves removal not of the penis but of the testicles. This, as we will see, is how castration is almost invariably imagined in early modern English writing, where the loss of "stones"—the most common name for the testes—is a recurrent obsession.[29] In a way that the excision of the penis did not, the removal of the testes fell very much into the provinces of Renaissance physiology and pathology. In particular, medical writing about castration was concerned with theories of the sanguineous form of semen and the unhealthy consequences of its loss.

Thomas Laqueur and Gail Kern Paster have shown how the physiology of the humors entailed a highly fungible economy of the body's fluids, especially the blood.[30] Hippocrates had argued that semen, like the froth of the sea, was a foam concocted from the blood. Aristotle likewise regarded *sperma* as refined blood, as did Galen. If Hippocrates and Aristotle saw the semen as the *end* point in a process of sanguineous refinement that led to generation, though, Galen saw the semen as the *origin* of the male body's perfection.[31] The loss of semen, therefore, entailed a crippling or effeminization of the male body. This is the assumption implicit in Shakespeare's "the expense of spirit in a waste of shame," where the narrator equates ejaculation with the wasteful/waistful spending of his body's life force, or spirit.[32] Such was the power of the semen that Galen sometimes included the testes, or *orcheis* (a term that famously denoted ovaries as well as testicles), among the body's principal organs, ranking them with the heart for their ability to infuse heat and spirit throughout the body.[33]

The Galenic view of the semen is crucial to an important early modern English account of the testes and castration. Helkiah Crooke's *Microcosmographia* (1618) was published just four years before Misselden and Malynes's debate; as I will argue, it shares much discursive ground with the latter. In a mammoth anatomical tome that seeks to offer exhaustive accounts of the various parts of the body and their functions, Crooke devotes an exceptionally large amount of space to the testicles—even more than he does to the penis.[34] His attitudes are for the most part conventionally Galenic. He endorses Galen's view that the testicular seed is sanguineous; noting that many have asked how the testicles can be "nourished" with blood, Crooke asserts, "I answere, as the Paps are nourished with Milke; for their bloud is not red but turned into Milke and Seed" (201). Like Galen, Crooke also argues that the testicles are principal organs to be ranked with—and in his opinion, even to be ranked *above*—the liver and the heart, because of the vital influence they have on these organs, and hence the rest of the body: "the Testicles haue no peculiar vessels by which they might deriue their influence into the whole body; but they impart this power and faculty of alteration, to the heart by the arteries, to the Liuer by the veines; from which it is againe reinfused into the particular members" (243). In Crooke's version of Galenism, then, the testicles become the *Arche,* or the origin of the body's life force—the liver that precedes the liver.

Unlike Shakespeare, Crooke illustrates the debilitating loss of testicular "spirit" by recourse not to the *petit mort* of ejaculation but to the living death of the eunuch. In his first section on the testes, he asserts, "They adde also to the body much strength and heate as appeareth by Eunuches, whose temperament, substance, habit and dispositions are all altered" (207). Crooke advances a similar argument in a section devoted to the controversies over the testes. To prove his Galenic conviction that the testes are principal organs that "make the body fruitefull, but also in the alteration of the temperament, the habit, the proper substance of the body, yea & of the maners themselues" (241), he again instances the example of the eunuch: "We see also that in gelt men called Eunuches, there is a change of the whole habite and proper substance of the body . . . the flower also of their blood decayeth and their vessels or veines loose their bredth and capacity, and all vigor . . . is extinguished" (242). In crucial fashion, then, Crooke's belief in the testes' immense power is predicated on fantasies of their removal. The loss of the testes cripples the body's hepatic economy by robbing it of not only its central motor but also its ability to engage in "fruitefull" exchange with the outside world—specifically, the business of "generation."

To represent the "vigor" generated by the testes, Crooke employs an arresting analogy: "in these doth *Galen* place, beside that in the heart, another hearth as it were of the inbred heate, and these are the houshold Goodes which doe blesse and warme the whole bodye" (241). In characterizing the testes as indispensable "houshold Goodes," Crooke glances obliquely at a common equation of those organs with valuable commodities. It was a small leap from "stones" to "precious stones" or "jewels," synonyms that were favored by early modern English playwrights. But other such economic similes abound in medical writing. Crooke himself refers to the scrotum as "a purse" (204), a common medical appellation; indeed, William Harvey refers to the testes in his anatomy lectures as "Primo scrotum, scortum, bursa, lik a lether purs with too pens."[35] Although his modern editor glosses "too pens" as "two compartments," it is hard not to hear in Harvey's remark a pun on "two pence."

If the testicles were often imagined as money in a purse, the analogy was also reversible: the common male practice of wearing one's purse next to the codpiece rendered the art of pickpocketing, or "purse cutting," easily representable as a form of castration. Hence Autolycus in *The Winter's Tale* can remark that "'twas nothing to geld a codpiece of a purse" (4.4.610–11), and Allom in Dekker and Webster's *Northward Ho* likewise complains that his "purse" has been "gelded."[36] John Davies' epigram, "Of Phormus his Gelded Purse," develops the links between purse cutting and castration in the most explicit detail:

Phormus had in his purse two rubies rich
When with his Turkesse (damnèd drab) he lay:
To find which purse and stone, she sought his britch
While he found sport—for which he dear did pay.
For when she found his purse, she made no bones
To geld it, ere he found it, of the stones.[37]

The English Phormus is robbed of his stones by a Turkish "drab": here we see not only the economic but also the political possibilities of castration as metaphor. These possibilities are spelled out in the second part of *Henry VI*, when Jack Cade asserts that the French-speaking "Lord Say hath gelded the commonwealth" and made it an "eunuch" (4.2.165).

The potential of testicular metaphors to represent national rather than simply personal treasure is also realized in *Microcosmographia*. For Crooke, the seminal vessels are like "Magazines or Store-houses," carrying the treasure of the generative seed (208); here, Crooke resorts to an explicitly mercantile pair of synonyms for the warehouses of entrepôts containing goods bound for transnational trade. A nationalized conception of treasure seems to be at play also in Marlowe's *Edward II*. In terms that recall Shakespeare's "expense of spirit" but equally suggest the national treasury, Mortimer Junior tells Edward that

The idle triumphs, masques, lascivious shows
And prodigal gifts bestowed on Gaveston
Have drawn thy treasure dry and made thee weak . . . .[38]

If Crooke offers a mercantile physiology of the testicles linked to that of blood, the association is all the more apparent in Mortimer's remark, whose reference to "drawn treasure" seems to imply a loss both of national lifeblood and of manly "spirit."

The overlapping physiologies of blood and semen legible in Crooke's and Marlowe's fantasies of treasure resonate powerfully with Misselden's and Malynes's divergent versions of "hepatitis." In both writers' pamphlets, the effects of the body politic's loss of treasure recall Crooke's account of the effects of the loss of the male body's precious stones. Misselden's *"marasmum"* of hepatitis, which "wounds" bodies "through the *sides,*" might just as well be applied to the wasting of the eunuch's body as described by Crooke: "the flower also of their blood decayeth and their vessels or veines loose their bredth and capacity, and all vigor . . . is extinguished" (242). In Malynes's allegory of the diseased body politic in *The Center of the Circle of Commerce,* the wasting effects of hepatitis sound even more like Crooke's account of the enfeebled eunuch and his decayed blood and vigor: "the externall parts thereof looke wan and pale"; "the *Vitall Spirits* of *Bullion* and *Money* doth languish with a continuall Flux of exportation"; "the *Hepaties* could not minister good bloud, with spirits sufficient to comfort the heart of *(our natiue commodities)* by a naturalle heate."[39] Here the liver takes the place of the Galenic testicles, the primary source of heat and spirit in the body. The potential overlaps between the physiologies of blood and semen are yet more apparent in *The Maintenance of Free Trade,* where Malynes's hepacentric Galenic terminology also recalls Shakespeare's more colloquial language of semen as "spirit": "Let the heart therfore by the liuer receiue his *Tinctured Chilus* by his owne mouth and stomacke, and the blood full of Spirits, shall fill all the *Veines,* and supplye the want of monyes."[40] The equation of blood and semen is suggested even more by the language of generative fertility and infertility he uses to articulate the doctrine of cosmopolitan economy. "God," Malynes argues, "caused nature to distribute her benefites, or his blessings to seuerall *Climates,* supplying the barrennesse of some things in one countrey, with the fruitfulnesse and store of other countries."[41]

Malynes's version of cosmopolitan economy is redolent of fetishism in its Freudian form, according to which a body marked by lack is made to reacquire a phantasmatic corporeal plenitude. In Malynes's argument, though, this plenitude takes the form not of a phallic wholeness but of a testicular "fruitfulnesse."[42] Much English mercantilist writing also entails the inverse fantasy, that the fruitful body politic can easily be rendered barren. Something like this fantasy informs Misselden's observation in *Free Trade* that "by *Foes* also this *Common-wealth* is lamentably *Passiue*, in the cruelty done by Turkish Pirats vpon *Men* and *Shippes*, and *Goods*."[43] This is an image less of sexual cruelty than of bodily violence committed against those of its *"Passiue"* merchants—merchants who otherwise, in Misselden's analysis, *actively* ensure the vigorous and healthy circulation of goods and treasure through the Christian nations of Europe. In this fantasy of piratical violence, which records the loss of English *"Goods,"* lurks the specter of testicular castration, a specter visible also in his claim that the loss of bullion makes "the *body* of this *Common-wealth* to be wounded sore, through the *sides* of many particular members thereof."[44]

Misselden's complaint recalls both Cade's invective against the French-speaking Lord Say and Mortimer's outburst against the French Gaveston; all three fantasies entail foreigners actively robbing a passive England of its stones or semen. But Misselden's complaint even more startlingly recalls the Turkish drab of Davies's epigram, who "gelds" the sleeping English Phormio of his "two rubies." I would suggest that the nationalities of Davies's castrator and her victim are particularly telling. The growing political and economic power of the Ottoman Empire had become something of an obsession in England during the early seventeenth century. The Turkish annexation of the North African Barbary States outside Morocco—the major port entrepôts of Algiers, Tripoli, and Tunis—together with King James's pursuit of peace with Spain in 1604 worked to divert English hostility from its old Catholic enemy to a new religious as well as economic bogeyman, in opposition to whom the two Christian powers could unite.[45] Under the guise of Christian antipathy toward infidel "Turkish" practices of bodily mutilation—circumcision of believers, castration of eunuchs—Jacobean English writers also lent voice to fears about the loss of national treasure. Misselden's complaints about "Turkish Pirats" robbing English merchants, and wounding all of *"Christendome"* into the bargain, is one local expression of this religioeconomic nexus. Early modern pirate drama, I shall argue, is another. And like its mercantilist co-texts, the genre is also preoccupied with the physiology of bullion accumulation in the body politic, whether at the royal center or the mercantile periphery.

Early Modern Pirate Drama: The Physiology of Currants

The details are so familiar that they barely need rehearsing. Several of the nation's vessels are hijacked; acts of violence follow. The nation's leaders attribute these acts to a largely Islamic axis of evil that they say threatens the ideals of civilization. The nation joins with others, including the erstwhile superpower that was once its fiercest enemy, in a new war against "terror." Yet even as they vigorously denounce "rogue" Islamic states, the nation's leaders are careful to maintain good trade relations with certain other Muslim powers—if only because those powers are rich in valuable resources such as oil or, as we will see, currants.

Well into the twentieth century, many English historians blithely repeated the mantra that Islamic pirates were the perennial scourge of Christian merchant venturers in the Mediterranean, capturing their ships, plundering their booty, and enslaving their crews in an ongoing "holy war."[46] This narrative informs Misselden's invectives against Turkish pirates as a principal cause of the decay of not only English but, more generally, Christian treasure. Yet Misselden's complaint, which is one of the earlier articulations of a position that was to become doctrinal, represented a major shift from Elizabethan English attitudes toward both Turks and pirates. Turks were easily denounced in Tudor England as Saracen infidels, of course, as they had been since the fall of Constantinople in 1453. But during Elizabeth's reign, Turkey had also come to be viewed somewhat sympathetically as England's fellow combatant against Spain. Queen Elizabeth cut political deals with the Ottoman sultan, and there was considerable English support for the Turks in their 1560 victory over the Spanish fleet near Jerba.[47]

Misselden's narrative of "holy war" against Turkish corsairs also represents a significant change from Elizabethan attitudes toward piracy. Statutes in the time of Henry VIII as well as Elizabeth had condemned pirates as thieves. Nevertheless, there is something of a Robin Hood-like quality in many dramatic representations of Elizabethan pirates who, in the words of Lois Potter, often embody "a kind of justice that cannot be found in supposedly civilized society."[48] Thomas Heywood and William Rowley's play, *A Fortune by Land and Sea*, exemplifies this romantic tradition. Though first performed after the ascension of James, it harks back nostalgically to Elizabeth's reign, depicting the sea adventures of two pirates executed in 1583, Purser and Clinton. The pair plunder the cargo of decent English merchants, but they are represented as men of honor who, "Though Out-laws, . . . keep laws amongst our selves" and command the respect of their adversaries as "valiant Pirats."[49]

This mode of representation was not just a function of literary genre. It was also very much a corollary of Elizabethan state ideology, for all its statutes against piracy. As many historians and critics have noted, pirating was but one step away from privateering. The latter proved a major source of English treasure from the 1570s to the 1590s, thanks to the missions of Sir Francis Drake, Sir John Hawkins, and later Sir Walter Raleigh and the Earl of Essex at Cadiz. By the last decades of Elizabeth's reign, the figure of the heroic privateer, plundering Spanish treasure in the Atlantic and the New World, had become the very model of the Protestant English patriot. In *The Trumpet of Fame* (1595), for example, the Devonshire sailor Henry Robarts celebrates the commercial adventures of Drake and Hawkins in terms that look forward to the chivalric language of *A Fortune by Land and Sea*: Robarts characterizes the two privateers as "Gallants bold, of *Albions* fertile soyle . . . By whom enriched is your Countries store, / And some made rich, which earst was held but poore."[50]

After Elizabeth's death, however, the crown lent its weight to a concerted demonization of piracy. One contributory factor was King James's 1604 peace settlement with Spain, which abruptly transformed the heroic English privateers and their Spanish plunder into diplomatic embarrassments. But other developments also contributed to the new attitude. Prior to the late sixteenth century, English merchant ships had made few forays into the Mediterranean. The closure of the Antwerp entrepôt in 1576 may have deprived English merchants of access to much-coveted Turkish silks, currants, and spices; but it also stimulated the creation of the Levant Company. The latter was chartered in 1581 with the financial support of the queen, who invested in the new company much of the plunder brought back by Drake from his voyage around the globe.[51] As the sea voyages from London to Constantinople and to Aleppo were of considerable duration, Levant Company merchant ships would customarily victual en route at the North African ports of Algiers or Tunis. This made them ready prey for the growing number of pirates in the region; and once the company started losing the lucrative spice trade to the new East India Company, chartered in 1601, the plundering of its Mediterranean vessels—which it could now ill afford to lose—became a more pressing concern. Although ships flying the English colors in the Strait of Gibraltar during the early years of the Levant trade arguably had more to fear from the Spanish, complaints about piracy off the Barbary Coast became increasingly vociferous during James's reign. With Spain's backing, an English war against "Turkish" piracy was waged, and an armada dispatched to wipe out the Barbary corsairs in 1621. The mission proved a dismal failure.[52]

Some of these Barbary corsairs were indeed Turks. But a significant number were Englishmen who, after the cessation of hostilities against Spain, had suddenly found their once acceptable privateering ventures stripped of legitimacy. A handful of English pirates, operating until 1614 out of the Moroccan port of Mamora, continued to uphold the anti-Spanish doctrine of Sir Francis Drake: the Oxford graduate turned corsair Captain Henry Mainwaring, who made the port his base after turning to piracy in 1612, claimed to attack Spanish galleys all the while sparing English merchant ships. Indeed, Mainwaring's raids were in large part responsible for Spanish proclamations against piracy and privateering in 1615.[53] Most English corsairs in the Mediterranean were equal-opportunity plunderers, however, attacking ships from their own nation as well as those of Spain, France, Holland, and Venice. These pirates often sought the protection of Turkish authorities in Tunis and Algiers, cities whose wealth depended in large part on the retail of plundered commodities and slaves. A letter sent to England from Portugal in the first decade of the seventeenth century remarks on "the infinity of goods, merchandise jewels and treasure taken by our English pirates daily from Christians and carried to Allarach, Algire and Tunis to the great enriching of Mores and Turks and impoverishing of Christians."[54] In return for protection, the English pirates usually gave the city authorities rights of monopoly over the sale of their plunder and sometimes converted to Islam.

One such renegado English pirate was John Ward, a.k.a. Yussuf Reis, who was based in Tunis from approximately 1605 until his death in 1622. Ward was a popular figure in English statutes, news pamphlets, ballads, and plays during the first ten years of James's reign.[55] Although much attention was focused on the scandal of Ward's conversion to Islam, the pamphlets that publicized his exploits were equally focused on the economic losses sustained by England as a result of his piracy. In his account of Ward's misdeeds, Andrew Barker wrote that "the infinite wealth that our nation hath suffered ruine of, by the *Turks* this last yeer it were without doubt . . . that *Londons* losses hath amounted to aboue 200000 pound."[56] Barker also complained that, thanks to Ward's and his fellow renegados' service to the Turks, England was also being robbed of its more advanced shipping technologies.[57] Whatever the validity of such allegations, they also entail a curious repudiation of former Elizabethan state policy. Accounts of English renegados repeatedly criticize the Barbary states' policy of doing business with pirates in order to fill their private and public coffers. Hence Barker complains that the head of the janissaries in Tunis, Cara Osman, has "held share with *Ward* in all his *Voyages, Prises,* and *Shippings,* and been his only supporter in all his disseignes."[58] What was once regarded by Elizabeth as a virtuous means of primitive accumulation had, under King James, become transformed into the enemy of lawful international commerce. As I will show, however, nearly all early modern literature about the Barbary corsairs entails this kind of shadow-boxing, whereby North African states provide fantastical mirrors in which English economic discourses and practices can be limned, critiqued, and disavowed as "Barbarous" or "Turkish."

I turn now to two pirate plays in order to plot shifting English attitudes toward piracy within the context of mercantilist discourses of national economy. The differences between the two plays bear witness to the mounting hostility to pirates during James's reign. In contrast to Thomas Heywood's pioneering *Fair Maid of the West* (c. 1600), which views the English pirate as a "gallant" and "honourable" patriot,[59] Philip Massinger presents Barbary corsairs as scourges of Christian civilization. In his play *The Renegado* (1623), the literary template for Massinger's pirate is no longer Robin Hood but Dr. Faustus, selling his soul to the (Turkish) devil: the Italian pirate Grimaldi is a sinner whose corsair activities must be renounced, under priestly guidance, for his Christian salvation. Yet early modern English pirate drama does far more than simply stage versions of the supposedly perennial "holy war" between Christianity and Islam. Any such facile Manichean binarism works in tandem with corporeal vocabularies of treasure and national economy that serve very different, competing conceptions of the relations between commercial activity and the state. When read in dialogue with each other, the two plays' corporeal vocabularies also resonate with the standoff between Misselden and Malynes about the nature of bullion flow and the "centers" of commerce.

Thomas Heywood's *Fair Maid of the West* is framed by bullionist preoccupations that reiterate Elizabeth's support for anti-Spanish piracy. In the play's first scene, the would-be privateer, Carrol, refers to Essex's recent success at Cadiz, which has left the English "on fire / To purchase from the Spaniard" and "tug with them / For golden spoil" (1.1.7–8, 9–10). This is but the first expression of the play's persistent valorization of anti-Spanish piracy as a mode of both patriotic heroism and economic nationalism. The play's heroine, Bess Hardwick, turns to piracy as she seeks revenge against the Spanish for the supposed death of her lover, Spencer. She declares her sea battles "gallantly perform'd" (4.4.2), and her chivalry is all the more supported by her Mainwaring-esque decision to spare the ships of fellow Protestant nations and only make "spoil / Of the rich Spaniard and the barbarous Turk." (4.5.7–8). Yet if Bess uses the language of chivalric romance and religious warfare to burnish her own pirate adventures, she also expresses a more clear-eyed economic nationalism with regard to piracy. Before leaving England, Bess confesses that she welcomes the pirates who frequent her tavern, for "Here they vent / Many brave commodities by which some gain accrues" (2.1.54–55).

When the Spanish captain is told to "pray for English Bess," he replies that "I know not whom you means, but be't your queen, / Famous Elizabeth, I shall report / She and her subjects both are merciful" (4.4.120–23). Critics have made much of this anamorphic doubling of maid and queen, which they have seen as a device designed to unite representatives of different classes within a pseudo-egalitarian nationalism.[60] But little attention has been paid to how Bess's justification of piracy as enabling the "vent" of "brave commodities by which some gain accrues" also doubles that of Mullisheg, the king of Morocco. In his first appearance, Mullisheg recounts how he has united disparate Moorish factions to create a new nation. He proceeds to offer an extended account of his policy as ruler, one that amounts to a veiled defense of piracy as a means of filling the state coffers:

> . . . we now have leisure
> To 'stablish laws, first for our kingdom's safety,
> The enriching of our public treasury,
> And last our state and pleasure. Then give order
> That all such Christian merchants as have traffic
> And freedom in our country, that conceal
> The least part of our custom due to us,
> Shall forfeit ship and goods. . . .
> These forfeitures must help to furnish up
> Th'exhausted treasure that our wars consum'd.
> Part of such profits as accrue that way
> We have already tasted. (4.3.12–19, 21–24)

On the one hand, Mullisheg sounds here like a law-abiding bullionist, the ideological bedfellow of Thomas Milles. Like Milles, Mullisheg values his national customs system as an important source of treasure for his fledgling state. Yet his "'stablishing" of national laws barely conceals an extended justification of piracy that is nevertheless every bit as English as Milles's customs system. As the last four lines of this passage suggest, Mullisheg actively wishes that his customs laws be infringed, precisely because his "exhausted" coffers depend on the larger revenue generated by the sale of goods forfeited by Christian merchants. Even though the play's "fair maid" later rescues French, Florentine, and English traders from such forfeitures, Mullisheg's piratical economics eerily mirror those of Bess—and not just Bess Hardwick, apologist for the venting of pirated "commodities," but also Bess Tudor, beneficiary of loot "forfeited" by Spanish galleons.

Mullisheg's expropriation of treasure from foreign visitors assumes a highly literal and embodied form in the play's last act. Upon meeting Spencer, Mullisheg orders that the Englishman be "gelded" and made to attend on him as his "chief eunuch" (5.2.92–93). Bess intervenes successfully on Spencer's behalf, but her apprentice drawer-cum-pirate sidekick, Clem, mishears "gelded" as "gilded" and foolishly rushes to takes Spencer's place. After his castration, he exclaims:

CLEM
No more of your honour, if you love me! Is this your Moorish preferment, to rob a man of his best jewels?
MULLISHEG
Hast thou seen our Alkedavy?
CLEM
Davy do you call him? He may be call'd shavy; I am sure he hath tickled my current commodity. No more your cutting honor, if you love me. (5.2.126–31)

Critics have read Clem's castration in very different ways. Focusing on his donning of Turkish dress (5.1.109), Jean Howard interprets Clem's mutilation as a "grotesquely hideous warning of the dangers of 'going native.' "[61] Barbara Fuchs has countered that Clem is castrated only because he takes Spencer's place; he is therefore punished not for "going native" but for upward social mobility.[62] Jonathan Burton offers a third interpretation, proposing that Clem's castration rewrites English fears about forced Islamic conversion and circumcision.[63] Indeed, English writers often linked Islamic conversion to bodily mutilations beyond circumcision itself. One pamphlet that details the kidnapping of an English ship in 1621 by "Turkish Pirates of Argier" recounts the alleged tortures that prompt English captives to convert to Islam: their Turkish jailers "strike the teeth out of their heads, pinch them by the tongues, and vse many other sorts of torture to conuert them," after which the English are "circumcised with new names."[64]

This narrative of mutilation is not entirely subsumed within the discourse of forced apostasy, however, for the bodily losses incurred by the English captives are represented as being of a piece with the larger losses of English ships and treasure that the pamphlet chronicles. I would argue that Clem's fate likewise lends comic expression to a fear haunting Elizabethan fantasies of privateering: namely, that bullion flows are not unidirectional, and treasure (or "best jewels") can be expropriated from England as much as appropriated by it. Indeed, Clem's remark about having his "current commodity" tickled entails a complex pun that suggests neither fears of going native, upward mobility, nor apostasy, but altogether different, economic sources of anxiety. "Current," or "currant," is another common early modern term for testicle; but it nods to one of the chief commodities of the Levant trade, a trade that North African piracy had threatened to trim. "Current" also recalls an early modern financial term that designated overvalued currency used to repay transnational debts: Misselden refers in *Free Trade* to Netherlandish *"Currant gelt,"* which helps "draw dry" English treasure. And, as Misselden's own puns on "geld" / "gelt" and "drawing dry" suggest, "current" in this last sense is readily commensurate with the castration of national treasure.[65]

Even as Clem's punishment lends a corporeal heft to *The Fair Maid of the West*'s vision of bullion flow out of England, the play also guards against the fear that English ventures abroad will result in the loss of its treasure. When he sees Mullisheg kiss Bess, the "girl worth gold" of the play's subtitle, Clem asks: "Must your black face be smooching my mistress's white lips with a Moorian?" (5.2.80–81). The pun on "with a murrain," or plague, invokes only to defuse the fear that England's treasure can be pathologically diminished and alienated to Morocco;[66] after all, Bess proves steadfast in her love for English Spencer. The synecdochic logic of Clem's remark typifies that of the play, according to which individual characters—whether Spanish sea captains, French merchants, kings of Morocco, or Bess as Elizabeth as England—are literally representatives of their nations in an ongoing global scramble for treasure. To this extent, *The Fair Maid of the West* articulates a recognizably bullionist fantasy in which piracy, privateering, and merchant venturing are all instruments of the nation-state.

Two decades later, early modern playwrights were fantasizing the centers of wealth production very differently. Philip Massinger's *Renegado* (1623) diverges from the *The Fair Maid of the West* by partially undoing the firm knot that lashes virtuous venturing to the state. In a fascinating reworking of Heywood's economics of castration, Massinger's play—which was written in the same year that Misselden and Malynes concluded their print exchange—probes the potential conflicts between the interests of the state and those of its "free-trading" servants whose business is the accumulation of treasure.[67] As a consequence, Massinger follows Misselden in obliquely fantasizing a transnational Christian polity within which the accumulation of treasure is more the responsibility of "manly" private merchants than of nation-states or their political and monetary institutions.

The location and the characters of *The Renegado* share much with Heywood's play. Like *The Fair Maid of the West,* Massinger's drama is chiefly set in North Africa—this time in Tunis; and like the earlier play, it presents a lustful Barbary potentate (Asambeg) who is rebuffed by a steadfast Christian maiden (Paulina) and a doltish Christian (Gazet) who fancies becoming a eunuch. Indeed, the most obvious echo of *The Fair Maid of the West* in *The Renegado* is its many anxious jokes about castration. More than in Heywood's play, castration is associated with the ever-present threat of a violent Islamic law, metonymically represented by the razor. Gazet, Vitelli the hero's idiotic servant, relates his eyewitness account of "an English pirate's whore with a green apron" (1.1.50), who had her clothes cut off in the Tunis marketplace by a razor-wielding mufti as punishment for wearing the sacred color of the prophet Mohammed. Gazet says that he himself " 'scaped a scouring," even though "my mistress' busk-point, of that forbidden color,/ Then tied my codpiece," and he adds: "Had it been discovered / I had been caponed" (1.1.55–58). Despite the religious colors of such fears, castration is equally associated throughout the play with economic loss. In a pun on mercantile units of measurement, Carazie, the English-born eunuch of the Ottoman princess Donusa, quips that he has been "made lighter / By two stoneweight" (1.2.25–26). Gazet tells Carazie that "I'll be an eunuch, though I sell my shop for't / And all my wares"; Carazie replies that "It is but parting with / A precious stone or two; I know the price on't" (3.4.50–53). The economic freight of these quips is compounded by Gazet's name, which was also the name of a small Venetian coin widely circulated in the Levant; implicit in his close calls with the Turkish razor, then, is a pun on coin-clipping, or debasement of currency—a recurrent source of English economic anxiety.[68]

Gazet's close shave with castration, and Clem's and Carazie's even closer ones, arguably serve a European orientalist vision of despotic economy similar to that outlined by Alain Grosrichard in *The Sultan's Court*. "This," Grosrichard claims, "is an absurd economy, its only goal the *jouissance* of the One, not the country's enrichment; its principle is *coupure*, the cutting-off of all that circulates (blood, merchandise, currency)."[69] Clem's and Carazie's castration not only metaphorically deprives England of its precious stones but also arbitrarily removes wealth in the form of human capital from circulation: immuring otherwise mobile Englishmen within the confines of the Muslim despot's seraglio, Clem's and Carazie's cuttings foster the *jouissance* of Mullisheg or Donusa without increasing the wealth of Morocco or Turkey. Grosrichard's analysis confines itself to eighteenth-century French fantasies of the Orient, and his physiological terms bear the stamp of that period's Physiocrat discourse, which understood economy on the principle of the circulation of the blood. Even to this extent, the Physiocrats' embodied conception of economy begs comparison to the English mercantilists'.[70] But Grosrichard's account of despotic *coupure* hints far more suggestively at the overlap between the economic physiologies of blood and castration that I have sketched throughout this chapter. As a result, Grosrichard's analysis casts light on Misselden's fantasy of money flowing through a Christian circuit of exchange to obviate a castrating Turkish threat that would likewise permanently remove "blood, merchandise, and currency" from circulation. Despite devoting a chapter to the figure of the eunuch, however, Grosrichard does not tether his analysis of despotic economy's *coupure* to the cutting of the testicles. By contrast, Heywood's and Massinger's fantasies of Christians' castration in North Africa suggest how the eunuch could serve as a figure not only for Oriental despotic *jouissance* but also for Christian fantasies of transnational economic competition.

Inasmuch as *The Renegado* presents castration as a pervasive Turkish threat, all the play's male Christian characters are potential eunuchs. It may seem that the only way in which a male Christian visitor to Tunis can fully avert the risk of castration is to receive the largesse of a powerful Turkish princess who, by filling his testicular purse with precious stones, also restores his manly vigor. Donusa, the niece of the Ottoman sultan Amurath, falls for Vitelli and gives him "bags stuffed full of our imperial coin" (2.4.83), which she also refers to as "seeds of bounty" (2.4.97). Yet these testicular gifts prove to be bogus sources of virility. Indeed, in a subtle departure from Galenic orthodoxy, the play seems to disqualify any metaphorical physiology grounded in a central organ, whether testes, liver, or heart. Upon learning from the Jesuit priest Francisco that Vitelli's sister Paulina, abducted by the pirate Grimaldi, is in Tunis, Vitelli exclaims that "my virtuous anger / Makes every vein an artery. I feel in me / The strength of twenty men" (1.1.121–23). Yet Vitelli's Galenic protestations of arterial vigor are as dubious as his aspirations to testicular virility, and Francisco eventually persuades him of the folly of both. Just as royal favor in Tunis almost results in Gazet's "promotion" to the office of eunuch, the testicular potency that supposedly accrues from Donusa's patronage is represented as a threat to Vitelli's manhood, one that threatens to "crack [his] best piece" (2.6.40). Vitelli's subsequent rejection of Donusa's gifts may be part of the play's narrative of Christian liberation from an effeminating Islamic bondage; but it easily shades into a more broad skepticism, inasmuch as this rejection also informs what I take to be the *The Renegado*'s concluding fantasy: a transnational community of Christian venturers liberated not only from Islamic masters but also from the emasculating sway of the state in general.

The Tunisian state in *The Renegado* lends its wholehearted support to pirate ventures. Francisco complains that Asambeg's associates are "all false pirates" (1.1.105), and another character claims that the viceroy tolerates the insults of the renegado corsair Grimaldi because Asambeg "receives profit / From the prizes he brings in" (1.3.94–95). These remarks arguably target more than just the criminality of Turkish potentates; I would suggest they also strike closer to home. Like the mirror that Vitelli sells in the Tunis mart ("steeled so exactly, neither taking from / Nor flattering the object it returns / To the beholder" [1.3.109–11]), the Tunis of the play reflects the society of its English audience in unexpected ways. Most notably, Carazie's long speech about how English vices parallel Turkish sins (1.2.27–48) serves to place Tunis in specular relation to London. Asambeg's receipt of "profit" from others' "prizes" is but one way in which Tunis mirrors early seventeenth-century England, whose rulers likewise acquired revenue from the bounty brought to port by foreign ships. For bullionist mercantilists such as Thomas Milles, as we have seen, such profit was the cornerstone of sound economic policy; and this policy finds expression in *The Fair Maid of the West*'s support for privateering. But in *The Renegado,* Grimaldi complains about Asambeg in a fashion that hints at a profound structural tension afflicting the partnership between state and venturer:

. . . how unmanly 'tis to sit at home
And rail at us, that run abroad all hazards,
If every week we bring not home new pillage
For the fatting his seraglio. (2.5.13–16)

Grimaldi's complaint once more conjures up a vision of the "absurd" despotic economy sketched by Grosrichard, in which the *jouissance* of the sultan in his seraglio demands the wasteful hoarding of wealth and an end to the circulation of "blood, merchandise and money." The gendered terms of Grimaldi's complaint also recall a passage in *A Christian Turned Turk* (1612), Robert Daborne's dramatization of John Ward's piracy. One of Ward's captives, the French merchant Ferdinand, tells the Englishman and his fellow pirates, "You rob the venting merchants, whose manly breast / (Scorning base gain at home) puts to the main / With hazard of his life and state."[71] But whereas Ferdinand contrasts the "manly" labors of the merchant with the indolence of the pirate, Grimaldi casts the pirate as the virile worker and the prince as the effeminate layabout. No matter how much his outburst may have been cheered on by the play's earliest audiences as the first intimation of his subsequent renunciation of Islam, Grimaldi's criticism of "unmanly" Turkish tyranny can equally be read as a private venturer's fantasy of freedom from state control, European as much as Asian or African.

This fantasy is realized at play's end. Eluding Asambeg's increasingly tyrannical clutches, an unlikely band—including the virtuous Vitelli, the repentant Grimaldi, the converted Donusa, and the loyal Carazie—escape Tunis by ship, with all their "choicest jewels . . . safe aboard" (5.8.27). This image of testicular integrity redounds here less to any one nation-state than to a Christian merchant community that, like the "free-trading" mart at the beginning of the play, represents "a confluence of all nations" (1.2.112). One might object that the band of escapees are not "free traders" so much as "true religious friend[s]" (5.7.11) under the spiritual guidance of Francisco.[72] Yet we might also recall here Edward Misselden's version of "free trading," which envisions bullion circulating within a Christian polity that staunchly protects its collective treasure from the Turkish "Enimies of *God* and *man*." Such stateless Christian solidarity suffuses Massinger's as much as Misselden's vision of global commerce. In the Tunisian marketplace, Gazet expresses a pan-Christian pragmatism that pointedly excludes the Turks:

GAZET
   Live I in England, Spain, France, Rome, Geneva:
   I'm of that country's faith.
VITELLI
   And what in Tunis?
   Will you turn Turk here?
GAZET
   No, so should I lose
   A collop of that part my Doll enjoined me

To bring home as she left it: 'tis her venture
Nor dare I barter that commodity
Without her special warrant. (1.1.36–42)

The Renegado may poke fun at Gazet's uxurious promise to his Doll; but the play's conclusion reclothes his (and Doll's) testicular, Turkish-fearing "venture" in more heroic colors. As the cosmopolitan Christian community sails off into the sunset with its "jewels" and "collops" safe from the threat of the Turkish razor, we might also glimpse a version of the virile, yet economically decentralized, Christian polity of Misselden's *Free Trade.* In both Misselden's treatise and Massinger's play, heroic venturers quietly displace the originary authority of European kings and queens and become the new sources of Christian polity's lifeblood and semen. As a result, however, Misselden and Massinger inaugurate a troubling narrative that is still part of our contemporary political landscape: namely, that despotic Islamic economy is the natural enemy of "free trade."

Economics into Physiology, Physiology into Economics

It may seem odd to include castration in a study of economic pathology, let alone in a chapter ostensibly about a disease of the liver. Yet the referential flexibility of Misselden's neologism allows early modern "hepatitis" to signify in ways that extend far beyond our modern conception of the disease. As we have seen, Galenic theory understands the physiological effects of castration in ways that are linked to its account of the dysfunctional liver. Aside from what these links might reveal to us about early modern conceptions of physiology and pathology, they also afforded early modern writers suggestive vocabularies for economic issues that had become pressing in the early seventeenth century— most notably, the circulation of wealth, the loss of treasure, and the central organs of commerce.

These issues surface prominently in seventeenth-century pirate drama, which employs the language of castration to represent not only the vicissitudes of bullion flow in and out of nations but also the increasingly fraught relations between the state and commercial venturing. In turn, these new economic concepts arguably reshaped the horizons of Renaissance physiology and pathology. Ernest Gilman has suggested that William Harvey's theory of circulation needs to be understood in relation not only to the intellectual contexts of Baconian empirical science and Aristotelian cosmology but also to the privateering ventures of Drake and his ilk: "Harvey specifies the idea of bodily circulation by opening a 'passage' between the arterial and venous systems for the flow of blood (moving in vessels, coincidentally) to unite the most distant points in the body with the heart. . . . In the 'lesser world' of man, Harvey has remapped the global voyages of the great circumnavigators."[73] Once again, then, as we have seen throughout this book, early modern medicine and mercantilism shaped each other's horizons of discursive possibility.

There is perhaps no better illustration of this mutuality than the fate of one early modern English medicoeconomic term: consumption. Like hepatitis, consumption was initially understood as a pathology of the blood; unlike hepatitis, it has migrated more or less entirely from the medical to the economic lexicon. This migration, however, has not been straightforward or unidirectional. As I will show in the next chapter, both economic and medical usages of "consumption" reveal a long history of semantic cross-pollination. To begin to plot this history—one that eventually leads to the mass production of consumer goods branded with TMs, or trademarks—I will turn to the work of two early modern TMs: the East India Company director, Thomas Mun, and the London playwright Thomas Middleton.

Consumption and Consumption: Thomas Mun, The Roaring Girl

Oh, worse than consumption of the liver!
Consumption of the patrimony!

—*Thomas Middleton*, Michaelmas Term, *2.1.116–17*

What is the meaning of "consumption" in Jacobean city comedy? Unusually preoccupied with the dealings and double-dealings of merchants and shopkeepers, the questionable glamor of luxury goods, and the fledgling self-consciousness of a recognizably bourgeois class, the genre would seem to lend itself particularly well to the study of early modern patterns of economic consumption.[1] But is this latter phenomenon in any way related to the pathological condition that these lines from Thomas Middleton's *Michaelmas Term* identify as "consumption"? As my title for this chapter suggests, in Middleton's plays, and indeed in early modern culture, there is consumption, and then there is consumption.[2]

Economic consumption—the purchase and use of commodities in such fashion as to exhaust their exchange value—has become a prominent category of analysis in recent scholarship on early modern culture. Since the publication in 1973 of Fernand Braudel's monumental *Capitalism and Material Life, 1400–1800,* there has been a growing tendency to explain the historical shift to capitalism in the West as driven not only by emergent means of production but also by new patterns of demand that anticipate those of modern consumer society. In particular, the desire of upper-class and upwardly mobile middle-class Londoners for fashionable, foreign luxury commodities—a desire satirized by Jonson in the figure of Lady Politic Would-Be—has been viewed as stimulating the rise of the English joint-stock companies devoted to trade with the Orient and the New World, the colonial institutions that brought these trades even more firmly into the orbit of English political authority, and the new industrial technologies of production that increased the availability of luxury goods.[3] For all the differences in their conclusions, studies of early modern English consumer society have tended to subscribe to an entirely modern conception of consumption as an interlinked set of practices and attitudes involving certain types of objects (commodities surplus to subsistence needs) and subjects (consumers divorced from the means of producing such objects). Although these studies do differentiate between patterns of modern and early modern consumption, they nonetheless presume enduring economic realities anterior to discourse, realities that early modern English culture is credited with having pioneered.[4]

But these studies' positive—not to mention positivist—conception of consumption is one that early modern writers would not have readily recognized. As my epigraph makes clear, the term "consumption" possessed in Thomas Middleton's England not simply a negative valence but, more specifically, a pathological one. In *Michaelmas Term*, "consumption" is associated less with the acquisition of goods than with a hepatic or tubercular wasting of wealth and health alike—a far cry from the more positive connotation lent the term by Adam Smith in *The Wealth of Nations*, where he famously argued that increasing individual consumption is the goal of all nations' economic activity.[5] This is not to insist that consumption as it is now often understood in the wake of Smith, that is, as a practice integral to the fortunes of the national economy, did not exist in Middleton's London. Rather, it is to suggest that any theorization of practices of consumption in early modern England and Europe stands to be complicated by the discursive history of the term, not least in the very nation within which consumption allegedly first emerged as a significant economic phenomenon.

This chapter untangles the twinned pathological and economic valences of consumption in early modern writing and its particular resonances in Middleton's city comedies. I look first at how economic and medical texts reconfigured the term during the course of the seventeenth century, producing for the first time a "consumption" that we might recognize—a reconfiguration evident in the influential tracts on foreign trade written in the 1620s by the London merchant and English East India Company director Thomas Mun. In his writings, consumption evinces the paradoxical logic of transnationalism with which I have been concerned throughout this book: at the same time that the term pathologizes foreign bodies, it also ratifies global connectedness as the basis of the healthy nation-state.

After sketching the larger, changing discursive fields within which consumption participated, I turn to an analysis of its meanings in Middleton's city comedies. The overriding sense of the term in his earlier plays is very much at odds with the way in which we now understand consumption. Yet something that looks more like Mun's reformulation of consumption is arguably visible in Middleton's later city comedy, *The Roaring Girl* (c. 1611), co-written with Thomas Dekker. By subjecting this play to a reading that attends to consumption as not only a material practice but also a shifting object of discourse, I seek to show how our more modern economic understanding of the term emerged from a medicalized vocabulary within which were fostered quite distinctive typologies of the domestic and the foreign, the healthy and the pathological. Conversely, the emergent early modern economic senses of consumption also substantially transformed its medical counterparts. The effects of this interplay between the mercantile and the medical, I shall argue, still haunt the valences of economic consumption in the present and have been crucial to the production of the modern notion of national economy.

This chapter, then, poses the question: what happens when we repathologize early modern consumption—that is, understand it as an object whose meanings are simultaneously generated in a medical as well as a mercantilist lexicon? How does *The Roaring Girl* dramatize consumption in both a pathological and an economic sense, and to what extent are the two senses dependent on each other? And what can consumption's shifting meanings in Middleton's plays in particular and in seventeenth-century writing in general reveal about the emergence of discourses not only of national economy but also of invasive pathology? In answering these questions, I will show how consumption has been instrumental in the production of "foreign bodies" in both mercantile and medical spheres.

From Pathological to Economic Consumption: Thomas Mun

The early modern disjunctions of consumption are partly a function of its two distinct etymologies. "Consumption" derives primarily from the Latin *consumere,* to use up, devour, or waste. But its meanings are also inflected by *consummare,* to sum up or carry to completion.[6] In English literature from the fourteenth to the seventeenth centuries, the "consumptive" meaning of the term largely eclipsed its "consummate" counterpart. The OED lists numerous early modern extrapolations of consumption in the sense of "wasting" or "devouring," including incineration, eating, and profligate spending. But both valences of the term appear in the lexicon of early modern medical writers. "Consumption" usually refers to the burning up of the humors, the wasting of the body, and specific ills of the blood; in its rarer, constructive sense of "consummate," however, to "consume" could occasionally refer also to the *purification* of the humors.[7] These medical usages delimited the range of meanings of economic consumption from the sixteenth to the eighteenth centuries. Although the wasteful sense eventually prevailed in medical parlance, its more positive connotation triumphed in Smithian economics. As I will show, though, early modern economic recuperations of "consumption" almost invariably draw on its pathological meanings.

Thomas Starkey's *Dialogue Between Reginald Pole and Thomas Lupset* (c. 1535), as we saw in Chapter 2, identifies eight diseases afflicting the body politic. All have an internal origin; and while many of them are strictly political ailments (such as the disease he terms "frenzy," caused by a mad "head" of state), the first and principal disease Starkey identifies is an economic one. Starkey argues that a nation's poverty is caused by a lack of population, and hence of a production base: "For like as in a consumption, when the body is brought to a great sklenderness there is lack of power and strength to maintain the health of the same, so in a country . . . where there is lack of people there wanteth power to maintain the flourishing state of the politic body, and so it falleth into manifest decay, and by little and little worneth away."[8] Starkey thus locates consumption not in the demand side of the traditional economic formula but in an etiolated domestic supply, the characteristic pathology of an insufficiently developed nation incapable of producing even subsistence goods for its citizenry.

Starkey's attribution of the origins of economic "consumption" to factors within the English body politic resonates with the prevailing humoral understanding of the disease in the early sixteenth century. Consumption, also called phthisis or "tisick," was not regarded as the determinate, invasive illness that we have understood it to be since Robert Koch (i.e., tuberculosis), residing in and transmitted by a bacterium. Although tuberculosis seems to have been responsible for nearly a third of the deaths in late fifteenth-century Kent, "consumption" was instead a catchall term designating a set of symptoms that included wasting accompanied by a cough.[9] These symptoms were occasionally regarded as contagious. Nevertheless, they were understood to have a primarily internal cause: a substantial diminishing of one of the four humors, blood. As John Trevisa noted in 1398, "Whanne blood is imade thinne it is nought dewe fedinge of membres, and so folewith consompcion and wastinge."[10] In his *Breuiary of Helthe*, Andrew Boorde distinguished between "natural" and "unnatural" consumptions but likewise insisted that both are caused by a lack of blood.[11] And as late as the 1650s, Sir Thomas Browne asserted that "there were few Consumptions in the Old World, when Men lived much upon Milk"—a substance that was regarded by Galenists as a concocted form of blood.[12] Early modern physicians' tendency to regard consumption as a depletion of the sanguine humor resulted in alcohol-intensive remedies designed to augment and enrich the blood. Boorde was of the mind that "swete wynes be good for them the whiche be in consumpcion, moderatly taken," and a mid-seventeenth-century pamphlet on consumption recommended "two Red-sage leaves, and one Bloodwort leaf . . . put . . . into a cup of small Bear" as a remedy.[13]

The humoral etiology of consumption lent itself to ready metaphorical appropriation by writers who attributed England's woes to a loss of blood—figurative and actual—well into the seventeenth century. In 1655, for example, William Gurnall asserted that owing to civil war, "the consumptive body of this our Nation, hath lost so much of her best blood."[14] Thomas Hobbes, following the examples of Edward Misselden and Gerard Malynes, famously compared money to blood in *Leviathan*; this analogy informs his catalog of the body politic's diseases, where he asserts, "*Consumption* [is caused by] Riot and Vain Expence," that is, a hemorrhaging of money.[15] The nation's loss of money and soldiers' blood was also conflated in an anonymous Elizabethan document titled "Distresses of the Commonwealth, With the Means to Remedy Them." This includes among the "many and most grievous diseases that our commonweal . . . travaileth with at this day" the identifiably humoral ailment of "the wars," which have "consumed our Captains, Men, Money."[16]

As these last two examples suggest, early modern economic usages of "consumption" or "to consume" almost invariably carried a pathological freight. But appropriations of consumption to figure the wasteful loss of national wealth also afford a proleptic glimpse of our modern and decidedly nonpathological understanding of the term. In his Proclamation of 1622, issued at the height of England's depression, King James attributed the crippling scarcity of money in the nation to a number of factors, including its overseas exportation. He singled out one particular "great waste and consumption of Coyne & Bullion of the Realme": the manufacture of gold and silver thread, a fashionable luxury accessory woven into costly garments.[17] "Consumption" here stands poised between its early and its modern senses. In his denunciation of immoral behavior that leads to the wasteful depletion of the nation's treasure, James's version of consumption partakes of the medieval discourse of luxury, which located the origins of sin in the pathological appetite.[18] But it also brings to visibility emerging practices of *conspicuous* consumption, whereby luxury commodities are purchased by a new kind of subject, the individual consumer, so that they may be both privately owned and publicly flaunted. The "wasteful" and "conspicuous" senses of consumption were to overlap for some time. In the late seventeenth century, the merchant William Petyt invoked both when he observed that "a consumptive trade," that is, one geared to satisfying the rapacious demands of the individual consumer for exotic luxury goods, "must render a nation weaker and weaker . . . because it must still exhaust more and more of the national riches, and sink the value of men's estates."[19] Nevertheless, consumption in its "conspicuous" sense increasingly came to shed its pathological associations.

In King James's and Petyt's models of the consumption of national riches, we can see a significant shift toward a consideration of the role played by foreign trade. However, both identified *domestic* factors—the removal of gold from circulation, the appetite of Englishmen for luxury commodities—as the causes of England's economic ills. So long as the nation's ailments could be attributed to imbalances within its modes of production and its patterns of demand, the humoral explanation of consumption as a deadly wasting disease of the blood (analogous to Misselden's *marasmum* of hepatitis) proved useful for early modern English economic writers. Yet the vicissitudes of England's increasingly global commerce also facilitated the shift to a more modern conception of consumption, a shift visible in the writings of Thomas Mun. Like James, Mun understood economic consumption as a pathological wasting of the body politic, caused primarily by domestic appetites. Yet he proceeded to recuperate the practice as a "necessary" evil whereby a controlled encounter with foreignness safeguards rather than pollutes the *corpus economicum*. As a consequence, consumption became in Mun's analysis of the global economy *both* a pathological *and* a positive category.

Like his fellow Hackney resident Edward Misselden, Mun wrote not as a state employee but as a successful businessman affiliated with a powerful trading company. He had spent many years as a merchant venturer in Italy, where he witnessed the remarkable growth of Livorno (or, as the English called it, Leghorn) into a successful free port, and he received extensive financial support from the grand duke of Tuscany for commercial undertakings in Turkey. In 1615, he was elected a director of the English East India Company. His subsequent experiences overseeing the company's trade resulted in two treatises, *A Discourse of Trade, From England Vnto the East-Indies* (1621) and the massively influential *Englands Treasure by Forraign Trade* (first published in 1664 but written as early as the late 1620s).

Like Malynes, Milles, and Misselden, Mun employed a determinedly pathological vocabulary to represent the vagaries of commerce across national borders. In *A Discourse of Trade,* for example, Mun insists that the scarcity of silver bullion "has been, and is, a general disease of all nations . . . but it seems that the malady is grown mortal here with us, and therefore cries out for remedy."[20] Mun gestures here to England's business depression of 1620–24, the causes of which were fiercely disputed by Misselden and Malynes in their pamphlet war. Amid a general bullionist suspicion that the loss of English treasure was not just a symptom but a cause of the crisis, the East India Company's patents to export silver coin had come under increasing attack. In 1621, Mun submitted statements to the crown that defended the commercial practices of the company.[21] These statements seem to have provided the germ for his *Discourse of Trade,* published in the same year, in which Mun asserts that "the *Trade* from *England* to the *East-Indies* doth not consume, but rather greatly increase the generall stocke and Treasure of this *Realme*" (sigs. A3–A3v).

Mun argues that the company's export of bullion for the purchase of the

East Indies' primary commodities—spices, drugs, indigo, calico, silk—aids England in several ways. First, in marked opposition to Timothy Bright and Thomas Milles, Mun asserts that Oriental spices and drugs are good for the bodily health of the nation: "the moderate vse of wholesome Druggs and comfortable Spices" serves not "to surfeit, or to please a lickorish tast (as it often happeneth, with many other fruites and wines) but rather as things most necessarie to preserue their health, and to cure their diseases" (sig. B3v). Second, the East India commodities save the nation money: Oriental drugs and spices cost less in the East Indies than they do in Levant entrepôts, where their prices are inflated by Turkish middlemen; calico and silk likewise cost less than luxury Continental European linens and fabrics. Third, the company often purchases Oriental goods in exchange for English "Broad-clothes, Kersies, Lead," and "Tinne" (sig. D2v), thereby stimulating the production of new markets for English commodities. Fourth, the use of indigo in dyes and the carding of silk both create domestic employment, as does the necessity of manning the East India Company's ships for the unusally long voyages to the Orient. Finally, and most importantly, Oriental imports can be resold for enormous profits in European markets—a double source of revenue, "for the commodities which are brought in, & after carried out vnto forren parts again, cannot hurt but doe greatly help the commonwealth, by encrease of his Maiesties Customes and Trades" (sig. G4).

Mun's discourse of "consumption" and "consuming" throughout *A Discourse of Trade* is in many ways conventionally pathological. He repeatedly associates either term with the wasting of wealth: Mun speaks of how the East India Company's opponents claim that by shipping out the nation's bullion, or lifeblood, its trade "wasteth and consumeth all" (sig. D7). He similarly bemoans how "the Commodities of this Kingdome, and also forraine wares, are the more consumed and wasted, a double meanes to abate the Common-wealth" (sig. H1). As this example shows, Mun envisages the consumption of commodities as a simultaneous consumption of the nation's wealth. In the process, he partially replicates earlier bullionist arguments against luxury goods. The opponents of drugs and spices should instead "exclaime against *Tobacco,* Cloth of gold and siluer, Lawnes, Cambricks, Gold and Siluer Lace, Veluets, Sattens, Taffaeties and diuers others manufactures, yearely brought into this Realme, for an infinite value; all which as it is most true, that whilest we consume them, they likewise deuoure our wealth" (sig. B4). Englishmen's appetite for luxury items like tobacco, Mun argues, converts the nation's wealth into "too much Smoake" (sig. D3v)—a common criticism of the time.[22] In all these cases, Mun's use of "consumption" seems to invoke its orthodox humoral and moral valence; foreign wares are immediately responsible for the nation's ills, but the root cause is excessive English appetites, which lead to the depletion of the body politic's internal resources.

Nevertheless, a counterdiscourse of consumption lurks in Mun's treatise. He pronounces himself less an unswerving opponent of the consumption of foreign commodities than an advocate of moderation: "we ought not to auoid the importation of forraine wares, but rather willingly to bridle our owne affections to the moderate consuming of the same" (sig. G4v). Mun's support for "moderate consuming" might again echo the humoral language of self-restraint. Yet this remark expresses the views not of Mun the moral physiologist but of Mun the pragmatic economist. Controlled consumption of luxury foreign goods, he argues, stimulates the export of domestic commodities, encouraging those nations from whom England buys luxury wares to purchase its goods in return. This attitude informs Mun's otherwise surprising reversal on those fashionable foreign textiles like cambric, linen, velvet, and taffeta, which he had denounced but a sentence earlier: "the moderate vse of all these wares hath euer suted well with the riches and Maiesties of this Kingdome" (sig. B4). Even as "suted" entails a witty pun on England's taste for foreign clothes, it also rhetorically refashions the "moderate" consumption of foreign luxury goods as a "suitable" means of increasing England's revenue.

Mun's partial recuperation of consumption is developed in his later and more famous treatise, *Englands Treasure by Forraign Trade*. Written in the late 1620s, its publication may have been initially thwarted by Mun's not so veiled criticism of Charles I's severe taxation policies; in any case, the treatise did not appear in print until 1664.[23] After its publication, however, it became the *locus classicus* of English mercantilism. Adam Smith paid Mun the dubious compliment of regarding *Englands Treasure by Forraign Trade* as the most lucid and systematic expression of a fundamentally flawed tradition of economic thought. Hence he criticized Mun's treatise for its bullionist equation of wealth with money and for sacrificing the interest of the consumer to that of the producer.[24] It is an index of Smith's enormous influence that this last assessment has gone largely unchallenged in studies of seventeenth-century economic and cultural history, where Mun has often been styled as a puritanical advocate for work and a fierce critic of fashionable luxury wares.[25] Such a characterization, however, fails to do justice to the complexity—and conflictedness—of Mun's theorization of consumption.

As in *A Discourse of Trade,* Mun often voices a profound antipathy toward foreign luxury goods. Tobacco once more serves as his favored target:

whilst we leave our wonted honourable Exercises and Studies, following our Pleasures, and of late years besotting our selves with Pipe and Pot, in a beastly manner, sucking smoak, and drinking healths, until death stares many in the face; the said Dutch have well-neer left this swinish vice, and taken up our wonted valour, which we have often so well performed both by Sea and Land. . . . The summ of all is this, that the general leprosie of our Piping, Potting, Feasting, Fashions, and mis-spending of our time in Idleness and Pleasure (contary to the Law of God, and the use of other Nations) hath made us effeminate in our Bodies, weak in our Knowledge, poor in our Treasure, declined in our Valour, unfortunate in our Enterprises, and contemned by our Enemies. I write the more of these Excesses, because they do so greatly wast our Wealth, which is the main subject of this whole Books discourse. (sigs. L2–L2v)

Mun's vision of the nation's "leprosie" presents tobacco as the wasteful poison par excellence, possessed of no ostensible use value. In a fashion that recalls Misselden's and Malynes's mercantilist physiologies of castration, tobacco—and luxury pleasures of all kinds—render virile bodies "effeminate," "weak," and "poor in . . . Treasure." This antipathy leads Mun to ponder the imposition of duties on foreign luxury goods: the latter, he speculates, "may be the more charged, which will turn to the profit of the Kingdom in the *Ballance of the Trade,* and thereby also enable the King to lay up the more Treasure out of his yearly incomes" (sig. C1v).

Yet these more conventional mercantilist positions are countered elsewhere in Mun's treatise by an abiding suspicion of state micromanagement of foreign trade. As is perhaps only to be expected from a key figure in the East India Company, Mun argues that the all-important balance of trade will not redound in England's favor by overlegislating against the flow of goods into the country or the flow of money out of it. For all that Mun denounces exotic luxury goods, he also repeatedly cautions against restrictions, arguing that if English authorities were to prohibit or obstruct the import of foreign commodities, similar restrictions would be laid upon English trade by foreign princes:

we must consider that all the ways and means which (in course of Trade) force Treasure into the Kingdom, do not therefore make it ours: for this can be done onely by a lawful gain, and this gain is no way to be accomplished but by the over-ballance of our Trade, and this over-ballance is made less by restrictions: therefore such restrictions do hinder the increase of our Treasure. The Argument is plain, and needs no other reasons to strengthen it, except any man be so vain to think that restrictions would not cause the less wares to be exported. . . . whatsoever courses we take to force money into the Kingdom, yet so much onely will remain with us as we shall gain by the ballance of our Trade. (sig. F4v)

The need to preserve the health of the English body politic is thus countermanded by Mun's faith in the operations of a global commerce that operates according to dependable laws. Chief among the latter is Mun's version of the law of the balance of trade, which, more than Misselden's counterpart, necessitates that the state adopt a laissez-faire attitude toward the movements of global commerce, including the flow of potentially poisonous luxury items into the nation. In the manner of modern discourses of transnational commerce, then, Mun's argument both stigmatizes the foreign and valorizes the global.

Mun's choice of terminology to discredit restrictions on global "trafficke" indicates the corporeal and, more specifically, pathological inflection of his economic theories. The flow of goods and specie is better left untampered with, for "the whole body of the Trade . . . will ever languish if the harmony of her health be distempered by the diseases of excess at home, violence abroad, charges and restrictions at home or abroad" (sigs. E8v–F1).[26] This remark hints at Mun's profoundly conflicted attitude toward consumption within the "body of Trade." On the one hand, he regards the consumption of tobacco and other luxuries as wasteful "diseases of excess at home"; on the other, "charges and restrictions at home or abroad" are equally noxious. And it is because of his profound opposition to the latter that Mun subtly yet significantly recodes consumption of luxury items as an occasionally *necessary* "disease of excess."

As in *A Discourse of Trade,* Mun often equates the consumption of commodities with the wasteful consumption of the nation: hence he states epigrammatically toward the end of *Englands Treasure by Forraign Trade* that "to lose and to consume doth produce one and the same reckoning" (sig. N1v). But one might also glimpse throughout his treatise a different view of consumption, one that lends rhetorical support to his defense of deregulated international commerce. Even as Mun understands consumption in vaguely Galenic fashion as a depletion of the nation's money or lifeblood, he also uses the term to signify less a wasteful attrition than a practice integral to global economic activity: "it is not therefore the keeping of our Money in the Kingdom which makes a quick and ample Trade," he argues against the likes of Malynes, "but the necessity and use of our Wares in forraign Countries, and our want of their Commodities which causeth the Vent and Consumption on all sides" (sig. C7). This last passage serves as a useful reminder that, for Mun, transnational "Consumption" is not necessarily a "wasteful" practice but instead the "consummate" engine of global economic prosperity.

Such an attitude leads Mun to positions that are a world away from the puritanical sentiments of moralists like Philip Stubbes. As we saw in Chapter 2, Stubbes attributed England's economic and moral ills to three "cankers," each of which entail the conspicuous consumption of luxury items: "daintie fare, gorgious buildings, and sumptuous apparel."[27] In pointed contrast, Mun argues that "the pomp of Buildings, Apparel, and the like, in the Nobility, Gentry, and other able persons, cannot impoverish the Kingdome" (sig. I4v). He justifies these (upper-class) practices of conspicuous consumption on two grounds. First, as in *A Discourse of Trade,* the import of foreign luxuries creates overseas markets for domestic commodities: "all kind of Bounty and Pomp is not to be avoided, for if we should become so frugal, that we would use few or no Forraign wares, how shall we then vent our own Commodities?" (sig. I4). And second, the production of luxury items abroad and in England creates employment opportunities for the poor: "if it be done with curious and costly works upon our Materials, and by our own people, it will maintain the poor with the purse of the rich, which is the best distribution of the Common-wealth" (sig. I4v). In this analysis, the effects of consumption are no longer grounded in the immediate use value (or lack of it) of the consumed goods themselves; rather, the effects are to be measured in terms of future revenue. In other words, Mun refashions wasteful consumption as a nationalist species of venture capital. By replacing the old bullionist end of hoarding specie with the new capitalist agenda of promoting a transnational class of upper-class consumers who stimulate the expansion of trade, Mun begins to divest economic consumption of its wasteful pathological valence.

Shadowing Mun's partial recuperation of consumption as a potential economic boon is another metaphor derived from pathological medicine. On the issue of taxation, Mun is divided. He sees taxation as an impermissible evil in some nations and a necessary one in others: "we must remember likewise that all bodies are not of one and the same constitution, for that which is Physick to one man, is little better than poyson to another" (sig. I8). Equally implied here is the converse position—that what is poison in one situation can be readily converted to medicine in another. This insistence is redolent of Paracelsan pharmacy, which famously argued that poison always possesses a medicinal potential.[28] In Mun's treatise, the semantic proximity of "Physick" and "poyson" suggests that a controlled encounter with seeming "illness" can serve a healthy function. I would argue that this quasi-Paracelsan pharmacy underwrites Mun's ambiguous recoding of consumption. No longer a straightforwardly humoral depletion of the lifeblood, consumption has become in *Englands Treasure by Forraign Trade* both an exogenous ailment (a wasting sickness caused by the invasion of "Forraign wares") and a potentially medicinal form of economic activity (a behavior that increases "the necessity and use of our Wares in Foreign Countries"). In the process, Mun arguably creates the template for later uses of consumption in pathological and economic discourse, as well as anticipating the more fundamental transformation of its meaning in Smith's *Wealth of Nations.*[29]

The slippage from the pathological to the economic evident in Mun's writing worked also in the opposite direction. Even as economic writers appropriated and transformed medical models of illness, so did medical writers increasingly rely on new economic theories of wealth. As Roy Porter notes in an important study of consumption's multiple meanings in the eighteenth century, the "model of the healthy body as a vital economy, demanding energetic stimulus, was widely accepted . . . by the medical profession itself." As a result, "medical materialism . . . conceived the pulsating body as a through-put economy whose efficient functioning depended upon generous input and unimpeded outflow."[30] Porter's analysis shows primarily how eighteenth-century models of economic consumption flowed back into the realm of physiology, where they acquired a largely positive connotation. But new habits of economic consumption also transformed understandings of its medical counterpart. The eighteenth-century physician George Cheyne's account of the "English Malady," which he understood largely in nervous rather than humoral terms, centered on consumption. Importantly, he attributed the disease to foreign goods: "Since our wealth has increas'd, and our Navigation has been extended, we have ransack'd all the Parts of the *Globe* to bring together its whole Stock of Materials for *Riot, Luxury,* and to provoke *Excess*."[31] Indeed, the association of luxury consumption with incursions of the foreign—an association already visible in Mun's work—arguably helped foster new understandings of the disease as an exogenous rather than endogenous entity. Thus was generated one of the discursive horizons within which Koch could first imagine, and then discover, the bacteria that cause tuberculosis.

The increased accent on dangerous foreign bodies in both economic and pathological understandings of consumption may have hindered what was to become the second and decisive shift in the term's range of meanings: Adam Smith's valorization of economic consumption as the basis of the healthy (because wealthy) nation. Nevertheless, we might glimpse the etiology of this second shift in Mun's gestures toward Paracelsan pharmacy. As economic consumption began to acquire its modern, positive valence during the eighteenth century, the metaphor of the medicinal disease came into vogue. Like Mun, the physician-turned-writer Bernard de Mandeville extolled the virtues of wasteful luxury consumption as a spur to prosperity and the creation of work for the poor.[32] Daniel Defoe went even further in *A Plan of the English Commerce* (1728), arguing that "the Home Consumption of our own Produce, and of the Produce of foreign Nations imported here is so exceeding great, that our Trade is raised up to such a Prodigy of Magnitude . . . by the Largeness of their Number the whole Country is supported."[33] By 1776, then, Smith had ample rhetorical precedent for his argument that "Consumption is the sole end and purpose of all production; and the interest of the producer ought to be attended to, only so far as it may be necessary for promoting that of the consumer. The maxim is . . . perfectly self-evident."[34] The pathological baggage of "consumption," however, remained a feature of the term even as Smith was writing. These residual meanings served to destabilize whatever "perfectly self-evident," positive effects Smith wished to attribute to consumption. As one French writer observed in 1792, "by the working of a system that seems paradoxical, the English have grown rich by consuming."[35]

It is only in the last century, subsequent to the discovery of a cure for tuberculosis and the disease's retreat from the popular Western imagination, that consumption has largely shed its negative medical connotations. In the various creeds of economic liberalism—particularly the supply-side theory that has been ideologically ascendant in the West during the last three decades—the term is now more or less exclusively deployed as an index of fiscal well-being rather than illness. But it may be worthwhile to retrieve the residual pathological vector of consumption in order to understand the peculiar configurations of the domestic and the foreign, the healthy and the sick, that still haunt the term. Consumption as an index of national economic health is, perhaps paradoxically, bound up with its history as a species of personal illness. As I will show, the overlaps between consumption's mercantile and pathological freight, and the first signs of its modern economic recoding as "healthy," are visible in the city comedies of Thomas Middleton.

From Terminal to Medicinal Consumption: *The Roaring Girl*

In the city comedies that Middleton wrote before 1610, the accumulation and loss of wealth is a recurrent theme; so it is no surprise that the wasteful, pathological sense of "consume" features strongly in their vocabularies.[36] *Michaelmas Term* (1606), for example, associates the word with the wasting of fortunes: Shortyard prays that the "mealy moth consume" the goods that Quomodo has offered him (2.3.180), and Rearage complains that "consumption of the patrimony" is an affliction far worse than "consumption of the liver" (2.1.117–18). The play also associates consumption with a syphilitically coded recklessness of appetite: Salewood, for example, complains that "I'll be damned, an these be not the bones of some quean that cozened me in her life and now consumes me after death" (2.1.125–26). Related to such destructive visions of consumption are a string of metaphors that, as Gail Kern Paster has observed, identify London and its commercial practices with a devouring, gastronomic consumption verging on the cannibalistic.[37] The Courtesan's Father, for example, dubs London "This man-devouring city" (2.2.21); and Shortyard, talking to Easy about Quomodo, observes that "you have fell into the hands of a most merciless devourer, the very gull o'the city" (3.4.73–74). Consumption is associated in all these instances not with the removal of luxury goods from circulation, therefore, but with a pathological wasting of wealth and health alike.

In *A Trick to Catch the Old One* (1606), Middleton develops this wasteful vision of consumption in particularly pathological detail. As in *Michaelmas Term*, the dual depletion of wealth and health by the excessive appetite is syphilitically coded. Hence Witgood asks: "Why should a gallant pay but two shillings for his ordinary that nourishes him, and twenty times two for his brothel that consumes him?" (1.1.3–5). The association of consumption with venereal illness is implicitly reinforced by a string of references to Witgood's dealings with the Courtesan. Witgood bitterly asks her, "Hast thou been the secret consumption of my purse, and now com'st thou to undo my last means, my wits?" (1.1.27–28); the Courtesan refers to herself as "the secret consumption of your purse" (1.1.41), and Onesiphorus wonders of Witgood: "I wonder how he breathes: h'as consumed all upon that courtesan!" (1.1.103–4).

Consumption's status as a species of both corporeal and economic sickness is elaborated with most force in *A Trick to Catch the Old One*'s subplot involving the lawyer-cum-usurer Harry Dampit. His is, at least initially, a seeming rags-to-riches story: Witgood says of Dampit that "his own boast is that he came to town but with ten shillings in his purse and now is credibly worth ten thousand pound!" (1.4.24–25). Yet we never see Dampit at the height of his powers. By act 3, he is renting a lodging in a seedy part of London, and his health has degenerated: he is permanently drunk and "very weak, truly; I have not eaten so much as the bulk of an egg these three days" (3.4.16–17). Indeed, for all his usurious consumption of others' money, he has avoided consuming food: "I eat not one penn'ort' of bread these two years. Give me a glass of fresh beer. I am not sick, nor am I not well" (3.4.27–28). As he physically wastes away, Dampit is also economically consumed. When Lamprey visits him in hopes of borrowing a hundred pounds, he replies, with a pun that conjoins the economic and the pathological, "Alas, you come at an ill time; I cannot spare it i'faith" (4.5.23). Dampit's consumptive illness, figured as it is in the familiar language of devouring and wasting, underscores what the play insists on—that consumption is a specifically *endogenous* disorder, arising from internal venal sins rather than trade between nations.

Michaelmas Term and *A Trick to Catch the Old One* are a world apart from Middleton's later collaboration with Thomas Dekker, *The Roaring Girl*, which dramatizes consumption very differently. This shift is partly the result of an interesting generic experiment: the play yokes Middleton's trademark brand of city comedy, brimful with crafty upper-class scoundrels and wasteful consumers of inherited fortunes, with Dekker's distinctive version of citizen comedy, populated by colorful artisans and shopkeepers. The marriage of the two genres results in a recognizably modern treatment of conspicuous luxury consumption. As I shall also argue, though, *The Roaring Girl*'s new vision of consumption is equally enabled by two crucial reworkings of pathological discourse, both of which parallel the gambits employed by Thomas Mun in his defense of the East India Company: first, the association of consumption with foreign agents; second, the recuperation of consumption as a medicinal practice that has both individual and national benefits.

In *The Roaring Girl*, first performed at the Fortune Theater by Prince Henry's Men in 1611,[38] Middleton and Dekker stage practices of consumption that are more familiar to modern eyes. Indeed, the play might be interpreted as an early modern paean to the universal powers of retail therapy. Nearly all *The Roaring Girl*'s characters—gallants and lowlife, men and women, villains and hero(in)es—spend a considerable portion of their time shopping for the ideal luxury commodity. "What d'ye lack?" asks the shopkeeper Mistress Gallipot (2.1.1), and it is a question that seems to possess a corporeal dimension: as many readers have noticed, the line glances slyly at the testicularly challenged Laxton (or "Lacks Stone").[39] But his anatomical lack is emblematic of a more widespread insufficiency shared by virtually all the characters, a lack for which material goods provide the fetishistic stopgap throughout *The Roaring Girl*. As a result, the play seems to offer a full-fledged depiction of a consumer society in which luxury items are the engines of both desire and identity.

One of the play's most daring pieces of theatrical business involves the onstage presentation of three shops—an apothecary's, a feather seller's, and a seamstress's. All three are examples of what was a relatively new phenomenon at the time the play was written: the luxury commodity outlet store. Of course, there were shops in London long before 1611; but the term "shop" was somewhat ambiguous and could also refer to an artisan's workplace, a stall in a market, or even a tray worn round the neck of a hawker. What we now regard as a shop, an indoor space catering primarily to consumers of luxury items, really only began to emerge in the late sixteenth century. The conjunction of three factors—substantial growth in the city's population, greater wealth amongst the middling sort, and increased availability of exotic luxury goods—had resulted in the proliferation throughout London of new retail outlets for foreign spices, drugs, clothes, and other fine items. Strolling shoppers in the early seventeenth century congregated in new fashionable areas dominated by such outlets: Cheapside, the Royal Exchange, and Britain's Burse in the Strand.[40]

The shops of *The Roaring Girl* respond to this new social phenomenon. Just as importantly, they also represent a new *theatrical* phenomenon. Plays from the 1580s and 1590s such as *Arden of Faversham* staged shop fronts but showed little interest in the goods inside them.[41] The most common interior "shop" location in plays from the 1590s was the cobblers' workshop, whose staging foregrounds artisanal labor rather than commodities for consumption. Hence *Locrine* (1591) depicts Strumbo, Dorothie, and Trompart "cobling shooes and singing"; *George a Greene* (1593) shows a shoemaker at work; Robert Wilson's *Cobbler's Prophecy* (1594) depicts Raph Cobler "with his stoole, his implements and shooes"; and Ben Jonson's *Case is Altered* (1597) displays the cobbler Juniper at work in his shop.[42] All of these scenes may depict goods destined to be retailed, but they do not represent processes of consumption; instead, they valorize the mystery of artisanal skill and the bonds of male fellowship. The props called for in these scenes are presented not as magical luxury items, then, but as material embodiments of relations of production.

By contrast, the Jacobean stage tended to parenthesize artisanal labor, reveling instead in the display of luxury commodities in their retail state. The transitional play was arguably Dekker's *Shoemaker's Holiday,* produced by the Admiral's Men in 1599. Like earlier cobbler plays, this citizen comedy depicts a cordwainers' workshop in which the property of male skill is celebrated over and above the physical items that the shoemakers produce. Yet the play also presents a shop retailing fine cloths, in which Jane the shopkeeper asks, "What is it you lack?"[43] This question is the mantra of subsequent plays that depict shops selling luxury goods: Mistress Gallipot's "What d'ye lack?" in *The Roaring Girl* is echoed by a veritable chorus of shopkeeper characters from Thomas Heywood's *Fayre Mayde of the Exchange* (1602) to Philip Massinger's *Renegado* (1623).[44]

Contrary to the myth of the bare Shakespearean stage, plays with shop scenes necessitated a myriad of expensive props. The playing companies may have been able to furnish from their own stock many of the scenes requiring the sale of clothes; as Peter Stallybrass has noted, the early modern theater was in crucial respects an extension of the English textile industry.[45] But certain other expensive goods required in shop scenes would have had to be specially procured or borrowed. This raises the distinct possibility that something resembling modern practices of product placement was a feature of the early modern theater.[46] The numerous goldsmith shop scenes from the 1590s to the 1630s, for example, would have necessitated the conspicuous display of items not normally found in theater companies' playing stock. In light of recent scholarship that has begun to illuminate the extensive business connections between the theater companies and the London goldsmiths,[47] it is fair to speculate that the theatrical display of expensive goldsmith's wares—for example, the gold plate displayed by apprentices in Heywood's *Edward IV,* the fine wares of the "Goldsmiths shoppe" in Chapman, Jonson, and Webster's *Eastward Hoe,* or the ornate drinking mugs of Jonson's *Epicoene*—may have been part of a commercial quid pro quo: the playing companies obtained goods with which to dazzle their audiences, and the goldsmiths secured an opportunity to advertise their handiwork for free.[48] A similar relationship with London glassmakers may have been required to stage the Tunisian market scene of Massinger's *Renegado*, in which Gazet and Vitelli retail luxury Venetian items, including crystal glasses and a dazzling mirror.[49]

The shops called for in *The Roaring Girl* are likewise brimful with fashionable exotic luxury items that may have required the temporary loan of properties to Prince Henry's Men from private artisans or merchants. The goods retailed by Mistress Overwork in her seamstress's shop are finished cloths imported from the Continent, including "holland linens" and other luxury textiles from the Low Countries—"fine bands and ruffs, fine lawns, fine cambrics" (2.1.2–3).[50] Mistress Tiltyard's feather store retails even more conspicuous luxury items: highly fashionable "spangled" plumage, possibly from Oriental and New World parakeets.[51] But while the company may have possessed sufficient cloth, costumes, and feathers to stock these two shops, it is most likely that the actors would have had to obtain new outlandish properties for Mistress Gallipot's apothecary shop. As we saw in Chapter 5, apothecaries tended to retail exotic commodities; Nathanael Carpenter asserted that "Apothecaries . . . owe most of the medicinable drugges to India."[52] But the apothecary's store also conventionally boasted *wunderkammers* of spectacular goods that were not necessarily for sale, yet added to the luster of their medicinal wares.[53] In *Romeo and Juliet*, Shakespeare describes "an apothecary" in whose "needy shop a tortoise hung, / An alligator stuff'd and other skins" (5.1.37, 42–43); and Thomas Nashe refers to "an Apothecaries Crocodile, or dride *Alligatur*."[54] The staging of apothecaries' shops in the London playhouses may have likewise demanded the display of such trademark properties. In Edward Sharpham's play *The Fleire* (1607), for example, the apothecary Signor Aluno enters "*his shop with wares about him.*"[55] It is quite possible that Mistress Gallipot's shop would have been similarly decorated.

Confronted with the spectacle of the three shops, members of the play's original audiences were given the opportunity to mimic the characters in their perusal of fashionable, eye-catching foreign goods. Such window shopping would not have been confined to the shopkeeper scenes. In addition to the exotic items on display in the apothecary's, seamstress's, and feather seller's shops, the play flaunts a veritable procession of foreign luxury items: the presumably Dutch "falling bands" (1.1.16) that the disguised Mary Fitzallard carries in the first scene; the "cup of rich orleans," a French plum drink, that Neatfoot offers her (1.1.23–24); the "German watch" with which Sir Alexander attempts to bait

Moll (4.1.11). Nor should we forget the audience's vicarious, olfactory consumption of the play's omnipresent North American tobacco (or, as it is also called, the "Indian potherbs" [2.1.10–11]), clouds of which are conspicuously exhaled by Laxton, Goshawk, and Moll in several scenes. Thus was the aptly named Fortune Theater turned into an early-seventeenth-century predecessor of the modern shopping mall, and its audiences cast as potential consumers of synesthetic exotica. As Margaret Ferguson has astutely noted of both the *Wunderkammer* and the early modern stage, "Those relatively new European institutions were coming to function as showcases for New World luxury objects."[56] What Ferguson does not spell out, however, are the ways in which such display implicated the theaters in the *interpellation* of consumer desire—desire both for the foreign goods they displayed and for drama itself as a new species of luxury commodity.

The playwrights were all too aware of this latter function. Middleton's opening letter "to the comic play-readers" literally sells the play as a luxury commodity available for consumption, whether in Thomas Archer's "shop in Popes head-pallace, neere the Royall Exchange" (as the 1611 title page says) or in the Fortune Theater. In his letter, Middleton compares the play to new fashions in clothes: "the fashion of play-making I can properly compare to nothing so naturally as the alteration in apparel" (1–3). The "epilogus" likewise compares its version of Moll to "the picture of a woman (every part / Limned to the life) hung out . . . to sell" (2–3). Other references to playgoing in *The Roaring Girl* draw attention to the commodification of the theater as a new luxury consumer item. Mistress Tiltyard refers to the "twelvepenny-stool gentlemen" (2.1.137), who paid what was then a substantial fee for the privilege of sitting onstage during the performances of plays by the children's companies. And Sir Alexander Wengrave, speaking to his party guests, turns *The Roaring Girl*'s theatrical consumers into his own expensive tchotchkes: under the pretext of showing the other characters his favorite "parlor," he instead displays the well-dressed audience: "when you look into my galleries, / How bravely they are trimmed up" (1.2.14–15). This is a reminder that early modern audience members paid to see not only the play but also each other. As the actors remark of the "goods" in Sir Alexander's parlor, "these sights are excellent!" (1.2.33).

Consumption, in other words, is not only *The Roaring Girl*'s theme; at least in performance, it is also the play's very ontological condition. Yet it is so only catachrestically, for the consumer practices that *The Roaring Girl* foregrounds—the purchase of luxury goods, including the watching of theater's commodified "sights"—do not ever go by the name "consumption" in the play itself. How does *The Roaring Girl*'s abiding fascination with what *we* recognize as practices of consumption square with the pathological discourses of consumption that I have sketched in *Michaelmas Term* and *A Trick to Catch the Old One*? And how might the play look forward to Thomas Mun's conflicted discourses of consumption as both foreign scourge and domestic panacea?

The play's two explicit usages of the term "consumption" and its cognates hark back to Middleton's earlier city comedies. The predatory Laxton, seeking to bleed the Mistress Gallipot of her husband's wealth under the pretext of seducing her, remarks: "She has wit enough to rob her husband, and I ways enough to consume the money" (2.1.93–5). And Master Gallipot fears that his wealth, including "my barns and houses / Yonder at Hockley-hole" are "consumed with fire" (3.2.96–97). These wasteful codings of consumption are implicitly supported by a rash of similar remarks with a pathological edge. Sebastian Wengrave, complaining that his father, Sir Alexander, has refused to allow him to marry Mary Fitzallard, the poor gentlewoman he loves, remarks: "He reckoned up what gold / This marriage would draw from him, at which he swore, / To lose so much blood could not grieve him more" (1.1.84–86). Sebastian's familiar equation of money with blood is hinted at also in Sir Davy Dapper's complaint about his son Jack's profligate habits. Sir Davy believes these to pathologically consume not only Jack's wealth but also his body:

A noise of fiddlers, tobacco, wine, and a whore,
A mercer that will let him take up more,
Dice, and a water-spaniel with a duck,—oh,
Bring him abed with these: when his purse jingles,
Roaring boys follow at's tail, fencers and ningles,
Beasts Adam ne'er gave name to; these horse-leeches suck
My son; he being drawn dry, they all live on smoke. (3.3.64–70)

Sir Davy's critique here sounds remarkably like Thomas Mun's blast against "piping and potting." Mun, we remember, asserts that tobacco sends wealth up "in too much Smoake"; he also sees it as robbing the nation of its virility. His remark that tobacco "hath made us effeminate in our Bodies, weak in our Knowledge, poor in our Treasure, declined in our Valour, unfortunate in our Enterprises" (sig. I2) describes to a tee Sir Davy's foppish son: Jack Dapper's jingling "purse" attracts "roaring boys" and "ningles" who (in language that also recalls the spermatic economies I examined in the last chapter) "suck" him "dry." But Mun's description applies just as well to Laxton, whose dubious virility sees him robbed not only of stones but also of intelligence, money, swordsmanship, and entrepreneurial skill.

Yet even as *The Roaring Girl* anticipates Mun's critiques of the effeminating and enfeebling effects of foreign luxury goods like tobacco, the play also manifests his aversion to restrictions on consumption. Despite Sir Jack Dapper's wasteful behaviors, Moll protects him from his father's mean-spirited attempts to control his spending and punish his profligacy. Instead, the play seems to endorse the voluntarist self-restraint championed by Mun. When Sir Alexander tries to tempt Moll into stealing a golden chain, a ruff, and a German watch, he fails miserably; for she knows how to control herself and her desires. And it is this self-control that distinguishes her consumption from that of the other consumers. Laxton and Dapper compulsively consume luxury goods to fill a lack that is metaleptically refashioned as their desire's effect as well as its cause. The more they get, the more they lose; witness Laxton, whose testicular "cutting" drives him to crave Moll as a kind of surrogate dildo, a "fat eel between a Dutchman's fingers" (2.1.191–92). But after obtaining money from Mistress Gallipot with which to woo Moll, he is "cut" yet more: "Here's blood would have served me this seven year in broken heads and cut fingers" (3.1.127–28), he exclaims after Moll has roundly beaten and scarred him with her sword, thereby forcing a metaphorical reenactment of his castration: "I yield both purse and body" (3.1.121).

Moll, by contrast, is the sublime object of consumer ideology.[57] An impossibly complete being, she is the one character who cannot answer Mistress Gallipot's question, "what d'ye lack?" because she is represented throughout the play as utterly self-sufficient. Her nickname is Cutpurse, but her own testicular "purse" is not cut. If the play's other characters, by consuming, are castrated as they try to remedy a lack within themselves, Moll's consumption is the mark of a unique hermaphroditic plenitude: her fashionable clothes mark her as "both man and woman" (2.1.220), possessed, in Sir Alexander's words, of "two trinkets" (2.2.82). Sir Alexander's term recalls the mercantilist disdain for luxury "trifles," but it simultaneously images a testicular wholeness that renders Moll's consumption "consummate" rather than "consumptive." Moll is less consumer, perhaps, than phantasmatic consumer icon, immaculate in her trendsetting power: as the tailor tells her, "You change the fashion" (2.2.87–88).[58]

Moll's consummate consumption is evident also in *The Roaring Girl*'s treatment of another fashionable commodity: language. Neatfoot the servingman and Jack Dapper are ardent, if awkward, collectors and spenders of the choice term. Likewise, Mistress Overwork says that before she met her husband, she had "my Latin tongue, and a spice of the French" (2.1.356–57). This commodification of fashionable language as foreign "spice" extends also to canting, the lowlife argot that Dapper refers to as "peddlar's French" (5.1.185). In the play's penultimate scene, Jack Dapper tells Lord Noland that "we are making a boon voyage to that nappy land of spice-cakes" (5.1.57–58)—not Cockaigne, let alone the Spice Islands, but Pimlico, a clearinghouse for exotic wares.[59] But the upper-class luxury consumers' planned day trip is interrupted by a chance en-

counter with the equally exotic commodity of "peddlar's French." Moll appre-
hends the cony-catchers Trapdoor and Tearcat, and together with them offers a
crash course in canting to Jack Dapper's band of voyagers. Defending her possession of such knowledge from charges of moral turpitude, Moll tells Sir Nolland:

> Suppose, my lord, you were in Venice—
>
> LORD NOLLAND
> Well.
>
> MOLL
> If some Italian pander there would tell
> All the close tricks of courtesans, would not you
> Hearken to such a fellow?
>
> LORD NOLLAND
> Yes.
>
> MOLL
> And here,
> Being come from Venice, to a friend most dear
> That were to travel thither, you would proclaim
> Your knowledge in these villainies, to save
> Your friend from their quick danger. Must you have
> A black ill name, because ill things you know? (5.1.349–57)

Moll presents her skill as a high-minded, nationalistic anthropology, whereby
consumption of luxurious (and lecherous) Venetian commodities no longer
causes damage but returns wealth to England in the form of protective knowledge. As in Mun's writing, this controlled luxury consumption is presented as a
nationalist form of venture capital, according to which an initial loss is the occasion for future revenue—like the profligate Bassanio's shooting of a second
arrow as a means of recovering the first and thereby acquiring a fortune (*The
Merchant of Venice*, 1.1.140–43).

   The healthy consumption of lowlife terms involves an altogether different
discourse of consumption from that of *Michaelmas Term* or *A Trick to Catch the
Old One*. And although the word "consumption" does not figure explicitly in
this discourse, we can glimpse its presence in the swarm of eating metaphors
that dominates the canting scene. Trapdoor tells Lord Nolland: "half a harvest
with us, sir, and you shall gabble your bellyful" (5.1.195–96). The harvest of canting terms promised by Trapdoor offers a wholesome repast that safeguards
rather than wastes the health of the English body politic. Trapdoor's images of
nutritious eating, which resonate also with Dapper's pursuit of "nappy spice-
cakes," work also to recode "consumption" as a mode of dietary health—just as
Mun suggests in *A Discourse of Trade* that "the moderate vse of wholesome

Druggs and comfortable Spices" serves not "to surfeit, or to please a lickorish tast (as it often happeneth, with many other fruites and wines) but rather as things most necessarie to preserue their health, and to cure their diseases" (sig. B3v).[60]

The Roaring Girl's conflicting attitudes toward consumption as both wasteful and nutritive are shadowed by its conflicting attitudes toward the ingestion of poison. On the one hand, Mistress Overwork insists that gustatory consumption can easily become poisonous: berating the predatory Goshawk, she asks him: "hast not thou / Sucked nourishment even underneath this roof, / And turn'd it all to poison?" (4.2.204–6). Yet in the previous scene, speaking of their dependence on Moll Cutpurse, Mary remarks to Sebastian, "No poison, sir, but serves us for some use" (4.1.148). Mary's maxim evokes Paracelsus's theory of the medicinal value of poisons, a version of which also haunts Mun's Englands Treasure by Forraign Trade. Something of this attitude also applies to the play's justification for the consumption of "peddlar's French." Valerie Forman has shown how The Roaring Girl is preoccupied with issues of commodity exchange and the fungibility of money and goods.[61] But in the play's recuperation of consumption, what is at stake is not straightforward monetary exchange; in the manner of Mun, the play instead invests in the future yield of venture capital. The moral for The Roaring Girl's audiences and for Mun's readers is thus the same—nothing ventured, nothing gained; but equally, nothing consumed, nothing ventured. In the process, Middleton and Dekker make a case for the Fortune Theater as a purveyor of luxury commodities that increase the nation's wealth, in the form of knowledge if not of treasure.

Sea Changes

In his No Wit, No Help Like A Woman's (c. 1611), Middleton uses the generic conventions of romance—separation of a family at sea, reunion and marriage as instruments of redemption—to add a transnational dimension to what is an otherwise equally generic city comedy. The character of the Dutch merchant, for example, an echo of Hans in The Interlude of Wealth and Health, lends the play's portrait of trade a global accent that it tends to lack in Middleton's other city comedies. Still, this innovation is hardly a break with his earlier treatments of consumption; it merely makes explicit what had been metaphorically hinted at in his other plays. Although The Roaring Girl is not a romance, it is still crammed with significant hints of the latter's generic trappings. Indeed, Sebastian and Mary's sea-tossed language in act 1 seems to belong more to the play-world of Pericles than to that of A Trick to Catch the Old One. Mary refers to

Sebastian's father's rejection of her dowry as her "shipwreck" (1.1.95); Sebastian replies that he must "sail . . . with a side-wind" (98, 97) and says that he hopes to force his father "to consent / That here I anchor, rather than be rent / Upon a rock so dangerous" (110–12). In the same vein, Sir Alexander compares the stage to a "floating island" (1.2.31) and calls Moll "a mermaid" who "Has tolled my son to shipwreck" (1.2.218–19). Such language underscores the argument I made in the Introduction: when romance's transoceanic frame of reference collides with the generic concerns of other forms—the Plautine "new" comedy (*The Comedy of Errors*), the Florentine novella (*The Merchant of Venice*), classical epic (*Troilus and Cressida*), satire (*Volpone*), tragicomedy (the pirate plays), and citizen/city comedy (*The Roaring Girl*)—the mercantile is translated from the domain of moral economy into that of national and transnational economy.

But as all the above plays also show, it is in the fertile soil of pathological discourse that the mercantilist drama of national economy first takes root. And conversely, it is in that drama that the language of disease is reformulated and reenergized. The title of this chapter, "Consumption and Consumption," may sound like the name of a Dickensian law firm or of a bad vaudeville agitprop comedy duo. But it is meant to underscore the homologies I have been suggesting throughout this book between the languages of pathology and commerce. The diptychal pairing of early modern disease and economic object that I have reproduced in the title of this and other chapters suggests a play of identity and difference that is at one and the same time discursive (the double helix of pathological and mercantilist writing) and historical (the interplay of past and present). Economic consumption is and is not pathological consumption; the consumption with which we are now familiar is and is not the consumption of early modern culture. There is consumption, and then there is consumption. And in that all-too-easily occulted play of identity and difference, we may spy one of the many etiologies of the modern national economy.

Afterword: Anthrax, Cyberworms, and the New Ethereal Economy

A citizen and his wife the other day
Both riding on one horse, upon the way
I overtook . . .
To get acquaintance with him I began
To sort discourse fit for so fine a man:
I asked the number of the Plaguy Bill,
Asked if the Custom Farmers held out still,
Of the Virginia plot, and whether Ward
The traffic of the Midland seas had marred,
Whether the Britain Bourse did fill pace,
And likely were to give th'Exchange disgrace;
Of new-built Aldgate, and the Moorfield crosses
Of store of bankrupts, and poor merchants' losses
I urged him to speak . . .

—John Donne, "A Tale of A Citizen and His Wife"

John Donne's sketch of London citizen chatter traces by-now familiar themes, themes that effectively summarize the preoccupations of mercantilist drama.[1] Like *The Comedy of Errors* and *The Merchant of Venice*, Donne's elegy lingers on the ill fortunes of commercial venturers ("poor merchants' losses"). In the manner of *Troilus and Cressida*, it fixates on the sources of value and national wealth ("the Britain Bourse," "likely were to give th'Exchange disgrace"). Following the lead of *Volpone*, it links talk of epidemic disease (the "Plaguy Bill") to surveillance of the nation's borders (the "Custom Farmers," or people to whom customs duties were farmed out). As do *The Fair Maid of the West* and *The Renegado*, it ponders the activities of Barbary corsairs in the Mediterranean ("Ward / The traffic of the Midland seas had marred"). And like *The Roaring Girl*, it conjures up the specter of wasteful consumption ("store of bankrupts") against a backdrop of London scenes of new economic prosperity ("new-built Aldgate") and deadly disease ("the Moorfield crosses").

In the process, Donne's elegy neatly summarizes and satirizes the points of connection that provided the chattering classes of early modern London with a "fit discourse"—or what we might call "news"—about the nation. Like the mercantilist dramas I have studied in this book, this discourse conjoins the economic and the pathological: for Donne's narrator and his citizen companion, "plague" and the funereal "Moorfield crosses" it helps erect are every bit as much players on the national stage as are "the Britain Bourse" and "th'Exchange." Also like the dramas of mercantilism, these domestic phenomena take their place within a global arena: talk of the nation leads to the activities of merchant venturing joint-stock companies and John Ward's Mediterranean piracy. And as these two last newsworthy topics suggest, the medium of global economy for both Donne's citizen and mercantilist drama is the sea.

How different is "news" about the economy at the beginning of the twenty-first century? The media for such chatter has changed: Donne's horseback banter has been replaced by the pronouncements of editorial pages, TV current affairs shows, and talk radio. The topics of economic news have changed too, even if John Ward's piracy has now yielded only to the white-collar pirates of Enron and World.com. But I would argue that the rhetorical strategies U.S. journalists employ to represent the national economy are often fundamentally similar to those of Donne's citizens. This continuity has been particularly evident since the traumatic events of September 11, 2001. In the immediate aftermath of the attack on the World Trade Center, the *New Yorker* characterized the hijackers who crashed planes into the two towers as "lethal viruses" that, targeting the monuments to global capitalism, "rode the flow of the world's aerial circulatory system."[2] In this version of economic pathology, as in early modern mercantilist drama, the foreign is stigmatized in order to naturalize the global: the two towers may fall under attack by "lethal" Middle Eastern terrorists, but the "circulatory system" that conveyed the "viruses" to their targets remains intact. Yet there is also one crucial difference: the medium of that global "system" has changed from sea to air.

The anthrax and smallpox scares of 2001 to 2003 have underlined this transformation. Unlike early modern humoral understandings of anthrax as "a Carbocle" which "doth come of . . . some euyll humour"[3] or of the "small pockes" as emerging from "houte and slimy" menstrual blood,[4] both diseases are now regarded as archetypes of the aerially transmitted foreign body. In the last months of 2001, U.S. media fears focused on how finely milled anthrax bacteria can be released into the atmosphere by crop dusters or circulated through public ventilation systems. Likewise in 2002, as mass inoculations of U.S. health workers against smallpox began, the media warned against a revival of the seemingly once extinct variola virus, which causes the illness by being absorbed through the respiratory tract. Because of both diseases' association in this country with the threat of foreign bioterror—despite the fact that the United States has been the world's largest producer of weapons-grade anthrax—each came to be doubly coded as invasive. Hence as Americans fretted about inhaling virulent viruses or spores, the news networks speculated (incorrectly, as it transpired) about a possible Iraqi source for the anthrax contained in the letters sent to NBC news anchor Tom Brokaw and Senators Tom Daschle and Patrick Leahy. And as the Bush administration geared up for war with Saddam Hussein in 2003, it entertained the possibility of attack from Al-Qaeda terrorists dispatched to unleash aerial payloads of the smallpox virus or nerve gas. Sales of duct tape (with which to seal cracked windows and troublesome gaps under doors) soared: air, or at least air from the *outside,* had become a source of pathogen panic.

The anthrax and smallpox scares have operated in a somewhat different register from the *New Yorker*'s reaction to September 11. But the two diseases' mode of transmission is profoundly implicated in how we are now accustomed to imagine the sphere of the economic. Theories of aerially transmitted diseases are hardly new: as we have seen, Hippocrates's miasmic pathology was organized around his understanding of polluted vapors, and Fracastoro and Paracelsus both proposed that infection was conveyed through the air by seeds of disease. Yet fantasies of diseased air have acquired a formidable charge in an age where the transnational movements of capital take place less upon the ocean than in the air—or its cybernetic and etymological equivalent, the ether.

As Fredric Jameson has noted, the finance capital moment of globalized society involves new forms of abstraction made available by computer technologies.[5] These forms have also begun to alter the ways in which we conceive of disease. The discourses of systems theory and electronic technology inflect, for example, new understandings of sickness as dysfunctional "information" "encoded" in genes and viral RNA.[6] Yet even if such understandings might seem to spell a partial return to endogenous models of pathology, the new electronic technologies have equally entailed heightened anxiety about the permeability of bounded systems. We speak of computer viruses infecting our hard drives, after all, and the brace of invasive e-pathologies to which computer users worldwide are becoming accustomed cannot be divorced from the transnational flows of capital through the Worldwide Web's ethereal "circulatory systems" of exchange. The "Slammer Worm," which disabled five of the Internet's thirteen servers in January 2003, for example, wrought not only electronic but also serious economic havoc: thousands of ATM machines operated by the Canadian Imperial Bank of Commerce and the Bank of America failed to dispense cash, and online trading ground to a halt in South Korea, bringing the national stock market to a thirteen-month low. This breakdown was initially attributed not to dysfunctions within the Worldwide Web itself, however, but to the machinations of evil foreign bodies. In the days following the Slammer Worm attack, *Computerworld* magazine published on its website an e-mail interview with an alleged member of the Pakistani radical group Harkat-ul-Mujahideen; the "Islamic" inter-viewee—subsequently exposed as an American prankster—claimed that the Worm was part of the campaign of terror against the United States, designed to inflict damage on its economy by exploiting the efficacy of the Worldwide Web.[7]

The ether and its related aerial abstractions, then, have provided yet an-other potent means of simultaneously pathologizing the foreign and ratifying the global. Fears that the United States is vulnerable to both metaphorical and "natural" diseases from abroad—whether the September 11 hijacker "viruses" or "Iraqi" anthrax, the ethereal "Asian flu" or the aerially-transmitted S.A.R.S. virus, the shadowy "Pakistani" Slammer Worm or "Al-Qaeda" nerve gas—have worked to lash the pathological more firmly to the foreign, and the foreign to the pathological. Yet these fears simultaneously confirm the efficacious "flow of the world's aerial circulatory system[s]," which are constituted as the neutral media of pathology rather than its cause. What tends to get effaced in such fears, in other words, is how the origin of the "pathological" need not be straight-forwardly foreign; it can be equally domestic or globally systemic.

The *New Yorker*'s tale of "lethal viruses," like the tale of the "Asian flu," high-lights how discourses of economic pathology are not simply *vocabularies*. They are also *narratives*, with explanatory beginnings and pathological endings: in the physis of global commerce, these narratives insist, it is only "natural" that a foreign pathogen will migrate from overseas, and with devastating effect. The narrative component of discourse is often forgotten in scholarship indebted to Foucault, who, for all his Panglossic erudition, was never a literary critic. If this neglected literary dimension is apparent in discourses of economic pathology, however, it is even more so in medical discourses of etiology. Any etiology of a disease is, after all, a narrative of pathological origin, motion, and ending. The etiological narrative goes under a fascinating pseudonym in medical discourse: "natural history." This immensely suggestive phrase potentially foregrounds even as it ostensibly occludes how any discourse of the "natural" always has a *history*, in the twin sense of a fictitious "story" that destabilizes that discourse's claim to facticity and a past that displaces the supposedly originary status of the "natural." In *Sick Economies*, I have provided a two-tiered "natural history" of the national economy in both these senses. I have critically recounted mercan-tilism's dramas of economic pathology to broaden our understanding of early modern fictions of the nation. But I have done so equally to illuminate the dis-cursive histories that have enabled, yet also throw into question, our own "nat-ural" dramas of the domestic, the foreign, and the global.

Notes

Chapter 1. The Asian Flu

1. The ongoing metaphorical use of the body in economic discourse has been acknowledged without ever being subjected to sustained analysis. Discussions of economic corporeal analogy tend to single out the theories of the eighteenth-century French Physiocrats: see, for example, Henry William Spiegel, *The Growth of Economic Thought*, 3rd ed. (Durham, N.C.: Duke University Press, 1991), 183–200, esp. 196–97. For an early modern discussion of the medical meanings of "inflation," see Andrew Boorde, *The Breuiary of Helthe, for All Maner of Syckenesses and Diseases the Whiche May Be in Man, or Woman* (London, 1547), sig. U3. I discuss the pathological dimensions of economic consumption in Chapter 7.

2. Romance, of course, is a notoriously tricky genre to define. For particularly useful discussions of the genre's form, see W. P. Ker, *Epic and Romance: Essays on Medieval Literature*, 2nd ed. (London: Macmillan, 1908); Erich Auerbach, *Mimesis: The Representation of Reality in Western Literature,* trans Willard Trask (Princeton, N.J.: Princeton University Press, 1953), 123–42; Northrop Frye, *The Secular Scripture: A Study of the Structure of Romance* (Cambridge, Mass.: Harvard University Press, 1976); Fredric Jameson, "Magical Narratives: Romance as Genre," *New Literary History* 7 (1975): 135–63; and Patricia A. Parker, *Inescapable Romance: Studies in the Poetics of a Mode* (Princeton, N.J.: Princeton University Press, 1979). Useful discussions devoted to Shakespeare's treatment of the genre include E. C. Pettet, *Shakespeare and the Romance Tradition* (London: Staples Press, 1949); and Howard Felperin, *Shakespearean Romance* (Princeton, N.J.: Princeton University Press, 1972).

3. See Richard Helgerson, *Forms of Nationhood: The Elizabethan Writing of England* (Berkeley: University of California Press, 1992); Claire McEachern, *Poetics of English Nationhood, 1590–1612* (Cambridge: Cambridge University Press, 1996); Jean E. Howard and Phyllis Rackin, *Engendering a Nation: A Feminist Account of Shakespeare's English Histories* (London: Routledge, 1997); John J. Joughin, ed., *Shakespeare and National Culture* (Manchester: Manchester University Press, 1997); and David J. Baker, *Between Nations: Shakespeare, Spenser, Marvell, and the Question of Britain* (Stanford, Calif.: Stanford University Press, 1997).

4. See the OED, economy, I.1. The term "the economy" does not appear until after the war—revealingly, perhaps, the OED does not include it in its list of definitions—but it has its roots in the concept of "political economy," coined by Sir John Stewart and Adam Smith and defined by the OED as "originally the art or practical science of managing the resources of a nation so as to increase its material prosperity" (economy, 3).

5. Charles W. Cole, "The Heavy Hand of Hegel," in Edward Mead Earle ed., *Na-

tionalism and Internationalism (New York: Columbia University Press, 1950), 64–78, esp. 75. Many other economic historians have similarly problematized the existence of mercantilism. See, for example, A. V. Judges, "The Idea of a Mercantile State," *Transactions of the Royal Historical Society* 4th ser. 21 (1939): 41–69, which concludes that mercantilism is an imaginary construction that falsely reconciles widely disparate ideas. For reviews of the debate over mercantilism as a historically coherent phenomenon, see Charles Wilson, " 'Mercantilism': Some Vicissitudes of an Idea," *Economic History Review* 2nd ser. 10 2 (1957): 181–88; and D. C. Coleman, ed., *Revisions in Mercantilism* (London: Methuen, & Co., 1969), passim.

6. Adam Smith, *An Inquiry into the Nature and Causes of the Wealth of Nations* (London, 1776), bk. 4, chap. 1.

7. Karl Marx, *A Contribution to the Critique of Political Economy* (London: Lawrence and Wishart, 1971), 158.

8. Gustav von Schmoller, *The Mercantile System and Its Historical Significance* (New York: Macmillan, 1897), 50.

9. Julie Robin Solomon, *Objectivity in the Making: Francis Bacon and the Politics of Inquiry* (Baltimore: Johns Hopkins University Press, 1998), 65.

10. Eli Heckscher, *Mercantilism*, 2 vols., 2nd ed., trans. Mendel Shapiro (London: Allen and Unwin, 1955), 1: 19, 21.

11. See Heckscher, *Mercantilism*, 1: 51.

12. Henry Robarts, *The Trumpet of Fame* (London, 1595), sig. A3.

13. Heckscher, *Mercantilism*, 1: 422.

14. Mary Poovey, *A History of the Modern Fact: Problems of Knowledge in the Sciences of Wealth and Society* (Chicago: University of Chicago Press, 1998). See also Michel Foucault, *The Order of Things: An Archaeology of the Human Sciences* (London: Tavistock, 1970), 174–80.

15. As some economic historians have recently pointed out, Smith's historical distinction between interventionist mercantilism and laissez-faire capitalism overlooks how the former often expressed versions of economic liberalism: both Mun and Misselden, for example, are far less defensive of protectionism than Malynes and Milles. See Terence Hutchison, *Before Adam Smith: The Emergence of Political Economy, 1622–1776* (Oxford: Basil Blackwell, 1988); and Lars Magnusson, *Mercantilism: The Shaping of an Economic Language* (London: Routledge, 1994). See also Anna Neill, *British Discovery Literature and the Rise of Global Commerce* (New York: Palgrave, 2002), esp. 18–22.

16. The term "bullionist" was coined by the nineteenth-century economist Richard Jones in his essay "Primitive Political Economy of England," *Edinburgh Review* (1847), reprinted in his *Literary Remains,* ed. W. Whewell (London: John Murray, 1859), 291–335. The best discussion of bullionism is Raymond de Roover, *Gresham on the Foreign Exchange* (Cambridge, Mass.: Harvard University Press, 1949).

17. For a discussion of the doctrine of cosmopolitan universal economy, see Douglas A. Irwin, *Against the Tide: An Intellectual History of Free Trade* (Princeton, N.J.: Princeton University Press, 1996), 11–15. Plutarch, for example, wrote of the sea that "this element, therefore, when our life was savage and unsociable, linked it together and made it complete, redressing defects by mutual assistance and exchange and so bringing about co-operation and friendship . . . the sea brought the Greeks the vine from India, from Greece transmitted the use of grain across the sea, thus preventing the greater part of mankind from being wineless, grainless, and unlettered." Quoted in Irwin, 11.

18. Edward Misselden, *Free Trade, or The Meanes to Make Trade Florish: Wherein, The Causes of the Decay of Trade in this Kingdome, are Discovered: And the Remedies also to Remove the Same, are Represented* (London, 1622), sig. C5.

19. Gerard Malynes, *Consuetedo, Vel, Lex Mercatoria; or, The Ancient Law-Merchant* (London, 1622), 1: 3–4.

20. On these distinctions, see Alfred F. Chalk, "Natural Law and the Rise of Economic Liberalism in England," *Journal of Political Economy* 59 (1951): 332–47. Chalk provides a useful account of the tension in mercantilist writing between support for natural laws of trade and endorsements of statutory law to control it.

21. Edward Misselden, *The Circle of Commerce: Or, the Balance of Trade, in Defence of Free Trade: Opposed to Malynes Little Fish and His Great Whale, and Poized Against Them in the Scale* (London, 1623), sig. Dd2. Compare Francis Bacon's famous articulation of the law: "Let the foundation of profitable trade be thus laid that the exportation of home commodities be more in value than the importation of the foreign, so we shall be sure that the stocks of the kingdom shall increase, for the balance of the trade must be returned in money or bullion." Cited in Spiegel, *Growth of Economic Thought*, 99.

22. "*Monsieur Bodine* the great *Polititian of France* . . . shewed that they had needed of the Stranger, and most especially of the *Traffique* with them. . . . God caused nature to distribute her benefites, or his blessings to seuerall *Climates*, supplying the barrennesse of some things in one countrey, with the fruitfulnesse and store of other countries, to the end that interchangeably one Common-weale should liue with an other." Gerard Malynes, *The Maintenance of Free Trade, According to the Three Essentiall Parts of Traffique; Namely, Commodities, Moneys, and Exchange of Moneys, by Bills of Exchanges for Other Countries* (London, 1622), sigs. E5v–E6.

23. Thomas More, *Utopia*, ed. George M. Logan and Robert M. Adams (Cambridge: Cambridge University Press, 1989), 107.

24. Misselden, *Circle of Commerce*, 17.

25. Thomas Mun, *Englands Treasure by Forraign Trade; Or, The Ballance of our Forraign Trade is The Rule of our Treasure* (London, 1669), sigs. G5v–G6.

26. Gerard Malynes, *Saint George for England Allegorically Described* (London, 1601); see also my discussion of this text in Chapter 3.

27. Thomas Milles, *The Custumers Alphabet and Primer: Conteining, Their Creede or Beliefe in the true Doctrine of Christian Religion* (London, 1608), sig. D2v.

28. Mun, *Englands Treasure by Forraign Trade*, sig. A6v.

29. A round of "hazard" is played in the opening scene of Robert Daborne's pirate drama, *A Christian Turned Turk*, in Daniel J. Vitkus, ed., *Three Turk Plays from Early Modern England: "Selimus," "A Christian Turned Turk," "The Renegado"* (New York: Columbia University Press, 2000), 157–58.

30. All references to *The Merchant of Venice* are to the Norton edition and are cited in the text. For a very useful discussion of how Bassanio's questing is suffused with language that echoes that of privateering and merchant adventurism, see Theodore B. Leinwand, *Theatre, Finance, and Society in Early Modern England* (Cambridge: Cambridge University Press, 1999), 113–19.

31. Leinwand, *Theatre, Finance, and Society*, 115.

32. G. W. H. Griffin, *Shylock: A Burlesque, As Performed by Griffin & Christy's Minstrels* (New York: Samuel French, 1876), 8.

33. Gerard Malynes, *A Treatise of the Canker of England's Commonwealth* (London,

1601), passim; *Saint George for England Allegorically Described*, 49; and *The Center of the Circle of Commerce; or, A Refutation of a Treatise, Intituled The Circle of Commerce, or The Ballance of Trade, Lately Published by E.M.* (London, 1623), sigs. R3v–S1.

34. Milles, *Custumers Alphabet*, sig. D2v.

35. Misselden, *Free Trade*, sig. B5v.

36. Mun, *Englands Treasure by Forraign Trade*, sig. L2v.

37. See Susan Sontag, *Illness as Metaphor* (New York: Farrar, Straus and Giroux, 1978), and *AIDS and Its Metaphors* (New York: Farrar, Straus and Giroux, 1989).

38. On the history of Galenism, see Owsei Temkin, *Galenism: Rise and Decline of a Medical Philosophy* (Ithaca, N.Y.: Cornell University Press, 1973).

39. Hippocrates blamed factors in the atmosphere for the appearance of infectious disease. For him and subsequent physicians, a "miasma" (derived from the Greek *Miasma*, related to *Miainein*, to pollute), composed of bad-smelling, poisonous particles created by the death and decay of organic matter, was implicated in a broad array of fevers. For a discussion of the miasmatic theory of disease in Shakespeare's London, see Leeds Barroll, *Politics, Plague, and Shakespeare's Theater: The Stuart Years* (Ithaca, N.Y.: Cornell University Press, 1991), chap. 3. I discuss providential models of disease in more detail in Chapter 5.

40. Galen's theory of the humors had long been dominant in English scholastic medicine, but it acquired additional authority with the 1521 translation by Dr. Thomas Linacre, founder of the College of Physicians in London, of Galen's most detailed treatise on the complexional theory of health, under the title *Galeni Pergamensis de Temperamentis, et de Inaequali Intemperie* (London, 1521). This version provided Thomas Elyot, a pupil of Linacre, with the source for his widely read *Castel of Helthe* (London, 1539), revised in 1541 and regularly reprinted until 1610. See also Boorde, *Breuiary of Helthe*. For a useful discussion of Galenic complexional theory and its adaptation by Renaissance physicians, see Linda Deer Richardson, "The Generation of Disease: Occult Causes and Diseases of the Total Substance," in A. Wear, R. K. French, and I. M. Lonie, eds., *The Medical Renaissance of the Sixteenth Century* (Cambridge: Cambridge University Press, 1985), 175–94.

41. Thomas Starkey, *A Dialogue Between Reginald Pole and Thomas Lupset*, ed. Kathleen M. Burton (London: Chatto and Windus, 1948), 64.

42. Milles, *Custumers Alphabet*, sig. G2.

43. Thomas Laqueur, *Making Sex: Body and Gender from the Greeks to Freud* (Cambridge, Mass.: Harvard University Press, 1990), 35.

44. Thomas Mun, *A Discourse of Trade, From England Vnto the East-Indies, Answering to Diuerse Objections Which Are Usually Made Against the Same* (London, 1621), 41. For a fine discussion of the "glutted, unvented" body politic of mercantilist writing, see Margaret Healy, *Fictions of Disease in Early Modern England: Bodies, Plagues, and Politics* (New York: Palgrave, 2001), esp. 195–99. For another excellent discussion of the mercantilist discourse of venting, see Mark Netzloff's paper, " 'Venting Trinculos': Race, Class, and the Language of Capital," presented at the 35th International Congress of Medieval Studies, Kalamazoo, Mich., May 2000. In her *Harmony and the Balance: An Intellectual History of Seventeenth-Century English Economic Thought* (Ann Arbor: University of Michigan Press, 2000), Andrea Finkelstein examines the relationship between the mercantilist theory of "balance of trade" and a physiologically conceived body politic,

though she does not consider how the mercantilists' language of balance resonates with humoral discourse.

45. Malynes, *Saint George for England Allegorically Described*, 14.

46. Girolamo Fracastoro, *De Contagione at Contagiosis Morbis et Eorum Curatione*, trans. Wilmer Care Wright (New York: Putnam, 1933), 34–35. For a useful overview of Fracastoro's conception of disease, see Vivian Nutton, "The Seeds of Disease: An Explanation of Contagion and Infection from the Greeks to the Renaissance," *Medical History* 27 (1983): 1–34. Fracastoro named syphilis, but his ontological model of disease was devoted largely to explaining plague; he himself believed syphilis to have primarily astrological causes. See *De Contagione*, 151. For Paracelsus's account of the *seminaria* of disease, see "Von Blatern, Lähmi, Beulen, Löchern, und Zitrachen der Franzosen und irs Gleichen," in Paracelsus, *Sämtliche Werke*, ed. Karl Sudhoff, 14 vols. (Munich: R. Oldenbourg: 1922), 6: 301–479, esp. bk. 2, chap. 10. The most thorough analysis of Paracelsus's pathology remains Walter Pagel's *Paracelsus: An Introduction to Philosophical Medicine in the Era of the Renaissance* (Basel: Karger, 1958), esp. 134–40. See also Paul Kocher, "Paracelsan Medicine in England," *Journal of the History of Medicine* 2 (1947): 251–80.

47. On the emergence of protomicrobiological or "ontological" notions of disease in the sixteenth century and earlier, see Pagel, *Paracelsus*, esp. 134–40; Nutton, "Seeds of Disease"; and Jonathan Gil Harris, *Foreign Bodies and the Body Politic: Discourses of Social Pathology in Early Modern England* (Cambridge: Cambridge University Press, 1998), chap. 2, esp. 22–30.

48. George Rosen, *A History of Public Health*, expanded ed. (Baltimore: Johns Hopkins University Press, 1993), 84.

49. For Paracelsus's considerable influence on seventeenth-century medicine, see Walter Pagel, *From Paracelsus to Van Helmont: Studies in Renaissance Medicine and Science*, ed. Marianne Winder (London: Variorum Reprints, 1986).

50. In book 6 of *De Rerum Natura*, Lucretius attempts to explain the etiology and form of plague in accordance with his atomic theory. Departing from Hippocratic orthodoxy, he sees plague as less a state caused by miasma or contaminated air than by particles that migrate from body to body. In her translation of Lucretius, which dates from the 1650s, Lucy Hutchinson renders the plague particles as "flowing seeds" that "spring up by chance / And, towards the troubled heavens, in throngs advance." Hugh de Quehen, ed., *Lucy Hutchinson's Translation of Lucretius: De Rerum Natura*, (Ann Arbor: University of Michigan Press, 1996), 205. See also Margaret Cavendish, *A Discovery of the New World Called the Blazing World*, in *The Blazing World and Other Writings*, ed. Kate Lilley (Harmondsworth: Penguin, 1994), 158–59. See also Chapter 5, in which I discuss Cavendish's and other seventeenth-century writers' interest in Lucretius.

51. Rosen, *History of Public Health*, 84.

52. Rosen, *History of Public Health*, 64. On the "Irish disease," see Eric Gruber von Arni, *Justice to the Maimed Soldier: Nursing, Medical Care, and Welfare for the Sick and Wounded Soldiers and Their Families During the English Civil Wars and Interregnum, 1642–1660* (Aldershot, Hampshire: Ashgate, 2001), 6.

53. Claude Quétel, *History of Syphilis*, trans. Judith Braddock and Brian Pike (Baltimore: Johns Hopkins University Press, 1992), 16.

54. See Ann Rosalind Jones and Peter Stallybrass, *Renaissance Clothing and the Materials of Memory* (Cambridge: Cambridge University Press, 2000), chap. 3, "Yellow

Starch: Fabrications of the Jacobean Court," 59–85; and Sara Warneke, "A Taste for New-fangledness: The Destructive Potential of Novelty in Early Modern England," *Sixteenth Century Journal* 26 (1995): 881–96.

55. John Deacon, *Tobacco Tortured, Or the Filthie Fume of Tobacco Refined* (London, 1616). I am grateful to Lloyd Edward Kermode for drawing my attention to this reference. See his essay "The Playwright's Prophecy: Robert Wilson's *The Three Ladies of London* and the 'Alienation' of the English," *Medieval and Renaissance Drama in England* 11 (1999): 60–87, esp. 69.

56. Jean-Noël Biraben, "Diseases in Europe: Equilibrium and Breakdown of the Pathocenosis," in Mirko D. Grmek, ed., *Western Medical Thought from Antiquity to the Middle Ages,* (Cambridge, Mass.: Harvard University Press, 1999), 319–53.

57. Jared Diamond, *Guns, Germs, and Steel: The Fates of Human Societies* (New York: Random House, 1997), esp. 197–210.

58. Malynes, *Saint George for England,* 14.

59. Mary Douglas, *Purity and Danger: An Analysis of the Concepts of Pollution and Taboo* (London: Routledge, 1996), 116.

60. Emily Martin, *Flexible Bodies: The Role of Immunity in American Culture from the Days of Polio to the Age of AIDS* (Boston: Beacon Press, 1994), 53.

61. Georges Canguilhem, *The Normal and the Pathological,* trans. Carolyn R. Fawcett and Robert S. Cohen (New York: Zone Books, 1991); René Girard, "The Plague In Literature," in his *To Double Business Bound: Essays on Literature, Mimesis, and Anthropology* (Baltimore: Johns Hopkins University Press, 1978), 136–54; Emile Durkheim, *Rules of Sociological Method,* trans. W. D. Halls (New York, Macmillan, 1982).

62. Foucault, *Order of Things,* xxiv.

63. Paul Slack, *The Impact of Plague in Tudor and Stuart England* (London: Routledge and Kegan Paul, 1985), 25.

64. Thomas Dekker, "London Looke Backe," in F. P. Wilson ed., *The Plague Pamphlets of Thomas Dekker* (Oxford: Clarendon Press, 1925), 181.

65. *An Interlude of Wealth and Health, Very Mery and Ful of Pastyme* (London: Malone Society Reprints, 1910). All references are cited in the text.

66. I adapt Cohen's immensely suggestive phrase, but I do so in order to characterize a very different genre—or, perhaps more accurately, tendency—of drama from the history play that he sees as the exemplum of early modern European dramatic nationalism. See Walter Cohen, *Drama of a Nation: Public Theater in Renaissance England and Spain* (Ithaca, N.Y.: Cornell University Press, 1985), 218–52.

67. Jean-Christophe Agnew, *Worlds Apart: The Market and the Theater in Anglo-American Thought, 1550–1750* (Cambridge: Cambridge University Press, 1986); and Douglas Bruster, *Drama and the Market in the Age of Shakespeare* (Cambridge: Cambridge University Press, 1992).

68. Barroll, *Politics, Plague, and Shakespeare's Theater;* passim.

69. Thomas White, *A Sermon Preached at Pawles Crosse on Sunday the Thirde of November 1577, In the Time of the Plague* (London, 1578), sig. C8.

70. Jameson, "Magical Narratives," 161.

71. Joan Pong Linton, *The Romance of the New World: Gender and the Literary Formations of English Colonialism* (Cambridge: Cambridge University Press, 1998). See also Roland Greene, *Unrequited Conquests: Love and Empire in the Colonial Americas* (Chicago: University of Chicago Press, 1999). For an argument that begins to bridge the

gap between Linton's and mine, see Leinwand, *Theatre, Finance, and Society,* esp. chap. 4, "Venture Capital," 110–39.

72. For a useful discussion of literary *contaminatio* in the context of empire and nation formation, see Heather James, *Shakespeare's Troy: Drama, Politics, and the Translation of Empire* (Cambridge: Cambridge University Press, 1997).

Chapter 2: Syphilis and Trade

1. See Greg W. Bentley, *Shakespeare and the New Disease: The Dramatic Function of Syphilis in "Troilus and Cressida," "Measure for Measure," and "Timon of Athens"* (New York: Peter Lang, 1989); Margaret Healy, *Fictions of Disease in Early Modern England: Bodies, Plagues, and Politics* (New York: Palgrave, 2001), esp. 172–85; and Johannes Fabricius, *Syphilis in Shakespeare's England* (London: Jessica Kingsley, 1994). I also discuss the problem of syphilis in Shakespeare's problem plays in Chapter 4.

2. All references to Shakespeare's works, unless specified otherwise, are to G. Blakemore Evans et al., eds., *The Riverside Shakespeare,* 2nd ed. (Boston: Houghton Mifflin, 1997).

3. Fabricius, *Syphilis in Shakespeare's England,* esp. chap. 11, "Shakespeare's Midlife Crisis," 231–54.

4. Formalist approaches to the play's treatment of its classical sources are offered by T. W. Baldwin, *On the Compositional Genetics of "The Comedy of Errors"* (Urbana: University of Illinois Press, 1965); A. C. Hamilton, "The Early Comedies: *The Comedy of Errors,"* in Hamilton, *The Early Shakespeare* (San Marino, Calif.: Huntington Library, 1967); John Arthos, "Shakespeare's Transformation of Plautus," *Comparative Drama* 1 (1967–68): 239–53; Leo Salingar, *Shakespeare and the Traditions of Comedy* (Cambridge: Cambridge University Press, 1974), esp. 59–67; and Catherine M. Shaw, "The Conscious Art of *The Comedy of Errors,"* in Maurice Charney, ed., *Shakespearean Comedy* (New York: New York Literary Forum, 1980), 17–28.

5. Discussions of commerce in the play have often paradoxically served to subordinate consideration of mercantile matters to analysis of the characters' psychological experiences. Richard Henze, for example, analyzes the circulations of the golden chain, or "carcanet," that Antipholus of Ephesus promises Adriana, but he is interested less in the commercial implications of its transactions than in the "distrust" and "confusion" that these engender: see "*The Comedy of Errors:* A Freely Binding Chain," *Shakespeare Quarterly* 22 (1971): 35–42, esp. 40. And in an influential reading of *The Comedy of Errors,* Barbara Freedman argues that "the play . . . is not simply about the payment of debts or the physical division and reunion of the family, but about the psychic division and integration of a personality"; see "Errors in Comedy: A Psychoanalytic Theory of Farce," in Charney, ed., *Shakespearean Comedy,* 233–43, esp. 235. Douglas Bruster offers a welcome if somewhat abbreviated corrective to these approaches in *Drama and the Market in the Age of Shakespeare* (Cambridge: Cambridge University Press, 1992), 73–77.

6. *The Works of Mr William Shakespear,* ed. Alexander Pope, 6 vols. (London, 1723), 1: v.

7. According to Edward H. Sugden, the Phoenix was the name of a London tavern as well as of a shop on Lombard Street; see Sugden, *A Topographical Dictionary to the*

Works of Shakespeare and His Fellow-Dramatists (Manchester: Manchester University Press, 1925), 409. For an early modern account of the central role played by Lombard Street in London's foreign trade, see John Stowe, *A Survey of London,* ed. Charles Lethbridge (Oxford: Clarendon Press, 1908), 1: 201.

8. As critics have noted, Shakespeare draws his framing story from romance sources such as Gower's *Apollonius, Prince of Tyre,* to which he was to return when he wrote *Pericles.* In reading his Plautine source play, however, Shakespeare's "romantic" imagination may have been influenced by the Latin farce's mercantile subtext. Interestingly, the *Menaechmi* separates the twins not through a shipwreck, as in *The Comedy of Errors,* but at a marketplace. In the English translation by "W. W." (probably William Warner), published in 1595 but perhaps circulated before then, Menaechmus the Citizen explains that "I went with my father to Tarentum, to a great mart, and there in the press I was stolen from him." See *Menaechmi,* 5.1, printed in William Shakespeare, *The Comedy of Errors,* ed. David Bevington (New York: Bantam, 1988), 115.

9. See Sandra K. Fischer, *Econolingua: A Glossary of Coins and Economic Language in Renaissance Drama* (Newark: University of Delaware Press, 1985).

10. On the technical details of foreign exchange and the role of the factor in early modern England and on the Continent, see Raymond de Roover, "What is Dry Exchange? A Contribution to the Study of English Mercantilism," in de Roover, *Business, Banking, and Economic Thought in Late Medieval and Early Modern Europe,* ed. Julius Kirshner (Chicago: University of Chicago Press, 1974), 183–99; and Brian E. Supple, "Currency and Commerce in the Early Seventeenth Century," *Economic History Review,* 2nd ser. 10 (1957): 239–55.

11. Compare, for example, "A witchcraft drew me hither" (*Twelfth Night,* 5.1.79); "How near the god drew to the complexion of a goose" (*Merry Wives of Windsor,* 5.5.8); and "Things outward / Do draw the inward quality after them" (*Antony and Cleopatra,* 3.13.33–34).

12. On the conceptual shift from moral to systemic notions of economy, see Joyce Oldham Appleby, *Economic Thought and Ideology in Seventeenth-Century England* (Princeton, N.J.: Princeton University Press, 1978), esp. chap. 1; and Henry William Spiegel, *The Growth of Economic Thought,* 3rd ed. (Durham, N.C.: Duke University Press, 1991), esp. chaps. 4 and 5.

13. See Angus Maddison, *The World Economy: A Millennial Perspective* (Paris: OECD, 2002), 91.

14. See A. G. Dickens, *The English Reformation,* 2nd ed. (London: Batsford, 1989), chap. 8, "The Great Transfer," 167–91.

15. See Y. S. Brenner, "The Inflation of Prices in Early Sixteenth Century England," *Economic History Review* 2nd ser. 14 (1961–62): 225–39; and J. D. Gould, "The Price Revolution Considered," *Economic History Review* 2nd ser. 17 (1964–65): 249–65.

16. For useful summaries of England's growing control of its foreign trade in the sixteenth century, see Robert Brenner, *Merchants and Revolution: Commercial Changes, Political Conflict, and London's Overseas Traders, 1550–1653* (Princeton, N.J.: Princeton University Press, 1993); and Alan K. Smith, *Creating a World Economy: Merchant Capital, Colonialism, and World Trade* (Boulder, Colo.: Westview Press, 1991).

17. See Ceri Sullivan, *The Rhetoric of Credit: Merchants in Early Modern Writing* (London: Associated University Presses, 2002).

18. Thomas Starkey, *A Dialogue Between Reginald Pole and Thomas Lupset,* ed.

Kathleen M. Burton (London: Chatto and Windus, 1948), 78, 83, 87. All further references are cited in the text. For a more extended discussion of Starkey's use of organic political analogy and his reliance upon humoral paradigms of disease, see Jonathan Gil Harris, *Foreign Bodies and the Body Politic: Discourses of Social Pathology in Early Modern England* (Cambridge: Cambridge University Press, 1998), 30–40.

19. Philip Stubbes, *The Anatomie of Abuses: Contayning a Discoverie, or Briefe Summarie, of Such Notable Vices and Imperfections, As Now Raigne in Many Christian Countreyes of the Worlde, But (Especiallie) in a Verie Famous Ilande Called Ailgna* (London, 1583), 106. For a discussion of the conflicted early modern understanding of "canker," see Chapter 4.

20. Spiegel, *Growth of Economic Thought,* 84. The work has also been attributed to John Hales and Shakespeare; the latter ascription is certainly spurious. I shall refer to the author as Thomas Smith because of the edition of the text I am using, though I am by no means convinced that Smith rather than Hales is the author.

21. Mary Dewar, ed., *A Discourse of the Commonweal of This Realm of England, Attributed to Sir Thomas Smith* (Charlottesville: University Press of Virginia, 1969), 12. All further references are cited in the text.

22. On Shakespeare's adaptations of humoral discourse, see John W. Draper, *The Humors and Shakespeare's Characters* (Durham, N.C.: Duke University Press, 1945); F. David Hoeniger, *Medicine and Shakespeare in the English Renaissance* (Newark: University of Delaware Press/Associated Press, 1992), esp. 175–89; Gail Kern Paster, *The Body Embarrassed: Drama and the Disciplines of Shame in Early Modern England* (Ithaca, N.Y.: Cornell University Press, 1993); and Michael C. Schoenfeldt, *Bodies and Selves in Early Modern England: Physiology and Inwardness in Spenser, Shakespeare, Herbert, and Milton* (Cambridge: Cambridge University Press, 1999), chap. 4.

23. Schoenfeldt, *Bodies and Selves,* passim.

24. There were numerous reasons for Spain's economic collapse, including the cost of its wars in the Low Countries and the depredations of English and Barbary pirates. For overviews of the Spanish problems in the larger context of early modern Europe, see Fernand Braudel, *The Mediterranean and the Mediterranean World in the Age of Phillip II,* vol. 1, trans. Sian Reynolds (Berkeley: University of California Press, 1995), esp. 393–493; Robert S. Duplessis, *Transitions to Capitalism in Early Modern Europe* (Cambridge: Cambridge University Press, 1997), 98–101; and J. H. Elliott, "The Decline of Spain," in Trevor Aston, ed., *Crisis in Europe, 1560–1660: Essays from "Past and Present"* (London: Routledge, 1965), 167–93. Early modern English writers were themselves aware of the inflationary pressures generated by the import of New World gold and silver. In an addendum to his *Discourse of the Commonweal of This Realm of England,* for example, Thomas Smith attributed inflation in England to the influx of specie from the Americas and the West Indies (143).

25. Cited in J. H. Lupton, *A Life of John Colet* (London, 1909), 308.

26. John Abernathy, *A Christian and Heavenly Treatise: Containing Physicke for the Soule* (London, 1630), 442.

27. Ulrich von Hutten, *De Guaiaci Medicina et Morbo Gallico* (London, 1533), fol. 4. As Greg Bentley points out, other writers attributed the causes of syphilis to melancholy; but the humoral etiologies they proposed were often confusingly interarticulated with exogenous models of infection. Von Hutten's humoral explanation of the disease, for example, is blended with a miasmic one redolent of Hippocrates, inasmuch as he attributes

the complexional disarray causing syphilis to bad vapors. See Bentley, *Shakespeare and the New Disease,* 10.

28. Andrew Boorde, *The Breuiary of Helthe, for All Maner of Syckenesses and Diseases the Whiche May Be in Man, or Woman* (London, 1547), sig. D3v.

29. On Galenic medicine's attempt to explain the contagious transmission of disease, see Vivian Nutton, "The Seeds of Disease: An Explanation of Contagion and Infection from the Greeks to the Renaissance," *Medical History* 27 (1983): 1–34.

30. William Horman, *William Horman's Vulgaria,* ed. M. R. James (London: Roxburghe Club, 1926), 57.

31. Peter Lowe, *An Easie, Certain and Perfect Method, to Cure and Prevent the Spanish Sicknes* (London, 1596), sig. B2. On the alleged attempt to infect Henry VIII, see Edward, Lord Herbert of Cherbury, *The Life and Raigne of King Henry the Eighth* (London, 1649), 267; and Fabricius, *Syphilis in Shakespeare's England,* 14.

32. Boorde, *Breuiary of Helthe,* sig. Y3.

33. Ruy Díaz de Isla, *Tractado Contra El Mal Serpentino: Que Vulgarmente en España es Llamado Bubas* (Seville, 1539), 181; translation taken from Fabricius, *Syphilis in Shakespeare's England,* 6–7. For a fuller discussion of the multinational names of syphilis, see Claude Quétel, *The History of Syphilis,* trans. Judith Braddock and Brian Pike (Baltimore: Johns Hopkins University Press, 1992), 19.

34. See Girolamo Fracastoro, *De Contagione at Contagiosis Morbis et Eorum Curatione,* trans. Wilmer Care Wright (New York: Putnam, 1930), esp. 34–35.

35. William Clowes, *A Short and Profitable Treatise Touching the Cure of the Disease Called Morbus Gallico by Unctions* (London, 1579), sig. B1.

36. Compare also Sonnet 144, "Till my bad angel fires my good one out" (14). Nevertheless, there are certainly occasions in Shakespeare's other works when he implies an exclusively humoral origin for the disease. *Venus and Adonis,* for example, refers to "The marrow-eating sickness whose attaint / Disorder breeds by heating of the blood" (741–42). Such references have prompted some scholars to misrecognize the ambivalences of syphilitic etiology in Shakespeare's writing. In his otherwise admirable study of desire in Shakespeare's sonnets, for example, Michael Schoenfeldt asserts that "venereal disease . . . was imagined to enter the desiring subject not as a contagious disease but rather as a moral and humoral imbalance" (*Bodies and Selves,* 94).

37. Martine Van Elk, "Urban Misidentification in *The Comedy of Errors* and the Cony-Catching Pamphlets," *Studies in English Literature* (2004).

38. Robert Greene, *The Life and Complete Works in Prose and Verse of Robert Greene,* ed. Alexander B. Grosart (New York: Russell, and Russell, 1886), 10: 198.

39. Thomas Dekker, *The Dead Tearme,* in *The Non-Dramatic Works of Thomas Dekker,* ed. Alexander B. Grosart (London: Hazell, Watson, and Viney, 1886), 4: 28.

40. Fischer, *Econolingua,* 65, 135.

41. Compare the punning on "hours" and "whores" after Dromio of Syracuse has improbably announced that time is going backward. Adriana declaims: "The hours come back! That did I never hear"; to which Dromio responds: "O yes, if any hour meet a sergeant, 'a turns back for very fear" (4.2.54–56).

Chapter 3: Taint and Usury

1. *"Richard Perryman and Mae Perryman v. Lee Hackler*: Supreme Court of Arkansas Opinion Delivered February 19, 1996"; see http://courts.state.ar.us/opinions/1996/95–788.txt. For a discussion of Amendment 60 to the Arkansas constitution, see Susan Wesson, "A Cost-Benefit Analysis of the Arkansas Usury Law and Its Effects on Arkansas Residents and Institutions," *Academic Forum* (2001), http://www.hsu.edu/faculty/afo/2000–01/wesson.htm.

2. OED, *taint*, sb., 3. See the definition in John Palsgrave, *Lesclarcissement de la langue francoyse* (London, 1530): "Taynte, *condamne*" (fol. 279).

3. On "taint" as an early modern disease in horses, see Thomas Blundeville, *The Foure Chiefest Offices Belonging to Horsemanship* (London, 1580): "a nether taint . . . is a little bladder full of iellie, much like vnto a wind-gall" (sig. Dd1).

4. Thomas Wilson, *Discourse on Usury* (London, 1572). For economic historians' narratives about softening attitudes toward usury, see Henry William Spiegel, *The Growth of Economic Thought*, 3rd ed. (Durham, N.C.: Duke University Press, 1991), 63–69, 81–83; and Norman Jones, *God and the Moneylenders: Usury and Law in Early Modern England* (Oxford: Oxford University Press, 1989). Ceri Sullivan examines what merchants wrote about usury in *The Rhetoric of Credit: Merchants in Early Modern Writing* (London: Associated University Presses, 2002), 44–52. James Shapiro discusses the impact of changing attitudes toward usury on early modern representations of Jews in *Shakespeare and the Jews* (New York: Columbia University Press, 1996), 98–100.

5. Francis Bacon, "On Usurie," in *The Essayes or Counsels Civill & Morall of Francis Bacon, Baron Verulam Viscount Saint Alban* (Norwalk, Conn.: Easton Press, 1980), 133. All further references are cited in the text.

6. Mun argued that usury gives the "*younger* and *poorer* Merchants" an opportunity "to rise in the world, and to enlarge their dealings." Thomas Mun, *Englands Treasure by Forraign Trade; or, The Ballance of our Forraign Trade is The Rule of our Treasure* (London, 1669), sig. I2v.

7. See especially Benjamin Nelson, *The Idea of Usury: From Tribal Brotherhood to Universal Otherhood*, 3rd ed. (Chicago: University of Chicago Press, 1969).

8. See Robert Wilson, *An Edition of Robert Wilson's "The Three Ladies of London" and "Three Lords and Three Ladies of London"*, ed. H. S. D. Mithal (New York: Garland, 1988); Christopher Marlowe, *The Jew of Malta*, ed. James R. Siemon (New York: Norton, 1994), 2.3.192; and George Wilkins, Samuel Rowley, and John Day, *The Travels of the Three English Gentlemen* in Anthony Parr, ed., *Three Renaissance Travel Plays* (Manchester: Manchester University Press, 1999). For comparative discussions of Gerontus, Barabas, Shylock, and Zariph, see Emily C. Bartels, *Spectacles of Strangeness: Imperialism, Alienation, and Marlowe* (Philadelphia: University of Pennsylvania Press, 1993); Daryl Palmer, "Merchants and Miscegenation: *The Three Ladies of London, The Jew of Malta,* and *The Merchant of Venice,*" in *Race, Ethnicity, and Power in the Renaissance,* ed. Joyce Green MacDonald (London: Associated University Presses, 1997); and Lloyd Edward Kermode, "The Playwright's Prophecy: Robert Wilson's *The Three Ladies of London* and the 'Alienation' of the English," *Medieval and Renaissance Drama in England* 11 (1999): 60–87.

9. Charles Johnson, ed., *The "De Moneta" of Nicholas Oresme and English Mint Documents* (London: Nelson, 1956). See also Marc Shell, *Money, Language, and Thought* (Baltimore: Johns Hopkins University Press, 1992), 51.

10. "Pecunia est res sterilis," in Martin Luther, *Tischreden*, 6 vols. (Weimar, 1912–21), 5: no. 5429.

11. Shell, *Money, Language and Thought*, 48–55.

12. Nelson, *Idea of Usury*, 141–64.

13. The notion of "brothers and others" was taken up with particular force by W. H. Auden, who argued that Shylock's bond involves no interest and is therefore more congruent with Christian conceptions of fair loans. See his "Brothers and Others," in *The Dyer's Hand and Other Essays* (New York: Random House, 1948), 218–37. Steven Mullaney develops Auden's argument in "Brothers and Others, or the Art of Alienation," in Marjorie Garber, ed., *Cannibals, Witches, and Divorce: Estranging the Renaissance* (Baltimore: Johns Hopkins University Press, 1986), 67–89.

14. Henry Smith, "The Examination of Usury: The First Sermon," in *The Works of Henry Smith*, ed. Thomas Fuller, 2 vols. (Edinburgh, 1866–67), 1: 97–98.

15. Thomas Milles, *The Customers Replie, Or Second Apologie* (London, 1604), sig. C4.

16. Gerard Malynes, *Consuetudo, Vel, Lex Mercatoria: Or, the Ancient Law-Merchant* (London, 1622), 114.

17. Gerard Malynes, *Saint George for England Allegorically Described* (London, 1601), 2. All further references are cited in the text.

18. Malynes was not alone in reconfiguring usury for the bullionist cause. Usury provided other mercantilists with a conventional language in which to voice new concerns that would become linchpins of mercantilist discourse. Thomas Milles argues that "so, as the *Standard* falls vncertaine, and Money engrost into priuate handes, all things grow deere, while the King becomes weake, and his Subiects poore, while Coyne it selfe by Usury in *Marchandizing Exchange*, eates out Industry and Trades." Milles, like Malynes, reconfigures usury as "merchandizing exchange," where money becomes a commodity that gets traded overseas. See Thomas Milles, *The Custumers Alphabet and Primer: Conteining, Their Creede or Beliefe in the True Doctrine of Christian Religion* (London, 1608), sig. G2v. We see the opposition to usury in later mercantilist works too; Edward Misselden names usury, which he regards as broadly as do Milles and Malynes, as the cause of "the decay" in England's trade. See Misselden, *Free Trade, or The Meanes to Make Trade Florish: Wherein, The Causes of the Decay of Trade in This Kingdome, are Discovered: And the Remedies also to Remoove the Same, are Represented,* (London, 1622), sig. C7. In mercantilist writing, "usury" as much as "Jew" often has an unclear meaning: it refers not only to the practice of charging interest but also to a large cluster of transnational economic practices that lead to the depletion of national bullion.

19. Bartholomew Traheron, trans., *The Most Excellent Workes of Chirurgerye, made and set forth by maister John Vignon* (London, 1543), fol. xxvi. Even in its humoral etiology, gangrene or cancrena was regarded as entailing a confusion or mixing of categories. Andrew Boorde writes that to treat the ailment, one needs to "purge coler and melancholy"; *The Breiuary of Helthe, for All Maner of Syckenesses and Diseases the Whiche May Be in Man, or Woman* (London, 1547), sig. C8v.

20. The letter C on the dragon's tail also recalls the depiction of Usurie in Robert Wilson's *Three Lords and Three Ladies of London* (1588), who is branded with "A little x standing in the middst of a great C" as a sign of the maximum interest rate he is allowed to take by law. See Mithal, sig. H3.

21. For a discussion of the legal status and etymology of "felony," see Frederick Pol-

lock and Frederic William Maitland, *The History of English Law Before the Time of Edward I*, 2 vols., 2nd ed. (Cambridge: Cambridge University Press, 1898), 2: 464–70.

22. See Frances E. Dolan, *Whores of Babylon: Catholicism, Gender, and Seventeenth-Century Print Culture* (Ithaca, N.Y.: Cornell University Press, 1999), passim. Dolan makes her argument with respect to seventeenth-century Catholics, who "hold the foreign and the familiar in disturbing tension" (219).

23. Milles, *Custumers Alphabet*, sig. K2v. Compare Milles's characterization of "*Iewish* Vsury" as "that Mistery of all Iniquity" in his later treatise, *The Misterie of Iniquitie* (London, 1611), sig. K2.

24. Shapiro, *Shakespeare and the Jews*, 177–78.

25. On the York Massacre and other episodes of English violence against Jews, see Zephira Entrin Rokeah, "The Expulsion of the Jews from England in 1290 A.D.: Some Aspects of Its Background," Ph.D. dissertation, Columbia University, 1986. Malynes might also be making reference to the mass execution of Jews for the clipping of coin in the reign of Edward I. John Stowe mentions that "The third of Edward the first, in a Parliament at London, vsury was forbidden to the Iewes, and that all Vsurers might be knowne, the king commaunded that euery Vsurer should weare a Table on their breast, the breadth of a pauelihe, or else to auoyde the Realme: the 6. of the said king Edward a reformation was made for clipping of the kings coyne, for which offence 267. Iews were drawne and hanged." John Stowe, *A Survey of London* (1603), ed. Charles Lethbridge, 2 vols. (Oxford: Clarendon Press, 1908), 1: 281.

26. John Strype, *Annals of the Reformation*, 4 vols. (Oxford, 1824), 4: 236, item no. 107, *Strangers, Flemings and French, in the city of London: and complaints of them, and libels againts them. Ann. 1593. MSS. Car. D. Halifax.*

27. My text of the libel is Arthur Freeman's transcription, included in his essay "Marlowe, Kyd, and the Dutch Church Libel," *English Literary Renaissance* 3 (1973): 44–52, esp. 50–51.

28. See Charles Nicholls, *The Reckoning: The Murder of Christopher Marlowe* (London: Harcourt, Brace, 1992), 284–88.

29. On the Dutch overcrowding of London tenements, see Andrew Pettegree, *Foreign Protestant Communities in Sixteenth-Century London* (New York: Oxford University Press, 1986), 284.

30. Strype, *Annals of the Reformation*, 4: 234.

31. Shapiro, *Shakespeare and the Jews*, 185.

32. Petegree, *Foreign Protestant Communities*, 10, 13.

33. Milles, *Custumers Alphabet*, sig. D2. For some mercantilists, this proved to be a problem of long duration. Compare Edward Misselden, who argued in 1622 that "the *Transportation* of the [raw] *Materials* of our *Cloth*" to the Low Countries meant a significant loss of revenue for the king and the country: "euery man is sensible to the losse to the *Commonwealth*, in robbing it of the *Materials:* whereby not onely our *Draperies* are *Impaired*, but the *Forreine* also are thereby much *Improued*" (*Free Trade*, sigs. G8–G8v).

34. For a more detailed discussion of the multiple meanings of "infection" in the late sixteenth and early seventeenth centuries, see Chapter 4.

35. Petegree, *Foreign Protestant Communities*, 78. I am greatly indebted to Petegree's study in this paragraph and throughout the chapter.

36. John Southerden Burns, *The History of the French, Walloon, Dutch and Other*

Foreign Protestant Refugees Settled in England, from the Reign of Henry VIII to the Revocation of the Edict of Nantes; with Notice of their Trade and Commerce, Copious Extracts from the Registers, Lists of the Early Settlers, Ministers (London: Longman, Brown, Green, and Longmans, 1846), 9.

37. See Petegree, *Foreign Protestant Communities*, 139. In a pamphlet written in 1553, for example, William Cholmely argued that it would be more profitable if English broadcloths were "finished" domestically rather than being exported to the Low Countries. His solution was to bring workmen to England to teach the art of finishing as it was performed in Flanders. Cholmely knew whereof he spoke: he himself had successfully introduced Continental techniques of dyeing to a business that he had set up in Southwark in 1551 with the aid of a skilled workman from Antwerp. More than half a century later, Thomas Milles reiterated Cholmely's solution to the problem of exporting unfinished textiles: "Our basest *Fell-wooll* of Shorlings, the refuse of the rest, and sweepings of our *Staples*, never vsed in Cloth is by our kindest Neighbours, in a new kinde of Drapery, made the glorie of our *Wolls*, and credite of our Kingdome, and might be a Patterne to reforme all our Clothing, and recouer our *Bullion*. . . . The Duch-Church at Sandwich, who flying the tyranny of Body and Conscience at home, admitted to refresh themselues but with our English ayre, layd the first foundation of true making of Bayes, Sayes, & Sarges there. (Trades neuer vnderstoode of vs before)." Milles, *Custumers Alphabet*, sig. D2.

38. The text of Sir Thomas Mildmay's suit is in Strype, *Annals of the Reformation*, 4: 296–301. All further references are cited in the text.

39. Strype, *Annals of the Reformation*, 4: 576.

40. Strype, *Annals of the Reformation*, 4: 577.

41. Petegree, *Foreign Protestant Communities*, 77 n. 4.

42. It is notable that in the anonymous *Interlude of Wealth and Health* (c. 1558), the Dutch character Hans is associated with a pair of Catholic-tinged saboteurs, Ill Will and Shrewd Wit. See my earlier discussion of the interlude in Chapter 1.

43. See Jonathan I. Israel, *European Jewry in the Age of Mercantilism, 1550–1750*, 3rd ed. (London: Littman Library of Jewish Civilization, 1998), 41.

44. Israel, *European Jewry*, 42.

45. Herbert I. Bloom, *The Economic Activities of the Jews of Amsterdam in the Seventeenth and Eighteenth Centuries* (Williamsport, Pa.: Bayard Press, 1937), 2.

46. For a discussion of the term "Portuguese Nation" as a synonym for Dutch Jewry, see Miriam Bodian, *Hebrews of the Portuguese Nation: Conversos and Community in Early Modern Amsterdam* (Bloomington: Indiana University Press, 1997), esp. 13: "Since the crypto-Jewish tendencies of the families who crossed the border from Portugal to Spain were notorious, the term 'Portuguese' became virtually synonymous with 'judaizer.' Collectively, the Portuguese conversos were known as *la nacion portuguesa* or *la gente portuguesa*. These terms were adopted in European countries outside the peninsula as well." The Portuguese Jesuit theologian António Viera complained about the misunderstanding this produced, noting that "in popular parlance, among most of the European nations, 'Portuguese' is confused with 'Jew.' " See António Viera, *Obras escolhidas* (Lisbon, 1951–54), 4:182. See also Alan Stewart's paper "The Portingale" for a discussion of how the confusion of "Jew" and "Portuguese" was also a feature of early modern English culture, including the literature about Dr. Lopez before and during his trial.

47. For a thorough study of early modern Amsterdam Jewry that complicates many of Herbert Bloom's findings, see Bodian, *Hebrews of the Portuguese Nation.*

48. Bloom, *Economic Activities of the Jews of Amsterdam,* 4.

49. Albert M. Hyamson, *A History of the Jews in England* (London: Chatto and Windus, 1908), 137. For the suggestion that Sarah Lopez was born in London rather than Antwerp, see Betty S. Travitsky and Anne Lake Prescott, eds., *Female and Male Voices in Early Modern England: An Anthology of Renaissance Writing* (New York: Columbia University Press, 2000), 187.

50. Burns, *History of the French, Walloon, Dutch and Other Foreign Protestant Refugees,* 11.

51. Bloom, *Economic Activities of the Jews of Amsterdam,* 106.

52. On the undecidable identity of the Marrano or converso, see Michael Alpert, *Crypto-Judaism and the Spanish Inquisition* (London: Palgrave, 2001); and Bodian, *Hebrews of the Portuguese Nation,* esp. x.

53. For the story of Maria Nuñes, I am drawing largely on Bodian, *Hebrews of the Portuguese Nation,* 23–24, and Bloom, *Economic Activities of the Jews of Amsterdam,* 6. Daniel Levi de Barrios claims that Maria Nuñes was displayed by Queen Elizabeth for her beauty and was sought in marriage by an English duke.

54. To this extent, then, Jews were crucial to the formation of modern capitalism. But my argument here is very different from Werner Sombart's infamously essentialist argument about the Jewish entrepreneurial spirit in *The Jews and Modern Capitalism,* trans. M. Epstein (New York: Macmillan, 1962).

55. Martin D. Yaffe, *Shylock and the Jewish Question* (Baltimore: Johns Hopkins University Press, 1997), 155.

56. Bodian, *Hebrews of the Portuguese Nation,* 3.

57. Thomas Elze remarked, "The Republic never had any direct communication with Mexico, nor even with America." Cited in Horace Howard Furness, ed., *A New Variorum Edition of Shakespeare: The Merchant of Venice,* 7th ed. (Philadelphia: Lippincott, 1888), note to 3.2.279–87. See also John Gillies, *Shakespeare and the Geography of Difference* (Cambridge: Cambridge University Press, 1992), 66.

58. Theodore B. Leinwand, *Theatre, Finance, and Society in Early Modern England* (Cambridge: Cambridge University Press, 1999), 114.

59. It is not just the mercantile axis of the play that recalls the Dutch; so, perhaps, does the courtroom scene. Thomas Elze noted in the *Shakespeare Jahrbuch* that "Although this Scene is correctly laid in a court of Justice, it is incorrect that Senators should appear as Judges, and the presence of the Doge, as presiding officer at least, is an anachronism" (cited in Furness, *Variorum Edition of Merchant of Venice,* note to 4.1). But perhaps this scene fits the traditions of Amsterdam polity, where magisters or *Regenten* did preside in such cases.

60. John Roche Dasent, ed., *Acts of the Privy Council of England, 1542–1604.* 32 vols (London: Stationery Office, 1890–1907), 24: 456.

61. Edward Misselden, *The Circle of Commerce: Or, the Balance of Trade, in Defence of Free Trade: Opposed to Malynes Little Fish and His Great Whale, and Poized Against Them in the Scale* (London, 1623), 25.

62. William Thomas, *The Historye of Italye* (London, 1561), fol. 85.

63. Andrew Petegree summarizes the political debates of 1593 about the status of the

Dutch community in *Foreign Protestant Communities,* 291–92. The possible connections between *The Merchant of Venice* and the situation of London's migrant Dutch community have been mooted before; see Andrew Tretiak, "*The Merchant of Venice* and the 'Alien' Question," *Review of English Studies* 5 (1929): 402–9. Benjamin Nelson dismisses Tretiak's suggestions out of hand in *Idea of Usury,* 87 n.

64. Shapiro, *Shakespeare and the Jews,* 187.

65. John Taylor, *All the Works of John Taylor the Water Poet Being 63 in Number* (London, 1630), sig. Aa3.

66. Fynes Moryson, *Itinerary* (London, 1617); quoted in Horace Howard Furness, ed., *A New Variorum Edition of Shakespeare: The Merchant of Venice,* 7th ed. (Philadelphia: Lippincott, 1888), note to 1.2.91–92.

67. John Stowe, "The Stilliyard, the Swan in Thames Street, The Swan in Crooked Lane, and the Sun at St. Mary Hill," in *A Survey of London* ed. Charles Lethbridge, 2 vols. (Oxford: Clarendon Press (1908), 2: 314.

68. It is striking how seventeenth-century Jewish criticisms of anti-Semitic rhetoric often performed the kind of division within Jewishness that Salarino offers. In the list that he presented to Oliver Cromwell of the primary slanders and calumnies against Jews, Israel ben Manasseh ranked uppermost the charge of usury: "As for usury, such dealing is not the essential property of the Jews, for though in Germany there be some indeed that practice usury, yet the most part of them that live in Turkey, Italy, Holland, and Hamburg, being come out of Spain, they hold it infamous to use." He adds that if some Jews commit usury, "they do it not as Jews simply, but as wicked Jews, as amongst all nations there are generally found some usurers" (Israel ben Menasseh, in Travitsky and Prescott, *Female and Male Voices in Early Modern England,* 202). Ben Menasseh's refutation of the slander is highly ambivalent. To exculpate the Sephardic Jews of Holland from the charge of usury, he vacillates between viewing it as a specifically Ashkenazi (i.e., German Jewish) crime and as a universal form of behavior. In the process, "Jew" becomes an unstable term that breaks down the Deuteronomic binarism of brother and Other: German Jew is "other" to Spanish or Portuguese Jew, who is "brother" to the Christians of his host nations.

69. John W. Draper, for example, complains that Shylock's "defence" of usury employs "the very reasons urged most bitterly against" the practice: see Draper, "Usury in *The Merchant of Venice,*" *Modern Philology* 33 (1935): 37–47, esp. 43. More recent studies have been inclined to suggest that the speech is about matters other than usury: see, for example, the study of *The Merchant of Venice* by Richard Halpern, who examines Shylock's speech in relation to Marxist paradigms of use value rather than mercantilist paradigms of usury, in *Shakespeare Among the Moderns* (Ithaca, N.Y.: Cornell University Press, 1997), 200–202.

70. Elizabeth A. Spiller, "From Imagination to Miscegenation: Race and Romance in Shakespeare's *The Merchant of Venice,*" *Renaissance Drama* n.s. 29 (2000 for 1998): 137–64, esp. 138.

71. Shell, *Money, Language, and Thought,* 49–50.

72. Coverdale renders the pertinent passage from Genesis as follows: "And that same daye, he sundered out the speckled and partye coloured goates, and all the spotted and partye coloured kyddes." *Biblia, The Byble: That Is The Holy Scripture of the Olde and New Testament, Faythfully Translated in to Englyshe* (London, 1535).

73. Henry Glapthorne, *The Hollander* (London, 1640), sig. E3. Glapthorne's play,

written in 1635, repeatedly blurs the Dutch into Jews. Sconce tells us that in "*Duke Alvas time, my ancestors kept the inquisition out of Amsterdam*" (sig. B4v) and reports an accusation that "all Hollanders were *Jewes*" (sig. C3v); his father, though "no Jew," was a usurer (sig. B4); and one of Sconce's fellow Dutch knights is named "*Sir Barrabas*" (sig. H2). These conflations, suggestive as they are, arguably belong to a very different historical moment from the Dutch-Jewish hybrids of the "Dutch Church Libel" and *The Merchant of Venice;* I would read them as a response to the openly Jewish community of Amsterdam, a phenomenon that belongs to the seventeenth century.

74. Auden, *Dyer's Hand,* 227–28. See also Shell, *Money, Language, and Thought,* 64–67; and Mullaney, "Brothers and Others," 81.

75. On early modern English myths of Jewish cannibalism, see Shapiro, *Shakespeare and the Jews,* 104–5, 109–11.

76. Gail Kern Paster, *The Body Embarrassed: Drama and the Disciplines of Shame in Early Modern England* (Ithaca, N.Y.: Cornell University Press, 1993), 84.

77. Homi K. Bhabha, "Signs Taken for Wonders: Questions of Ambivalence and Authority under a Tree Outside Delhi, May 1817," in *Race, Writing, and Difference,* ed. Henry Louis Gates (Chicago: University of Chicago Press, 1986), 163–84.

78. See my earlier argument about early modern representations of Jewish vengeance as mimesis in *Foreign Bodies and the Body Politic: Discourses of Social Pathology in Early Modern England* (Cambridge: Cambridge University Press, 1998), chap. 4.

79. Indeed, the Venetian Launcelot is arguably the play's nonpareil of indeterminate hybridity. His first speech in the play, so redolent of the conventions of English morality drama, casts him as a Christian Everyman figure, stuck between a good angel and a bad angel (2.2.1–24); later in the same scene, he symbolically stands in for a Jewish figure in his exchange with his blind father, which parodically echoes Isaac's blessing of Jacob, "coloured" as Esau; yet, according to Shylock, he is "Hagar's" offspring, which would seem to render him an Arab or a Turk (2.5.42). And Launcelot bequeaths his hybridity to his next generation: Portia's Moorish maidservant, we learn, is pregnant with Launcelot's child.

80. This stereotype of the English was common. Thomas Dekker observed that "an English-mans suit is like a traitors bodies that hath beene hanged, drawne, and quartered, and set up in seuerall places: the collar of his doublet and the belly in France; the wing and narrow sleeue in Italy; the shorte waist hangs over a Dutch botcher stall in Utrich; his huge sloppes speakes Spanish; Polonia gives him his bootes." See *The Seuen Deadly Sinnes of London* (1606), in *The Non-Dramatic Works of Thomas Dekker,* ed. Alexander Grosart (London: Hazell, Watson, and Viney, 1884–86), 2: 59–60.

81. On the details of Malynes's biography, see Raymond de Roover, "Gerard de Malynes as an Economic Writer: From Scholasticism to Mercantilism," in de Roover, *Business, Banking, and Economic Thought in Late Medieval and Early Modern Europe,* ed. Julius Kirshner (Chicago: University of Chicago Press, 1974), 346–66, esp. 346–49. Misselden's libel appears in *The Circle of Commerce,* 31; for documentation regarding the subscription of "Garet de Malines" (totaling £200), see Burns, *History of the French, Walloon, Dutch, and Other Foreign Protestant Refugees,* 10.

Chapter 4. Canker/Serpego and Value

1. Chapter epigraph: Ezra Pound, *The Cantos of Ezra Pound* (New York: New Directions, 1948), Addendum to Canto 100, 798.

2. Robert Wilson, *The Three Ladies of London,* in W. Carew Hazlitt, ed., *A Select Collection of Old English Plays,* 4th ed. (London: Reeves and Turner, 1874), 369.

3. Nicholas Breton, "The Good and the Bad; or, Descriptions of the Worthies and Unworthies of this Age," in Henry Morley, ed., *Character Writings of the Seventeenth Century* (London: George Routledge and Sons, 1891), 271.

4. John Blaxton, *The English Usurer, or Usury Condemned* (London, 1634), sig. C2.

5. Francis Bacon, "Of Usurie," in *The Essayes or Counsels Civill & Morall of Francis Bacon, Baron Verulam Viscount Saint Alban* (Norwalk, Conn.: Easton Press, 1980), 134.

6. Gerard Malynes, *Saint George for England Allegorically Described* (London, 1601), sig. B6v.

7. Edward Misselden, *Free Trade, or The Meanes to Make Trade Florish: Wherein, The Causes of the Decay of Trade in this Kingdome, are Discovered: And the Remedies also to Remooue the Same, are Represented* (London, 1622), sig. G8.

8. Wyndham Beauwes, *Lex Mercatoria Rediviva, or The Merchant's Directory* (London, 1752), 36.

9. John Aubrey, *Brief Lives,* ed. Andrew Clark, 2 vols. (Oxford: Oxford University Press, 1898), 1: 286; cited in Stephen Greenblatt, "Invisible Bullets: Renaissance Authority and its Subversion, *Henry IV, Henry V,*" in Jonathan Dollimore and Alan Sinfield, eds., *Political Shakespeare: New Essays in Cultural Materialism* (Manchester: Manchester University Press, 1985), 18.

10. For a useful discussion of the convention of "biting" usury, see Ceri Sullivan, *The Rhetoric of Credit: Merchants in Early Modern Writing* (London: Associated University Presses, 2002), 44–52.

11. I am very grateful to Pat Parker for drawing this passage to my attention.

12. See the work of Raymond de Roover, especially "What Is Dry Exchange? A Contribution to the Study of English Mercantilism," in de Roover, *Business, Banking, and Economic Thought in Late Medieval and Early Modern Europe,* ed. Julius Kirshner (Chicago: University of Chicago Press, 1974), 183–99. See also Brian E. Supple, "Currency and Commerce in the Early Seventeenth Century," *Economic History Review* 2nd ser. 10 (1957): 239–55.

13. David Hawkes, *Idols of the Marketplace: Idolatry and Commodity Fetishism in English Literature, 1580–1680* (New York: Palgrave, 2001), 20. See also Jean-Joseph Goux, *The Coiners of Language,* trans. Jennifer Curtiss Gage (Norman: University of Oklahoma Press, 1994); and Marc Shell, *Money, Language, and Thought* (Baltimore: Johns Hopkins University Press, 1992).

14. The "problem play" category is, of course, itself problematic. In the century since F. S. Boas applied the label to *All's Well That Ends Well, Measure for Measure, Troilus and Cressida,* and *Hamlet* in *Shakespeare and His Predecessors* (New York: Scribners, 1896), 344–408, there has been an ongoing debate—the contributions to which are too voluminous to itemize here—about which plays from this list are or are not "problems," and what indeed a "problem play" might be. A useful summary of the debate's highlights is offered by Michael Jamieson in "The Problem Plays, 1920–1970," *Shakespeare Survey* 25 (1972): 1–10.

15. *Hamlet*, 5.1.166; *Measure for Measure*, 1.2.52; *All's Well That Ends Well*, 2.2.22; *Troilus and Cressida*, 2.3.18–19, 5.3.101–6, and 5.10.35–56.

16. *Hamlet*, 1.5.71; *Troilus and Cressida*, 5.1.23; "sciatica" and "serpego" ("suppeago" or "sapego" in some editions) are referred to in both *Measure for Measure* (1.2.59, 3.1.31) and *Troilus and Cressida* (5.1.21, 2.3.74). All further references to the three plays are cited in the text.

17. Caroline F. E. Spurgeon, *Shakespeare's Imagery and What It Tells Us* (Cambridge: Cambridge University Press, 1952), 129, 131.

18. Johannes Fabricius, *Syphilis in Shakespeare's England* (London: Jessica Kingsley, 1994), 231, 234: see chap. 11, "Shakespeare's Midlife Crisis."

19. René Girard, "The Plague In Literature," in his *To Double Business Bound: Essays on Literature, Mimesis, and Anthropology* (Baltimore: Johns Hopkins University Press, 1978), 136–54, esp. 136. See also Girard's essay "The Politics of Desire in *Troilus and Cressida*," in Patricia Parker and Geoffrey Hartman, eds., *Shakespeare and the Question of Theory* (New York and London: Methuen, 1985), 188–209; and the chapters on *Troilus* in his *A Theatre of Envy: William Shakespeare* (Oxford: Oxford University Press, 1991). Compare Greg W. Bentley, *Shakespeare and the New Disease: The Dramatic Function of Syphilis in* Troilus and Cressida, Measure for Measure, *and* Timon of Athens (New York: Peter Lang, 1989): "Shakespeare uses syphilis as one of the central images, in fact the *ne plus ultra* of individual, social, and political decay. It is the word picture *[sic]* that he consistently and coherently employs to satirize the physical, moral, and spiritual degeneration of English society" (4).

20. Eric S. Mallin, *Inscribing the Time: Shakespeare and the End of Elizabethan England* (Berkeley: University of California Press, 1995), 65. In her important essay " 'So Unsecret to Ourselves': Notorious Identity and the Material Subject in *Troilus and Cressida*," chap. 3 of *Notorious Identity: Materializing the Subject in Shakespeare* (Cambridge, Mass: Harvard University Press, 1993), 70–102, Linda Charnes offers a celebratory psychoanalytic variant of this approach, arguing for the "subversive signifying power" of *Troilus and Cressida*'s pathological imagery (72), which she reads as symptoms of the erosion of a symbolic order that never existed in the first place.

21. On Shakespeare's adaptations of humoral discourse, see F. David Hoeniger, *Medicine and Shakespeare in the English Renaissance* (Newark: University of Delaware Press/Associated Press, 1992), esp. 175–89; and Gail Kern Paster, *The Body Embarrassed: Drama and the Disciplines of Shame in Early Modern England* (Ithaca, N.Y.: Cornell University Press, 1993), passim.

22. See Hoeniger, *Medicine and Shakespeare*, 189–90. Shakespeare implicitly alludes to the battle between humoralism and the new pharmacies when he makes satiric reference to the followers of "Galen and Paracelsus" in *All's Well That Ends Well*, 2.2.12.

23. Although Shakespeare's editors tend to gloss "Winchester goose" as "prostitute," the term had a specific pathological application. In *The Nomenclator, or Remembrancer of Adrianus Junius* (London, 1585), 439, a "bubo" is defined as "a sore in the grine or yard, which if it come by lecherie, it is called a Winchester goose, or botch"; John Taylor refers in his "Praise of Cleane Linnen" to "A Groyne Bumpe, or a Goose from *Winchester*," in *All the Workes of Iohn Taylor The Water Poet Being 63 in Number* (London, 1630), sig. Pp2v.

24. Andrew Boorde, *The Breuiary of Helthe, for All Maner of Syckenesses and Diseases the Whiche May Be in Man, or Woman* (London, 1547) sig. Hh4v; Bartholomew Tra-

heron, trans., *The Most Excellent Workes of Chirurgerye, made and set forth by maister John Vignon* (London, 1543), fol. cxxxixv.

25. Boorde, *Breuiary of Helthe,* sig. Hh4v.

26. *The Dramatic Works of Thomas Heywood* (London: John Pearson, 1874), 6: 50.

27. See Jonathan Gil Harris, *Foreign Bodies and the Body Politic: Discourses of Social Pathology in Early Modern England* (Cambridge: Cambridge University Press, 1998), passim.

28. For details of Malynes's biography, I am drawing on Leslie Stephen and Sidney Lee, eds., *The Dictionary of National Biography* (Oxford: Oxford University Press, 1921–22), 12: 894–96.

29. Joyce Oldham Appleby, *Economic Thought and Ideology in Seventeenth-Century England* (Princeton, N.J.: Princeton University Press, 1978), passim.

30. Craig Muldrew, *The Economy of Obligation: The Culture of Credit and Social Relations in Early Modern England* (New York: St. Martin's Press, 1998), 2.

31. Sullivan, *Rhetoric of Credit,* introduction.

32. On early modern English coin, its minting, and its fluctuations of value, see C. E. Challis's magisterial *Tudor Coinage* (Manchester: Manchester University Press, 1978); and Sandra K. Fischer, *Econolingua: A Glossary of Coins and Economic Language in Renaissance Drama* (Newark: University of Delaware Press, 1985). For very useful discussions of Henry VIII's debasement of the coinage, see J. D. Gould, *The Great Debasement* (Oxford: Oxford University Press, 1970); and C. E. Challis, ed., *A New History of the Royal Mint* (Cambridge: Cambridge University Press, 1992), 228–44.

33. Thomas Smith, *A Discourse of the Commonweal of This Realm of England, Attributed to Sir Thomas Smith,* ed. Mary Dewar (Charlottesville: University Press of Virginia, 1969), 104–5.

34. For a useful collection of essays on Sir Thomas Gresham's Royal Exchange and its financial innovations, see Ann Saunders, ed., *The Royal Exchange* (London: London Topographical Society, 1997).

35. See Glyn Davies, *A History of Money from Ancient Times to the Present Day* (Cardiff: University of Wales Press, 1994), 233–79.

36. Gerard Malynes, *A Treatise of the Canker of England's Commonwealth* (London, 1601), sig. B2. All further references are cited in the text. For discussions of Malynes's economic theories, see Appleby, *Economic Thought and Ideology,* 41–47; Andrea Finkelstein, *Harmony and Balance: An Intellectual History of Seventeenth-Century English Economic Thought* (Ann Arbor: University of Michigan Press, 2000), chap. 2, "Gerard de Malynes: *Institutio Mercatoris Christiani*," 26–53; Jonathan Gil Harris, " 'The Canker of England's Commonwealth': Gerard de Malynes and the Origins of Economic Pathology," *Textual Practice* 13 (1999): 311–28; Eli F. Heckscher, *Mercantilism,* 2 vols., 2nd ed. trans. Mendel Shapiro (London: George Allen & Unwin, 1955), 2: 238–48; Lynn Muchmore, "Gerrard de Malynes and Mercantile Economics," *History of Political Economy* 1 (1969): 336–58; Raymond de Roover, "Gerard de Malynes as an Economic Writer: From Scholasticism to Mercantilism," in de Roover, *Business, Banking, and Economic Thought,* 346–66; and Henry William Spiegel, *The Growth of Economic Thought,* 3rd ed. (Durham, N.C.: Duke University Press, 1991), 100–106.

37. On Hippocrates's and Galen's diagnoses of cancer, and the history of attitudes toward cancer and oncology in general, see Erwin H. Ackerknecht, "Historical Notes on Cancer," *Medical History* 2 (1958): 114–19; L. J. Rather, *The Genesis of Cancer: A Study in*

the History of Ideas (Baltimore: Johns Hopkins University Press, 1978), esp. 9–21; and Susan Sontag, *Illness as Metaphor* (New York: Farrar, Straus and Giroux, 1978). Thomas Paynell observed in 1528, "A canker is a melancholy impostume, that eateth the parts of the body": *Regimen Sanitatis Salerni: or, the Schoole of Salernes Regiment of Health* (London, 1649 [1528]), sig. T2v. Andrew Boorde replicated this view: "This infyrmyte doth come of a melancoly humour, or a coleryke humour adusted": *Breiuary of Helthe*, sig. G4v.

38. Paynell, *Regimen Sanitatis Salerni*, sig. T2v.

39. Malynes, *Saint George for England Allegorically Described*, sigs. A7v, B6v.

40. Randle Cotgrave, *A Dictionarie of the French and English Tongues* (London, 1611), sig. P5v. For discussions of the origins of the term "chancre," see Fabricius, *Syphilis in Shakespeare's England*, 185–86, and Harry Keil, "The Evolution of the Term Chancre and Its Relation to the History of Syphilis," *Journal of the History of Medicine* 4 (1949): 407–16.

41. Traheron, *Most Excellent Workes of Chirurgerye*, dedication, sig. +ii.

42. Robert Wilson, *Three Ladies and Three Lords of London*, in Hazlitt, ed., *A Select Collection of Old English Plays*, 499.

43. For Sennert's and Van Helmont's theories of the etiology of cancer, see Rather, *Genesis of Cancer*, 28–29.

44. For a fuller version of my argument here, see Harris, "Canker of England's Commonwealth," esp. 318–20.

45. Gerard Malynes, *Consuetudo, Vel, Lex Mercatoria: Or, the Ancient Law-Merchant*, 3 vols. (London, 1622), 1: 254.

46. Malynes repeatedly attempted to fashion such compromises throughout his work. In his *Englands View, in the Unmasking of Two Paradoxes* (London, 1603), he acknowledges the "diuersities of mens opinions" concerning the value of "pearls and precious stones," yet insists that "a generall estimation doth approue the value of things" (sigs. G3v–G4). As Jesse M. Lander has pointed out with respect to this passage, "Malynes provides a typical early modern account of value in which disagreement over value is acknowledged while the idea of intrinsic value is maintained": see " 'Crack'd Crowns' and Counterfeit Sovereigns: The Crisis of Value in *1 Henry IV*," *Shakespeare Studies* 30 (2002): 137–61, esp. 157. My treatment of Malynes's compromise is indebted to Pierre Macherey and Etienne Balibar's theory of the linguistic compromise formation, which they outline in "Literature As an Ideological Form: Some Marxist Hypotheses," *Praxis* 5 (1980): 43–58, esp. 48. For an illuminating application of Macherey and Balibar's theory to Shakespeare's presentation of artisanal labor in *A Midsummer Night's Dream*, see James H. Kavanagh, "Shakespeare in Ideology," in John Drakakis, ed., *Alternative Shakespeares* (London: Methuen, 1985), 144–65.

47. In this respect, Malynes performs what Julie Robin Solomon has identified as one of the characteristic gambits of mercantilist discourse: the coordination of royal and private interests through the representation of "the monarch as the disinterested representative of the public weal, while casting aspersions upon the unregulated pursuit of private interests." See Solomon, *Objectivity in the Making: Francis Bacon and the Politics of Inquiry* (Baltimore: Johns Hopkins University Press, 1998), 75. For a useful discussion of the distinction between *bonitas intrinseca* and *bonitas extrinseca*, see Spiegel, *Growth of Economic Thought*, 71.

48. On the fixed versus fluid values of money in seventeenth-century mercantilist

discourse, see Appleby, *Economic Thought and Ideology*, 42–47. See also Michael Foucault's discussion of the seventeenth-century epistemic shift in representations of value in "Exchanging," in *The Order of Things: An Archaeology of Human Knowledge* (London: Tavistock, 1970), 166–214.

49. *Troilus and Cressida*'s pervasive mercantile metaphors have been the subject of a large number of essays from an almost equally large variety of critical perspectives. See Raymond Southall, "*Troilus and Cressida* and the Spirit of Capitalism," in Arnold Kettle, ed., *Shakespeare in a Changing World* (London: Lawrence and Wishart, 1964), 217–32; T. J. Stafford, "Mercantile Imagery in *Troilus and Cressida*," in Stafford, ed., *Shakespeare in the Southwest: Some New Directions* (El Paso: Texas Western Press, 1969), 36–42; Douglas B. Wilson, "The Commerce of Desire: Freudian Narcissism in Chaucer's *Troilus and Criseyde* and Shakespeare's *Troilus and Cressida*," *English Language Notes* 21 (1983): 11–22; C. C. Barfoot, "*Troilus and Cressida*: 'Praise Us As We Are Tasted,'" *Shakespeare Quarterly* 39 (1988): 45–57; Douglas Bruster, "'The Alteration of Men': *Troilus and Cressida*, Troynovant, and Trade," chap. 7 of *Drama and the Market in the Age of Shakespeare* (Cambridge: Cambridge University Press, 1992), 97–117; Lars Engle, "Always Already in the Market: The Politics of Evaluation in *Troilus and Cressida*," chap. 7 of *Shakespearean Pragmatism: Market of His Time* (Chicago: University of Chicago Press, 1993), 147–63; and Hugh Grady, "'Mad Idolatry': Commodification and Reification in *Troilus and Cressida*," chap. 2 of *Shakespeare's Universal Wolf: Postmodernist Studies in Early Modern Reification* (Oxford: Clarendon Press, 1996), 58–94.

50. Discussions of the play's presentation of the origin of value include Winifred M. T. Nowottny, "'Opinion' and 'Value' in *Troilus and Cressida*," *Essays in Criticism* 4 (1954): 282–96; Frank Kermode's very useful riposte to Nowottny (including her invocation of Hobbes), "Opinion, Truth, and Value," *Essays in Criticism* 5 (1955): 181–87; W. R. Elton's enduringly illuminating essay, "Shakespeare's Ulysses and the Problem of Value," *Shakespeare Studies* 2 (1966): 95–111; Gayle Greene's pair of essays, "Shakespeare's Cressida: 'A Kind of Self,'" in Carolyn Ruth Swift Lenz, Gayle Greene, and Carol Thomas Neely, eds., *The Woman's Part: Feminist Criticism of Shakespeare* (Urbana: University of Illinois Press, 1980), 133–49, which approaches the question of value from the point of view of patriarchal economies of female subject formation, and "Language and Value in Shakespeare's *Troilus and Cressida*," *Studies in English Literature* 21 (1981): 271–85, which reapplies her argument to issues of signification; Girard, "Politics of Desire in *Troilus and Cressida*," which analyzes value in terms of mimetic desire and violence; Engle, *Shakespearean Pragmatism*, which relates Shakespeare's treatment of ancient codes of value to the emergence in the late sixteenth century of a ubiquitous market economy; Charnes, "'So Unsecret to Ourselves,'" which provides a powerful development of and corrective to Greene's and Girard's arguments through an analysis of value as it is produced within the play's male homosocial structures of desire; and Heather James's "'Tricks We Play on the Dead': Making History in *Troilus and Cressida*," chap. 3 of *Shakespeare's Troy: Drama, Politics, and the Translation of Empire* (Cambridge: Cambridge University Press, 1997), 85–118, which treats value through the prism of the play's heterogeneous, conflicting literary sources.

51. The most extensive treatment of early modern theories of plague transmission, including miasmic models of infection, is Leeds Barroll's *Politics, Plague, and Shakespeare's Theater: The Stuart Years* (Ithaca, N.Y.: Cornell University Press, 1991); see esp. chap. 3. I treat this issue in extensive detail in Chapter 5. On Shakespeare's largely mias-

mic understanding of infection, see Hoeniger, *Medicine and Shakespeare in the English Renaissance*, 187–90.

52. William Clowes, *A Briefe and Necessary Treatise, Touching the Cure of the Disease Now Usually Called Lues Venera, by Unctions and Other Approued Waies of Curing*, in *A Profitable and Necessarie Booke of Obseruations* (London, 1596), sig. U1. Fabricius discusses Clowes's theories of the causes and cures of venereal disease in *Syphilis in Shakespeare's England*, 106–12.

53. Compare Heather James's argument in *Shakespeare's Troy*, 110–11, that Troilus's desire for Cressida is complicated by his investment in a "truthful" ego-ideal predicated on her faithlessness; according to this reading, his Petrarchan love already teeters on the brink of sanctimonious disgust.

54. See, for example, Thomas Starkey, *Dialogue Between Reginald Pole and Thomas Lupset*, ed. Kathleen M. Burton (London: Chatto and Windus, 1948 [c. 1535]), which suggests that the body politic suffers from "palsy" as a result of merchants' importing foreign "trifles and conceits," especially "French cloth" (82, 92); Stephen Gosson, *Playes Confuted in Fiue Actions, Prouing That They Are Not To Be Suffred in a Christian Common Weale* (London, 1582 [?]), which complains about "wanton Italian bookes, which being translated into english, haue poysoned the olde manners of our Country with foreine delights" (sig. B6); and Thomas Tryon, *The Good Housewife Made Doctor* (London, 1685), which declaims against Spanish fruits, arguing that "the eating and drinking of *Forreign Ingredient*" is what most "destroys and hurts [the] health" of bodies natural and politic (90).

55. Charnes, " 'So Unsecret to Ourselves,' " 81.

56. "Contamination" derives from the same etymological root as "contagion"; in medieval Latin, "contamen" meant "infection." Hence "contaminate" and its various cognates appear repeatedly in early modern medical discourse, most notably in relation to syphilis: the English translation of Oswald Gaebelkover's *Boock of Physicke* (London, 1599) analyzes "Contamination in [the] bodye, be it either of the French disease, or of anye other such like infectious diseases" (sig. Bb3v). Interestingly, both "infect" and "contaminate" came to have a twinned medical and numismatic application: in his *Metallographia, or An History of Metals* (London, 1671), the physician John Webster speaks of "imperfect metals" that have been "infected, or contaminated with terrestrial faeculency" (sig. S2v). My thoughts on Helen's "contamination" by her male evaluators owe a great debt to Heather James's astute reading of Diomedes' lines; see *Shakespeare's Troy*, 104–5.

57. By contrast, Robert Weimann has argued that *Troilus and Cressida*'s "bifold authority" springs from the divided *locus* and *platea* of the Elizabethan platform stage: see "Bifold Authority in Shakespeare's Theatre," *Shakespeare Quarterly* 39 (1988): 401–17; and "Representation and Performance: The Uses of Authority in Shakespeare's Theater," *PMLA* 107 (1992): 497–510.

58. Bruster, *Drama and the Market*, 98–99.

59. In her important essay "Unbodied Figures of Desire," *Theater Journal* 38 (1986): 34–52, Carol Cook observes that Cressida's lines elsewhere in the play sound "like an effect of ventriloquism" (51). See also Alan Sinfield's reading of Cressida's "character" in *Faultlines: Cultural Materialism and the Politics of Dissident Reading* (Berkeley: University of California Press, 1992), 54.

60. Compare Marx and Engels's famous epithet about the transformations of value by capitalist production: "all that is solid melts into air, all that is holy is profaned," "The

Communist Manifesto," in *The Marx-Engels Reader,* ed. Robert C. Tucker, 2nd ed. (New York: W. W. Norton, 1978), 476. W. R. Elton writes of the "market-fluctuations" that underwrite the play's theme of mutability in general and Ulysses' speech on time in particular, "Shakespeare's Ulysses," 104; Lars Engle likewise sees Ulysses' speech as espousing a "market ethic," in *Shakespearean Pragmatism,* 157.

61. Georg Simmel, *The Philosophy of Money* (London: Routledge, 1978), 67. For an illuminating explication and adaptation of Simmel's theory of the commensuration of demand in the production of value, see Arjun Appadurai, "Introduction: Commodities and the Politics of Value," in Appadurai ed., *The Social Life of Things: Commodities in Cultural Perspective* (Cambridge: Cambridge University Press, 1986), 3–63.

62. Thomas Hobbes, *The Collected Works of Thomas Hobbes,* ed. Sir William Molesworth, 2nd impression (London: Routledge/Thoemmes Press, 1994), 3: 76. See Elton, "Shakespeare's Ulysses," esp. 100–107; and Greene, "Language and Value," 272.

63. Grady, *Shakespeare's Universal Wolf,* 58–59. See also Jeanne Newlin, "The Modernity of *Troilus and Cressida,*" *Harvard Library Bulletin* 17 (1969): 353–73, which documents the many early twentieth-century stage treatments of *Troilus and Cressida* that viewed the play as addressing fundamentally "modern" concerns.

64. Robert Henryson, *Testament of Cresseid,* ed. Denton Fox (London: Thomas Nelson, 1968), line 395. Cressida may have been depicted as leprous also in Henry Chettle and Thomas Dekker's lost *Troilus and Cressida* (1599). A fragmentary "plot" of Chettle and Dekker's play has survived, and it indicates a great debt to Henryson's poem; as in the latter, Cressida is shown to enter "wth Beggars," which suggests strongly that Chettle and Dekker followed Henryson in afflicting Cressida with leprosy. If so, Shakespeare's deviation from this tradition, given its freshness in his audience's minds, would have been all the more noteworthy. See Harold Jenkins, *The Life and Work of Henry Chettle* (London: Sidgwick and Jackson, 1934), 222.

65. Kermode, "Opinion, Truth, Value," 182.

66. Ulrich von Hutten, *De Guaiaci Medicina et Morbo Gallico* (London, 1533), fol. 4. As Greg Bentley points out, other writers attributed the causes of syphilis to melancholy; but the humoral etiologies they proposed were often confusingly interarticulated with exogenous models of infection. Von Hutten's humoral explanation of the disease, for example, is blended with a miasmic one, inasmuch as he attributes the complexional disarray causing syphilis to bad vapors. See Bentley, *Shakespeare and the New Disease,* 10.

67. Kermode's assumption of an objective value that the deluded will misapprehends has been repeated by subsequent critics. Gayle Greene says of Troilus and the other male evaluators, "assuming that value is assigned by 'will,' these characters subvert reason with passion and invert the proper working of the mind": "Language and Value," 277 Douglas B. Wilson similarly asserts that "Shakespeare's play directs a world of trivial combat and mannered passion where infected will strains to replace objective merit". "Commerce of Desire," 15. For a critique of the implicit essentialism of such presumptions, see Charnes, "So Unsecret to Ourselves," 70.

68. Ulysses's theory of value is in many respects a precursor of a phenomenon that was to emerge with increasing forcefulness throughout the seventeenth century: that is, the valuation of a commodity less according to any allegedly intrinsic use-value it might possess than by an appeal to an ineffable source outside it that determines its market or exchange value. Perhaps the best example of such an appeal is provided not by the play

itself but by the epistle to the 1609 quarto edition, dedicated by the "Never Writer" to the "Ever Reader." *Troilus and Cressida,* the Never Writer claims, has avoided the taint of the stage, where it would have been "stal'd" or contaminated by its audiences' assessments, both contagiously ("clapper-clawd with the palmes of the vulger") and miasmically ("sullied, with the smoaky breath of the multitude"). The Never Writer insists that the play's "scape" from the stage to print has been necessary for it not only to avoid such infection but also to disclose a stable value that derives from an external "sovereign" source, the playwright's "power of wit." All quotes are from *Troilus and Cressida,* ed. Kenneth Palmer (London: Methuen, 1982), 95. For more on the tendency to attribute an artistic commodity's market value to the power of an external creator, see Ann Rosalind Jones and Peter Stallybrass's recent work on fetishism and the origin of value in early modern Europe, particularly the introduction to their *Renaissance Clothing and the Materials of Memory* (Cambridge: Cambridge University Press, 2000), 1–14.

69. Paracelsus, *Selected Writings,* ed. Jolande Jacobi, trans. Norbert Guterman (New York: Pantheon, 1958), 107. For a discussion of the broader application of this notion in late Elizabethan and early Stuart political discourse, see Harris, *Foreign Bodies and the Body Politic,* chap. 3. The reversibility of the sun's curative and noxious properties is hinted at in *Timon of Athens* when Timon exhorts the "blessed breeding sun" to "infect the air" (4.3.1, 3).

70. On the ambivalent politics of the speech, see Thomas Cartelli, *Marlowe, Shakespeare, and the Economy of Theatrical Experience* (Philadelphia: University of Pennsylvania Press, 1991), 147–51.

71. It is worth noting that Hobbes proposes a similar compromise. Although he endorses an exogenous notion of value, he is disturbed by its civil consequences, which he notably figures in pathological terms: "the *diseases* of a commonwealth . . . proceed from the poison of seditious doctrines, whereof one is, *that euery private man is judge of good and evil actions.* This is true in the condition of mere nature, where there are no civil laws . . . But otherwise, it is manifest, that the measure of good and evil actions, is the civil law" (*Collected Works,* 3: 310). For Hobbes as for Malynes, in other words, subjection to civil law imposed by a monarch arrests the potential anarchy of multiple valuation. See also Elton, "Shakespeare's Ulysses," 106–7.

72. "Drawing attention to the narrative techniques—rhetoric, genre, and disposition—that stamp interpretive values on the legendary events and heroes at Troy, [Shakespeare] exposes lack of authenticity in a legend which exists only to bequeath authoritative origins. . . . In the play's very dramatic construction, Shakespeare reiterates Troilus' notorious query, "'What's aught but as 'tis valued?'" James, *Shakespeare's Troy,* 89–90. For a related reading of the intertextual ensembles that constitute character in *Troilus and Cressida,* see Cook, "Unbodied Figures of Desire," 52. Compare Lars Engle's richly suggestive argument that "aesthetic evaluations of the two major sources, Homer's *Iliad* and Chaucer's *Troilus and Criseyde,* and personal evaluations within the play are subject to a forceful thought experiment in perspective reversal." *Shakespearean Pragmatism,* 23.

73. James, *Shakespeare's Troy,* 91.

74. Compare Homer, *The Iliad,* trans. Richmond Lattimore (Chicago: University of Chicago Press, 1951), 17.123; Vergil, *The Aeneid,* trans. L. R. Lind (Bloomington: Indiana University Press, 1963), 2.438; and Ovid, *Metamorphoses,* trans. Rolfe Humphries (Bloomington: Indiana University Press, 1955), 13.291.

75. Compare James's remarks about Achilles' valuation of Hector in *Shakespeare's Troy,* 105.

76. George Chapman, *The Iliads of Homer Translated According to the Greek,* 2 vols. (London: J. M. Dent, 1898), 1: xiii. See also Joseph Loewenstein, "Plays Agonistic and Competitive: The Textual Approach to Elsinore," *Renaissance Drama* 19 (1988): 63–90, for similar conclusions about Shakespeare's contamination of his Iliadic materials. In Hamlet's rendering of the "rugged Pyrrhus" set-piece before the players, Loewenstein argues, "one can easily find a furiously empowered effacement of all distinction between Trojan Homer, Trojan Virgil, and Trojan Shakespeare . . . the speech conflates the manner of ranting tragedy and of Virgilian epic. This is *contaminatio,* practiced in such a way that it elides the distinction between *imitatio* and the adoption of stylistic fashion" (75–76).

77. Pandarus may indeed have bequeathed the Winchester goose to the play's audiences or readers. His syphilis is perhaps responsible for what is widely regarded as a compositor's error in the first published version of John Marston's *Insatiate Countess:* a line from Signior Claridia's extended admonition to husbands in V.i, which editors agree should read "The box unto Pandora is given," was rendered in the 1613 quarto edition "The poxe is unto Panders given." See *The Plays of John Marston,* ed. H. Harvey Wood (London: Oliver and Boyd, 1939), 3: 81.

78. These figures are taken from John Craig, *The Mint: A History of the London Mint from A.D. 287 to 1948* (Cambridge: Cambridge University Press, 1953), esp. xv, 133. On the vicissitudes of coordinating competing systems of measurement in the sixteenth and seventeenth centuries, see Heckscher, *Mercantilism,* 1: 110–27. Challis provides a useful comparative breakdown of troy, avoirdupois, and tower weight systems in *The Tudor Coinage,* app. 1, 303. For a suggestive discussion of troy weight in relation to *Troilus and Cressida,* see Bruster, *Drama and the Market,* 100–101.

79. Thomas Middleton and William Rowley, *The Old Law,* ed. Catherine M. Shaw (New York: Garland, 1982), 4.1.77–79.

Chapter 5. Plague and Transmigration

1. Ben Jonson, *Volpone, or The Fox,* ed. Philip Brockbank (London and New York: A and C Black/Norton, 1991), 1.3.29. All further references are cited in the text.

2. Georg Simmel, *The Philosophy of Money* (London; Routledge, 1978); quoted in George Rosen, *A History of Public Health,* expanded ed. (Baltimore: Johns Hopkins University Press, 1993), 59.

3. See, for example, Andrew Wear, "Medicine in Early Modern Europe: 1500–1700," in Lawrence I. Conrad et al., *The Western Medical Tradition: 800 B.C. to A.D. 1800* (Cambridge: Cambridge University Press, 1995), 215–361, esp. 339–40.

4. Thomas Dekker, *London Looke Backe,* in F. P. Wilson, ed., *The Plague Pamphlets of Thomas Dekker* (Oxford: Clarendon Press, 1925), 181. All further references to Dekker's plague pamphlets are to Wilson's volume.

5. See Girolamo Fracastoro, *De Contagione at Contagiosis Morbis et Eorum Curatione,* trans. Wilmer Care Wright (New York: Putnam, 1933), 34–35. The only explicit reference to Fracastoro that I have managed to locate in English plague writing is in Stephen Bradwell's *Physick for the Sicknesse, Commonly Called the Plague, With All the*

Particular Signes and Symptoms, Whereof the Most Are Ignorant (London, 1636), where the author refers to Fracastoro's observation about the contagiousness of a Veronese gown (sig. B4).

6. Dekker, *London Looke Backe,* 187.

7. Dekker, *The Meeting of the Gallants,* 109. See Stephen Greenblatt, "Invisible Bullets: Renaissance Authority and its Subversion, *Henry IV, Henry V,*" in Jonathan Dollimore and Alan Sinfield, eds., *Political Shakespeare: New Essays in Cultural Materialism* (Manchester: Manchester University Press, 1985), 18–47. I critique Greenblatt's reading of Renaissance pathology in *Foreign Bodies and the Body Politic: Discourses of Social Pathology in Early Modern England* (Cambridge: Cambridge University Press, 1998), 8–12.

8. Bradwell, *Physick for the Sicknesse,* sig. B3v.

9. Dekker, *News from Graves End,* 84, 85–86.

10. Thomas Lodge, *A Treatise of the Plague: Containing the Nature, Signes, and Accidents of the Same* (London, 1603), sig. B4; Thomas Thayre, *A Treatise of the Pestilence* (London, 1603), sig. B1.

11. See Rosen, *History of Public Health,* 80–81.

12. Gilbert Skayne, *Ane Breve Description of the Pest Quhair in the Causis, Signis, and Sum Speciall Preseruation and Cure Thairof Ar Contenit* (Edinburgh, 1568), sig. A2v.

13. S. H., *A New Treatise of the Pestilence* (London, 1603), sig. A2.

14. Skayne, *Breve Description,* sig. A3.

15. John Strype, *Annals of the Reformation and Establishment of Religion, and Other Various Occurrences in the Church of England During Queen Elizabeth's Happy Reign* (Oxford: Clarendon Press, 1824), 4: 294.

16. Lodge, *Treatise of the Plague,* sig. B3. I discuss Lodge's confused etiology of the plague in *Foreign Bodies and the Body Politic,* 24–26.

17. Margaret Healy, *Fictions of Disease in Early Modern England: Bodies, Plagues, Politics* (New York: Palgrave, 2001), 51.

18. Bradwell, *Physick for the Sicknesse,* sig. B4.

19. Bradwell, *Physick for the Sicknesse,* sig. B2v.

20. Dekker, *News from Graves End,* 87.

21. F. P. Wilson, *The Plague in Shakespeare's London* (Oxford: Oxford University Press, 1927), 86.

22. Paul Slack, *The Impact of Plague in Tudor and Stuart England* (London: Routledge and Kegan Paul, 1985), 221. See also Leeds Barroll, *Politics, Plague, and Shakespeare's Theater: The Stuart Years* (Ithaca, N.Y.: Cornell University Press, 1991).

23. *Certain Necessary Direction, As Well for the Cure of the Plague, As for Preuenting the Infection* (London, 1636), sig. B3v.

24. John Roche Dasent, ed., *Acts of the Privy Council of England, 1542–1604,* 32 vols. (London: Stationery Office, 1890–1907), 24: 472, 400, 347.

25. Margaret Cavendish, *A Discovery of the New World Called the Blazing World,* in Kate Lilley, ed., *The Blazing World and Other Writings* (Harmondsworth: Penguin, 1994), 158–59. Lucretius himself offers in book 6 of *De Rerum Natura* an exogenous, ontological model of the origin and form of plague. In Lucy Hutchinson's translation from the 1650s, with which Margaret Cavendish may have been familiar, we are told that the disease comes from "flowing seeds" that "spring up by chance / And towards the troubled heaven, in throngs advance." See *Lucy Hutchinson's Translation of Lucretius:* De Rerum Natura, ed. Hugh de Quehen (Ann Arbor: University of Michigan Press, 1996), 205. For

a discussion of the early modern rehabilitation of Lucretius in the realm of pathology—in this case, by Shakespeare in the "Queen Mab" speech from *Romeo and Juliet*—see Jonathan Gil Harris, "Atomic Shakespeare," *Shakespeare Studies* 30 (2002): 41–45. For a fascinating discussion of Lucretian and other classical theories of metamorphic motion in the Renaissance, see Michel Jeanneret, *Perpetual Motion: Transforming Shapes in the Renaissance from da Vinci to Montaigne,* trans. Nidra Poller (Baltimore: Johns Hopkins University Press, 2001).

26. "The rich, unhappy that they are—what ills are they not subject to through intemperance? Gout and consumption and pneumonia and dropsy are the consequences of those splendid dinners." Lucian, "The Dream, or the Cock," in *Lucian in Eight Volumes,* trans. A. M. Harmon (Cambridge, Mass.: Harvard University Press, 1968), 2: 219; compare *Volpone,* 1.2.125–28.

27. "D'autres morceaux demanderaient à être supprimés complètement, tels les divertissements improvisés que Volpone se fait donner à deux reprises par ses esclaves familiers." Maurice Castelain, *Ben Jonson, l'Homme et l'Oeuvre* (Paris, 1907), 301.

28. See *Volpone, or the Fox,* J. D. Rea ed. (New Haven, Conn.: Yale University Press, 1919), xxvii.

29. Harry Levin, "Jonson's Metempsychosis," *Philological Quarterly* 22 (1943): 231–39.

30. Douglas Duncan, *Ben Jonson and the Lucianic Tradition* (Cambridge: Cambridge University Press, 1979), chap. 7.

31. See, for example, Anthony's remarks about the Egyptian crocodile, in William Shakespeare, *Anthony and Cleopatra,* ed. Michael Neill (Oxford: Oxford University Press, 1994), 2.7.44.

32. Thomas Westcote, *A View of Devonshire in MDCXXX,* ed. George Oliver and Pitman Jones (Exeter, 1845), 51.

33. For a contemporary description of the game, see Thomas Freeman, *Runne, and a Great Cast* (London, 1614), epigram 95.

34. Arjun Appadurai, "Introduction: Commodities and the Politics of Value," in Appadurai, ed., *The Social Life of Things: Commodities in Cultural Perspective* (Cambridge: Cambridge University Press, 1986), 3–63, esp. 5.

35. "Quacksalver," from which we derive our modern medical slang term "quack," was an early modern Dutch term applied to people who talk up ("quack") their ointments ("salves"); compare the modern Dutch word *kwaksalver.* Given Jonson's extraordinary sensitivity to etymology, his choice of an alien term here is arguably highly significant.

36. On the poisonous properties of medicines in Jacobean Italianate drama, see Tanya Pollard, "Beauty's Poisonous Properties," *Shakespeare Studies* 27 (1999): 187–210.

37. My information about Lady Politic Would-Be's "remedies" is drawn from the following early modern medical and lay health texts: for seed-pearl, Robert Burton, *The Anatomy of Melancholy* (London, 1632), 376; for mint, Gervase Markham, *The English Housewife: Containing the Inward and Outward Virtues Which Ought to Be in a Complete Woman* (London, 1615), 1: ¶ 27; and for elecampane root, bugloss, myrobalanes, and saffron, Robert Lovell, *PAMBOTANOLOGIA Sive Enchiridion Botanicum: Or A Compleat Herball* (Oxford, 1659), 62–63, 303–4, 399–402.

38. In *The English Housewife,* for example, Gervase Markham directs his female readers to primarily local and inexpensive remedies; only rarely does he prescribe exotic drugs such as "bole armeniac" (1: ¶ 123, 193) or *"unguentum Aegyptiacum"* (1. ¶ 202): here

we see an intriguing overlap between the domestic as the "household" and the "national." For an extensive overview of this overlap, see Wendy Wall, *Staging Domesticity: House-hold Work and English Identity in Early Modern English Drama* (Cambridge: Cambridge University Press, 2002). On women's roles in Stuart English medical practice, see Doreen Evenden Nagy, *Popular Medicine in Seventeenth-Century England* (Bowling Green, Ohio: Bowling Green State University Popular Press, 1988), chap. 5.

39. As Lovell's *Pambotanologia* makes clear, these New World drugs were all initially regarded as medicinal. Tobacco was marketed as an all-purpose panacea for a wide array of ailments, including "fits of the mother," gout, toothache, ulcers, "kibed heeles," vertigo, deafness, asthma, and tumors (451); sassafras, also known as the "Ague-Tree," was applied to all "cold diseases and obstructions of the liver and spleen" (4); and guiacum, or "Pock-Wood," was the miracle drug of the time for syphilis (365), although both tobacco and sassafras were also used to mitigate its symptoms.

40. See Thomas Elyot, *The Castel of Helthe* (London, 1539), fol. 22b; and William Harrison, *Harrison's Description of England*, ed. Frederick J. Furnivall (London: N. Trübner, 1877), 1: 327.

41. On the spicers' trade, see R. S. Roberts, "The Early History of the Import of Drugs into Britain," in F. N. L. Poynter, ed., *The Evolution of Pharmacy in Britain* (Springfield, Ill.: Charles C. Thomas, 1965), 165–85, esp. 166. The "Drug Section" of the 1604 Rate Book, which includes the spices I have listed, is reproduced by Roberts on 173–83.

42. John Milton, *Paradise Lost,* ed. Alastair Fowler (London: Longman, 1998), 2: 640–41.

43. Christopher Marlowe, *The Jew of Malta,* ed. James R. Siemon (New York: Norton, 1994), 4.1.63–67. Barabas's famous first scene, in which he inventories his wealth, is certainly an influence on Volpone's counting-house scene.

44. Roberts, "Early History," 178, 175.

45. The subtitle of Lovell's treatise revealingly advises the reader that, among the items in its exhaustive list of medicinal plants, *"all that are not in the Physick Garden in Oxford are noted with asterisks."*

46. *The Libele of Englyshe Polycye* (c. 1436), quoted in Roberts, "Early History," 167.

47. Timothy Bright, *A Treatise: Wherein is Declared the Sufficiencie of English Medicines, for Cure of All Diseases* (London, 1580), sig. Aiii. All further references are cited in the text.

48. For an extremely useful analysis of the etiologies of illness in Galenic medicine, including the hints of exogenous explanations in Galen's infrequent comments about "seeds" of illness, see Vivian Nutton, "The Seeds of Disease: An Explanation of Contagion and Infection from the Greeks to the Renaissance," *Medical History* 27 (1983): 1–34.

49. Robert Greene, *A Quip for an Vpstart Courtier: Or, a Quaint Dispute betweene Velvet-breeches and Cloth-breeches* (London, 1635), sig. D3.

50. Thomas Starkey, *A Dialogue Between Reginald Pole and Thomas Lupset,* ed. Kathleen M. Burton (London: Chatto and Windus, 1948), 82.

51. The term "bullionist" was coined by the nineteenth-century economic historian Richard Jones: see his essay "Primitive Political Economy of England," *Edinburgh Review* (April 1847); reprinted in W. Whewell, ed., *Literary Remains* (London: John Murray, 1859), 291–335.

52. On the details of Milles's career, see Leslie Stephen and Sidney Lee, eds., *The Dictionary of National Biography* (Oxford: Oxford University Press, 1921–22), 13: 434.

53. My discussion of the history of the English national customs system draws heavily on Eli F. Heckscher, *Mercantilism,* 2nd ed., 2 vols., trans. Mendel Shapiro (London: George Allen and Unwin, 1955), 1: 51–52.

54. See John Wheeler, *A Treatise of Commerce, Wherin Are Shewed the Commodities Arising by a Well Ordered, and Ruled Trade, Such As That of the Societie of Merchantes Adventurers Is Proved to Bee* (London, 1601), especially sig. M2, which includes the marginal heading "Customers of the out-Portes, back-byte the M. M. Adventurers."

55. Thomas Milles, *The Custumers Alphabet and Primer: Conteining, Their Creede or Beliefe in the True Doctrine of Christian Religion* (London, 1608), sig. G1v.

56. Thomas Milles, *Custumers Apology: That is to Say, a Generall Answere to Informers of All Sortes, and Their Iniurious Complaints, Against the Honest Reputation of the Collectors of her Maiesties CUSTUMES, Specially in the OUT-PORTES of this Realme* (London, 1599), sig. B2.

57. Milles, *Custumers Apology,* sig. B2v. Compare Thomas Milles, *The Customers Replie, or Second Apologie* (London, 1604), sig. A5, and *Custumers Alphabet,* sig. G1v.

58. Milles, *Custumers Alphabet,* sig. G1v.

59. Milles, *Customers Replie,* sig. A5v.

60. Milles, *Customers Replie,* sig. D1v.

61. Milles, *Custumers Alphabet,* sig. D1v.

62. Milles, *Custumers Alphabet,* sigs. D2–D2v.

63. Thomas Milles, *The Misterie of Iniquitie* (London, 1611), sig. K1, attached page.

64. Milles argues that taxes "might happily ayme at the beating back of some Forraine idle Commodities": *Custumers Alphabet,* sig. D1v. Edward Misselden argues that tobacco was a foreign commodity well worth regulating, for the health of English bodies natural and politic alike. He blasts "the great *Excesse* of the *Kingdome,* in consuming the Commodities of forreine Countries in such abundance, to our own losse. And amongst those, the great excess in *Tobacco* is none of the least: which if it might seeme good to the High Wisdome of HIS *Maiestie,* to restraine, or at least to give a tolleration of the *Virginia* and *Barmudo's* only: there might be a great deale of *Pietie* and *Policy* shewed in this *Remedy.* For in the one respect, it would tend to a great enriching of that plantation, which so happily succeedeth through Gods blessing: and in the other it would aduantage the KING and the *Kingdome,* in the redresse of the disorder of the *Spanish Trade,* and in bringing in *Treasure* in stead of that *Toye,* more then the Rent that is now raised to HIS *Maiestie* for the same." *Free Trade, Or The Meanes To Make Trade Florish: Wherein, the Causes of the Decay of Trade in this Kingdome, are Discovered: And the Remedies also to Remoove the Same, are Represented* (London, 1622), sigs. H6v–H7.

65. The symptoms of leprosy and syphilis were often conflated, as is hinted by the once popular canard that syphilis was caused by the fornication of a Jew and a leper. As Johannes Fabricius has noted, the overlap between discourses of leprosy and syphilis is evident in *Hamlet* when the Ghost describes the effects of Claudius's poison on him; see Fabricius, *Syphilis in Shakespeare's England* (London: Jessica Kingsley, 1994), 42, 259. For discussions of the etiology and treatment of leprosy and its relationship to the emergent discourses of syphilis, see Anna Foa, "The New and the Old: The Spread of Syphilis (1494–1530)," in Edward Muir and Guido Ruggiero, eds., *Sex and Gender in Historical Perspective,* trans. Margaret A. Gallucci et al. (Baltimore: Johns Hopkins University Press, 1990), 26–45; and Michel Foucault, *Madness and Civilization: A History of Insanity in the Age of Reason,* trans. Richard Howard (New York: Pantheon, 1965), 1–19.

66. On onions as a remedy for the plague, see *Orders, Thought Meete by her Maiestie, and her Priuie Counsell, to be Executed throughout the Countries of this Realme, in such Townes, Villages, and Other Places, as Are, or May be hereafter Infected with the Plague* (London, 1592), sigs. B3v–B4; and *Present Remedies Against the Plague* (London, 1594), sig. B3v.

67. Michel Foucault, *Discipline and Punish: The Birth of the Prison,* trans. Alan Sheridan (New York: Pantheon, 1977), 144.

68. Such intermingling is particularly strong in Jonson's Venice, which plays host to numerous foreign bodies shipped from abroad. Most notable in this regard, perhaps, is the swarm of foreign currencies name-checked by the characters: in addition to the Venetian chequeen, gazet, and bagatine (1.3.65, 2.2.223, 2.2.258), one finds also the Spanish pistolet (2.2.267), the French livre and sol (4.1.110, 4.5.97), and the English groat and pound (2.2.70, 4.1.111).

69. On emergent late medieval quarantine regulations in Venice and the Adriatic, see Rosen, *History of Public Health,* 44–45; and Mirko D. Grmek, "Le Concept d'infection dans l'antiquité at au moyen age: les anciennes mesures sociales contre les maladies contagieuses et la fondation de la première quarantaine à Dubrovnik," *Rad Jugoslavneske Akademje* 384 (1980): 9–55. For a discussion of England's comparatively late adoption of quarantine regulations, see Slack, *Impact of Plague,* 221.

70. Stone was whipped in the spring of 1605 at Bridewell for "a blasphemous speech" in which he called the admiral a fool; see Brockbank's note to 2.1.53. It is intriguing that Stone was thus associated with the state's leading maritime authority; perhaps this helped prompt Jonson's fantasy of Stone's "subversion."

71. This is not to suggest that Sir Politic Would-Be was written as a satirical portrait of Thomas Milles, with whom Ben Jonson would have in all likelihood been unacquainted. Other real-life models for Sir Pol have been mooted, especially Sir Henry Wotton, English ambassador to Venice.

72. For a useful description of Plato's theories of physiology and medicine, see Jacques Jouanna, "The Birth of Western Medical Art," in Mirko D. Grmek, ed., *Western Medical Thought from Antiquity to the Middle Ages,* trans. Antony Shugaar (Cambridge, Mass.: Harvard University Press, 1998), 22–71, esp. 68–71. Lady Politic Would-Be is herself a travesty of Plato's ideal of the physician; in the *Laws,* Plato presents the physician not only as a master of the art but also as a master of persuasion.

73. Robert Fludd, *Utrusque Cosmi . . . Historia* (Oppenheim, 1619), 109; Michael C. Schoenfeldt, *Bodies and Selves in Early Modern England: Physiology and Inwardness in Spenser, Shakespeare, Herbert, and Milton* (Cambridge: Cambridge University Press, 1999), 3, 5. I discuss Fludd's theory of *spiritus mali* in *Foreign Bodies,* 29–30.

74. See OED, *infection,* 8.

Chapter 6. Hepatitis/Castration and Treasure

1. See J. D. Gould, "The Trade Depression of the Early 1620s," *Economic History Review* 7 (1954): 81–88; Brian E. Supple, *Commercial Crisis and Change in England, 1600–1642: A Study in the Instability of a Mercantile Economy* (Cambridge: Cambridge University Press, 1959), 52–72; and Joyce Oldham Appleby, *Economic Thought and Ideol-*

ogy in Seventeenth-Century England (Princeton, N.J.: Princeton University Press, 1978), 42.

2. Edward Misselden, *Free Trade, or The Meanes to Make Trade Florish: Wherein, The Causes of the Decay of Trade in this Kingdome, are Discovered: And the Remedies also to Remooue the Same, are Represented* (London, 1622), sig. B5v. All further references are cited in the text.

3. This standoff culminated the following year in the Dutch massacre of the English at Amboyna. For a contemporary English account of the events, see *News Out of East India of the Cruell Usage of Our English Merchants at Amboyna* (London, 1625).

4. Misselden, *Free Trade*, sig. H5v.

5. Gerard Malynes, *The Maintenance of Free Trade, According to the Three Essentiall Parts of Traffique; Namely, Commodities, Moneys, and Exchange of Moneys, by Bills of Exchanges for Other Countries* (London, 1622), sig. B7.

6. Edward Misselden, *The Circle of Commerce. Or, the Ballance of Trade, in Defence of Free Trade: Opposed to Malynes Little Fish and His Great Whale, and Poized Against Them in the Scale* (London, 1623), sigs. Aa1, K3.

7. Gerard Malynes, *The Center of the Circle of Commerce. Or, A Refutation of a Treatise, Intituled The Circle of Commerce, or The Ballance of Trade, Lately Published by E. M.* (London, 1623), sig. B3.

8. Malynes, *Center of the Circle of Commerce*, sig. R4.

9. See, for instance, Appleby, *Economic Thought and Ideology*, 41–47; Andrea Finkelstein, *Harmony and Balance: An Intellectual History of Seventeenth-Century English Economic Thought* (Ann Arbor: University of Michigan Press, 2000), 54–73; and Henry William Spiegel, *The Growth of Economic Thought*, 3rd ed. (Durham, N.C.: Duke University Press, 1991), 104–6.

10. Misselden, *Circle of Commerce*, sig. Ee4v.

11. Mary Poovey, *A History of the Modern Fact: Problems of Knowledge in the Sciences of Wealth and Society* (Chicago: University of Chicago Press, 1998), 76–79.

12. Finkelstein, *Harmony and Balance*, chap. 1, "Merchants and the Body Politic," 15–25.

13. The OED cites the entry for the condition in the 1727–51 edition of *Chambers' Cyclopedia:* "The hepatitis bears a near resemblance to the pleurisy."

14. Gervase Markham, *Cavelarice. Of the English Horseman* (London, 1607), 73.

15. Andrew Boorde, *The Breuiary of Helthe, for All Maner of Syckenesses and Diseases the Whiche May Be in Man, or Woman* (London, 1547), sigs. F5–F5v.

16. *The Anatomical Lectures of William Harvey: Prelectiones Anatomie Universalis, De Musculis*, ed. and trans. Gweneth Whitteridge (Edinburgh: E. and S. Livingstone, 1964), 137, 241.

17. Of these, jaundice seems the most likely to have overlapped with what we now regard as hepatitis. In his *Breuiary of Helthe*, for example, Boorde describes "jaunes" as a sickness "which hath consumed the bloud and then the skyn and the exteriall partes muste nedes turne to yeloweness, for lacke of bloud, coler hauyng the dominion ouer it" (sig. H7v).

18. For useful discussions of Galen's views of the liver in regard to the production of the blood, see Walter Pagel, *William Harvey's Biological Ideas: Selected Aspects and Historical Background* (Basel: Karger, 1967), esp. 127–32; and Gweneth Whitteridge, *William Harvey and the Circulation of the Blood* (New York: American Elsevier, 1971), esp. 41–44.

19. Boorde, *Breuviary of Helthe,* sig. P4.

20. Helkiah Crooke, *Microcosmographia: A Description of the Body of Man, Together With the Controuersies and Figures Thereto Belonging* (London, 1618), 129. In fact the Greek *hepar* derives from a related word meaning "reddish-brown."

21. Barnabe Barnes, *Foure Bookes of Offices: Enabling Privat Persons for the Speciall Service of All Good Princes and Policies* (London, 1606), sig. B1v.

22. Thomas Milles, *The Custumers Apology: That is to Say, a Generall Answere to Informers of All Sortes, and Their Iniurious Complaints, Against the Honest Reputation of the Collectors of her Maiesties CUSTUMES, Specially in the OUT-PORTES of this Realme* (London, 1599), sig. D2v. Milles repeated this remark, without the "inflamed," in his later pamphlet *The Misterie of Inquitie* (London, 1611), sig. N1.

23. Malynes, *Center of the Circle of Commerce,* sig. R4.

24. Malynes, *Center of the Circle of Commerce,* sig. S1.

25. See Pagel, *Harvey's Biological Ideas,* "Circular Symbolism, Heart and Blood Before Harvey," 87–124.

26. Malynes, *Center of the Circle of Commerce,* sig. B3v.

27. In Misselden's writing, there is a persistently uneasy accommodation of what might otherwise seem like advocacy for merchant venturer aspirations within the language of monarchical government. In *Free Trade,* he argues that "*Gouernment* is a representation of the *Maiestie* and *Authoritie* of the KING" (sig. E3), but then goes on to praise the excellent government displayed by the most powerful merchant venturing companies. Similarly, he argues in *The Circle of Commerce* that "the States and States-men, Gouernours, Counsellers, and Magistrates of *Venice, Luca, Genoa, Florence, the Vnited Prouinces of the Low Countries,* and many other well gouerned Commonwealths, are by education Merchants: In so much as I may truely say, and I hope without any suspition or offence, there's none more fit to make a minister for a King, then an expert and iudicious Merchant" (sig. D2).

28. Gary Taylor, *Castration: An Abbreviated History of Western Manhood* (New York: Routledge, 2000), 54.

29. The testicles are referred to in sixteenth-century medical textbooks as "ballockes," "hyngers," "kind," "stones," and, occasionally, "testicles"; see Juhani Norri, *Names of Body Parts in English, 1400–1550,* Finnish Academy of Science and Letters (Saarijärvi: Gummerus Oy, 1998), 287.

30. Thomas Laqueur, *Making Sex: Body and Gender from the Greeks to Freud* (Cambridge, Mass.: Harvard University Press, 1990); and Gail Kern Paster, *The Body Embarrassed: Drama and the Disciplines of Shame in Early Modern England* (Ithaca, N.Y.: Cornell University Press, 1993).

31. Laqueur, *Making Sex,* 35.

32. For a discussion of the Galenic physiology of Shakespeare's sonnet, see Michael C. Schoenfeldt, *Bodies and Selves in Early Modern England: Physiology and Inwardness in Spenser, Shakespeare, Herbert, and Milton* (Cambridge: Cambridge University Press, 1999), chapter 2, esp. 82–83. On the links between Shakespeare's physiologies of blood and semen, see Byung-Eun Lee, "Shakespeare's Villeinizing of Jack Cade," in Peter C. Rollins and Alan Smith, eds., *Shakespeare's Theories of Blood, Character, and Class: A Festschrift in Honor of David Shelley Berkeley* (New York: Peter Lang, 2001), 109–22.

33. The key text here is Galen's *Peri Spermatos (On The Seed);* its arguments are briefly but usefully summarized by Laqueur in *Making Sex,* 40.

34. Crooke devotes one section to the penis, but no less than four to the testicles, including several sections on the controversies and questions surrounding the functioning of the testes. For a useful discussion of Crooke's testocentric physiology, see Rebecca Ann Bach, "Tennis Balls: *Henry V* and Testicular Masculinity, or, According to the OED, Shakespeare Doesn't Have Any Balls," *Renaissance Drama* 30 (2001): 3–23, esp. 6–9.

35. Harvey, *Anatomical Lectures,* 190.

36. Thomas Dekker, *Northward Ho,* 4.2.9; in *The Dramatic Works of Thomas Dekker,* ed. Fredson Bowers, 3 vols. (Cambridge: Cambridge University Press, 1995), vol. 2.

37. John Davies, *Of Phormus his Gelded Purse,* cited in Taylor, *Castration,* 106. Although Taylor offers a useful discussion of the poem, he does not pay attention to the nationalities of the epigram's characters.

38. Christopher Marlowe, *Edward II,* ed. Charles R. Forker (New York: St. Martin's Press, 1994), 2.2.156–58.

39. Malynes, *Center of the Circle of Commerce,* sigs. R3v, R4.

40. Malynes, *Maintenance of Free Trade,* sig. D3v.

41. Malynes, *Maintenance of Free Trade,* sig. E5v.

42. One might also argue that Malynes's obsessive desire to restore a center to the circle of commerce reeks of the fetishist's desire, according to Freud's classic account. See "Fetishism," in *On Sexuality: The Pelican Freud Library,* vol. 7, ed. Angela Richards (Harmondsworth: Penguin, 1977), 351–57. At times, there is certainly something phallic about Malynes's "center": "it is recorded that when *Giotto* had made his Circle for his masterpeece, another Painter (perceiuing the same to be without a Center) did instantly with a pinsell make a point within the same, which made a perfect center; whereupon his Art was much extolled and preferred before *Giotto*'s conceit" (*Center of the Circle of Commerce,* sig. B3). But in the passage that concludes his treatise, the center serves as a fetishistic replacement, not for the phallus, but for something similar to Crooke's originary testes—that is, an organ that can ensure the health of blood and spirit alike: "*Bullion* being the Chylus, *Money* is but the Bloud, *Exchange* the Spirit that quickens all the Body. . . . To be short, *Bullion* is the very Body and Bloud of Kings, *Money* is but the Medium betweene Subiects and their Kings, *Exchange* the heauenly Mistery that ioynes them both together. . . . Next therefore let the exportation of moneys, the profusion of bloud, be preuented by the meanes of this *Center*" (sig. T1).

43. Misselden, *Free Trade,* sig. H2.

44. Misselden's inclusion of Christian ships in the list of Turkish victims may have made the specter of castration even more apparent to early modern readers. The language of phallic and testicular potency was a notable feature of English privateers' terminology for the parts of "man-o'war" ships. In an account of a Spanish war vessel, Captain John Smith refers to "the tops and yards well manned with stones and brass balls." John Smith, *An Accidence for all Young Sea-men* (London, 1626), 19.

45. There was considerable uncertainty in early modern Europe about what constituted the "Barbary Coast." For Leo Africanus, it was the coastal area of northern Africa, extending from Tripoli in the east to the Atlantic Moroccan shore. For many English, however, the term referred simply to the kingdoms and later empire of Morocco or to the Atlantic Moroccan coast. In its current application, however, the term refers to the Turkish regencies (Algiers, Tunis, Tripolis), as well as the three kingdoms of Fez, Morocco, and Sus, which were later united under the sherif (or emperor) of Morocco. See

Godfrey Fisher, *Barbary Legend: War, Trade, and Piracy in North Africa, 1415–1830* (Oxford: Clarendon Press, 1957), 17–18.

46. For the standard view that Christians were the hapless targets of Islamic corsairs, see Stanley Lane-Poole, *The Barbary Corsairs* (London: T. Fisher Unwin, 1890). As recently as 1970, one account of early modern Mediterranean piracy attempted to explain it in terms of a timeless, Manichean "holy war" between Christianity and Islam. See Peter Earle, *Corsairs of Malta and Barbary* (London: Sigwick and Jackson, 1970).

47. For a useful summary of attitudes toward Turks in Elizabethan England, see Daniel J. Vitkus's introduction to *Three Turk Plays from Early Modern England: "Selimus," "A Christian Turned Turk," "The Renegado"* (New York: Columbia University Press, 2000), 1–53.

48. Lois Potter, "Pirates and 'Turning Turk' in Renaissance Drama," in Jean-Pierre Maquerlot and Michèle Willems, eds., *Travel and Drama in Shakespeare's Time* (Cambridge: Cambridge University Press, 1996), 124–40, esp. 124.

49. Thomas Heywood and William Rowley, *A Critical Edition of A Fortune by Land and Sea*, ed. Herman Doh (New York: Garland, 1980), 4.1.1585, 4.2.1693.

50. Henry Robarts, *The Trumpet of Fame* (London, 1595), sig. A3. For a good discussion of early modern English privateers and their relations to the state, see Kenneth Andrews, *Elizabethan Privateering: English Privateering During the Spanish War, 1585–1603* (Cambridge: Cambridge University Press, 1964). See also Harry Kelsey, *Sir Francis Drake: The Queen's Pirate* (New Haven, Conn.: Yale University Press, 1998).

51. See Christopher Lloyd, *English Corsairs on the Barbary Coast* (London: Collins, 1981), 83–84; Alfred C. Wood, *The History of the Levant Company* (Oxford: Oxford University Press, 1935); and T. S. Willan, "Some Aspects of English Trade with the Levant in the Sixteenth Century," *English History Review* 70 (1955): 399–410.

52. Fisher, *Barbary Legend*, 114. For a contemporary report of the mission, led by Sir Robert Mansell, see *Algiers Voyage, In a Iournall or Briefe Reportary of All Occurents Happning in the Fleet of Ships Sent Out by the King His Most Excellent Maiestie, As Well Against the Pirates of Algiers, As Others* (London, 1621).

53. Henry Mainwaring, "Of the Beginnings, Practices, and Suppression of Pirates," in G. E. Manwaring, ed., *The Life and Works of Sir Henry Mainwaring*, 2 vols. (London: Navy Records Society, 1920), 2: 3–49, esp. 9–10; see also Manwaring's introduction to vol. 1: 26.

54. Salisbury MSS. xiv. 246; cited in Fisher, *Barbary Legend*, 130.

55. The figure of the English convert to Islam, or renegado, has attracted much attention in recent early modern cultural studies. See especially Nabil Matar, " 'Turning Turk': Conversion to Islam in English Renaissance Thought," *Durham University Journal* 86 (1994): 33–43; Potter, "Pirates and 'Turning Turk' "; Daniel J. Vitkus, "Turning Turk in Othello: The Conversion and the Damnation of the Moor," *Shakespeare Quarterly* 48 (1997): 145–76; Patricia Parker, "Preposterous Conversions: Turning Turk, and Its Pauline Rerighting," *Journal for Early Modern Cultural Studies* 2 (2002): 1–34; and Jonathan Burton, "English Anxiety and the Muslim Power of Conversion: Five Perspectives on 'Turning Turk' in Early Modern Texts," *Journal for Early Modern Cultural Studies* 2 (2002): 35–67.

56. Andrew Barker, *True and Certaine Report of the Beginning, Proceedings, Ouerthrowes, and Now Present Estate of Captaine Ward and Danseker, the Two Late Fa-*

mous Pirates: From Their First Setting Foorth to This Present Time (London, 1609), sig. A2v.

57. See Barker, *A True and Certaine Report,* sig. A2: "it is most lamentable to report, how many Ships of *London,* and other parts of England haue beene taken and made prey vnto them: without the help of which English, the *Turks* by no means could haue gouerned and conducted them through theirs vnskilfulnes and insufficiencie in the art of *Nauigation.*"

58. Barker, *True and Certaine Report,* sig. B4v. Compare also the account in the anonymous *Ward and Danseker, Two Notorious Pyrates, Ward an Englishman, and Danseker a Dutchman* (London, 1609), sig. B3v: Ward, "hauing growne very rich by the spoile of many nations, crept vnto their fauours by his often comming to *Tunis,* to make sale of such goods as he made wrongfull purchase of at sea, which liberty he had by all tolleration, and allowance from the great Turke, so as he might goe and come at his pleasure, for they had them at such prises, as they made great profit of them, insomuch that the Viceroy of *Tunis* gaue him a large peece of ground, that sometimes before was an old Castle, and all the store that belonged vnto it, vpon which it is reported he hath built a very stately house, farre more fit for a Prince, then a pirate." In light of Barker's remarks, it is notable that in Robert Daborne's dramatization of John Ward's career, *A Christian Turned Turk* (1612), Ward operates without the support of the very nation-state that allegedly sponsored his historical counterpart's ventures. Although Daborne's Ward attracts the attention of the Tunis governor, the latter is more concerned with procuring his soul than his plunder. Even after Ward has converted, the state displays greater interest in his faith than his finances. After wounding his wicked Turkish wife Voada, Ward is fined in accordance with Muslim law. He frustratedly begs the governor to "set me to sea again," as "The tenth of what I'll bring you in shall countervail / The revenue of the Indies" (16.246–48). But safeguarding the nation's religion rather than accumulating treasure is the priority of the play's Tunisian leaders. If, as Andrew Barker asserted, the historical John Ward had a business arrangement with Cara Osman, the captain of the Tunis janissaries and the de facto ruler of the city, Daborne chooses to finesse any implication that Ward's commercial activities enjoy the backing of the Tunisian state. He dramatizes Cara Osman in the character of Crosman, but the janissary captain's commercial relationship with Ward has been downplayed and displaced. Instead, the pirate's factor is not Crosman or any state representative but a private citizen, Benwash the Jew, who enjoys a monopoly on all plundered goods that are brought into Tunis's port (5.55, 6.170). All references are to Robert Daborne, *A Christian Turned Turk,* in Vitkus, ed., *Three Turk Plays.*

59. Thomas Heywood, *The Fair Maid of the West, Parts I and II,* ed. Robert K. Turner, Jr. (Lincoln: University of Nebraska Press, 1967), 4.4.2, 4.4.84. All further references are cited in the text.

60. See, for example, Jean E. Howard, "An English Lass Amid the Moors: Gender, Race, Sexuality, and National Identity in Heywood's *The Fair Maid of the West,*" in Margo Hendricks and Patricia Parker, eds., *Women, "Race," and Writing in the Early Modern Period* (London: Routledge, 1994), 101–17, esp. 102.

61. Howard, "An English Lass Amid the Moors," 115.

62. Barbara Fuchs, *Mimesis and Empire: The New World, Islam, and European Identities* (Cambridge: Cambridge University Press, 2001), 133.

63. Burton, "English Anxiety," 54–55.

64. *The Famous and Wonderfull Recoverie of a Ship of Bristoll, Called the Exchange, from the Turkish Pirates of Argier, With the Unmatchable Attempts and Good Successe of John Rawlins, Pilot in Her, And Other Slaves* (London, 1622), sigs. B1v–B2.

65. Misselden, *Free Trade*, sig. B5v. The term "geld" is itself connected to "gelt"; it was the name of an early land tax paid to the Crown.

66. Heywood's punning association of the "Moorian" with "murrain" is a patholo-gizing gesture found elsewhere in early modern English drama. In Anthony Munday's *John a Kent and John a Cumber*, ed. J. Payne Collier (London: Shakespeare Society, 1851), a character "drest like a Moore" is called a "monstrous murrian blak-a-moore" (1.1). I am grateful to Pat Parker for this reference.

67. Philip Massinger, *The Renegado*, in Vitkus, ed., *Three Turk Plays*, 1.1.46. All fur-ther references are cited in the text.

68. Sandra K. Fischer, *Econolingua: A Glossary of Coins and Economic Language in Renaissance Drama* (Newark: University of Delaware Press, 1985), 79.

69. Alain Grosrichard, *The Sultan's Court: European Fantasies of the East*, trans. Liz Heron (London: Verso, 1998), 68.

70. On the French Physiocrats and their corporeal vocabularies of economy, see Spiegel, *Growth of Economic Thought*, 183–200.

71. Daborne, *A Christian Turned Turk*, 1.62–64.

72. Barbara Fuchs argues that "the shadowy Jesuit Francisco" is thoroughly impli-cated in *The Renegado*'s depiction of commerce and "carries out the most successful transactions" in the play—though as "a redeemer," his "transactions are ideally final and absolute. What he buys back goes out of circulation." Fuchs, *Mimesis and Empire*, 137.

73. Ernest B. Gilman, "The Arts of Sympathy: Dr. Harvey, Sir Kenelm Digby, and the Arundel Circle," in Peter C. Herman, ed., *Opening the Borders: Inclusivity in Early Modern Studies, Essays in Honor of James V. Mirollo* (Newark: University of Delaware Press, 1999), 265–97, esp. 282, 284.

Chapter 7. Consumption and Consumption

1. For studies of Jacobean city comedy that approach the genre through the prism of the market, see Douglas Bruster, *Drama and the Market in the Age of Shakespeare* (Cambridge: Cambridge University Press, 1992), esp. chap. 3, " 'City Comedy' and the Materialist Vision," 29–46; and Theodore B. Leinwand, *The City Staged: Jacobean City Comedy, 1603–1613* (Madison: University of Wisconsin Press, 1986), esp. chap. 3, "The Merchant-Citizen in City Comedy," 44–80.

2. References to plays solely authored by Middleton (i.e., not including *The Roar-ing Girl*) are taken from Michael Taylor, ed., *A Mad World, My Masters, and Other Plays* (Oxford: Oxford University Press, 1995). All further references are cited in the text.

3. See Fernand Braudel, *Capitalism and Material Life, 1400–1800* (New York: Harper and Row, 1973); Neil McKendrick, John Brewer, and J. H. Plumb, eds., *The Birth of a Con-sumer Society: The Commercialization of Eighteenth-Century England* (Bloomington: In-diana University Press, 1982); Chandra Mukerji, *Graven Images: Patterns of Modern Materialism* (New York: Columbia University Press, 1983); Daniel Roche, *A History of Everyday Things: The Birth of Consumption in France, 1600–1800*, trans. Brian Pearce

(Cambridge: Cambridge University Press, 2000); Joan Thirsk, *Economic Policy and Projects: The Development of a Consumer Society in Early Modern England* (Oxford: Oxford University Press, 1978). For useful critiques of consumer-oriented approaches to cultural studies in general and the development of capitalism in particular, see Ben Fine and Ellen Leopold, "Consumerism and the Industrial Revolution," *Social History* 15:1 (1990): 151–79; and Jean-Christophe Agnew, "Coming up for Air: Consumer Culture in Historical Perspective," in John Brewer and Roy Porter, eds., *Consumption and the World of Goods* (New York: Routledge, 1994), 19–39.

4. There has been considerable debate about when exactly "consumer society" emerged. Neil McKendrick locates it in the eighteenth century; Daniel Roche in the seventeenth century; Joan Thirsk and Chandra Mukerji push the *terminus a quo* back to the sixteenth century.

5. See Adam Smith, *An Inquiry into the Nature and Causes of the Wealth of Nations* (London, 1776), bk. 4, passim.

6. On the bivalences of consumption's etymologies, see Pasi Falk, *The Consuming Body* (London: Sage, 1994), 93.

7. The OED lists numerous instances of the destructive set of meanings; but it also lists an example of the constructive meaning from Robert Copland's 1541 handbook on Galenic therapies: "the one is holpen, made perfyte, and consumed by the other." See "consume, v.2."

8. Thomas Starkey, *A Dialogue Between Reginald Pole and Thomas Lupset*, ed. Kathleen M. Burton (London: Chatto and Windus, 1948), 87, 78. For a more extended discussion of Starkey's use of the organic analogy and his reliance upon the humoral paradigm, see Jonathan Gil Harris, *Foreign Bodies and the Body Politic: Discourses of Social Pathology in Early Modern England* (Cambridge: Cambridge University Press, 1998), 30–40.

9. Mary Dobson, *Contours of Death and Disease in Early Modern England* (Cambridge: Cambridge University Press, 1997), 235n32. For discussions of the history of conceptions of consumption, phthisis, and tuberculosis, see H. D. Chalke, "The Impact of Tuberculosis on History, Literature, and Art," *Medical History* 6 (1962): 301–18; René J. Dubos and Jean Dubos, *The White Plague: Tuberculosis, Man, and Society* (New Brunswick, N.J.: Rutgers University Press, 1987); Gregory G. Kayne, *The Control of Tuberculosis in England, Past and Present* (London: Oxford University Press, 1937); Vivian Nutton, "The Seeds of Disease: An Explanation of Contagion and Infection from the Greeks to the Renaissance," *Medical History* 27 (1983): 1–34; and Susan Sontag, *Illness as Metaphor* (New York: Farrar, Straus and Giroux, 1978).

10. John Trevisa, *On the Properties of Things: John Trevisa's Translation of Bartholomaeus Anglicus De Proprietatibus Rerum*, 2 vols. (Oxford: Clarendon Press, 1975), 1: 381.

11. Andrew Boorde, *The Breuiary of Helthe, for All Maner of Syckenesses and Diseases the Whiche May Be in Man, or Woman* (London, 1547), sig. Gg1.

12. Sir Thomas Browne, "A Letter to a Friend, upon Occasion of the Death of his Intimate Friend," in Thomas Browne, *The Major Works*, ed. C. A. Patrides (Harmondsworth: Penguin, 1977), 399. On the Galenic theory that milk is concocted uterine blood, see Thomas Laqueur, *Making Sex: Body and Gender from the Greeks to Freud* (Cambridge, Mass.: Harvard University Press, 1990), 36; and Gail Kern Paster, *The Body Embarrassed: Drama and the Disciplines of Shame in Early Modern England* (Ithaca, N.Y.: Cornell University Press, 1993), 194.

13. Andrew Boorde, *A Compendyous Regyment or A Dyetary of Helth made in*

Mountpyllier, compyled by Andrewe Boorde of Physycke Doctour, ed. F. J. Furnivall (London: Kegan Paul, Trench, Trübner, 1870), 296; *The Good Angel of Stamford, Or An Extraordinary Cure Of An Extraordinary Consumption, In A True and Faithful Narrative Of SAMUEL WALLAS Recovered, By The Power of God, and Prescription Of an Angel* (London, 1659), 4.

14. William Gurnall, *The Christian in Compleat Armour, or A Treatise of the Saints War Against the Devil, Wherein a Discovery is Made of that Great Enemy of God and his People* (London, 1655), dedication.

15. Thomas Hobbes, *Leviathan,* ed. Richard Tuck (Cambridge: Cambridge University Press, 1997), 173, 230.

16. Quoted in Henry Gee, ed., *The Elizabethan Prayer-Book & Ornaments* (London: Macmillan, 1902), app. 3, 210.

17. King James I, *A Proclamation for Restraint of the Exportation, Waste, and Consumption of Coine and Bullion* (London, 1622), 2.

18. For a useful intellectual history of the discourses of luxury, see John Sekora, *Luxury: The Concept in Western Thought, Eden to Smollett* (Baltimore: Johns Hopkins University Press, 1978).

19. William Petyt, *Britannia Languens, or A Discourse of Trade* (London, 1680), 137. On the issue of "conspicuous consumption" in this time, see F. J. Fisher, "The Development of London as a Centre of Conspicuous Consumption in the Sixteenth and Seventeenth Centuries," *Transactions of the Royal Historical Society* 4th ser. 30 (1948): 37–50.

20. Thomas Mun, *A Discourse of Trade, From England Vnto the East-Indies: Answering to Diuerse Obiections Which Are Usually Made Against the Same* (London, 1621), sig. F3v. All further references are cited in the text. For discussions of Mun's thought in relation to broader trends within mercantilism, see Joyce Oldham Appleby, *Economic Thought and Ideology in Seventeenth-Century England* (Princeton, N.J.: Princeton University Press, 1978), 38–41; Andrea Finkelstein, *Harmony and Balance: An Intellectual History of Seventeenth-Century English Economic Thought* (Ann Arbor: University of Michigan Press, 2000), chapter 4, "Thomas Mun and the Finite *Zeitgeist*," 74–88; Eli F. Heckscher, *Mercantilism,* 2 vols., 2nd ed., trans. Mendel Shapiro (London: George Allen and Unwin, 1955), 2: 238–61; and Henry William Spiegel, *The Growth of Economic Thought,* 3rd ed. (Durham, N.C.: Duke University Press, 1991), 106–18.

21. See Leslie Stephen and Sidney Lee, eds., *The Dictionary of National Biography* (Oxford: Oxford University Press, 1921–22), 13: 1184.

22. See Jeffrey Knapp's excellent discussion of early modern literature about tobacco in *An Empire Nowhere: England, America, and Literature from* Utopia *to* The Tempest (Berkeley: University of California Press, 1992), esp. 174.

23. Mun not only critiques the illicit levying of taxes by kings—a bald reference to Charles I—but also asserts that "the invention of Parliaments is an excellent policie of Government" and, in an oblique yet ominous reference to Menenius's fable of the rebellion of the body's members against the stomach, warns that "a Prince (in this case) is like the stomach in the body, which if it cease to digest and distribute to the other members, it doth no sooner corrupt them, but it destroyes it self": *Englands Treasure by Forraign Trade; or, The Ballance of our Forraign Trade is The Rule of our Treasure* (London, 1664), 166. Notably, the second edition of 1669 is missing sigs. K1–K8, which contain the offending passages. All further references are to this edition and are cited in the main body of the text.

24. Smith, *Inquiry into the Wealth of Nations*, 155: "In the mercantile system the interest of the consumer is almost constantly sacrificed to that of the producer."

25. See, for example, the remarks of the otherwise scrupulous Joan Thirsk: "It was anathema to Mun to observe in the frequent changes of fashion in food and clothing—many of them imported from France, Italy and Spain—the signs of a developing home market in goods"; *Economic Policy and Projects*, 134.

26. Indeed, Mun's fondness for pathological metaphors can be seen most clearly in the medical bromides he dispenses throughout *Englands Treasure by Forraign Trade:* "the State knew well that there needed no remedy where there was no disease" (sig. H7v); "if we mistake the nature of the Malady, we shall ever apply such cures as will at least delay, if not confound the Remedy" (sig. I2); "for that which is Physick to one man, is little better than poyson to another" (sig. I8).

27. Philip Stubbes, *The Anatomie of Abuses: Contayning a Discoverie, or Briefe Summarie, of Such Notable Vices and Imperfections, As Now Raigne in Many Christian Countreyes of the Worlde, But (Especiallie) in a Verie Famous Ilande Called Ailgna* (London, 1877 [1583]), 106.

28. This conviction had longstanding roots that predate the sixteenth century, as is made clear by the string of disjunctive terms in numerous European languages that signify both medicine and poison: the Greek *pharmakon*, the Latin *medicamentus*, and the German *Gift*. For a discussion of Paracelsan pharmacy and its reproduction of the disjunctions embodied in European languages' conceptions of medicine and poison, see chapters 3 and 4 of Harris, *Foreign Bodies and the Body Politic*.

29. To be sure, Mun was not alone among seventeenth-century writers in recoding consumption positively. Eli Heckscher has noted that for most mercantilists, consumption's meanings varied according to its location. Domestic consumption tended to be regarded as dangerous; but this allowed for its positive recuperation in *other* nations. Charles Davenant, for example, insisted that "all Foreign Consumption is a Clear and Certain Profit" (see Heckscher, *Mercantilism*, 115–16). In a zero-sum global economy, other nations' loss was England's gain. Indeed, Mun himself asserts that "wee must ever observe this Rule; to sell more to strangers yearly than we consume of theirs in value" (*Englands Treasure by Forraign Trade*, sig. B1). For the most part, though, the bullionist residue of Mun's writing is overshadowed by his conviction that genuine wealth springs from money in motion, stimulating labor, industry, exchange—and consumption.

30. Roy Porter, "Consumption: Disease of the Consumer Society?", in John Brewer and Roy Porter, eds., *Consumption and the World of Goods* (London: Routledge, 1994), 58–81, esp. 60.

31. George Cheyne, *The English Malady; Or, A Treatise of Nervous Diseases* (London: Routledge, 1991), 49.

32. Bernard de Mandeville, *The Fable of the Bees: Private Vices, Public Benefits* (London, 1729).

33. Daniel Defoe, *A Plan of the English Commerce, Being a Compleat Prospect of the Trade of this Nation, as well as the Home Trade as the Foreign* (Oxford: Basil Blackwell, 1928), 76–77.

34. Smith, *Inquiry into the Wealth of Nations*, 424.

35. Cited in François Crouzet, "Les Français et le miracle anglais," *L'Histoire* 28 (1980): 21–30, esp. 28.

36. Margot Heinemann observes that in Middleton's city comedies, "society has

ceased to be based on inherited status; it is now a trading, venturing society based on exchange and credit." *Puritanism and Theatre: Thomas Middleton and Opposition Drama Under the Early Stuarts* (Cambridge: Cambridge University Press, 1980), chap. 6, "Money and Morals in Middleton's City Comedies," 88–106, esp. 95. See also Brian Gibbons, *Jacobean City Comedy: A Study of Satiric Plays by Jonson, Marston, and Middleton,* 2nd ed. (London: Methuen, 1980).

37. Gail Kern Paster, *The Idea of the City in the Age of Shakespeare* (Athens: University of Georgia Press, 1985), chap. 6, "Parasites and Sub-Parasites: The City as Predator in Jonson and Middleton," 150–77.

38. I am persuaded by the evidence mustered by Elizabeth Cook for a date of 1611, which makes the play a later one than some earlier editors have adduced. See Thomas Middleton and Thomas Dekker, *The Roaring Girl,* ed. Elizabeth Cook (New York: Norton, 1997), xix. All references to the play are from this edition and are cited in the text.

39. See, for example, Marjorie Garber, "The Logic of the Transvestite," in David Scott Kastan and Peter Stallybrass, eds., *Staging the Renaissance: Reinterpretations of Elizabethan and Jacobean Drama* (London: Routledge, 1991), 221–34, esp. 224–27.

40. Dorothy Davis, *A History of Shopping* (London: Routledge and Kegan Paul, 1966), 101, 55. James Knowles describes Britain's Burse as "a commercial Utopia of wonders," including exotic luxury items such as wax fruit, parrots, porcelain, sundials, and gold chains: see "Cecil's Shopping Centre: The Rediscovery of a Ben Jonson Masque in Praise of Trade," *Times Literary Supplement,* February 7, 1997, 14–15.

41. *Arden of Faversham,* ed. Hugh Macdonald (London: Malone Society Reprints, 1949), 3.51.1.

42. W. S., *Locrine,* ed. R. B. McKerrow (London: Malone Society Reprints, 1908), ll. 569–70; *George a Greene,* ed. F. W. Clarke (London: Malone Society Reprints, 1911), ll. 971–72; Robert Wilson, *The Cobblers Prophecy* (London, 1594), sigs. A3v–A4; Ben Jonson, *The Case is Altered* (London, 1609 [1597]), sig. A2. For these and all subsequent references to shop scenes, I am profoundly grateful for the generous assistance of Leslie Thomson. The value to the researcher of Alan C. Dessens and Thomson's *Dictionary of Stage Directions from Early Modern English Drama* (Cambridge: Cambridge University Press, 2000) is immeasurable.

43. Thomas Dekker, *The Shoemaker's Holiday,* ed. Anthony Parr, 2nd ed. (New York: Norton, 1990), 12.22. For an enlargement of the points I make in this paragraph, see also Jonathan Gil Harris, "Properties of Skill: Product Placement in Early Artisanal Drama," in Jonathan Gil Harris and Natasha Korda, eds., *Staged Properties in Early Modern English Drama* (Cambridge: Cambridge Unversity Press, 2002), 35–66, in which I discuss *The Shoemaker's Holiday*'s conflicted attitudes toward property in relation to medieval mystery drama's presentation of artisanal skill.

44. Thomas Heywood, *The Fayre Mayde of the Exchange, With the Pleasant Humours of the Cripple of Fanchurch* (London, 1607 [1602]), sig. F1; Middleton and Dekker, *The Honest Whore, With the Humours of the Patient Man and the Longing Wife* (London, 1604), sig. B4; Dekker, *The Honest Whore, Part Two* (London, 1630 [1605]), sig. F2; George Chapman, Ben Jonson, and John Webster, *Eastward Hoe* (London, 1605), sig. A2v; Edward Sharpham, *The Fleire* (London, 1607), sig. G2v; Dekker, *A Tragi-Comedy: Called, Match Mee in London* (London, 1631 [1611]), sig. C3v; John Cooke, *Greene's Tu Quoque, or The Citie Gallant* (London, 1614 [1611]), sig. B1; Middleton and John Webster, *Any Thing for a Quiet Life* (London, 1664 [1621]), sig. C3; Philip Massinger *The Renegado* (1623), in

Daniel J. Vitkus, ed., *Three Turk Plays from Early Modern England: "Selimas," "A Christian Turned Turk," "The Renegado"* (New York: Columbia University Press, 2000), 1.3.1.

45. Peter Stallybrass, "Worn Worlds: Clothes and Identity on the Renaissance Stage," in Margreta de Grazia, Maureen Quilligan, and Peter Stallybrass, eds., *Subject and Object in Renaissance Culture* (Cambridge: Cambridge University Press, 1996), 289–320. Seamstress's shops are explicitly called for in the stage directions of not only *The Roaring Girl* (2.1.0) but also *The Shoemaker's Holiday,* 12.0, and Thomas Heywood, *The Wise-Woman of Hogsdon* (London, 1638 [1604]), sig. A4v. The shop in John Cooke's *Greene's Tu Quoque* is explicitly "A Mercers Shop" (sig. B1), and the anonymous play *Knave in the Grain* (London, 1625) involves a transaction with a Mercer who retails "Boults of Sattin" (sig. I1).

46. See William Ingram, "Robert Keysar, Playhouse Speculator," *Shakespeare Quarterly* 37 (1986): 476–88; and John H. Astington, "The Career of Andrew Cane, Citizen, Goldsmith, and Player," *MARDIE* (2003): forthcoming. I am grateful to Professor Astington for sharing a copy of his paper in advance of its publication.

47. Thomas Heywood, *Edward IV* (London, 1599), sig. H1v; Chapman, Jonson, and Webster, *Eastward Hoe,* sig. A2. Juana Green has speculated that the mugs of *Epicoene* may have been provided by Robert Keysar, a master goldsmith who was an organizer of the Children of the Queen's Revels—the company that first performed the play. See her "Properties of Marriage: Proprietary Conflict and the Calculus of Gender in *Epicoene,*" in Harris and Korda, eds., *Staged Properties,* 261–87, esp. 269.

48. See Harris, "Properties of Skill," esp. 41–7.

49. Philip Massinger, *The Renegado,* 1.3.2–3.

50. For a discussion of the fashionability of Low Country clothes in early seventeenth-century London, see Ann Rosalind Jones and Peter Stallybrass, *Renaissance Clothing and the Materials of Memory* (Cambridge: Cambridge University Press, 2000), chap. 3, "Yellow Starch: Fabrications of the Jacobean Court," 59–85.

51. See Margaret W. Ferguson, "Feathers and Flies: Aphra Behn and the Seventeenth-Century Trade in Exotica," in de Grazia, Quilligan, and Stallybrass, eds., *Subject and Object in Renaissance Culture,* 235–59; and Jones and Stallybrass, *Renaissance Clothing,* 53.

52. Nathanael Carpenter, *Geography Delineated Forth in Two Bookes, Containing the Spaericall and Topicall Parts Thereof* (Oxford, 1625), sig. G3.

53. Some London apothecaries, like James Petiver, earned reputations as collectors of foreign goods; but such goods seem to have been part of the apothecary's traditional paraphernalia. On Petiver, see Marjorie Swann, *Curiosities and Texts: The Culture of Collecting in Early Modern England* (Philadelphia: University of Pennsylvania Press, 2001), 3.

54. Thomas Nashe, *Have With You to Saffron-walden; or, Gabriel Harueys Hunt is vp* (London, 1596), sig. F2.

55. These include boxes of "*Arringus,*" bottles of "ciuet," and "spirit of roses"; Sharpham, *The Fleire,* sigs. G2v–G3.

56. Ferguson, "Feathers and Flies," 247.

57. I am, of course, referring to Slavoj Žižek, *The Sublime Object of Ideology* (London: Verso, 1989).

58. There is a significant body of critical literature on the meanings of Moll's hermaphroditic cross-dressing: see Garber, "Logic of the Transvestite"; Jean E. Howard, "Cross-Dressing, the Theatre, and Gender Struggle in Early Modern England," *Shakespeare Quarterly* 39 (1988), 417–39; and Mary-Beth Rose, "Women in Men's Clothing: Ap-

parel and Social Stability in *The Roaring Girl*," *English Literary Renaissance* 14 (1984): 367–91. All these essays, however, understand Moll's transvestism largely in terms of gender and sexuality. I wish to suggest that if Middleton and Dekker invoke the old Platonic ideal of the "consummate" hermaphrodite, they do so equally in the (no less gendered) economic context of consumption.

59. Pimlico, in Hogsdon, seems to have become stereotypically associated with the exotica of other lands. In the anonymous pamphlet *Pimlyco, or Runne Red-Cap: Tis A Mad World at Hogsdon* (London, 1609), the author states: "You that weare out your liues and weary your bodies, in *Discouery of strange Countries,* (been for pleasure or profite) rig out a *Fleet,* and make a *Voiage* to an *Iland* which could neuer be found out by the *Portugals, Spaniards,* or *Hollanders,* but only (and that now of late) by *Englishmen.* The name of its *Pymlico*" (sig. A2). Interestingly, the pamphlet also presents Pimlico as a competitor with the Fortune Theater (where *The Roaring Girl* was first performed) and the Bull Theater in the display of exotic pleasures: "each afternoone thy *house* being fill, / Makes *Fortune* blind, or *Gelds the Bull*" (sig. D2).

60. For a useful discussion of the links between economic and gastronomic consumption in early modern drama, see Margaret Healy, *Fictions of Disease in Early Modern England: Bodies, Plagues, and Politics* (New York: Palgrave, 2001), 202–28.

61. Valerie Forman, "Marked Angels: Counterfeits, Commodities, and *The Roaring Girl*," *Renaissance Quarterly* 54 (2001): 1531–60.

Chapter 8. Afterword

1. John Donne, Elegy 14, "A Tale of a Citizen and His Wife," lines 11–13, 19–29, in *The Complete English Poems*, ed. A. J. Smith (Harmondsworth: Penguin, 1986), 114–15.

2. Hendrik Hertzberg, "Comment: Tuesday, and After," *New Yorker*, September 24, 2001, 27.

3. Andrew Boorde, *The Breuiary of Helthe, For All Maner of Syckenesses and Diseases the Whiche May Be in Man, or Woman* (London, 1547), sig. B7v.

4. Simon Kellwaye, *A Defensative Against the Plague* (London, 1593), fol. 39.

5. Fredric Jameson, "Culture and Finance Capitalism," *Critical Inquiry* 24 (1997): 246–65.

6. See Emily Martin, *Flexible Bodies: The Role of Immunity in American Culture from the Days of Polio to the Age of AIDS* (Boston: Beacon Press, 1994), 113–59.

7. Russell Brown, "Spoofs and Scoops," *New Zealand Listener*, March 1, 2003, 40. For a helpful account of the history of the hoax surrounding *Computerworld*'s online interview, see www.brianmcwilliams.com/why.html.

Bibliography

Abernathy, John. *A Christian and Heavenly Treatise: Containing Physicke for the Soule.* London, 1630.

Ackerknecht, Erwin H. "Historical Notes on Cancer." *Medical History* 2 (1958): 114–19.

Agnew, Jean-Christophe. "Coming Up for Air: Consumer Culture in Historical Perspective." In John Brewer and Roy Porter, eds., *Consumption and the World of Goods.* London: Routledge, 1994. 19–39.

———. *Worlds Apart: The Market and the Theater in Anglo-American Thought, 1550–1750.* Cambridge: Cambridge University Press, 1986.

Alpert, Michael. *Crypto-Judaism and the Spanish Inquisition.* London: Palgrave, 2001.

Algiers Voyage, In a Iournall or Briefe Reportary of All Occurents Hapning in the Fleet of Ships Sent Out by the King His Most Excellent Maiestie, As Well Against the Pirates of Algiers, As Others. London, 1621.

Andrews, Kenneth. *Elizabethan Privateering: English Privateering During the Spanish War, 1585–1603.* Cambridge: Cambridge University Press, 1964.

Appadurai, Arjun, ed. *The Social Life of Things: Commodities in Cultural Perspective.* Cambridge: Cambridge University Press, 1986.

Appleby, Joyce Oldham. *Economic Thought and Ideology in Seventeenth-Century England.* Princeton, N.J.: Princeton University Press, 1978.

Arden of Faversham. Ed. Hugh Macdonald. London: Malone Society Reprints, 1949.

Arthos, John. "Shakespeare's Transformation of Plautus." *Comparative Drama* 1 (1967–88): 239–53.

Astington, John H. "The Career of Andrew Cane, Citizen, Goldsmith, and Player." *MARDIE* (2003).

Aubrey, John. *Brief Lives.* Ed. Andrew Clark. 2 vols. London: Oxford University Press, 1898.

Auden, W. H. *The Dyer's Hand and Other Essays.* New York: Random House, 1948.

Auerbach, Erich. *Mimesis: The Representation of Reality in Western Literature.* Trans. Willard Trask. Princeton, N.J.: Princeton University Press, 1953.

Bach, Rebecca Ann. "Tennis Balls: *Henry V* and Testicular Masculinity, or, According to the OED, Shakespeare Doesn't Have Any Balls." *Renaissance Drama* 30 (2001): 3–23.

Bacon, Francis. *The Essayes or Counsels Civill & Morall of Francis Bacon, Baron Verulam Viscount Saint Alban.* Norwalk, Conn.: Easton Press, 1980.

Baker, David J. *Between Nations: Shakespeare, Spenser, Marvell, and the Question of Britain.* Stanford, Calif.: Stanford University Press, 1997.

Baldwin, T. W. *On the Compositional Genetics of "The Comedy of Errors".* Urbana: University of Illinois Press, 1965.

Barfoot, C. C. "*Troilus and Cressida*: 'Praise Us as We Are Tasted.'" *Shakespeare Quarterly* 39 (1988): 45–57.

Barker, Andrew. *A True and Certaine Report of the Beginning, Proceedings, Ouerthrowes, and Now Present Estate of Captaine Ward and Danseker, the Two Late Famous Pirates: From Their First Setting Foorth to This Present Time.* London, 1609.

Barnes, Barnarbe. *Foure Bookes of Offices: Enabling Privat Persons for the Speciall Service of All Good Princes and Policies.* London, 1606.

Barroll, Leeds. *Politics, Plague, and Shakespeare's Theater: The Stuart Years.* Ithaca, N.Y.: Cornell University Press, 1991.

Bartels, Emily C. *Spectacles of Strangeness: Imperialism, Alienation, and Marlowe.* Philadelphia: University of Pennsylvania Press, 1993.

Beauwes, Wyndham. *Lex Mercatoria Rediviva, Or The Merchant's Directory.* London, 1752.

Bentley, Greg W. *Shakespeare and the New Disease: The Dramatic Function of Syphilis in "Troilus and Cressida," "Measure for Measure," and "Timon of Athens".* New York: Peter Lang, 1989.

Bhabha, Homi K. "Signs Taken for Wonders: Questions of Ambivalence and Authority Under a Tree Outside Delhi, May 1817." In *Race, Writing, and Difference,* ed. Henry Louis Gates. Chicago: University of Chicago Press, 1986. 163–84.

Biblia, The Byble: That Is The Holy Scripture of the Olde and New Testament, Faythfully Translated in to Englyshe. Trans. Miles Coverdale. London, 1535.

Biraben, Jean-Noël. "Diseases in Europe: Equilibrium and Breakdown of the Pathocenosis." In Mirko D. Grmek, ed., *Western Medical Thought from Antiquity to the Middle Ages.* Cambridge, Mass.: Harvard University Press. 319–53.

Blaxton, John. *The English Usurer, or Usury Condemned.* London, 1634.

Bloom, Herbert I. *The Economic Activities of the Jews of Amsterdam in the Seventeenth and Eighteenth Centuries.* Williamsport, Pa.: Bayard Press, 1937.

Blundeville, Thomas. *The Foure Chiefest Offices Belonging to Horsemanship.* London, 1580.

Boas, F. S. *Shakespeare and His Predecessors.* New York: Scribner's, 1896.

Bodian, Miriam. *Hebrew of the Portuguese Nation: Conversos and Community in Early Modern Amsterdam.* Bloomington: Indiana University Press, 1997.

Boorde, Andrew. *The Breuiary of Helthe, for All Maner of Syckenesses and Diseases the Whiche May Be in Man, or Woman.* London, 1547.

———. *A Compendyous Regyment or A Dyetary of Helth made in Mountpyllier, compyled by Andrewe Boorde of Physycke Doctour.* Ed. F. J. Furnivall. London: Kegan Paul, Trench, Trübner, 1870.

Bradwell, Stephen. *Physick for the Sicknesse, Commonly Called the Plague, With All the Particular Signes and Symptoms, Whereof the Most Are Ignorant.* London, 1636.

Braudel, Fernand. *Capitalism and Material Life 1400–1800.* New York: Harper and Row, 1973.

———. *The Mediterranean and the Mediterranean World in the Age of Phillip II.* Vol. 1. Trans. Sian Reynolds. Berkeley: University of California Press, 1995.

Brenner, Robert. *Merchants and Revolution: Commercial Changes, Political Conflict, and London's Overseas Traders, 1550–1653.* Princeton, N.J.: Princeton University Press, 1993.

Brenner, Y. S. "The Inflation of Prices in Early Sixteenth Century England." *Economic History Review* 2nd ser. 14 (1961–62): 225–39.

Bright, Timothy. *A Treatise: Wherein is Declared the Sufficiencie of English Medicines, for Cure of All Diseases.* London, 1580.

Brown, Russell. "Spoofs and Scoops." *New Zealand Listener,* March 1, 2003, 40.

Browne, Thomas. *The Major Works.* Ed. C. A. Patrides. Harmondsworth: Penguin, 1977.

Bruster, Douglas. *Drama and the Market in the Age of Shakespeare.* Cambridge: Cambridge University Press, 1992.

Burns, John Southerden. *The History of the French, Walloon, Dutch and Other Foreign Protestant Refugees Settled in England, from the Reign of Henry VIII to the Revocation of the Edict of Nantes; with Notice of their Trade and Commerce, Copious Extracts from the Registers, Lists of the Early Settlers, Ministers.* London: Longman, Brown, Green, and Longmans, 1846.

Burton, Jonathan. "English Anxiety and the Muslim Power of Conversion: Five Perspectives on 'Turning Turk' in Early Modern Texts." *Journal for Early Modern Cultural Studies* 2 (2002): 35–67.

Burton, Robert. *The Anatomy of Melancholy.* London, 1632.

Canguilhem, Georges. *The Normal and the Pathological.* Trans. Carolyn R. Fawcett and Robert S. Cohen. New York: Zone Books, 1991.

Carpenter, Nathanael. *Geography Delineated Forth in Two Bookes, Containing the Spaericall and Topicall Parts Thereof.* Oxford, 1625.

Cartelli, Thomas *Marlowe, Shakespeare, and the Economy of Theatrical Experience.* Philadelphia: University of Pennsylvania Press, 1991.

Castelain, Maurice. *Ben Jonson, l'homme et l'oeuvre.* Paris, 1907.

Cavendish, Margaret. *The Blazing World and Other Writings.* Ed. Kate Lilley. Harmondsworth: Penguin, 1994.

Certain Necessary Direction, As Well for the Cure of the Plague, As for Preuenting the Infection. London, 1636.

Chalk, Alfred F. "Natural Law and the Rise of Economic Liberalism in England." *Journal of Political Economy* 59 (1951): 332–47.

Chalke, H. D. "The Impact of Tuberculosis on History, Literature and Art." *Medical History* 6 (1962): 301–18.

Challis, C. E. ed. *A New History of the Royal Mint.* Cambridge: Cambridge University Press, 1992.

———. *The Tudor Coinage.* Manchester: Manchester University Press, 1978.

Chapman, George. *The Iliads of Homer Translated According to the Greek.* 2 vols. London: J. M. Dent, 1898.

Chapman, George, Ben Jonson, and John Webster. *Eastward Hoe.* London, 1605.

Charnes, Linda. *Notorious Identity: Materializing the Subject in Shakespeare.* Cambridge, Mass.: Harvard University Press, 1993.

Cheyne, George. *The English Malady; Or, A Treatise of Nervous Diseases.* London: Routledge, 1991.

Clowes, William. *A Briefe and Necessary Treatise, Touching the Cure of the Disease Now Usually Called Lues Venera, by Unctions and Other Approued Waies of Curing.* In *A Profitable and Necessarie booke of Observations.* London, 1596.

———. *A Short and Profitable Treatise Touching the Cure of the Disease Called Morbus Gallico by Unctions.* London, 1579.

Cohen, Walter. *Drama of a Nation: Public Theater in Renaissance England and Spain.* Ithaca, N.Y.: Cornell University Press, 1985.

Cole, Charles W. "The Heavy Hand of Hegel." In Edward Mead Earle, ed., *Nationalism and Internationalism.* New York: Columbia University Press, 1950. 64–78.

Coleman, D. C., ed. *Revisions in Mercantilism*. London: Methuen, 1969.

Cook, Carol. "Unbodied Figures of Desire." *Theater Journal* 38 (1986), 34–52.

Cooke, John. *Greene's Tu Quoque, Or the Citie Gallant*. London, 1614.

Cotgrave, Randle. *A Dictionarie of the French and English Tongues*. London, 1611.

Craig, John. *The Mint: A History of the London Mint from A.D. 287 to 1948*. Cambridge: Cambridge University Press, 1953.

Crooke, Helkiah. *Microcosmographia: A Description of the Body of Man, Together With the Controuersies and Figures Thereto Belonging*. London, 1618.

Crouzet, François. "Les Français et le miracle anglais." *L'Histoire* 28 (1980): 21–30.

Dasent, John Roche, ed. *Acts of the Privy Council of England, 1542–1604*. 32 vols. London: Stationery Office, 1890–1907.

Davis, Dorothy. *A History of Shopping*. London: Routledge and Kegan Paul, 1966.

Deacon, John. *Tobacco Tortured, Or the Filthie Fume of Tobacco Refined*. London, 1616.

Defoe, Daniel. *A Plan of the English Commerce, Being a Compleat Prospect of the Trade of this Nation, as well as the Home Trade as the Foreign*. Oxford: Blackwell, 1928.

Dekker, Thomas. *The Dramatic Works of Thomas Dekker*. Ed. Fredson Bowers, 3 vols. Cambridge: Cambridge University Press, 1955.

———. *The Honest Whore, Part Two*. London, 1630.

———. *The Non-Dramatic Works of Thomas Dekker*. Ed. Alexander B. Grosart. 5 vols. London: Hazell, Watson, and Viney, 1886.

———. *The Plague Pamphlets of Thomas Dekker*. Ed. F. P. Wilson. Oxford: Clarendon Press, 1925.

———. *The Shoemaker's Holiday*. Ed. Anthony Parr. 2nd ed. New York: Norton, 1990.

———. *A Tragi-Comedy: Called, Match Mee in London*. London, 1631.

Dessens, Alan C. and Leslie Thomson. *Dictionary of Stage Directions from Early Modern English Drama*. Cambridge: Cambridge University Press, 2000.

Diamond, Jared. *Guns, Germs, and Steel: The Fates of Human Societies*. New York: Random House, 1997.

Díaz de Isla, Ruy. *Tractado contra el mal serpentino: que vulgarmente en España es llamado bubas*. Seville, 1539.

Dickens, A. G. *The English Reformation*. 2nd ed. London: Batsford, 1989.

A Discourse of the Commonweal of This Realm of England, Attributed to Sir Thomas Smith. Ed. Mary Dewar. Charlottesville: University Press of Virginia, 1969.

Dobson, Mary. *Contours of Death and Disease in Early Modern England*. Cambridge: Cambridge University Press, 1997.

Dolan, Frances E. *Whores of Babylon: Catholicism, Gender, and Seventeenth-Century Print Culture*. Ithaca, N.Y.: Cornell University Press, 1999.

Donne, John. *The Complete English Poems*. Ed. A. J. Smith. Harmondsworth: Penguin, 1986.

Douglas, Mary. *Purity and Danger: An Analysis of the Concepts of Pollution and Taboo*. London: Routledge, 1996.

Draper, John W. *The Humors and Shakespeare's Characters*. Durham, N.C.: Duke University Press, 1945.

———. "Usury in *The Merchant of Venice*." *Modern Philology* 33 (1935): 37–47.

Dubos, René J. and Jean Dubos. *The White Plague: Tuberculosis, Man, and Society*. New Brunswick, N.J.: Rutgers University Press, 1987.

Duncan, Douglas. *Ben Jonson and the Lucianic Tradition.* Cambridge: Cambridge University Press, 1979.

Duplessis, Robert S. *Transitions to Capitalism in Early Modern Europe.* Cambridge: Cambridge University Press, 1997.

Durkheim, Emile. *Rules of Sociological Method.* Trans. W. D. Halls. New York, Macmillan, 1982.

Earle, Peter. *Corsairs of Malta and Barbary.* London: Sigwick and Jackson, 1970.

Elliott, J. H. "The Decline of Spain." In Trevor Aston, ed., *Crisis in Europe, 1560–1660: Essays from "Past and Present".* London: Routledge, 1965. 167–93.

Elyot, Thomas. *The Castel of Helthe.* London, 1539.

Elton, W. R. "Shakespeare's Ulysses and the Problem of Value." *Shakespeare Studies* 2 (1966): 95–111.

Engle, Lars. *Shakespearean Pragmatism: Market of his Time.* Chicago: University of Chicago Press, 1993.

Fabricius, Johannes. *Syphilis in Shakespeare's England.* London: Jessica Kingsley, 1994.

Falk, Pasi. *The Consuming Body.* London: Sage, 1994.

The Famous and Wonderfull Recoverie of a Ship of Bristoll, Called the Exchange, from the Turkish Pirates of Argier, With the Unmatchable Attempts and Good Successe of John Rawlins, Pilot in Her, And Other Slaves. London, 1622.

Felperin, Howard. *Shakespearean Romance.* Princeton, N.J.: Princeton University Press, 1972.

Ferguson, Margaret W. "Feathers and Flies: Aphra Behn and the Seventeenth-Century Trade in Exotica." In Margreta de Grazia, Maureen Quilligan, and Peter Stallybrass, eds., *Subject and Object in Renaissance Culture.* Cambridge: Cambridge University Press, 1996. 235–59.

Fine, Ben and Ellen Leopold. "Consumerism and the Industrial Revolution." *Social History* 15, 1 (1990): 151–79.

Finkelstein, Andrea. *Harmony and Balance: An Intellectual History of Seventeenth-Century English Economic Thought.* Ann Arbor: University of Michigan Press, 2000.

Fischer, Sandra K. *Econolingua: A Glossary of Coins and Economic Language in Renaissance Drama.* Newark: University of Delaware Press, 1985.

Fisher, F. J. "The Development of London as a Centre of Conspicuous Consumption in the Sixteenth and Seventeenth Centuries." *Transactions of the Royal Historical Society* 4th ser. 30 (1948): 37–50.

Fisher, Godfrey. *Barbary Legend: War, Trade and Piracy in North Africa, 1415–1830.* Oxford: Clarendon Press, 1957.

Fludd, Robert. *Utrusque Cosmi . . . Historia.* Oppenheim, 1619.

Foa, Anna. "The New and the Old: The Spread of Syphilis (1494–1530)." In Edward Muir and Guido Ruggiero, eds., *Sex and Gender in Historical Perspective.* Trans. Margaret A. Gallucci et al. Baltimore: Johns Hopkins University Press, 1990. 26–45.

Forman, Valerie. "Marked Angels: Counterfeits, Commodities, and *The Roaring Girl.*" *Renaissance Quarterly* 54 (2001): 1531–60.

Foucault, Michel. *Discipline and Punish: The Birth of the Prison.* Trans. Alan Sheridan. New York: Pantheon, 1977.

———. *Madness and Civilization: A History of Insanity in the Age of Reason.* Trans. Richard Howard. New York: Pantheon, 1965.

———. *The Order of Things: An Archaeology of the Human Sciences.* London: Tavistock, 1970.

Fracastoro, Girolamo. *De Contagione at Contagiosis Morbis et Eorum Curatione.* Trans. Wilmer Care Wright. New York: G. P. Putnam, 1933.

Freedman, Barbara. "Errors in Comedy: A Psychoanalytic Theory of Farce." In Maurice Charney, ed., *Shakespearean Comedy.* New York: New York Literary Forum, 1980. 233–43.

Freeman, Arthur. "Marlowe, Kyd, and the Dutch Church Libel." *English Literary Renaissance* 3 (1973): 44–52.

Freeman, Thomas. *Runne, and a Great Cast.* London, 1614.

Freud, Sigmund. "Fetishism." In *On Sexuality: The Pelican Freud Library,* vol. 7, ed. Angela Richards. Harmondsworth: Penguin, 1977. 351–57.

Frye, Northrop. *The Secular Scripture: A Study of the Structure of Romance.* Cambridge, Mass.: Harvard University Press, 1976.

Fuchs, Barbara. *Mimesis and Empire: The New World, Islam, and European Identities.* Cambridge: Cambridge University Press, 2001.

Gaebelkover, Oswald. *Boock of Physicke.* London, 1599.

Galen. *Galeni Pergamensis de Temperamentis, et de Inaequali Intemperie.* Trans. Thomas Linacre. London, 1521.Brian Brian

Garber, Marjorie. "The Logic of the Transvestite." In David Scott Kastan and Peter Stallybrass, eds., *Staging the Renaissance: Reinterpretations of Elizabethan and Jacobean Drama.* London: Routledge, 1991. 221–34.

Gee, Henry, ed. *The Elizabethan Prayer-Book & Ornaments.* London: Macmillan, 1902.

George a Greene. Ed. F. W. Clarke. London: Malone Society Reprints, 1911.

Gibbons, Brian. *Jacobean City Comedy: A Study of Satiric Plays by Jonson, Marston and Middleton,* 2nd ed. London: Methuen, 1980.

Gillies, John. *Shakespeare and the Geography of Difference.* Cambridge: Cambridge University Press, 1992.

Gilman, Ernest B. "The Arts of Sympathy: Dr. Harvey, Sir Kenelm Digby, and the Arundel Circle." In Peter C. Herman, ed., *Opening the Borders: Inclusivity in Early Modern Studies, Essays in Honor of James V. Mirollo.* Newark: University of Delaware Press, 1999. 265–97.

Girard, René. *To Double Business Bound: Essays on Literature, Mimesis and Anthropology.* Baltimore: Johns Hopkins University Press, 1978. 136–54.

———. "The Politics of Desire in *Troilus and Cressida.*" In Patricia Parker and Geoffrey Hartman, eds., *Shakespeare and the Question of Theory.* New York: Methuen, 1985. 188–209.

———. *A Theatre of Envy: William Shakespeare.* Oxford: Oxford University Press, 1991.

Glapthorne, Henry. *The Hollander.* London, 1640.

The Good Angel of Stamford, Or An Extraordinary Cure Of An Extraordinary Consumption, In A True and Faithful Narrative Of SAMUEL WALLAS Recovered, By The Power of God, and Prescription Of an Angel. London, 1659.

Gosson, Stephen. *Playes Confuted in Fiue Actions, Prouing That They Are Not To Be Suffred in a Christian Common Weale.* London, 1582 (?).

Gould, J. D. *The Great Debasement.* Oxford: Oxford University Press, 1970.

———. "The Price Revolution Considered." *Economic History Review* 2nd ser. 17 (1964–65): 249–265

————. "The Trade Depression of the Early 1620s." *Economic History Review* 7 (1954): 81–88.

Goux, Jean-Joseph. *The Coiners of Language.* Trans. Jennifer Curtiss Gage. Norman: University of Oklahoma Press, 1994.

Grady, Hugh. *Shakespeare's Universal Wolf: Postmodernist Studies in Early Modern Reification.* Oxford: Clarendon Press, 1996.

Green, Juana. "Properties of Marriage: Proprietary Conflict and the Calculus of Gender in *Epicoene.*" In Jonathan Gil Harris and Natasha Korda, eds., *Staged Properties in Early Modern English Drama.* Cambridge: Cambridge University Press, 2002. 261–87.

Greenblatt, Stephen. "Invisible Bullets: Renaissance Authority and Its Subversion, *Henry IV, Henry V.*" In Jonathan Dollimore and Alan Sinfield, eds., *Political Shakespeare: New Essays in Cultural Materialism.* Manchester: Manchester University Press, 1994. 18–47.

Greene, Gayle. "Shakespeare's Cressida: 'A kind of self,'" in Carolyn Ruth Swift Lenz, Gayle Greene, and Carol Thomas Neely, eds., , *The Woman's Part: Feminist Criticism of Shakespeare.* Urbana, IL: University of Illinois Press, 1980. 133–49

————. "Language and Value in Shakespeare's *Troilus and Cressida.*" *Studies in English Literature* 21 (1981): 271–85.

Greene, Robert. *The Life and Complete Works in Prose and Verse of Robert Greene.* Ed. Alexander B. Grosart. New York: Russell and Russell, 1886.

————. *A Quip for an Vpstart Courtier: Or, a Quaint Dispute betweene Velvet-breeches and Cloth-breeches.* London, 1635.

Greene, Roland. *Unrequited Conquests: Love and Empire in the Colonial Americas.* Chicago: University of Chicago Press, 1999)

Griffin, G. W. H. *Shylock: A Burlesque, As Performed by Griffin & Christy's Minstrels.* New York: Samuel French, n.d.

Grmek, Mirko D. "Le Concept d'infection dans l'antiquité at au Moyen Age: les anciennes mesures sociales contre les maladies contagieuses et la fondation de la première quarantaine à Dubrovnik." *Rad Jugoslavneske Akademje* 384 (1980): 9–55.

Grosrichard, Alain. *The Sultan's Court: European Fantasies of the East.* Trans. Liz Heron. London: Verso, 1998.

Gruber von Arni, Eric. *Justice to the Maimed Soldier: Nursing, Medical Care, and Welfare for the Sick and Wounded Soldiers and Their Families During the English Civil Wars and Interregnum, 1642–1660.* Aldershot, Hampshire: Ashgate, 2001.

Gurnall, William. *The Christian in Compleat Armour, or A Treatise of the Saints War Against the Devil, Wherein a Discovery is Made of that Great Enemy of God and his People.* London, 1655.

S. H. *A New Treatise of the Pestilence.* London, 1603.

Halpern, Richard. *Shakespeare Among the Moderns.* Ithaca, N.Y.: Cornell University Press, 1997.

Hamilton, A. C. *The Early Shakespeare.* San Marino, Calif.: Huntington Library, 1967.

Harris, Jonathan Gil. "Atomic Shakespeare." *Shakespeare Studies* 30 (2002): 41–45.

————. "'The Canker of England's Commonwealth': Gerard de Malynes and the Origins of Economic Pathology." *Textual Practice* 13 (1999): 311–28.

————. *Foreign Bodies and the Body Politic: Discourses of Social Pathology in Early Modern England.* Cambridge: Cambridge University Press, 1998.

————. "Properties of Skill: Product Placement in Early Artisanal Drama." In Jonathan Gil Harris and Natasha Korda, eds., *Staged Properties in Early Modern English Drama*. Cambridge: Cambridge Unversity Press, 2002. 35–66.

Harrison, William. *Harrison's Description of England*. Ed. Frederick J. Furnivall. London: Trübner, 1877.

Harvey, William. *The Anatomical Lectures of William Harvey: Prelectiones Anatomie Universalis, De Musculis*. Ed. and trans. Gweneth Whitteridge. Edinburgh: Livingstone, 1964.

Hawkes, David. *Idols of the Marketplace: Idolatry and Commodity Fetishism in English Literature, 1580–1680*. New York: Palgrave, 2001.

Hazlitt, W. Carew, ed. *A Select Collection of Old English Plays*. 4th ed. London: Reeves and Turner, 1874.

Healy, Margaret. *Fictions of Disease in Early Modern England: Bodies, Plagues, Politics*. New York: Palgrave, 2001.

Heckscher, Eli F. *Mercantilism*. 2nd ed. Trans. Mendel Shapiro. 2 vols. London: Allen and Unwin, 1955.

Heinemann, Margot. *Puritanism and Theatre: Thomas Middleton and Opposition Drama Under the Early Stuarts*. Cambridge: Cambridge University Press, 1980.

Helgerson, Richard. *Forms of Nationhood: The Elizabethan Writing of England*. Berkeley: University of California Press, 1992.

Henryson, Robert. *Testament of Cresseid*. Ed. Denton Fox. London: Thomas Nelson, 1968.

Henze, Richard. "*The Comedy of Errors:* A Freely Binding Chain." *Shakespeare Quarterly* 22 (1971): 35–42.

Herbert, Edward, Lord Herbert of Cherbury. *The Life and Raigne of King Henry the Eighth*. London, 1649.

Hertzberg, Hendrik. "Comment: Tuesday, and After." *New Yorker,* September 24, 2001.

Heywood, Thomas. *The Dramatic Works of Thomas Heywood*. 6 vols. London: John Pearson, 1874.

————. *Edward IV*. London, 1599.

————. *The Fair Maid of the West, Parts I and II*. Ed. Robert K. Turner, Jr. Lincoln: University of Nebraska Press, 1967.

————. *The Fayre Mayde of the Exchange, With the Pleasant Humours of the Cripple of Fanchurch*. London, 1607.

————. *The Wise-Woman of Hogsdon*. London, 1638.

Heywood, Thomas and William Rowley, *A Critical Edition of A Fortune by Land and Sea*. Ed. Herman Doh. New York and London: Garland, 1980.

Hobbes, Thomas. *The Collected Works of Thomas Hobbes*. Ed. Sir William Molesworth. 2nd impression. London: Routledge/Thoemmes, 1994.

————. *Leviathan*. Ed. Richard Tuck. Cambridge: Cambridge University Press, 1997.

Hoeniger, F. David. *Medicine and Shakespeare in the English Renaissance*. Newark: University of Delaware Press, 1992.

Homer. *The Iliad*. Trans. Richmond Lattimore. Chicago: University of Chicago Press, 1951.

Horman, William. *William Horman's Vulgaria*. Ed. M. R. James. London: Roxburghe Club, 1926.

Howard, Jean E. "Cross-Dressing, the Theatre, and Gender Struggle in Early Modern England." *Shakespeare Quarterly* 39 (1988): 417–39.

————. "An English Lass Amid the Moors: Gender, Race, Sexuality and National Identity in Heywood's *The Fair Maid of the West.*" In Margo Hendricks and Patricia Parker, eds., *Women, "Race," and Writing in the Early Modern Period.* London: Routledge, 1994. 101–17.

Howard, Jean E. and Phyllis Rackin, *Engendering a Nation: A Feminist Account of Shakespeare's English Histories.* London: Routledge, 1997.

Hutchinson, Lucy. *Lucy Hutchinson's Translation of Lucretius:* De Rerum Natura. Ed. Hugh de Quehen. Ann Arbor: University of Michigan Press, 1996.

Hutchison, Terence. *Before Adam Smith: The Emergence of Political Economy 1622–1776.* Oxford: Blackwell, 1988.

Hutten, Ulrich von. *De Guaiaci Medicina et Morbo Gallico.* London, 1533.

Hyamson, Albert M. *A History of the Jews in England.* London: Chatto Windus, 1908.

Ingram, William. "Robert Keysar, Playhouse Speculator." *Shakespeare Quarterly* 37 (1986): 476–88.

An Interlude of Wealth and Health, Very Mery and Ful of Pastyme. London: Malone Society Reprints, 1910.

Irwin, Douglas A. *Against the Tide: An Intellectual History of Free Trade.* Princeton, N.J.: University Press, 1996.

Israel, Jonathan I. *European Jewry in the Age of Mercantilism 1550–1750,* 3rd ed. London: Littman Library of Jewish Civilization, 1998.

James I. *A Proclamation for Restraint of the Exportation, Waste, and Consumption of Coine and Bullion.* London, 1622.

James, Heather. *Shakespeare's Troy: Drama, Politics, and the Translation of Empire.* Cambridge: Cambridge University Press, 1997.

Jameson, Fredric. "Culture and Finance Capitalism." *Critical Inquiry* 24 (1997): 246–65.

———. "Magical Narratives: Romance as Genre." *New Literary History* 7 (1975): 135–63.

Jamieson, Michael. "The Problem Plays, 1920–1970." *Shakespeare Survey* 25 (1972): 1–10.

Jeanneret, Michel. *Perpetual Motion: Transforming Shapes in the Renaissance from da Vinci to Montaigne.* Trans. Nidra Poller. Baltimore: Johns Hopkins University Press, 2001.

Jenkins, Harold. *The Life and Work of Henry Chettle.* London: Sidgwick and Jackson, 1934.

Johnson, Charles, ed. *The "De Moneta" of Nicholas Oresme and English Mint Documents.* London, 1956.

Jones, Ann Rosalind and Peter Stallybrass. *Renaissance Clothing and the Materials of Memory.* Cambridge: Cambridge University Press, 2000.

Jones, Norman. *God and the Moneylenders: Usury and Law in Early Modern England.* Oxford: Oxford University Press, 1989.

Jones, Richard. *Literary Remains.* Ed. W. Whewell. London: John Murray, 1859.

Jonson, Ben. *The Case is Altered.* London, 1609.

———. *Volpone, or The Fox.* Ed. Philip Brockbank. London and New York: A & C Black/Norton, 1991.

———. *Volpone, or the Fox.* Ed . J. D. Rea. New Haven, Conn.: Yale University Press, 1919.

Jouanna, Jacques. "The Birth of Western Medical Art." In Mirko D. Grmek, ed., *Western Medical Thought from Antiquity to the Middle Ages.* Trans. Antony Shugaar. Cambridge, Mass.: Harvard University Press, 1998. 22–71.

Joughin, John J. ed. *Shakespeare and National Culture.* Manchester: Manchester University Press, 1997.

Judges, A. V. "The Idea of a Mercantile State." *Transactions of the Royal Historical Society* 4th ser. 21 (1939): 41–69.

Kavanagh, James H. "Shakespeare in Ideology." In John Drakakis, ed., *Alternative Shakespeares.* London: Methuen, 1985. 144–65.

Kayne, Gregory G. *The Control of Tuberculosis in England, Past and Present.* London: Oxford University Press, 1937.

Keil, Harry. "The Evolution of the Term Chancre and Its Relation to the History of Syphilis." *Journal of the History of Medicine* 4 (1949): 407–16.

Kellwaye, Simon. *A Defensative Against the Plague.* London, 1593.

Kelsey, Harry. *Sir Francis Drake: The Queen's Pirate.* New Haven, Conn.: Yale University Press, 1998.

Ker, W. P. *Epic and Romance: Essays on Medieval Literature.* 2nd. ed. London: Macmillan, 1908.

Kermode, Frank. "Opinion, Truth and Value." *Essays in Criticism* 5 (1955): 181–87.

Kermode, Lloyd Edward. "The Playwright's Prophecy: Robert Wilson's *The Three Ladies of London* and the 'Alienation' of the English." *Medieval and Renaissance Drama in England* 11 (1999): 60–87.

Knapp, Jeffrey. *An Empire Nowhere: England, America, and Literature from* Utopia *to* The Tempest. Berkeley: University of California Press, 1992.

Knave in the Grain. London, 1625.

Knowles, James. "Cecil's Shopping Centre: The Rediscovery of a Ben Jonson Masque in Praise of Trade." *Times Literary Supplement,* February 7, 1997, 14–15.

Kocher, Paul. "Paracelsan Medicine in England." *Journal of the History of Medicine* 2 (1947): 251–80.

Lander, Jesse M. " 'Crack'd Crowns' and Counterfeit Sovereigns: The Crisis of Value in *1 Henry IV.*" *Shakespeare Studies* 30 (2002): 137–61.

Lane-Poole, Stanley. *The Barbary Corsairs.* London: T. Fisher Unwin, 1890.

Laqueur, Thomas. *Making Sex: Body and Gender from the Greeks to Freud.* Cambridge, Mass.: Harvard University Press, 1990.

Lee, Byung-Eun. "Shakespeare's Villeinizing of Jack Cade." In Peter C. Rollins and Alan Smith, eds., *Shakespeare's Theories of Blood, Character, and Class: A Festschrift in Honor of David Shelley Berkeley.* New York: Peter Lang, 2001. 109–22.

Leinwand, Theodore B. *The City Staged: Jacobean City Comedy, 1603–13.* Madison: University of Wisconsin Press, 1986.

———. *Theatre, Finance and Society in Early Modern England.* Cambridge: Cambridge University Press, 1999.

Levin, Harry. "Jonson's Metempsychosis." *Philological Quarterly* 22 (1943): 231–39.

Linton, Joan Pong. *The Romance of the New World: Gender and the Literary Formations of English Colonialism.* Cambridge: Cambridge University Press, 1998.

Lloyd, Christopher. *English Corsairs on the Barbary Coast.* London: Collins, 1981.

Lodge, Thomas. *A Treatise of the Plague: Containing the Nature, Signes and Accidents of the Same.* London, 1603.

Loewenstein, Joseph. "Plays Agonistic and Competitive: The Textual Approach to Elsinore." *Renaissance Drama* 19 (1988): 63–90.

Lovell, Robert. *PAMBOTANOLOGIA sive Enchiridion Botanicum: Or A Compleat Herball.* Oxford, 1659.

Lowe, Peter. *An Easie, Certain and Perfect Method, to Cure and Prevent the Spanish Sicknes.* London, 1596.

Lucian. *Lucian in Eight Volumes.* Trans. A. M. Harmon. Cambridge, Mass.: Harvard University Press, 1968.

Luther, Martin. *Tischreden.* 6 vols. Weimar, 1912–21.

Lupton, J. H. *A Life of John Colet.* London, 1909.

Macherey, Pierre and Etienne Balibar. "Literature as an Ideological Form: Some Marxist Hypotheses." *Praxis* 5 (1980): 43–58.

Maddison, Angus. *The World Economy: A Millennial Perspective.* Paris: OECD, 2002.

Magnusson, Lars. *Mercantilism: The Shaping of an Economic Language.* London: Routledge, 1994.

Mainwaring, Henry. *The Life and Works of Sir Henry Mainwaring.* Ed. G. E. Manwaring. 2 vols. London: Navy Records Society, 1920.

Mallin, Eric S. *Inscribing the Time: Shakespeare and the End of Elizabethan England.* Berkeley: University of California Press, 1995.

Malynes, Gerard. *The Center of the Circle of Commerce, Or, A Refutation of a Treatise, Intituled The Circle of Commerce, or The Ballance of Trade, Lately Published by E. M.* London, 1623.

———. *Consuetedo, Vel, Lex Mercatoria: Or, the Ancient Law-Merchant.* London, 1622.

———. *Englands View, in the Unmasking of Two Paradoxes.* London, 1603.

———. *The Maintenance of Free Trade, According to the Three Essentiall Parts of Traffique; Namely, Commodities, Moneys, and Exchange of Moneys, by Bills of Exchanges for Other Countries.* London, 1622.

———. *Saint George for England Allegorically Described.* London, 1601.

———. *A Treatise of the Canker of England's Commonwealth.* London, 1601.

Mandeville, Bernard de. *The Fable of the Bees: Private Vices, Public Benefits.* London, 1729.

Markham, Gervase. *Cavelarice. Of the English Horseman.* London, 1607.

———. *The English Housewife: Containing the Inward and Outward Virtues Which Ought to Be in a Complete Woman.* London, 1615.

Marlowe, Christopher. *Edward II.* Ed. Charles R. Forker. New York: St. Martin's Press, 1994.

———. *The Jew of Malta.* Ed. James R. Siemon. New York: Norton, 1994.

Marston, John. *The Plays of John Marston.* Ed. H. Harvey Wood. 3 vols. London: Oliver and Boyd, 1939.

Martin, Emily. *Flexible Bodies: The Role of Immunity in American Culture from the Days of Polio to the Age of AIDS.* Boston: Beacon Press, 1994.

Marx, Karl. *A Contribution to the Critique of Political Economy.* London: Lawrence and Wishart, 1971.

Marx, Karl and Friedrich Engels. *The Marx-Engels Reader.* Ed. Robert C. Tucker. 2nd ed. New York: W.W. Norton, 1978.

Matar, Nabil. " 'Turning Turk': Conversion to Islam in English Renaissance Thought." *Durham University Journal* 86 (1994): 33–43.

McEachern, Claire. *Poetics of English Nationhood, 1590–1612.* Cambridge: Cambridge University Press, 1996.

McKendrick, Neil, John Brewer, and J. H. Plumb, eds. *The Birth of a Consumer Society: The Commercialization of Eighteenth-Century England.* Bloomington: Indiana University Press, 1982.

Middleton, Thomas. *A Mad World, My Masters, and Other Plays.* Ed. Michael Taylor. Oxford: Oxford University Press, 1995.

Middleton, Thomas and Thomas Dekker. *The Honest Whore, With the Humours of the Patient Man and the Longing Wife.* London, 1604.

———. *The Roaring Girl.* Ed. Elizabeth Cook. New York: Norton, 1997.

Middleton, Thomas and William Rowley. *The Old Law.* Ed. Catherine M. Shaw. New York: Garland, 1982.

Middleton, Thomas and John Webster. *Any Thing for a Quiet Life.* London, 1664.

Milles, Thomas. *The Custumers Alphabet and Primer: Conteining, Their Creede or Beliefe in the true Doctrine of Christian Religion.* London, 1608.

———. *The Custumers Apology: That is to Say, a Generall Answere to Informers of All Sortes, and Their Iniurious Complaints, Against the Honest Reputation of the Collectors of her Maiesties CUSTUMES, Specially in the OUT-PORTES of this Realme.* London, 1599.

———. *The Customers Replie, Or Second Apologie.* London, 1604.

———. *The Misterie of Iniquitie.* London, 1611.

Milton, John. *Paradise Lost.* Ed. Alastair Fowler. London: Longman, 1998.

Misselden, Edward. *The Circle of Commerce: Or, the Balance of Trade, in Defence of Free Trade: Opposed to Malynes Little Fish and His Great Whale, and Poized Against Them in the Scales.* London, 1623.

———. *Free Trade or, The Meanes To Make Trade Florish: Wherein, The Causes of the Decay of Trade in this Kingdome, are Discovered: And the Remedies also to Remooue the Same, are Represented.* London, 1622.

More, Thomas. *Utopia.* Ed. George M. Logan and Robert M. Adams. Cambridge: Cambridge University Press, 1989.

Morley, Henry, ed. *Character Writings of the Seventeenth Century.* London: George Routledge & Sons, 1891.

Muchmore, Lynn. "Gerrard de Malynes and Mercantile Economics." *History of Political Economy* 1 (1969): 336–58.

Mukerji, Chandra. *Graven Images: Patterns of Modern Materialism.* New York: Columbia University Press, 1983.

Muldrew, Craig. *The Economy of Obligation: The Culture of Credit and Social Relations in Early Modern England.* New York: St. Martin's Press, 1998.

Mullaney, Steven. "Brothers and Others, or the Art of Alienation." In Marjorie Garber, ed., *Cannibals, Witches and Divorce: Estranging the Renaissance.* Baltimore: Johns Hopkins University Press. 67–89.

Mun, Thomas. *A Discourse of Trade, From England Vnto the East-Indies: Answering to Diuerse Obiections Which Are Usually Made Against the Same.* London, 1621.

———. *Englands Treasure by Forraign Trade; Or, The Ballance of our Forraign Trade is The Rule of our Treasure.* London, 1669.

Munday, Anthony. *John a Kent and John a Cumber.* Ed. J. Payne Collier. London: Shakespeare Society, 1851.

Nagy, Doreen Evenden. *Popular Medicine in Seventeenth-Century England.* Bowling Green, Ohio: Bowling Green State University Popular Press, 1988.

Nashe, Thomas. *Have With You to Saffron-walden. Or, Gabriel Harueys Hunt is vp.* London, 1596.

Neill, Anna. *British Discovery Literature and the Rise of Global Commerce.* New York: Palgrave, 2002.

Nelson, Benjamin. *The Idea of Usury: From Tribal Brotherhood to Universal Otherhood,* 3rd ed. Chicago: University of Chicago Press, 1969.

Netzloff, Mark. " 'Venting Trinculos': Race, Class, and the Language of Capital." Paper presented at the 35th International Congress of Medieval Studies, Kalamazoo, Michigan, May 2000.

Newlin, Jeanne. "The Modernity of *Troilus and Cressida.*" *Harvard Library Bulletin* 17 (1969): 353–73.

News Out of East India of the Cruell Usage of Our English Merchants at Amboyna. London, 1625.

Nicholls, Charles. *The Reckoning: The Murder of Christopher Marlowe.* London: Harcourt and Brace, 1992.

The Nomenclator, or Remembrancer of Adrianus Junius. London, 1585.

Norri, Juhani. *Names of Body Parts in English, 1400–1550.* Finnish Academy of Science and Letters. Saarijärvi: Gummerus Oy, 1998.

Nowottny, Winifred M. T. " 'Opinion' and 'Value' in *Troilus and Cressida.*" *Essays in Criticism* 4 (1954): 282–96.

Nutton, Vivian. "The Seeds of Disease: An Explanation of Contagion and Infection from the Greeks to the Romans." *Medical History* 27 (1983): 1–34.

Orders, Thought Meete by her Maiestie, and her Priuie Counsell, to be Executed throughout the Countries of this Realme, in such Townes, Villages, and Other Places, as Are, or May be hereafter Infected with the Plague. London, 1592.

Ovid. *Metamorphoses.* Trans. Rolfe Humphries. Bloomington: Indiana University Press, 1955.

Pagel, Walter. *From Paracelsus to Van Helmont: Studies in Renaissance Medicine and Science,* ed. Marianne Winder. London: Variorum Reprints, 1986.

———. *Paracelsus: An Introduction to Philosophical Medicine in the Era of the Renaissance.* Basel: Karger, 1958.

———. *William Harvey's Biological Ideas: Selected Aspects and Historical Background.* Basel: Karger, 1967.

Palmer, Daryl. "Merchants and Miscegenation: *The Three Ladies of London, The Jew of Malta,* and *The Merchant of Venice.*" In Joyce Green MacDonald, ed., *Race, Ethnicity, and Power in the Renaissance.* London: Associated University Presses, 1997.

Palsgrave, John. *Lesclarcissement de la langue francoyse.* London, 1530.

Paracelsus. *Sämtliche Werke.* Ed. Karl Sudhoff. 14 vols. Munich: R. Oldenbourg, 1922.

———. *Selected Writings.* Ed. Jolande Jacobi, trans. Norbert Guterman. New York: Pantheon, 1958.

Parker, Patricia A. *Inescapable Romance: Studies in the Poetics of a Mode.* Princeton, N.J.: Princeton University Press, 1979.

———. "Preposterous Conversions: Turning Turk, and Its Pauline Rerighting." *Journal for Early Modern Cultural Studies* 2 (2002): 1–34.

Parr, Anthony, ed. *Three Renaissance Travel Plays.* Manchester: Manchester University Press, 1999.

Paster, Gail Kern. *The Body Embarrassed: Drama and the Disciplines of Shame in Early Modern England.* Ithaca, N.Y.: Cornell University Press, 1993.

———. *The Idea of the City in the Age of Shakespeare.* Athens: University of Georgia Press, 1985.

Paynell, Thomas. *Regimen Sanitatis Salerni: or, the Schoole of Salernes Regiment of Health.* London, 1649.

Pettegree, Andrew. *Foreign Protestant Communities in Sixteenth-Century London.* London: Oxford University Press, 1986.

Pettet, E. C. *Shakespeare and the Romance Tradition.* London: Staples Press, 1949.

Petyt, William. *Britannia Languens, or a Discourse of Trade.* London, 1680.

Pimlyco, or Runne Red-Cap: Tis A Mad World at Hogsdon. London, 1609.

Pollard, Tanya. "Beauty's Poisonous Properties." *Shakespeare Studies* 27 (1999): 187–210

Pollock, Frederick and Frederic William Maitland. *The History of English Law Before the Time of Edward I.* 2 vols. 2nd ed. Cambridge: Cambridge University Press, 1898.

Poovey, Mary. *A History of the Modern Fact: Problems of Knowledge in the Sciences of Wealth and Society.* Chicago: University of Chicago Press, 1998.

Pope, Alexander, ed. *The Works of Mr William Shakespear.* 6 vol. London, 1723.

Porter, Roy. "Consumption: Disease of the Consumer Society?" In John Brewer and Roy Porter, eds., *Consumption and the World of Goods.* London: Routledge, 1994. 58–81.

Potter, Lois. "Pirates and 'Turning Turk' in Renaissance Drama." In Jean-Pierre Maquerlot and Michèle Willems, eds., *Travel and Drama in Shakespeare's Time.* Cambridge: Cambridge University Press, 1996. 124–40.

Pound, Ezra. *The Cantos of Ezra Pound.* New York: New Directions, 1948.

Present Remedies Against the Plague. London, 1594.

Quétel, Claude. *The History of Syphilis.* Trans. Judith Braddock and Brian Pike. Baltimore: Johns Hopkins University Press, 1992.

Rather, L. J. *The Genesis of Cancer: A Study in the History of Ideas.* Baltimore: Johns Hopkins University Press, 1978.

Richard Perryman and Mae Perryman v. Lee Hackler: Supreme Court of Arkansas Opinion delivered February 19, 1996. http://courts.state.ar.us/opinions/1996/95–788.txt.

Richardson, Linda Deer. "The Generation of Disease: Occult Causes and Diseases of the Total Substance." In A. Wear, R. K. French, and I. M. Lonie, eds., *The Medical Renaissance of the Sixteenth Century.* Cambridge: Cambridge University Press, 1985. 175–94.

Robarts, Henry. *The Trumpet of Fame.* London, 1595.

Roberts, R. S. "The Early History of the Import of Drugs into Britain." In F. N. L. Poynter, ed., *The Evolution of Pharmacy in Britain.* Springfield, Ill.: Charles C. Thomas, 1965. 165–85.

Roche, Daniel. *A History of Everyday Things: The Birth of Consumption in France, 1600–1800.* Trans. Brian Pearce. Cambridge: Cambridge University Press, 2000.

Rokeah, Zephira Entrin. "The Expulsion of the Jews from England in 1290 A.D.: Some Aspects of Its Background." Ph.D. dissertation, Columbia University, 1986.

de Roover, Raymond. *Business, Banking, and Economic Thought in Late Medieval and Early Modern Europe.* Ed. Julius Kirshner. Chicago: University of Chicago Press, 1974.

———. *Gresham on the Foreign Exchange.* Cambridge, Mass.: Harvard University Press, 1949.

Rose, Mary-Beth. "Women in Men's Clothing: Apparel and Social Stability in *The Roaring Girl.*" *English Literary Renaissance* 14 (1984): 367–91.

Rosen, George. *A History of Public Health.* Expanded Edition. Baltimore: Johns Hopkins University Press, 1993.

W. S. *Locrine.* Ed. R. B. McKerrow. London: Malone Society Reprints, 1908.

Salingar, Leo. *Shakespeare and the Traditions of Comedy.* Cambridge: Cambridge University Press, 1974.

Saunders, Ann, ed. *The Royal Exchange.* London: London Topographical Society, 1997.

Schmoller, Gustav von. *The Mercantile System and its Historical Significance.* New York: Macmillan, 1897.

Schoenfeldt, Michael C. *Bodies and Selves in Early Modern England: Physiology and Inwardness in Spenser, Shakespeare, Herbert, and Milton.* Cambridge: Cambridge University Press, 1999.

Sekora, John. *Luxury: The Concept in Western Thought, Eden to Smollett.* Baltimore: Johns Hopkins University Press, 1978.

Shakespeare, William. *Anthony and Cleopatra,* ed. Michael Neill. Oxford: Oxford University Press, 1994.

———. *The Comedy of Errors.* Ed. David Bevington. New York: Bantam, 1988.

———. *A New Variorum Edition of Shakespeare: The Merchant of Venice.* Ed. Horace Howard Furness. 7th ed. Philadelphia: J.B. Lippincott, 1888.

———. *The Riverside Shakespeare.* Ed. G. Blakemore Evans et al. 2nd ed. Boston: Houghton Mifflin, 1997.

———. *Troilus and Cressida.* Ed. Kenneth Palmer. London: Methuen, 1982.

Shapiro, James. *Shakespeare and the Jews.* New York: Columbia University Press, 1996.

Sharpham, Edward. *The Fleire.* London, 1607.

Shaw, Catherine M. "The Conscious Art of *The Comedy of Errors.*" In Maurice Charney, ed., *Shakespearean Comedy.* New York: New York Literary Forum, 1980. 17–28.

Shell, Marc. *Money, Language, and Thought.* Baltimore: Johns Hopkins University Press, 1992.

Simmel, Georg. *Philosophy of Money.* London: Routledge, 1978.

Sinfield, Alan. *Faultlines: Cultural Materialism and the Politics of Dissident Reading.* Berkeley: University of California Press, 1992.

Skayne, Gilbert. *Ane Breve Description of the Pest Quhair in the Causis, Signis and Sum Speciall Preseruation and Cure Thairof Ar Contenit.* Edinburgh, 1568.

Slack, Paul. *The Impact of Plague in Tudor and Stuart England.* London: Routledge, 1985.

Smith, Adam. *An Inquiry into the Nature and Causes of the Wealth of Nations.* London, 1776.

Smith, Alan K. *Creating a World Economy: Merchant Capital, Colonialism, and World Trade.* Boulder, Colo.: Westview Press, 1991.

Smith, Henry. *The Works of Henry Smith.* Ed. Thomas Fuller. 2 vols. Edinburgh, 1866–67.

Smith, John. *An Accidence for all Young Sea-men.* London, 1626.

Solomon, Julie Robin. *Objectivity in the Making: Francis Bacon and the Politics of Inquiry.* Baltimore: Johns Hopkins University Press, 1998.

Sombart, Werner. *The Jews and Modern Capitalism.* Trans. M. Epstein. New York: Macmillan, 1962.

Sontag, Susan. *AIDS and Its Metaphors.* New York: Farrar Straus Giroux, 1989.

———. *Illness as Metaphor.* New York: Farrar, Straus & Giroux, 1978.

Southall, Raymond. "*Troilus and Cressida* and the Spirit of Capitalism." In Arnold Kettle, ed., *Shakespeare in a Changing World.* London: Lawrence and Wishart, 1964. 217–32.

Spiegel, Henry William. *The Growth of Economic Thought.* 3rd ed. Durham, N.C.: Duke University Press, 1991.

Spiller, Elizabeth A. "From Imagination to Miscegenation: Race and Romance in Shakespeare's *The Merchant of Venice.*" *Renaissance Drama* n.s. 29 (2000 for 1998): 137–64.

Spurgeon, Caroline F. E. *Shakespeare's Imagery and What It Tells Us.* Cambridge: Cambridge University Press, 1952.

Stafford, T. J. "Mercantile Imagery in *Troilus and Cressida.*" In Stafford, ed., *Shakespeare in the Southwest: Some New Directions.* El Paso: Texas Western Press, 1969. 36–42.

Stallybrass, Peter. "Worn Worlds: Clothes and Identity on the Renaissance Stage." In Margreta de Grazia, Maureen Quilligan, and Peter Stallybrass, eds. *Subject and Object in Renaissance Culture.* Cambridge: Cambridge University Press, 1996. 289–320.

Starkey, Thomas. *A Dialogue Between Reginald Pole and Thomas Lupset.* Ed. Kathleen M. Burton. London: Chatto and Windus, 1948.

Stephen, Leslie and Sidney Lee, eds., *The Dictionary of National Biography.* Oxford: Oxford University Press, 1921–22.

Stewart, Alan. "The Portingale." Paper presented at the 30th convention of the Shakespeare Association of America, Minneapolis, 2002.

Stowe, John. *A Survey of London.* Ed. Charles Lethbridge. Oxford: Clarendon Press, 1908.

Strype, John. *Annals of the Reformation and Establishment of Religion, and Other Various Occurrences in the Church of England During Elizabeth's Happy Reign.* 4 vols. Oxford: Oxford University Press, 1824.

Stubbes, Philip. *The Anatomie of Abuses: Contayning a Discoverie, or Briefe Summarie, of Such Notable Vices and Imperfections, As Now Raigne in Many Christian Countreyes of the Worlde, But (Especiallie) in a Verie Famous Ilande Called Ailgna.* London, 1583.

Sugden, Edward H. *A Topographical Dictionary to the Works of Shakespeare and his Fellow-Dramatists.* Manchester: Manchester University Press, 1925.

Sullivan, Ceri. *The Rhetoric of Credit: Merchants in Early Modern Writing.* London: Associated University Presses, 2002.

Supple, Brian E. *Commercial Crisis and Change in England 1600–1642: A Study in the Instability of a Mercantile Economy.* Cambridge: Cambridge University Press, 1959.

———. "Currency and Commerce in the Early Seventeenth Century." *Economic History Review* 2nd ser. 10 (1957): 239–55.

Swann, Marjorie. *Curiosities and Texts: The Culture of Collecting in Early Modern England.* Philadelphia: University of Pennsylvania Press, 2001.

Taylor, Gary. *Castration: An Abbreviated History of Western Manhood.* New York: Routledge, 2000.

Taylor, John. *All the Works of John Taylor the Water Poet Being 63 in Number.* London, 1630.

Temkin, Owsei. *Galenism: Rise and Decline of a Medical Philosophy.* Ithaca, N.Y.: Cornell University Press, 1973.

Thayre, Thomas. *A Treatise of the Pestilence.* London, 1603.

Thirsk, Joan. *Economic Policy and Projects: The Development of a Consumer Society in Early Modern England.* Oxford: Oxford University Press, 1978.

Thomas, William. *The Historye of Italye.* London, 1561.

Travitsky, Betty S. and Anne Lake Prescott, eds. *Female and Male Voices in Early Modern England: An Anthology of Renaissance Writing.* New York: Columbia University Press, 2000.

Tretiak, Andrew. "*The Merchant of Venice* and the 'Alien' Question." *Review of English Studies* 5 (1929): 402–9.

Trevisa, John. *On the Properties of Things: John Trevisa's Translation of Bartholomaeus Anglicus De Proprietatibus Rerum.* 2 vols. Oxford: Clarendon Press, 1975.

Tryon, Thomas. *The Good Housewife Made Doctor.* London, 1685.

Van Elk, Martine. "Urban Misidentification in *The Comedy of Errors* and the Cony-Catching Pamphlets." *Studies in English Literature,* forthcoming.

Vergil. *The Aeneid.* Trans. L. R. Lind. Bloomington: Indiana University Press, 1963.

Vignon, Jean. *The Most Excellent Workes of Chirurgerye, made and set forth by maister John Vignon.* Trans. Bartholomew Traheron. London, 1543.

Vitkus, Daniel J., ed. *Three Turk Plays from Early Modern England: "Selimus," "A Christian Turned Turk," "The Renegado".* New York: Columbia University Press, 2000.

———. "Turning Turk in Othello: The Conversion and the Damnation of the Moor." *Shakespeare Quarterly* 48 (1997): 145–76.

Wall, Wendy. *Staging Domesticity: Household Work and English Identity in Early Modern English Drama.* Cambridge: Cambridge University Press, 2002.

Ward and Danseker, Two Notorious Pyrates, Ward an Englishman, and Danseker a Dutchman. London, 1609.

Warneke, Sara. "A Taste for Newfangledness: The Destructive Potential of Novelty in Early Modern England." *Sixteenth Century Journal* 26 (1995): 881–96.

Wear, Andrew. "Medicine in Early Modern Europe: 1500–1700." In Lawrence I. Conrad et al., *The Western Medical Tradition: 800 BC to AD 1800.* Cambridge: Cambridge University Press, 1995. 215–361.

Webster, John. *Metallographia, or An History of Metals.* London, 1671.

Weimann, Robert. "Bifold Authority in Shakespeare's Theatre." *Shakespeare Quarterly* 39 (1988): 401–17

———. "Representation and Performance: The Uses of Authority in Shakespeare's Theatre." *PMLA* 107 (1992): 497–510.

Wesson, Susan. "A Cost-Benefit Analysis of the Arkansas Usury Law and Its Effects on Arkansas Residents and Institutions." *Academic Forum* (2001). www.hsu.edu/faculty/afo/2000–01/wesson.htm

Westcote, Thomas. *A View of Devonshire in MDCXXX.* Ed. George Oliver and Pitman Jones. Exeter, 1845.

Wheeler, John. *A Treatise of Commerce, Wherin Are Shewed the Commodities Arising by a Well Ordered, and Ruled Trade, Such As That of the Societie of Merchantes Adventurers Is Proved to Bee.* London, 1601.

White, Thomas. *A Sermon Preached at Pawles Crosse on Sunday the Thirde of November 1577, In the Time of the Plague.* London, 1578.

Whitteridge, Gweneth. *William Harvey and the Circulation of the Blood.* New York: American Elsevier, 1971.

Willan, T. S. "Some Aspects of English Trade with the Levant in the Sixteenth Century." *English History Review* 70 (1955): 399–410.

Wilson, Charles. "'Mercantilism': Some Vicissitudes of an Idea." *Economic History Review* 2nd ser. 10, 2 (1957): 181–88.

Wilson, Douglas B. "The Commerce of Desire: Freudian Narcissism in Chaucer's *Troilus and Criseyde* and Shakespeare's *Troilus and Cressida*." *English Language Notes* 21 (1983): 11–22.

Wilson, F. P. *The Plague in Shakespeare's London.* Oxford: Oxford University Press, 1927.

Wilson, Robert. *The Cobblers Prophecy.* London, 1594.

———. *An Edition of Robert Wilson's "The Three Ladies of London" and "Three Lords and Three Ladies of London"*. Ed. H. S. D. Mithal. New York: Garland, 1988.

Wilson, Thomas. *Discourse on Usury*. London, 1572.

Wood, Alfred C. *The History of the Levant Company*. Oxford: Oxford University Press, 1935.

Yaffe, Martin D. *Shylock and the Jewish Question*. Baltimore: Johns Hopkins University Press, 1997.

Žižek, Slavoj. *The Sublime Object of Ideology*. London: Verso, 1989.

Index

Abernathy, John, 42
Achilles, 101, 104, 110
Adriana, 29–30, 34, 45, 49; observations of, 39
de Affaitati, Johan Karel, 69, 70
Agamemnon, 100, 104
Agnew, Jean-Christophe, 24
Ajax, 105
Al-Qaeda, 188, 189
Alexander, 105
All's Well That Ends Well (Shakespeare), 85–86
alopecia, 46, 47
Alva, Duke of, 69
Amphitruo (Plautus), 31
Amsterdam, plague in, 114
Amurath, 158
The Anatomy of Abuses (Stubbes), 36–37
Androgyno, 116
Angelo, 31–32
anthrax, 187–88
Antipholus, 29, 31, 39, 40, 47, 50
Antonio, 11, 52, 54–55, 72, 73; Shylock and, 79–80
Antwerp, 5, 72; capture of, 69
Apemantus, 96
Apollonius, Prince of Tyre (Gower), 198n8
Appadurai, Arjun, 119
Appleby, Joyce Oldham, 89, 141
Aquinas, Thomas, 54, 58, 94, 103
Archer, Thomas, 180
Arden of Faversham, 178
Aristotle, 93, 143, 146
Arkansas, 52
Asambeg, 157, 159, 160
Asian flu, 12, 189; as metaphor, 2, 23; outbreak of, 1
Aubrey, John, 84
Auden, W. H., 78, 202n13
avoirdupois system, 107

Bacon, Francis, 4, 55, 61, 193n21; on canker, 83–84; on Judaism, 62; language of, 56; on usury, 54, 57

Balthasar, 29, 31
Bank of America, 188
Barbary Coast, 136–37, 150, 152; corsairs at, 139; definition of, 224n45
Barker, Andrew, 153
Barnes, Barnabe, 143
de Barrios, Daniel Levi, 70
Barroll, Leeds, 24
Bartholomew Fair (Jonson), 39
Bassanio, 10, 11, 80, 183
Beauwes, Wyndham, 84
ben Menasseh, Israel, 69
Bentley, Greg, 199n27, 214n66
Biraben, Jean-Noël, 18
Blaxton, John, 83
The Blazing World (Cavendish), 115
Bloom, Herbert, 70
Bodian, Miriam, 70
Bolingbroke, 84
Boorde, Andrew, 13–14, 88, 142, 222n17; on consumption, 166; on liver, 143; on syphilis, 42–43
Bradwell, Stephen, 112, 113; on plague, 114
Braudel, Fernand, 163
Breton, Nicholas, 84
Breuiary of Helthe (Boorde), 13–14, 166, 222n17
Bright, Timothy, 26, 109, 127, 129, 134; drugs and, 120–25, 122–23, 125; on humoral model, 124; Mun, Thomas, and, 169. See also *Treatise: Wherein is Declared the Sufficiencie of English Medicines*
Brokaw, Tom, 188
Browne, Thomas, 166
Bruster, Douglas, 24, 99
bubonic plague, 16
Burns, John Southerden, 67
Burton, Jonathan, 156

Cade, Jack, 148, 150
Canadian Imperial Bank of Commerce, 188
Canguilhem, Georges, 19

canker, 2, 110; Bacon on, 83–84; description of, 91; etiology of, 92; Malynes on, 83–84; Misselden on, 83; serpego and, 92–93; usury and, 83–84

Canker of England's Commonwealth. See *A Treatise of the Canker of England's Commonwealth* (Malynes)

Cantos (Pound), 83

capitalism, mercantilism and, 3

Capitalism and Material Life, 1400–1800 (Braudel), 163

Carazie, 157, 158, 159

Cardano, Girolamo, 16

Carpenter, Nathanael, 179

Carrol, 154

The Case is Altered (Jonson), 178

The Castel of Helthe (Elyot), 121

Castelain, Maurice, 116

castration, 137, 146–50, 156, 157, 158; liver and, 161

Castration: An Abbreviated History of Manhood (Taylor), 146

Catholicism, 5, 68

Cavendish, Margaret, 16, 115

Cecil, William, 74

Celia, 118, 121, 129, 130

The Center of the Circle of Commerce (Malynes), 12, 149

Cervantes, 10

Chapman, George, 105

Charles I, 170, 229n23

Charles V, 65

Charnes, Linda, 98, 209n20

Chaucer, Geoffrey, 104

Cheyne, George, 174

Cholmely, William, 204n37

A Christian Turned Turk (Daborne), 160

Christianity, 123; Judaism and, 80

The Circle of Commerce (Misselden), 9, 73, 140–41, 144

Clem, 155–57, 158

Clowes, William, 44, 96

Cobham, Lord, 114

Cobbler's Prophecy (Wilson), 178

Cobler, Raph, 178

Cohen, Walter, 23

Colet, John, 42

Columbus, Christopher, 123, 124

The Comedy of Errors (Shakespeare), 29–51, 185, 186; date of, 31; on international trade, 38–39; mercantilism in, 33; pathology in, 49–51; syphilis in, 44–46

commonwealth, 8–9; mercantilism and, 22

Constantinople, 151, 152

consumption, 2, 27, 162; Boorde on, 166; definition of, 163, 165–66; Dekker on, 176–84; in England, 164; humoral model on, 166–67; as metaphor, 12; in *Michaelmas Term*, 164; Middleton on, 175–84; Mun on, 165–75; Starkey on, 166

contamination, 213n56

Cook, Elizabeth, 231n38

Copland, Robert, 228

Corbaccio, 120

Corvino, 118

Cotgrave, Randle, 92

Crooke, Helkiah, 147–48, 224n34

currency, 89–90; of England, 107; Malynes on, 94–95; Scottish, 106–7; of Troy, 106

The Customers Replie (Milles), 126, 127–28

The Custumers Apology (Milles), 126, 127, 144

The Custumers Alphabet and Primer (Milles), 9, 126, 127

Daborne, Robert, 226n58

Dampit, Harry, 176

Dapper, Davy, 181

Dapper, Jack, 181, 182

Daschle, Tom, 188

Davies, John, 148

De Coster, Peter, 70

De Motu Cordis (Harvey), 137, 143

Deacon, John, 17, 18

The Dead Tearme (Dekker), 46

Dekker, Thomas, 20, 46, 111; on consumption, 176–84; on disease, 114; on Englishmen, 207n80. See also *The Dead Tearme; London Looke Backe; News from Graves End; Northward Ho; The Roaring Girl; The Shoemaker's Holiday*

Description of England (Harrison), 121

Dialogue Between Reginald Pole and Thomas Lupset (Starkey), 14, 30, 36–38, 166

Diamond, Jared, 18

Dictionarie of the French and English Tongues (Cotgrave), 92

Diomedes, 98

Discipline and Punish (Foucault), 131

Discourse of the Commonweal of This Realm of England (Smith), 30, 37–38, 89–90

Discourse of Trade, From England Vnto the East-Indies (Mun), 168–70, 172–73

disease: defining, 20; Dekker on, 114; economics and, 21–22; interpreting, 86–87; language

disease (*continued*)
of, 12, 15, 53, 77; Malynes on, 12; mercantilism
and, 12; as metaphor, 59; Milles on, 12;
models of, 16; modern, 20; usury and, 82;
in *Volpone*, 129–33
*A Disputation Between a Hee and a Shee Conny
Catcher* (Greene), 46
Dolan, Francis E., 60
Donne, John, 186, 187
Donusa, 157, 158–59, 160
Douglas, Mary, on body, 19
Dr. Pinch, 40
Drake, Francis, 5, 151, 152
drama, economy and, 23
Draper, John W., 206n69
Dromio, 29, 32, 39, 40, 41, 47, 50
drugs, 109–10, 119, 169; Bright and, 120–25, 122;
in England, 122; in Italy, 122
Duncan, Douglas, 117
Durkheim, Emile, 20
Dutch Church Libel, 25, 53, 62–66, 81; content
of, 62–63; England and, 64; Judaism and, 66;
populations during, 68; readings of, 64; on
trade, 79
Dutch Reformed Church, 67–68
The Dyer's Hand (Auden), 78
dysentery, 16

East India Company, 5, 35, 128, 139, 140, 152, 162;
Mun and, 164, 168, 171, 177
Eastward Hoe (Chapman, Jonson, and Web-
ster), 178–79
Edward II (Marlowe), 148
Edward IV (Heywood), 178
Edward VI, 66
Egeon, 31–32, 33–34, 38–39, 49
Egerton, Thomas, 57
Elizabeth (queen of England), 138, 151, 153; on
piracy, 154
Elton, W. R., 99
Elyot, Thomas, 121
Elze, Thomas, 72, 205n59
England, 5; consumption in, 164; currency
of, 90, 106–7; depression in, 167; drugs in,
122; Dutch Church Libel and, 64; epidemics
in, 18; national identity of, 7–8; ports
of, 168; Rome and, 35; under Cromwell,
4, 69
Englands Treasure by Forraign Trade (Mun),
136, 168, 170–73, 184
*Englands View, in the Unmasking of Two Para-
doxes* (Malynes), 211n46

English Mint, 89
The English Housewife (Markham), 218n38
The English Usurer, or Usury Condemned
(Blaxton), 83
Ephesus, 32–33
Epicoene (Jonson), 179
epidemic constitution, 112
Erasistratus, 143
Erasmus, 116
Essex, Earl of, 151
etiology, 27, 85; of canker, 92; of disease, 189
eunuchs, 147
Eurovision Song Contest, 10
Every Man in His Humor (Jonson), 134
exports, valorization of, 36

Fabricius, Johannes, 86, 220n65
The Fair Maid of the West (Heywood), 26,
136–37, 153–57, 186
Fascism, 83
The Fayre Mayde of the Exchange (Heywood),
178
Federal Reserve Discount Rate, 52
Ferguson, Margaret, 180
Feste, 105
Fiorentino, Giovanni, 10
Fitzallard, Mary, 179, 181
Fludd, Robert, 16, 133
foreign trade, effects of, 85
Forman, Valerie, 184
A Fortune by Land and Sea (Heywood and
Rowley), 151
Fortune Theater, 177, 180, 184
Foucault, Michel, 6, 20, 21, 189; on ports, 131
Fracastoro, Girolamo, 15–16, 44, 87, 111, 124, 188,
195n46
free trade, 3; Malynes on, 7–8; Misselden on,
7–8
*Free Trade, or The Meanes to Make Trade Flor-
ish* (Misselden), 7, 83, 138–41, 145, 150,
223n27; Christian policy in, 161
Freud, Sigmund, 146
Fuchs, Barbara, 156, 227n72

Galen, 39, 44, 50, 91, 112, 124, 194n40; on heart,
143; humoral model of, 13–15, 112; Milles on,
143–44; pathological models of, 40; on
semen, 146
Gallipot, Mistress, 177, 178, 181
gangrene, 59–60
Gazet, 157, 160–61
Geoffrey of Monmouth, 104

Germany, currency of, 90
Gillies, John, 72
Gilman, Ernest, 161
Girard, René, 19, 86–87
Glapthorne, Henry, 77
Gobbo, 80
Goshawk, 180, 184
Goux, Jean-Joseph, 85
Grady, Hugh, 99
Graziano, 80
Greenblatt, Stephen, 111
Greene, Gayle, 99, 214n67
Greene, Robert, 46, 125
Gresham, Thomas, 90
Grimaldi, 159, 160
Grosrichard, Alain, 158, 160
Gurnall, William, 167

Hales, John, 37
Hamlet (Shakespeare), 29, 42, 85–86
Hardwick, Bess, 154–55
Harriot, Thomas, death of, 84
Harrison, William, 121
Harvey, William, 137, 142, 143, 148; on circula-
     tion, 161
Hawkes, David, 85
Hawkins, John, 151
Healy, Margaret, 15, 113
Heckscher, Eli, on mercantilism, 4, 5, 230n29
Hector, 96, 97, 100, 103
Hegel, G. W. F., 4, 5
Helen, 96, 98
Henry IV Part 2 (Shakespeare), 84
Henry V (Shakespeare), 48
Henry VI Part 2 (Shakespeare), 148
Henry VII, 35
Henry VIII, 43, 90, 151
Henryson, Robert, 100, 104
Henze, Richard, 197n5
hepatitis, 2, 12, 137, 138, 142–45, 161–62; defini-
     tions of, 142–43
heroism, 95–96
Heywood, Thomas, 26, 88, 136–37, 151, 153, 157;
     Massinger and, 158. See also *The Fair Maid
     of the West*; *The Fayre Mayde of the
     Exchange*; *A Fortune by Land and Sea*; *A
     Royall King and Loyall Subject*
Hippocrates, 13, 91, 96, 112, 194n39; miasma
     theory of, 113; on semen, 146
A History of the Modern Fact (Poovey), 6
Hobbes, Thomas, 167, 215n71
The Hollander (Glapthorne), 77

Homer, 104, 105, 106
Hong Kong, 1
Horman, William, 43
Hotdspur, 84
humoral model, 13–15, 40, 88, 96–97, 109;
     Bright on, 124; on consumption, 166–67; of
     Galen, 112
Hussein, Saddam, 188
Hutchinson, Lucy, 16, 195n50
Hythlodaeus, Raphael, 8

The Idea of Usury (Nelson), 55
Iliad (Homer), 104, 105
inflation, origin of, 1
Inquisition, 70
An Interlude of Wealth and Health, 21–23, 184
international commerce, 8–9, 11, 25, 32, 33,
     120–21; body and, 14; Milles on, 9; Mun on,
     9; syphilis and, 17
invasive model, 88
de Isla, Rey Díaz, 43, 46
Israel, Jonathan, 68
Italy: currency of, 90; drugs in, 122; Fascist, 83

James (king of England), 152, 153, 167
James, Saint, 84
Jameson, Fredric, 24, 188
The Jew of Malta (Marlowe), 54, 64, 121
John (king of England), 126
John of Salisbury, 8
Jones, Richard, 192n16; terms coined by, 219n51
Jonson, Ben, 18, 26, 108, 131, 133, 163; on drugs,
     119; etymological choices of, 218n35. See also
     Bartholomew Fair; *The Case is Altered*; *East-
     ward Hoe*; *Epicoene*; *Every Man in His
     Humor*; *Volpone*
Judaism, 57, 61, 68–72, 79, 206n68; Christianity
     and, 80; Dutch and, 64, 68; Dutch Church
     Libel and, 66; Malynes on, 61–62; in *Mer-
     chant of Venice*, 53, 71; problematizing,
     75–76

Kermode, Frank, 100–101, 214n67
King, John, 113
Kirchner, Athanasius, 16
Koch, Robert, 13, 166

Lamprey, 176
Lander, Jesse M., 211n46
Laqueur, Thomas, 14, 146
Launcelot, 80, 207n79
Laxton, 177, 180, 181, 182

Leahy, Patrick, 188
Leontes, 96
leprosy, 18
Levant Company, 5, 35, 152
Leviathan (Hobbes), 167
Levin, Harry, 116
Lex Mercatoria (Malynes), 7, 11, 81, 140
Lex Mercatoria Rediviva (Beauwes), 84
The Libele of Englyshe Polycye, 122
Linacre, Thomas, 194n40 ,
Linton, Joan Pong, 24
liver, 143, 144; castration and, 161
Lodge, Thomas, 112, 113
London, 5, 72, 152; ports of, 114, 131
London Looke Backe (Dekker), 111
Lopez, Roderigo, 81
Love Connection, 10
Lovell, Robert, 122, 219nn39, 45
Lowe, Peter, 43
Lucian, 116
Luciana, 39–40, 45
Lucretius, 16, 195n50; theories of, 115
luxury goods, 170–71

The Maintenance of Free Trade (Malynes), 8, 140, 149
Mainwaring, Henry, 152
Mallin, Eric S., 87
Malynes, Gerard, 2, 3, 23; background of, 81–82; on blood, 167; on canker, 83–84, 84–85, 92; on currency, 94–95, 99; on disease, 12; financial actions of, 126; on free trade, 7–8; on gangrene, 60; on Judaism, 61–62; language of, 15, 19, 58; mercantilist model of, 64; Misselden and, 137, 138–46; on ports, 134; positions held by, 89; Shakespeare and, 108; theories of, 6; on troy system, 106–7; on. usury, 53, 56, 57–58, 202n18; on value, 102. See also *The Center of the Circle of Commerce*; *Englands View, in the Unmasking of Two Paradoxes*; *Lex Mercatoria*; *The Maintenace of Free Trade*; *Saint George for England Allegorically Described*; *A Treatise on the Canker of England's Commonwealth*
de Mandeville, Bernard, 174
Markham, Gervase, 120, 142, 218n38
Marlowe, Christopher, 64, 121, 148
Marranos, 69–70, 81
Martin, Emily, 19
Marx, Karl, 4, 21, 213n60

The Massacre at Paris (Marlowe), 64
Massinger, Philip, 26, 136–37, 157, 161; Heywood and, 158. See also *The Renegado*
McKendrick, Neil, 228n4.
Measure for Measure (Shakespeare), 29, 45–46, 85–86
Menaechmi (Plautus), 31
Mendes, Diego, 69
mercantilism: on blood, 79; capitalism and, 3; colored identities in, 78; in *The Comedy of Errors*, 33; commercial pathology before, 35–38; commonwealth and, 22; definitions of, 3, 4, 12; on disease, 130; disease and, 12, 18–19; drama and, 23; era of, 34; Heckscher on, 4; national economy and, 38–39; nation-hood and, 2; pathological metaphors in, 127; pirate-drama and, 136–62; on royalty, 145; Smith on, 4; theories of value of, 102; types of, 6; typology of, 19–20; usury and, 53; vocabulary of, 15
Merchant Adventurers, 5, 9, 35, 126, 128, 131; patents of, 138; threats presented by, 134–35
The Merchant of Venice (Shakespeare), 10–12, 21, 24, 25, 31, 51–57, 71–82, 183, 185, 186; blood in, 79; color in, 78; Dutch in, 75–76; Judaism in, 71, 81–82; taint of usury in, 52–53; trade in, 10–12
metempsychosis, 26, 115; in *Volpone, or The Fox*, 116–19
miasma theory, 113
Michaelmas Term (Middleton), 163, 175, 176, 181, 183; consumption in, 164
Microcosmographia (Crooke), 147–48
Middle East, 18
Middleton, Thomas, 162, 163, 165; on consumption, 175–84 See also *Michaelmas Term*; *No Wit, No Help Like a Woman's*; *The Old Law*; *The Roaring Girl*; *A Trick to Catch The Old One*
A Midsummer Nights Dream (Shakespeare), 106
Mildmay, Thomas, 67, 68
Milles, Thomas, 2, 3, 23, 26, 132, 138, 155; background of, 126; on body, 14; on disease, 12; on Dutch, 65; on foreign trade, 9; on Galen, 143–44; on money, 57; Mun and, 169; on ports, 134; on profit, 159; on protectionism, 125–29; rhetorical strategies of, 109; on taxes, 220n64; theories of, 6; on usury, 61, 202n18. See also *The Customers Replie*; *The Customers Apologie*; *The Customers Alphabet and Primer*; *The Misterie of Iniquitie*

Milton, John, 121
miscegenation, 76
Misselden, Edward, 2, 3, 5, 23, 26, 224n44; on
    blood, 167; on canker, 83; on common-
    wealth, 9; on free trade, 7–8; on free trading,
    160; language of, 19; Malynes and, 137,
    138–46; on merchant ventures, 223n27; on
    pirates, 150–51; on spice trade, 73; on taxes,
    220n64; theories of, 6. See also *The Circle of
    Commerce*; *Free Trade or the Meanes to Make
    Trade Florish*
The Misterie of Iniquitie (Milles), 128
Mohammed, 157
Moll, 180, 182, 183, 184
More, Thomas, 8
Moryson, Fynes, 75
Mosca, 116
Much Ado About Nothing (Shakespeare), 48
Mukerji, Chandra, 228n4
Muldrew, Craig, 89
Mullisheg, 154–55
Mun, Thomas, 2, 3, 5, 23, 27, 54, 162; Bright
    and, 169; on commonwealth, 9; on con-
    sumption, 165–75; East India Company and,
    164, 168, 171, 177; on foreign trade, 9; on free
    trade, 8; Milles and, 169; pathological vocab-
    ulary of, 168–69, 230n26; Stubbes and, 172;
    on taxes, 229n23; theories of, 6; on usury,
    201n6; vocabulary of, 15; writings of, 136.
    See also *Discourse of Trade, from England
    Vnto the East-Indies*; *Englands Treasure by
    Forraign Trade*
Muscovy Company, 5
Myrmidon, 101

Nano, 116, 134
Nashe, Thomas, 179
nationhood: development of, 8; mercantilism
    and, 2
Neatfoot, 179
Nell, 40–41
Nelson, Benjamin, on usury, 55–56
Nestor, 100, 101
News from Graves End (Dekker), 112
No Wit, No Help Like A Woman's (Middleton),
    184
Noland, Lord, 182
Northward Ho (Dekker and Webster), 148
Nuñes, Maria, 70–71, 72

The Old Law (Middleton and Rowley), 107
orcheis, 146

The Order of Things (Foucault), 6, 20
Oresme, Nicholas, 55
Osman, Cara, 153, 226n58
Othello (Shakespeare), 29
Ottoman Empire, 5, 7, 150–51
Overwork, Mistress, 182, 184
Ovid, 104, 105

Pambotanologia (Lovell), 122, 219n39
Pandarus, 100, 101, 106
Paracelsus, 15–16, 87, 173, 174, 184, 188, 230n28
Paradise Lost (Milton), 121
Paster, Gail Kern, 79, 146
Pasteur, Louis, 13
pathenogenesis, models of, 16
Paulina, 157, 159
Il Pecorone (Fiorentino), 10
Peregrine, 118, 119
Pereira, Isaac Raphael Haim. *See* Pereira,
    Manuel Lopes
Pereira, Manuel Lopes, 70, 71
Petiver, James, 232n52
Petyt, William, trade model of, 167–68
Philosophy of Money (Simmel), 110
Physiocrats, theories of, 1
Pimlico, 233n59
plague, 109–15, 127–34; causes of, 112–13
Plato, 7, 314
Plautus, 31
playhouses, 23–24
Plutarch, 7, 192n17
Politic Would-Be, Lady, 120–21, 122, 133–34
Politic Would-Be, Sir, 109, 118, 121, 130, 132
Poovey, Mary, 6, 141
Pope, Alexander, 31
Porter, Roy, 174
Portia, 10–11, 57, 79, 80
ports, 131, 134; Malynes on, 134–35; Milles on,
    134
Portugal, trades of, 35
Pound, Ezra, 83, 84
Priam, 104
Prince Henry's Men, 177, 179
protectionism, 192n15
Protestant Reformation, 35, 55, 65, 66
Pythagoras, 116

quarantine regulations, 131
A Quip for an Vpstart Courtier (Greene), 125

Raleigh, Walter, 24, 67, 151
Rea, J. D., 116

Reformation, 5
The Renegado (Massinger), 26, 136–37, 157–61, 178, 186, 227n72
Richardson, Linda Deer, 194n40
Riolan, Jean, 142
The Roaring Girl (Dekker and Middleton), 27, 164–65, 176–85, 186; consumption in, 176–84
Roche, Daniel, 228n4
romance, 191n1; conventions of, 10, 12, 24, 184; language of, 154
Rome, 18; England and, 35; imperialism of, 104
Rowley, William, 151
de Roover, Raymond, 81
A Royall King and Loyall Subject (Heywood), 88
Rules of Sociological Method (Durkheim), 20

Saint George for England Allegorically Described (Malynes), 9, 25, 57–62, 66, 81, 83; canker in, 90–92; usury in, 57
Salarino, 73, 79
Sanctes, Balthazar, 70
Schoenfeldt, Michael, 39, 133
Scoto, 129
sea trade, development of, 5
semen, 146–47
semiology, 85
Sennert, Daniel, 92
serpego, 85–88, 110; canker and, 92–93
Shakespeare, 10, 23; on canker, 84; on castration, 146; economics and, 26; Malynes and, 108; myths used by, 104; physiological concepts of, 39; romances of, 24; on serpego, 85–88; sovereign will used by, 105; on syphilis, 47–49; on taint, 77–78; on usury, 53. See also *All's Well That Ends Well*; *Henry V*; *Henry VI Part 2*; *Measure for Measure*; *The Merchant of Venice*; *A Midsummer Nights Dream*; *Much Ado About Nothing*; *Timon of Athens*; *Titus Andronicus*; *Troilus and Cressida*; *Twelfth Night*; *Venus and Adonis*; *The Winter's Tale*
Shakespeare's Imagery and What It Tells Us (Spurgeon), 86
Shapiro, James, 61, 64, 74
Sharpham, Edward, 179
Shell, Marc, 55, 76, 85
The Shoemaker's Holiday (Dekker), 178
Shylock, 11, 54–55, 56, 71, 72, 73; Antonio and, 79–80; parable of, 75–77; usury of, 78
silk trade, 35
Simmel, Georg, 99, 110

Skayne, Gilbert, 113
Slack, Paul, 20
Slammer Worm, 188, 189
smallpox, 18, 25, 187–88
Smith, Adam, 1, 164, 170, 175, 192n15; influence of, 2; on mercantilism, 4
Smith, Henry, 56
Smith, John, 224n44
Smith, Thomas, 30, 34, 37, 38, 41, 89. See also *Discourse of the Commonwealth of This Realm of England*
Solinus, 33, 39, 41
Solomon, Julie Robin, 4, 211
Sombart, Werner, 205n54
Sontag, Susan, on disease, 12
sovereign will, 102–3; Shakespeare's use of, 105
Spain, 7, 41, 65, 152; economic collapse of, 199n24
Spencer, 154–55
Spice Islands, 121
spice trade, 35, 169; Misselden on, 73
Spiegel, Henry William, 37
Spiller, Elizabeth, 76
Spurgeon, Caroline, 86
Stallybrass, Peter, 178
Starkey, Thomas, 8, 13, 30, 34, 36, 38, 128; on consumption, 166; on imports, 125. See also *Dialogue Between Reginald Pole and Thomas Lupset*
statecraft, 3–4
Stevenson, Robert Louis, 136
Stowe, John, 75
Stubbes, Philip, 36, 38, 128; Mun and, 172. See also *The Anatomy of Abuses*
Sugden, Edward H., 197
Sullivan, Ceri, 89
The Sultan's Court (Grosrichard), 158
Summa Theologica (Aquinas), 54
Supreme Court, 52
Sydenham, Thomas, 112
syphilis, 15, 20–21, 25, 29–51, 85, 111; Boorde on, 42; in *The Comedy of Errors*, 44–46; curing, 129; emergence of, 87; literature on, 44; as metaphor, 49–50; migration of, 17; names for, 98; naming of, 195n46; Shakespeare on, 47–49; spread of, 96; symptoms of, 220n65; views on, 41; vocabulary of, 30; word-play and, 48
Syracuse, 32–33

taint, 60, 82, 84; definition of, 77
Tamburlaine (Marlowe), 64

Taylor, Gary, on castration, 146
Taylor, John, 75
Tearcat, 183
temperance, 50
terrorism, 187–89
Testament of Cresseid (Henryson), 100
Thayre, Thomas, 112
Thersites, 88
Thirsk, Joan, 228n4
Thomas, William, 74
The Three Ladies of London (Wilson), 54, 83
The Three Lords and Three Ladies of London
    (Wilson), 92
Tiltyard, Mistress, 179, 180
Timon of Athens (Shakespeare), 21, 42, 49, 96
Titus Andronicus (Shakespeare), 48
tower system, 106
Tractado Contra El Mal Serpentino (de Isla), 43
trade, pathologization of, 21
Traheron, Bartholomew, 59
transmigration, 117
Trapdoor, 183
Travels of Three English Gentlemen (Day, Row-
    ley, and Wilkins), 54
Treasure Island (Stevenson), 136
*A Treatise of the Canker of England's Common-
    wealth* (Malynes), 12, 85, 90–95, 97, 138–40;
    on authority, 103; on value, 106
Treatise of the Plague (Lodge), 112
*Treatise: Wherein is Declared the Sufficiencie of
    English Medicines* (Bright), 26, 122–25
Trevisa, John, 166
A Trick to Catch the Old One (Middleton), 176,
    181, 183
Troilus and Cressida (Shakespeare), 29, 42, 49,
    85–88, 91, 95–107, 119, 185, 186; disease in,
    87–88; female characters in, 105; mechanistic
    philosophies in, 110; sovereign will in, 105–6;
    value in, 95–102
Trojan Horse, 106
Troy, Trojans: currency of, 106; history of, 104
troy system, Malynes on, 106–7
The Trumpet of Fame (Robarts), 152
tuberculosis, 13
Tudors, 35–36
Twelfth Night (Shakespeare), 95
typhus fever, 16

Ulysses, 99, 101, 102, 110, 111, 119
urbanization, 18
usury, 52–64, 67, 76; Bacon on, 54, 57; defini-
    tions of, 58; disease and, 82; justifying, 78;
    Malynes on, 56, 57–58; mercantilism and, 53;
    Milles on, 61; Nelson on, 55–56
Utopia (More), 8
Utrusque Cosmi (Fludd), 133

Van Elk, Martine, 46
Van Helmont, J. B., 16, 92
van Leeuwenhoek, Antony, 16
Vanderperre, Jacques. *See* Pereira, Manuel
    Lopes
Velasquez, Manuel. *See* Pereira, Manuel Lopes
Venice, 5, 72, 74
Venus and Adonis (Shakespeare), 200n36
Vergil, 104
Virginia Company, 5
Vitelli, 157, 158–59
Volpone, or the Fox (Jonson), 108–10, 115–21,
    129–34, 185; cargo in, 134; metempsychosis
    in, 116–19
von Hutten, Ulrich, 42, 101, 214n66
von Schmoller, Gustav, 4; on mercantilism, 5

War of the Roses, 35
Ward, John, 153, 160, 226n58
The Wealth of Nations (Smith), 3, 164, 173
Weimann, Robert, 213n57
Wengrave, Alexander, 179, 180, 182, 185
Wengrave, Sebastian, 181
Westcote, Thomas, 117
Wheeler, John, 126
White, Thomas, 24
Wilson, Robert, 54, 83, 92, 178
Wilson, Thomas, 54
The Winter's Tale (Shakespeare), 96, 148
Witgood, 176
Woolley, John, 74
World Trade Center, 187
World War II, 35; economies after, 2
Worldwide Web, 188

Yaffe, Martin D., 71
York Massacre, 203n25
Yussuf Reis. *See* Ward, John

Acknowledgments

This book was born of a twofold desire to make amends. First, I wanted to re-dress certain omissions and oversights in my earlier book, *Foreign Bodies and the Body Politic,* in which I had sought to foreground the political coordinates of the new notions of disease that emerged in the sixteenth and seventeenth centuries, yet neglected the important pathological vocabulary of the period's mercantilist literature. And second, I wished to correct my more general lack of knowledge about economics and economic history—a deficiency all the more embarrass-ing given the supposedly materialist bent of my work.

To the extent that I have been able to remedy these ills, the following peo-ple have helped me with their suggestions, intellectual support, and/or criti-cisms: Edmund Campos, Tom Cartelli, Jeffrey Cohen, Larry Danson, Heather Dubrow, Will Fisher, Valerie Forman, Rebecca Garden, Brad Greenburg, Eliza-beth Hanson, Peter Herman, Martha Howell, Heather James, Joel Kaye, Carole Levin, Carla Mazzio, Stephanie Moss, Michael Neill, Mark Netzloff, Louise Noble, Lena Orlin, Gail Paster, Carol Ann Pech, Kaara Peterson, Tanya Pollard, Bryan Reynolds, Rachana Sachdev, Lee Salamon, Alan Sinfield, Peter Stallybrass, Alan Stewart, Leslie Thomson, Grace Tiffany, Mike Torrey, Wendy Wall, and Giovanni Zanelda. Without their helpful interventions—even if in some cases they don't realize they made them!—this book would not have assumed the form it now has. Likewise, the comments of auditors at the University of Auck-land, Barnard College, the George Washington University, the University of Kansas, and McMaster University have helped me refine my argument. Shilpa Prasad provided me with an invaluable sounding board, and so much else, dur-ing the early stages of the project. And I owe a very special debt to Pat Parker, lively exchanges with whom (always over excellent food!) have sparked a good many of the ideas in this book.

I have been very fortunate with my students, past and present, at Ithaca College, many of whom have taught me far more, I fear, than I have taught them: in particular, I must thank Karin Chun-Taite, Kim Huth, Ashley Shelden, and Pavitra Sundar. I have also been immensely lucky with my friends. In Ithaca, I have benefited immeasurably from the love and laughter of Asma Barlas, Ulises Mejias, Rob Odom, and Greg Tomso. Judith Brown, Lee Edelman, the Gopinadh clan, Joe Litvak, Indira Menon, Kalyani Menon, Mohan Menon, Martin Murray, Ian Narev, Margaret Pappano, and Rebecca Walkowitz may live further afield, but their friendship, love, and support have made the task of writing this book a good deal easier. Shekhar Aiyar and Franziska Ohnsorge provided me with a roof, and considerable generosity, during the book's last stages. I am delighted also to record strong debts of gratitude to three dear friends. I wish to thank my collaborator, Natasha Korda, whose thinking has had such an irrevocable impact on my own; my long-time pal and fellow Kiwi expatriate, Anna Neill, who always manages to pop up in the same locales, physical and intellectual, in which I have taken up residence and make me understand them afresh; and my buddy Henry Turner, whose comradeship and brilliance have always pushed me to new levels of rigor and self-scrutiny.

I am grateful also to the Folger Institute for the award of a summer fellowship, to Ithaca College's Center for Faculty Research and Development for the award of several semesters' release time and summer funding to work on the project, and to the late Robert Ryan of Ithaca College's Department of History, whose generous bequest of a chair helped fund and generate valuable time for my research. My department chair at Ithaca College, Michael Twomey, lent support to my project and my applications for research funding. I am endebted to my two anonymous readers at the University of Pennsylvania Press for their meticulous reports on the first draft of this project, which helped make this a much better book. And I owe a huge debt of gratitude to my editor at the press, Jerry Singerman, who has safely shepherded this book to its completion from when it was barely a glimmer of an idea. Few readers realize the difference a good editor can make; in the case of Jerry, that difference is truly humbling. Many thanks also to Alison Anderson, my anonymous copyeditor, Theodore Mann, and John Hubbard, all of whom provided invaluable assistance during the production stage.

And finally, I wish to record several debts that are simply unpayable. My parents, Norman and Stella Harris, and my sister, Miriam Harris, have always modeled for me the value of intellectual inquiry, *metta* and *ahava*. But in recent years I have learned much more about some of the subject material in this book than I will ever be able to communicate from my little sister, Naomi Harris Narev. Her joie-de-vivre, courage, and imagination put mine to shame. It is with great love and pride that I dedicate this book to her. My biggest debt of all, however, is to Madhavi Menon. Her loving companionship, shimmering intellect, and contagious laughter have sustained me throughout the completion of this book. Through thick and very thin, she has been my anchor, emotionally and intellectually. Many of the better ideas here have emerged from my conversations with her. All the irredeemably sick ones, however, are entirely my own and hence, contrary to most of the ideas of disease that I examine here, endogenous rather than externally contracted.

Some of this book has already appeared in print. Portions of several chapters first appeared in " 'The Canker of England's Commonwealth': Gerard de Malynes and the Origins of Economic Pathology," *Textual Practice* 13, 2 (1999): 124–39. A version of Chapter 2 appeared in Stephanie P. Moss and Kaara Peterson, eds., *Disease, Diagnosis, and Cure on the Early Modern Stage* (Burlington, Vt.: Ashgate Press, 2004). A version of Chapter 4 was published in *Renaissance Drama* 29 (2000): 3–37. Portions of Chapter 5 appeared in *Literature and Medicine* 21, 2 (2001): 109–32. I thank Routledge, Ashgate Press, Northwestern University Press, and Johns Hopkins University Press for their permission to reproduce those pieces here.